Managerial Practice Issues in Strategy and Organization

A Volume in Research in Strategy Science

Series Editor

T. K. Das
City University of New York

Research in Strategy Science

T. K. Das, Series Editor

Published

Time Issues in Strategy and Organization (2019)
edited by T. K. Das

Cultural Values in Strategy and Organization (2021)
edited by T. K. Das

Managerial Practice Issues in Strategy and Organization (2023)
edited by T. K. Das

In Development

International Issues in Strategy and Organization
Edited by T. K. Das

Managerial Practice Issues in Strategy and Organization

edited by

T. K. Das
City University of New York

INFORMATION AGE PUBLISHING, INC.
Charlotte, NC • www.infoagepub.com

Library of Congress Cataloging-in-Publication Data

CIP record for this book is available from the Library of Congress
http://www.loc.gov

ISBNs: 979-8-88730-021-4 (Paperback)

979-8-88730-022-1 (Hardcover)

979-8-88730-023-8 (ebook)

CONTENTS

v

ABOUT THE BOOK SERIES

The field of strategy science has grown in both the diversity of issues it addresses and the increasingly interdisciplinary approaches it adopts in understanding the nature and significance of problems that are continuously emerging in the world of human endeavor. These newer kinds of challenges and opportunities arise in all forms of organizations, encompassing private and public enterprises, and with strategies that experiment with breaking the traditional molds and contours. The field of strategy science is also, perhaps inevitably, being impacted by the proliferation of hybrid organizations such as strategic alliances, the upsurge of approaches that go beyond customary emphasis on competitiveness and profit making, and the intermixing of time-honored categories of activities such as business, industry, commerce, trade, government, professions, and so on. The blurring of the boundaries between various areas and types of human activities points to a need for academic research to address the consequential developments in strategic issues. Hence, research and thinking about the nature of issues to be tackled by strategy science should also cultivate requisite variety in issues recognized for research inquiry, including the conceptual foundations of strategy and strategy making, and the examination of the critical roles of strategy makers, strategic thinking, time and temporalities, business and other goal choices, diversity in organizing modes for strategy implementation, and the complexities of managing strategy, to name a few. This book series on *Research in Strategy Science* aims to provide an outlet for ideas and issues that publications in the field do not provide, either expressly or adequately, especially as regards the comprehensive coverage deserved by certain emerging areas of interest. The topics of the volumes in the series will keep in view this objective to

Managerial Practice Issues in Strategy and Organization, pp. vii–viii
Copyright © 2023 by Information Age Publishing
www.infoagepub.com

expand the research areas and theoretical approaches routinely found in strategy science, the better to permit expanded and expansive treatments of promising issues that may not sufficiently align with the usual research coverage of publications in the field.

—T. K. Das
City University of New York

Series Editor
Research in Strategy Science

CHAPTER 1

MANAGING IN THE COLLECTIVE
The Practice of Big Science Collaborations

Mark Robinson and Susanne Braun

ABSTRACT

The scientific results of Big Science increasingly hit the headlines as they provide welcome hope to address a range of complex cross-border problems. However, their collaborative style governance and managerial practice have gone relatively unseen. Collaborative leadership can be seen as an oxymoron, yet it regularly works in Big Science domains; a success that demands attention by scholars and practitioners alike. Through leadership-as-practice research in three iconic scientific communities (CERN, ISS, and ITER) we reveal effective collaborative managerial practice as well as counterfactual examples of ineffective practice. Our analysis is in line with the distinction between the emerging leadership-as-practice and traditional leadership research concerning conceptual agency. We show that the source of agency in Big Science is mostly collective and collaborative (rather than mostly about individuals), that power emerges through enactment of participants' competing choices and practices (rather than through the influence of top leaders), and dialogue is used to focus on mutual learning, deep understanding, and collaborative actions (rather than to convince the other of one's point of view). Using Big Science collaborations as a site to explore these issues is exciting. It is an example of the very latest thinking on the key issues concerning the role and significance of managerial practice in strategic management and organization studies. We are bold in our conclusion by suggesting that the post-heroic, not-authoritarian view of leadership rooted in Big Science

Managerial Practice Issues in Strategy and Organization, pp. 1–37

collaborations, which we term *light-touch management*, will inspire a wider critical and constructive debate of collective approaches to managerial practice.

INTRODUCTION

The ex-astronaut, Ron Garan in his 2015 book *The Orbital Perspective* asks several searching rhetorical questions of his readers:

> How did we go from those early days of mistrust and suspicion to building and operating the space station? What was the secret ingredient that enabled a coalition of fifteen nations to work together systematically, in a fully integrated manner, to construct and operate the most complex structure ever built in space? Is there something we can learn from how the members overcome differences and cultural misunderstandings to accomplish remarkable things together? And can we use these same techniques to reach agreement on things such as alleviating poverty, mitigating climate change, or achieving peaceful solutions to long-term conflicts? (Garan, 2015, p. 34)

Garan also pointedly suggests that one does not have to be in orbit in the space station to have the orbital perspective he espouses. In answer to the questions he posed, he suggests several lessons learned from his experience (Garan, 2015, pp. 35, 39, 42, and 43), including:

> Check pride at the door, solutions can come from anywhere.... If you create something meaningful then the inevitable bumps in the road do not derail the partnership.... Be in it for the long run.... Plan for incremental collaboration and Establish relationships and build trust.

These statements provide a motivation to better understand how these types of transformation took place and how the behaviors in line with values (no pride, solution driven) were implemented (driven by managerial practices) in the Big Science organizational context.

The Royal Society (RS) and American Academy for Arts and Science (AAAS) jointly challenged and dismissed the romantic notion of the scientist as a lone creative genius (Royal Society, 2010). In today's world to be alone in science means to be cut-off from ideas, concepts, funding, and equipment that are all needed to tackle today's problems. Scientific enterprise is now premised on the need to connect with the best minds in each field; the emphasis being on the necessity to work in well-funded groups with cutting edge equipment. This reality coupled with the financial need to pool resources efficiently should be kept in mind throughout the themes developed in this chapter.

We consider Big Science collaborations as a site to explore effective and ineffective collaborative managerial practice. We thereby seek to bring together theories of leadership in the collective and their extension as well as critical reflection in the Leadership-as-Practice (L-A-P) paradigm. We seek to identify L-A-P in the management of Big Science projects as well as their implications for power and agency. We see the combination of these approaches as a potential avenue toward exploration of three questions: (1) Do collaborative forms of leadership exist in these projects, if so, who leads and who follows, when and why?; (2) How do collaborative agency and power emerge in the space of L-A-P in this specific context?; and (3) Which constraints to collaborative agency emerge in this space and what are potential solutions? In the next section we position managing in the collective in L-A-P research.

Where we use the term Big Science its meaning is derived from that of Alvin Weinberg (1967) when introducing the phrase in his book on the impact of Large-Scale Science on the United States. He focused on the emerging large research infrastructures. Here we expand the term to mean large research projects, their communities, and infrastructures. The criterion for these terms is explained in the case studies section together with how the sites for the research were identified. The analysis section then continues this path by illustrating results from each of the three sites obtained under the L-A-P paradigm. From three emerging themes—agency, power, and dialogue—we derive a new concept that we term light-touch management. We conclude with thoughts for the implementation and further study of this paradigm.

POSITIONING MANAGING IN THE COLLECTIVE IN LEADERSHIP PRACTICE RESEARCH

Emerging Views of Leadership

In this chapter we will present the results of L-A-P research in three iconic scientific communities that represent key elements in the Big Science context: CERN (Conseil Européen pour la Recherche Nucléaire) is expanding human knowledge in fundamental physics, ITER (International Thermonuclear Experimental Reactor) is endeavoring to provide a route to carbon-free, commercial power generation, and the ISS (International Space Station) is carrying out unique micro-gravity science and building the knowledge mankind will need for deep space travel.

The purpose of our work is three-fold: First, we seek to observe how managers and non-managerial employees contribute to leadership in each of these projects, which are exemplary of Big Science research but come with its unique set of challenges for collaboration. Second, we are looking to understand and explain the collaboration and related challenges under a L-A-P paradigm. Questions that we seek to address with the paradigm comprise: Does leadership and followership exist in these projects, and if so, who leads and who follows, when and why? Themes that we explore on this basis relate to agency, power, and dialogue between all members of these Big Science collaborations, especially how managers interact with and influence others, and vice versa. Finally, with these observations we aim to derive implications for managerial practice. We demonstrate several ways in which Big Science organizations practice leadership and follower-ship that can open up new perspectives for organizations and businesses with currently more traditional leadership structures.

Leadership and Followership

The views of leadership as power resting in the hands (or abilities) of one exceptional individual are the beginning of a long-standing tradition of leadership research (Lord, Day, Zaccaro, Avolio, & Eagly, 2017; also see Antonakis & Day, 2018, for a historical overview). However, these views are not necessarily well-suited to address the complexities that modern orga-nizations must face today (e.g., in the wake of the COVID-19 pandemic; Antonakis, 2021; Kniffin et al. 2021). Looking backwards over the past 30 years, the evolution of leadership scholarship shows what started as individual-focused power and influence research (e.g., an individual's abil-ity to influence others through reward and punishment), has evolved into manifold views of how leadership develops between and within individuals, groups, and collectives (Zhu, Song, Zhu, & Johnson, 2018, for an overview).

It is now well-accepted that leadership "involves a process whereby intentional influence is exerted over other people to guide, structure, and facilitate activities and relationships in a group or organization" (Yukl & Gardner, 2020, p. 22). However, who leads and who follows in this process, when and why, appears up for debate. Publications in key outlets evidence that what leaders do, how they are perceived by others, and the situational contingencies that they experience all represent important contextual fac-tors that affect leadership and its outcomes (Lord et al., 2017).

Rather than focusing on one powerful individual, emerging perspec-tives in the literature now seek to capture leadership as a "contextualized, dynamic, multi-level, multi-person construct that guides emerging roles and identities, and in the process affects many organizational outcomes" (Lord, Gatti, & Chui, 2016, p. 129). In other words, leadership does not happen without the involvement of multiple individuals (i.e., there is no leadership without followership; Uhl-Bien, Riggio, Lowe, & Carsten,

2014). Leadership is not static but rather an interplay of collaboration and communication that crosses boundaries (e.g., of organizational roles or responsibilities) and has the potential to help solve complex problems. We argue in this chapter that Big Science collaborations have recognized this advantage, and in fact necessity, of shared agency to resolve complex problems. They are therefore informative cases to study and learn from. Moreover, we see them as exciting opportunities to study new forms of leadership in practice, especially those that focus on the leadership from a process-oriented, collective perspective.

Leading and Managing in the Collective

Lord et al. (2017) observed that "social relationships in which leadership transpires are in transition in ways that will change how people theorize, investigate, and practice leadership in organizations, communities, and nations" (p. 445). That leadership originates and can be shared in collectives is an emerging perspective in the leadership literature (Pearce & Conger, 2003; for reviews see Bolden, 2011; Day, Gronn & Salas, 2004; Denis, Langley, & Sergi, 2012; Zhu, Liao, Yam, & Johnson, 2018). However, the theoretical as well as practical understanding how this process happens and how to facilitate it remains "at best rudimentary" (Lord et al., 2017, p. 445).

Critical questions about leadership as it emerges in the collective remain insufficiently addressed by the current research. These questions particularly pertain to the intersections between (informal) collective leadership structures and (formal) managerial roles as they may facilitate or hinder each other. Whether leadership emerges in a collective appears to depend at least in part on the managerial practices (sometime described as "vertical leadership") and belief systems in organizations. To begin with, when team members believe in hierarchical leadership structures, competence is more likely to be centralized and shared leadership less likely to emerge (DeRue, Nahrgang, & Ashford, 2015). This is concerning especially complex contexts, where success or failure depend naturally on decentralized competence structures. In fact, past research has demonstrated that while both shared and vertical leadership behaviors predicted team effectiveness, the explanatory value of sharing leadership in the collective was consistently higher than that of the individual manager's leadership (Pearce & Sims, 2002). One explanation for these findings may be that formal managerial practice feeds into shared leadership (through vision/purpose, but also access to resources, team, and process design as well as boundary management; Pearce, 2004).

Researchers have more recently started to address the potential issues and opportunities at the intersections of managerial practice and leadership in the collective (Holm & Fairhurst, 2018), addressing questions of power, competition, and conflict. These initial insights bring to light that the dualism between management and leadership appears to continue in the sphere of collective approaches, leading to calls for the analysis of hybrid leadership configurations and their embeddedness in a field of power relationships (Gronn, 2009, 2015).

In a nutshell, how informal leadership structures and formal managerial practice intersect remains to be understood—and a better understanding will in turn inform organizations that seek to embed these emerging and increasingly decentralized leadership approaches within more traditional, often hierarchical managerial structures. A critical rethink of current models and managerial practices appears necessary, to render what may seem outwardly challenging or even incompatible, a successful and worthwhile endeavor for organizations and their members.

The Leadership-as-Practice Paradigm

The Leadership-as-Practice (L-A-P) paradigm is representative, or some would argue constituent, of a new and radical movement in leadership studies (Raelin, 2016; Raelin, Kempster, Youngs, Carroll, & Jackson, 2018). Its purpose is to move away from a role-driven, entitative perspective on relationships in organizations. Instead, L-A-P studies leadership "wherever and however it appears" (Raelin, 2017, p. 216). Its collaborative agency approach seeks to reframe what leadership means and how it is practiced. L-A-P forms a counterpoint to heroic, individual or dyadic focused approaches to relationships between managers and employees in organizations. Instead, in L-A-P organizational actors are those who create the knowledge as they experience leadership through their day-to-day practice (Raelin, 2016).

The themes of power and agency are central to L-A-P. Raelin (2012, 2016) refers to a collaborative agency as "a fair dialogical exchange among those committed to a practice" (Raelin, 2017, p. 137), including the interest in listening to and reflecting on each other's perspectives as well as the openness to change through the dialogue. Such dialogue must be free of judgment, meaning that those who interact talk freely. The outcome of the dialogue is open-ended as opposed to predetermined. At the end of the dialogue, it may have changed the very structures that it emerged from. In other words, L-A-P changes the practices of leadership. Managers were originally seen as facilitators of such dialogue (Raelin, 2012), although the more recent take of L-A-P would appear to be that they form part of the inter-actors within the dialogue independent of role or positional stance.

L-A-P's assumptions as to how and when collaborative agency emerges may at best sound idealistic when one thinks of common power structures in (hierarchical) organizations. In fact, recent criticism of L-A-P emphasizes that collective agency and the enactment of power often create considerable tensions as "owners seek to control, … leaders seek to lead and … managers seek to manage" (Collinson, 2018, p. 366). As such, we concur with the view that if L-A-P seeks to make substantive contributions to a new understanding of leadership, issues of power asymmetry and agency cannot be ignored but must be understood through its lens on power relationships in organizations.

As a starting point to this exploration, Raelin (2016), building on Caldwell's (2012) critique of Senge's learning organization, proposes a set of constraints to collaborative agency that warrant further examination; (a) autonomy—is a precondition to individual agency, which to an extent may have to be foregone in order for collaborative agency to emerge; (b) rationality—while inter-actors may like to assume that they are acting rationally, emotional or "extra-rational" activity may be required to require to get dialogue "unstuck"; (c) expertise—as a knowledge driven society we value expertise; however, in resolving complex problems, where no individual actor has sufficient expertise to find a solution, collective agency means resolving from individual expertise to creating shared knowledge structures (and acknowledging individual limitations); and finally (d) reflexivity—albeit valued in dialogue, reflexivity can create power imbalances between individuals (e.g., due to communication strength or emotions management) and thus may require a form of meta-reflexivity.

In sum, the L-A-P paradigm opens up new avenues for the research of managerial practices in organizations. Specifically, individual and collaborative agency, and their enactment in Big Science organizations drives our work with the purpose to better understand effective and ineffective collaborative managerial practices.

BIG SCIENCE COLLABORATIONS CASE STUDIES

The case study titles, abbreviations, HQ location, founding date, and membership are shown in Table 1.1.

The Case Study Selection Process

The case study selection process adopted by the first author has been a successive one, firstly covering the cost factors, then the international norms used for demarcating large projects, the attributes and criteria for global status and concludes with the rationale for the three case studies that are our focus here.

Table 1.1

Big Science Case Studies

Case Study (abbreviation)	HQ location (founding date)	Full Members (Founding members are shown first; other members that have joined later are shown second).	Notes
European Council for Nuclear Research (in French Conseil Européen pour la Recherche Nucléaire (CERN)	Geneva, Switzerland (1953)	Belgium, Denmark, France, Germany, Greece, Italy, Netherlands, Norway, Sweden, Switzerland, and United Kingdom.	There are also six associate members: Croatia, India, Lithuania, Pakistan, Turkey, and Ukraine.
		Austria, Bulgaria, Czech Republic, Finland, Hungary, Israel, Poland, Portugal, Romania, Serbia, Slovak Republic, and Spain	Observer states include Japan and the United States.
International Thermonuclear Experimental Reactor (ITER)	Cadarache, France (2006)	The People's Republic of China, Europe (27 states bound together through a European atomic research cooperation treaty), India, Japan, the Republic of Korea, the Russian Federation, and the United States.	The 7 founding members have not been added to, although there are bilateral research agreements with others such as Australia. The abbreviation only is always used by the community rather than the full words.
International Space Station (ISS)	Washington DC, United States. (1998)	Canada, Japan, the Russian Federation, the USA, and the European Space Agency (comprising eleven participating member states: Belgium, Denmark, France, Germany, Italy, The Netherlands, Norway, Spain, Sweden, Switzerland, and the United Kingdom).	The 5 founding members have not been added to.

Cost Factors

Miller and Lessard (2000) in their work at the Massachusetts Institute of Technology use a practical construction cost threshold of greater than US$1B when defining large engineering projects. The amount does not consider inflation nor that there are different costs in different parts of the world, but it does provide an apt order of magnitude and has been widely accepted within academia researching mega-project management.

This chapter uses the same threshold as part of the Big Science facility status criteria.

International Norms for Demarcating Big Science Facilities.

The role of the European Strategy Forum for Research Infrastructures (ESFRI) is to support European states in determining a coherent and strategy-led approach to science research policymaking. It comprises a well-respected body of experts from several fields who together facilitate multinational initiatives leading to development and/or better use of European science research infrastructures. One product is a bi-annual roadmap that demarcates between projects and landmark status projects (ESFRI, 2016), which we use for definitional purposes in this chapter.

A Group of Senior Officials (GSO) composed of experts from Australia, Brazil, Canada, China, the European Commission, France, Germany, India, Italy, Japan, Mexico, Russia, South Africa, the United Kingdom, and United States produced a Framework for Global Research Infrastructures (GRI). This sets three broad categories for GRI: (1) Single-sited global facilities that are geographically localized unique facilities whose governance is fundamentally international in character; (2) Globally distributed research infrastructures formed by national or institutional nodes, which are part of a global network and whose governance is fundamentally international in character; and (3) National facilities of global interest with unique capabilities that attract wide interest from researchers outside of the host nation (EC, 2017).

Attributes and Criteria for Global Big Science Facility Status

Utilizing the criteria above results in a list of over one hundred Big Science facilities. Despite the somewhat inflated claims of many science communities only a select few are global in that they have taken decades to form into collaborations under intergovernmental treaty obligations, have members that span continents, have a specially created central headquarters (HQ) or a specially created new entity within an existing international HQ, have highly complex technical challenges to deal with ground-breaking iconic research, share their results world-wide within a global expert community and enjoy a high visibility within both the scientific and public realms.

The final justification in selecting the three case studies is when the following attributes are considered: all three meet the global criteria bar outlined above, they are equal in the sense of all being in the foremost position within their domains, and each have members who are also involved in other global communities that are functioning less well and therefore the analysis provides fertile ground to examine what the case study governance and leadership regimes are doing that the others are not. Also, access to key interviewees that provided primary data is feasible together with ready access to reputable secondary data including founding documents, treaties, negotiation positions, and leadership material including the minutes of governing bodies.

Field Research

Field data was collected via semi-structured interviews over a two-year period (2017–2018) with world leading executives and academics with experience and knowledge of the three case studies and the wider Big Science management landscape. Interviewees were drawn from both the central managerial teams and the member states management teams. Interviewee roles included the very highest levels in the HQ organizations with a serving Director General (DG), several former DGs (Herwig Schopper and Chris Llewellyn-Smith), division leaders and middle management contributing. Academic interviewees included noted science historians such as John Krige, the Directors of the Space Policy Institute at George Washington University (John Logsdon and Henry Hertzfeld) and Professors of International Management such as Don Lessard at Sloan School of Management, Cambridge, United States and Janet Smart of Saïd Business School, University of Oxford. Aguinis and Solarino (2019) provide a ready guide for the case of interviews with elite informants that was followed here: the research method was through case studies, the setting was Big Science organizations, the corresponding author was the interviewer and in the period the interviews were conducted was an outsider and former insider of the ITER project.

Interviews were conducted at the case study HQs in Geneva, Switzerland, Cadarache, France, and in Washington DC, United States. Data was also collected at international conferences of the American Association for the Advancement of Science in Austin, Texas and Washington DC, United States, and at a CERN symposium held in December 2017. Introductions and consent to interviews was achieved with the support of points of contact in each case study community. Information sheets were provided to all the participants, describing the nature of the research, why and how it was being conducted together with an explanation of why they had been asked to take part. All interviews were conducted within the considerations of informed consent, confidentiality and anonymity, interviewee details of those who have agreed to be named and/or already have their comments publicly presented is available from the corresponding author.

The study design has at its core the three questions that need to be addressed: (1) Do collaborative forms of leadership exist in these projects, if so, who leads and who follows, when and why? (2) How do collaborative agency and power emerge in the space of L-A-P in this specific context? (3) Which constraints to collaborative agency emerge in this space and what are potential solutions? The questions were concise enough to reduce the problem space area but deep enough to address the fundamental L-A-P issues at hand. Marian Petre and Gordon Rugg (2010) point out that resolving the questions this way, into more tractable pieces, helps keep fresh the original motivation of why it was an important overall topic (p. 96). The research analysis needed to satisfy the test of "answering the research questions" for a readership that would include the wider managerial and L-A-P community. The data collection and analysis were therefore conducted and recorded in as jargon free style that the subject matter allowed.

Booth, Colomb, and Williams (2008, p. 82) point out that striking a balance between not freezing the interviewee with too scripted questions while not questioning aimlessly can only be overcome by determining exactly what you want to know. Individual interviews were therefore conducted in a straightforward manner and typically lasted around 90 minutes. The structure was (A) an introductory question to put the interviewee at ease, such as "you work as part of the senior management team here, please tell me about your role and responsibilities," (B) core questions such as "this project has reportedly long-standing, good collaboration between the member states and the central organization, what would you say is the most significant factor that has led to this?", "what would you say have been the greatest disagreements and difficulties with the members states on this project and are there any lingering, unresolved problems?" and " what new measures would you say could be introduced to the project management that would improve schedule and cost performance?" and C) concluding and follow-up questions depending on the specific role of the interviewee and items of interest, such as "What—if any—are the managerial lessons learned by the project governance and management regimes that may provide clues in advancing global collaboration more generally?"

This data capture helped to identify, in the way that Ives (2005) describes, contextual elements in the case studies' management that impacted on project success. Pre-work with the points of contact in the case study Big Science facilities HQs showed how willing subjects were to take part. It was important to maintain this momentum while conducting the interviews as systematically and sensitively as possible. Maylor and Blackmon (2005, p. 243) describe this as "controlled opportunism" whereby researchers take advantage of new themes to improve resultant theory. The few reticent interview participants were gently encouraged to relate their experiences of high-level management relevant to the three core questions.

Counterfactual Evidence

The research conclusions have the potential to contest prevailing L-A-P thinking. Such conclusions would only have credibility if counter evidence had also been gathered, analyzed, and considered. Reasonable skepticism would also serve to reflect on and challenge the adequacy of the questions themselves.

Consequently, as David Dooley (1984) points out, plausible alternative explanations to observations and gathered data should not be ruled-out in the research design and methodology. The research design therefore has ensured that no data either primary (interviews) or secondary (literature) has been dismissed as irrelevant or unreliable evidence. The analytical methods of testing the results include counterfactual evidence, which has served to understand the problem better and identify any weaknesses/simplifications in the research questions. The methods of dealing with latent interviewee bias and researcher bias are covered below.

Researcher Confirmation Bias and Latent Interviewee Bias

The risk of interviewer bias has been recognized and while it can never be eliminated it can be managed; in this research by implementing three mitigation actions. Firstly, the research questions are open ones, in that they ask how managing in the collective is achieved. They do not predispose that any Big Science collaborative L-A-P are "good" "or bad." Secondly, the breadth and quality of the literature incorporated the analysis of a secondary data pool that included counterevidence. Thirdly, the field work interviewee information sheets included the research questions but not our supposition. This calculated omission was to remove interviewer or respondent biases and maximize the opportunity for complete and accurate communication between the interviewer and the respondent (Cannell & Kahn, 1968, pp. 526–595). The tone of the interviews was an open one encouraging each participant to recount in their own way what they believed was important, thus revealing both supporting and opposing evidence and reducing the risk of distractive prompting of the respondents by the interviewer.

Many Big Science facilities compete with rival projects to gain formal go-ahead and be established. They have optimism bias and what Flyvbjerg, Bruzelius, and Rothengatter, when examining large engineering projects and risk, termed "strategic misrepresentation" (2003, p. 73) built into their founding genes as evidenced in their pre-approval phase bid documentation. Participants in Big Science projects are justifiably proud of their own contribution and that of the institutions and organizations that are addressing these types of global challenges. With this understandable pride comes the risk of excessive defensiveness when these individuals are faced with criticism. Sergei Krikalev is an icon of Russian space exploration and a current Russian Space Agency Director. He provided this comment in a 2017 interview when asked to recall good and bad days on the ISS: "for sure, we had difficult days, probably it is a sign of human memory to remember more positive things than the negative one." (Česká televize, 2017). This trait was not encountered during the field work: pride in accomplishments was equally matched with admission of the failings. Indeed, it is the openness and insights into how difficulties and constraints were overcome that are some of the key analytical materials we cover.

The collection and analysis of data was conducted keeping this latent defensive bias in mind. Booth et al. (2008, p. 82) reveal that experienced researchers understand that for research of any substance, any one interviewee's version of the truth is complicated, usually ambiguous, and always contestable. That is why they argue a sufficiently large sample of interviews needs to be conducted in order to even out any bias; a recommendation that has been ardently followed here with over 70 interviews being conducted.

ANAYSIS OF LEADERSHIP-AS-PRACTICE STUDY RESULTS

Research Context—Governance and Management Structures

A shared mission alone cannot sustain a Big Science collaboration for the decades that it will take for it to be established, built, commissioned, and provide research results. Their administrative framework is designed to accommodate the member states' scientists and politicians as much as possible over the lengthy life cycle.

The ultimate authority for each Big Science project rests in its governing Council that will normally meet three times per year and hold extraordinary sessions when needed (ITER, 2022, CERN, 2022a). The Council is usually advised by a range of specialist topic sub-committees such as Management, Science/Technology and Finance/Audit matters. Each sub-committee has delegates from the member states and invited expert advisers as issues dictate. The governing Councils appoint a Director General (DG) who is granted authority to make operational decisions and run the project. We will cover the process for this appointment later.

Typically, a Big Science DG will have five or six Executive Directors as direct reports, who themselves may have their appointments ratified or noted by the Council. These roles will include a Project Director (who runs the Project Office and drives project performance), a Technical Director (who exercises design authority on behalf of the DG), a Science Director (who preserves the requirements and raison d'être for the whole endeavor), an International Relations Director (who assists the DG in dealing with the member state affairs) and an Administration and Finance Director (CERN, 2022b; ITER, 2022). The central workforce, supported by the dispersed community experts and suppliers reports to middle management who then report to the Directors. The size of the central workforce changes over the life cycle of the projects but can be large. Currently, CERN has around 2,500 direct employees and ITER around 1,100. Figure 1.1 shows the generic arrangement including the concept of mini-epistemic communities of experts that we also cover later.

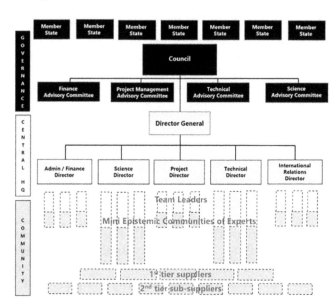

Figure 1.1.   Big Science generic management structure.

Consensual Governance—Unanimity of Voting

At CERN each member state gets Council two seats: one reserved for a scientist and the other for an administrator. One member, one vote has been maintained throughout CERN's existence (Rule 15 of CERN, 2022a) and, as we will explain, the member states have appropriately empowered the central management team as the organization evolved. The member states in all three case studies consistently exercise consensual governance. This can be seen though the [public at least] unanimity of voting and the fact that they deal with constraints fairly.

In contrast to an earlier golden period when the budget was increasing, Herwig Schopper, DG of CERN from 1981 to 1988, took over when the funds from the contributing members were being reduced. Tough decisions had to be taken to close existing projects and concentrate on securing funding for new and essential core work. He provided first-hand insight into how members voting was managed during this challenging period:

> what I introduced was before each Finance Committee and each Council meeting there was a dinner of all the delegates and my team, where we could openly discuss serious questions and we asked delegates, do you have instructions to vote against something? They would say yes; I have these instructions and we would then ask if you were overruled by a majority then would that create serious problems in your country or not? Then delegates would say either if you overrule me, yes, it will create serious problems, or they would tell us it is manageable. If the answer was the first, then we would try hard to find another solution acceptable to everyone ahead of any closed sessions of Council. This pre-meeting dinner forum continues to this day. There was then and is now an active spirit of fairness in the collaboration that we always try and maintain.

Lack of credibility of the schedule to harness fusion energy for commercial power generation has been a feature of the fusion landscape from the onset of pioneers raising expectations to gain backing and funds, all adding to common semi-serious quip that fusion is always 10 years away and US$10B away. Efforts by the first two DGs in tackling—albeit difficult schedule issues—were unsuccessful in changing this perception. A report by the 2008 Management Advisory Committee deliberations revealed the prevailing gloomy mood (International Thermonuclear Experimental Reactor Newsline, 2008). Ten years was the original estimate for the combined length of the construction, commissioning, and initial operation phases. The basic first plasma is now forecast for the mid-2020s almost twice that original estimate. Even considering the optimism bias and strategic misrepresentation that Flyvbjerg et al. (2003) and Flyvbjerg (2006) have described, no one foresaw that the delay would be of this magnitude. This has placed a considerable strain on all the members due to the prolonged funding that the delays have caused. Publicly at the very least, Council consensus has prevailed as without it the project's critics would have exploited any unresolved major conflicts between the members and between the members and the DG and his central team.

Consensual Governance—Dealing With Constraints Fairly

The approach taken to other members by the central organization leadership (as with the CERN HQ) or to other members by the principal member leadership (as with Europe for ITER and the U.S. for the ISS) has been key to their success and longevity. They have consistently acted fairly and openly and thereby gained and maintained the other members' respect. This leadership has been most strongly evident in times of crisis that could have otherwise de-railed the projects. Lengthy and complex projects of this type suffer from three main and interlocking types of constraints: political turmoil, partner funding shortfalls, and technical setbacks; examples from each case study follow (Robinson, 2021).

For CERN, when Germany, due to the costs of re-unification in 1990, was forced to reduce its cash contribution to the central capital funds, just at the time when the organization needed more funds for the Large Hadron Collider (LHC) infrastructure, the remarkable decision reached was to reduce the cash contributions of all the member states by the same proportion. The management team recognized that the overriding need was to maintain fairness, a judgement call that was then endorsed by the Council. When Germany again reduced her contribution in 1997, the Council maintained the members funding ratios and permitted construction finance through advantageous European Investment Bank loans for the first time.

The risks of political appointees in large scale national projects are widely accepted and well researched (Kelman, 2010; and Dahlström & Holmgrem, 2018). These risks are magnified in projects that have high delegated powers of the DG and his/her immediate team. ITER suffered from the consequences of political appointees to its early high-level management team. The constraint of these political appointees has been steadily mitigated by recruiting suitably experienced replacements as the best person for the job. An ITER Director typified the views of many involved at the time:

> In a sense you could imagine that the DG could be a political appointment; that is OK as it is a political facing role. That is reasonable. The problem has also been the next level down; there is still some of it left in place, but it is not as bad as it was in the first round of appointments. The next level are department heads and therefore should be operational managers but, in the beginning, they included political appointees that had little appropriate skills.

The most notable technical ISS set-back surrounded the Space Shuttle Columbia disaster on re-entry in February 2003 that threatened to terminate the project. In the immediate aftermath the Russians filled the launch capability gap. This gave time for the Americans to deal internally with budget pressures and maintain their commitments to the program, thereby bolstering its technical and collaborative reputation with its international partners.

A further reason for the member states tendency to exercise consensual governance stems from the need to maintain the institutions and industries in their own territories bound by the project's detailed in-kind contribution commitments. One of the drawbacks of the in-kind funding system is that the control of the main supply base is not with a central team [who would need to be given the cash to place all the contracts] but remains with the contributing members. Consequently, when there are changes to the long-negotiated in-kind contributions they must be agreed by all parties, not just by the directly affected members. The leadership recognize this and respect the need for members to have full transparency and fairness in funding sharing; an administrative burden that takes considerable management effort to get right.

Finally, consensus is maintained through a need for community survival. ITER interviewees all emphasized that the project's focality added to the pressure on the community to deliver. There is a realization that the set of circumstances that established this nuclear collaboration between arch-rivals in other domains would be very difficult to repeat in today's increasingly nationalistic political climate. There will therefore not be a second chance for generations; failure is not an option for the planet or the fusion community. National interest from non-European ITER member states also features whereby they want to avoid the possibility of Europe taking over the remnants of the project should the international collaboration collapse.

Mechanism for Appointment of the Director General and Top-Level Management Team

A meticulously thorough selection process is followed for the appointment of a DG, typically for a 5-year term. A search committee of Council appointed experts carry out an extensive set of interviews aimed at ensuring that the person will be of the required stature to be accepted by the Big Science community. The reason for this care is how crucial the DG leadership role. It is more than a CEO in an industrial complex. The incumbent sets the tone, work ethic and behavioral example of these endeavors, represents the central organization to external stakeholders, the science community and the public and is ultimately responsible for safety and the granting of a license to operate from national regulators. This individual helps establish a productive collaborative culture that both the internal and external workforce can get behind and believe in.

Another governance system controlling measure at CERN is the accepted protocol on the appointment of a DG that if that person is a CERN "insider" (i.e., an existing member of the central staff), the direct reports will then be from "outside" CERN. The reverse would apply if the DG was an "outsider" appointee. This process enables a regular freshening up of the top-level central management and helps break up any cliques that may form. Similarly, the CERN Council President is limited to a 3-year term allowing the Member States, who elect the President, to have regular input into how governance is operationally exercised. Power, at two crucial levels, is therefore openly, regularly, and seamlessly passed on.

For CERN, the structural arrangement is that the embedded experiment instrument programs and core infrastructure form one integrated research facility. The experiments are managed separately but no results would be produced if they did not act in a fully cohesive manner. The recognized management teams of the longer established LHC do not overbear the more recently established instrument teams; they must and do work seamlessly within a collaborative approach. Both sets of technical groups have devised legitimate and effective processes that the other groups respect. The embedded scientific instrument teams are led by what are known as "spokespersons." These individuals are chosen by voting by their peers. The incumbents have no contractual levers over the team members from the collaboration partner institutes. Given that these embedded projects are multimillion-dollar endeavors, with the all the project control, risk, and reporting pressures that this brings, the fact that they work is remarkable. They demonstrate the benefit of taking time in selecting first-rate leaders who have proven team building and communication skills and a track record of delivering within a collaborative environment.

The way that the ISS project selects its mission commanders is based on a de facto agreement that the lead position should be rotated. This demonstrates that the U.S. does not exclude other members from the lead person on ISS Expeditions. The U.S. could have used its pre-eminence in the project to not share or severely limit these high-profile appointments; it has purposively chosen not to do so.

Case Study L-A-P Results

Here we will consider three aspects of the case study L-A-P results. Firstly, we will outline counterfactual results from both the literature and interviews. Secondly, we will investigate the case studies as epistemic communities of experts. Finally, we will examine the case studies belief systems, culture, and the importance of meaningfulness in these endeavors.

Counterfactual L-A-P Results

The proposition that the Big Science members are an elitist club of the most powerful developed nations who work to their own hidden agenda does have supporting circumstantial evidence from the research. The case study projects all fail to include developing nations, and field work revealed that they have no meaningful plans to include any. Also, it is true that at the core of each project's memberships are the world's nuclear powers who certainly have strategic reasons for staying close to each other. This counterfactual argument continues with the reasoning that the case for nuclear powers to stay close to each other is weaker in other non-strategically relevant domains and therefore the same states' leadership teams do not make sufficient efforts to achieve meaningful collaboration in these other domains. In other words, Big Science is too special to merit wider consideration. The push back on this argument is that key elements of these endeavors are breakthrough science research and development of cutting-edge technology. Both areas that are increasingly at the core of many regular large ventures. Also, meaningful engagement and retention of an educated, knowledgeable, and mobile workforce is faced by many management teams. Our core finding regarding what we can learn from Big Science light-touch management leadership traits is therefore relevant despite the undeniable special nature of the case studies themselves. In doing so and although concentrating on physics global Big Science, we note and acknowledge the wealth of other natural science projects which also have a select few projects in the global category such as the Human Genome Project and International Brain Initiative.

Several high-profile Big Science major projects have been beset by schedule delays and cost overruns. In that sense they demonstrate no immunity from what Bent Flyvbjerg identified as the "Iron Law" and main challenge in megaproject management: "Over budget, over time, under benefits, over and over again" (2017, p. 1). However, what does set them apart is their ability to ride out constraints and setbacks and maintain the full support of their stakeholders. Also, the complexity of these endeavors means that they are pushing the boundaries of technical capabilities which they are in part designed to overcome.

It is also true that Big Science is not devoid of poor leadership. Indeed, the research highlighted where this has had a detrimental effect on project performance, moral and followship loyalty. However, we will show that fundamental to the success of the three main light-touch management approach elements we feature in the emerging themes section of this chapter, is the standing of the person who exercises them. Therefore, anyone who does not have or loses this respect is bluntly exposed. The community, in the form of the governing Council, then acts. An example of this is when the second ITER DG was struggling to lead the project through the deep and diverse difficulties it was faced with in 2013, the individual's position became progressively untenable. This culminated in the 2013 Management Assessors report to Council including a recommendation to "Accelerate the DG Transition" (Madia and Associates, 2013, p. 7).

Case Studies Viewed as Epistemic Communities

To be understood Big Science project management needs also to be seen through the concept of an epistemic community which Peter Haas (1992, p. 3) defines as "a network of professionals with recognized expertise and competence in a particular domain and an authoritative claim to policy-relevant knowledge within that domain." The three case studies are all estimable examples of epistemic communities in their respective fields. For CERN it comprises the high energy physics community who have developed since the founding of the field in the 1950s. For ITER it comprises the nuclear fusion community and particularly those embracing magnetic confinement fusion. For the ISS it comprises all of those involved from the constituent national space agencies. Figure 1.1 therefore is a generic representation of a Big Science epistemic community.

Claire Dunlop (2012, p. 229) highlights that understanding the structure and power dynamics that exist within an epistemic community is important in understanding their behavior. Here, these dynamics can be viewed by the degree that the members grant the central element autonomy and the performance of the community to adapt to shifts in organizational structure as more power is delegated to the center as the project matures. The central leadership team have to earn this greater autonomy by showing they are capable of being trusted with it. Quite naturally, given their different project life-cycle phases, the research has shown that the level of autonomy granted to the center by the members varies across the three case studies. Nevertheless, despite this the central leadership teams actively manage any ensuing multi-polarity into good outcomes.

The early CERN management teams quickly established an international institution that commanded global respect and consistently drew funds from the member states. The community has encouraged the embedded experimental projects to exercise autonomy in deciding how they tackle science enquiry. Interviewees from both the central teams and the member states confirmed that this helps to attract and retain the world's best scientific and technological talent to the central entities. They find "champions" they can willingly follow. For example, a Science Director and the leaders of their instrument teams, and the niche technical areas and their group leaders support the Technical Director; again, see Figure 1.1. The former DG, Chris Llewellyn Smith, summarized the position: "The governing structure was pretty hands-off … there was never a tendency to micromanage; they let the CERN management just get on with it."

For ITER the Members are both Stakeholders (through the Council) and Suppliers (through the in-kind contributions they are responsible for). This is a dilemma that must be continually and sensitively handled if the legitimacy of the Council is to be maintained. Two interviewees believed that at the start of the project there was a power struggle between the international central HQ team based in France and the main (Europe) member team based in Barcelona and, to a lesser extent the six other members' teams based worldwide. While the overall design authority rests with the DG and thereby his staff, and is respected for areas such as nuclear safety, there has been a reluctance from the members to provide project control levers to the central organization in other areas. Evidence for this is in the analysis of independent Management Review Reports such as that provided by Madia and Associates (2013, p. 7). This power struggle made the appointment of a DG who could achieve effective collaboration between the parties even more vital.

When the respected French physicist Bernard Bigot took office in 2015 as the third ITER DG, he openly set as one of his conditions of appointment that he and his team needed to be given more executive authority. Bigot has restored faith in the leadership through personal example and by a series of apposite, firm, and timely decisions. Team moral has consequently improved as evidenced by an executive staff survey results (International Thermonuclear Experimental Reactor Council Working Group, 2016, p. 51). A current ITER Division Head, with over 10 years on the project, summed up Bigot's effect on international collaboration thus: "In Bigot's dealing with the USA, I think he has made magic. He has managed to communicate and convince major players …, which was the complete opposite before he came." A long-serving and respected ITER Science and Operations Team Section Leader added:

> And what is good now is that Bernard Bigot has insisted on more central team control over the members and much more dialogue, so things are clearer. How things are written is clearer, the way documents are reviewed and assessed is getting better and so communication channels are much improved. It also helps when you see that the project has come to life in the last few years. Now you hear good things, not just bad things. That inertia is very important and that has come from the very top…. Bigot is so well connected that he has opened up influential contacts everywhere. Something his predecessors struggled to do.

A current ITER Head of Department noted: "One of the things Bernard Bigot is very good at is 'ask what you want' and 'say what you think.' Do not play political games on the project as it is viewed differently in different cultures." Dr James Van Dam, the acting associate director, Fusion Energy Sciences, Office of Science, Department of Energy, in his 2016 testimony to Congress stated: "The ITER Organisation has significantly improved its project management performance under DG Bigot, and we thank him for that." Three interviewees indicated however that there is a lingering tension between the central team and the ring of supporting members; a tension that needs, and now receives, constant attention from the highest management levels.

For the ISS, governance of the project is inexorably linked to the leadership that the dominant member state has provided. The lead role of the United States in the management arrangements was accepted by all the parties when they agreed to take part. The international reputation of the U.S. to deal with its partners fairly has therefore been under scrutiny from the outset. Interviewees attested that reaching consensus with the other Space Agencies has been at the center of NASA's approach to ISS operations throughout the project's life cycle. The success of the U.S. in doing so has elevated the ISS to become an iconic beacon of what can be done when there is a collective will for peaceful collaboration. It has also laid the foundation for further collaboration in space such as the James Webb Space Telescope (NASA, 2021) which includes three of the original ISS members (NASA, the Canadian Space Agency, and the European Space Agency); see Table 1.1.

The Abbott and Hale (2014, p. 9) paper, "Orchestrating Global Solution Networks; A Guide for Organizational Entrepreneurs" identifies characteristics of successful orchestrator organizations that include "focality" and "legitimacy." This research has assessed the level and quality of both features within the three case studies drawing on evidence from field work interviews to supplement the available literature. The granting of autonomy is made by the members (their representatives at Council and other sub-committees) to the DG and the central team of directors and managers. The process is a steady evolutional one rather than in revolutionary jumps. For example, more power is delegated to the central project management office as an integrated master schedule is capable of showing the task and associated resource loading to achieve the work. More power is delegated to the central engineering team to enable their control of systems engineering processes as the design matures.

Case Studies Belief Systems, Culture, and the Importance of Meaningfulness

We have shown that, the common key to success in all three case studies has been the emergence of epistemic communities of experts with their own norms and expectations who work well together. However, it is deeper than just organizational efficiency that has led to the success of these challenging projects it is that the key participants operate within a shared belief system. This belief system can be seen through the four knowledge elements that Peter Haas (1992) identified: (1) a shared set of normative and principled beliefs, (2) shared causal beliefs, (3) shared notions of validity and 4) a common policy enterprise. Interviewees invariably demonstrated a deep holding of these beliefs. They have overcome national boundaries, albeit with occasional setbacks usually because of national funding shortfalls, by working in their specialist areas to establish effective and legitimate processes to deliver their portion of the work. The prevailing organizational culture is best illustrated by direct quotations from interviewees.

A senior CERN manager provided a high-level context:

> the successful collaboration comes back to this idea of science for peace, it is a bit of a cliché almost, but it sums up so much, we get people coming here that are motivated by the science, they meet people from other countries and cultures and they have this shared passion and they discover they have a lot more in common than they maybe thought they would have.

A young and award-winning post-doctoral physicist made a telling observation that:

> As a scientist you are trained to think that there is a fundamental truth and this helps unify people and many scientists come from a background of international experience, many people go abroad already as students ... and so, when you bring people together at a place like CERN there is already a component that has had that exposure in the past and what they have been exposed in the field of physics has been the same regardless of where they come from. They already have the mindset that to collaborate internationally is normal.

The 2013 ITER Management Assessor (Madia and Associates, 2013, p. 4) pointed out the difficulties in establishing a shared project culture between fusion systems designers, scientists, and nuclear industry construction engineers. The groups have differing backgrounds and priorities. For example, the design groups are stereotyped as having difficulty in embracing the concept of "this is good enough." This view was supported by a highly experienced ITER Division Head:

> We talk a lot about cultural differences and conflicts and people like to relate this to nationalities. In my opinion this is completely wrong. We do have a big cultural problem but that is between the science community and the nuclear industry community which are two extremes, and everything is different in these two worlds, and we continually have conflicts.... The science community on ITER has adapted and become a little stronger to push back.

While much of this chapter discusses the collaborative facets of science, it is also a highly competitive field. There is a worldwide competition between groups and institutions to discover knowledge and to secure research and innovation funds. Competition is also encouraged and indeed essential to the way CERN operates internally, typified by the rigor employed in the detection of the Higgs boson. The findings were only made public when the results from two instrument teams were independently confirmed. While there was a need for the dual confirmation there was also keen and natural competition as to which investigational group would be first. However, the prevailing culture is that it is a healthy rivalry. A long-serving ITER Director, noted with respect to analyzing the project culture that:

> There is not a single relationship. For example, every procurement responsible officer in the central organization has a relationship with their counterparts in the member states agencies; each one has a plus or minus that contributes to the overall depth and quality of the central organization to members' relationships. This observation has read across to a series of specialist mini epistemic communities that are led by the central organization staff who have counterparts in the member organizations. For example, a veteran ITER technical team leader put it this way: I organized bi-annual meetings and ITER became the leading entity in an emerging specialist field of technology. People attended to find out what to do and went and did it, this has benefited everyone in the end. What we have seen is that the less experienced countries see the collaboration as a possibility to learn. An example is China where they have learned. It is a win-win for our community as they learn, and we get the work done cheaply, well and on time.

This effective collaboration does not mean the total lack of conflict. It is constructive conflict which CERN DG Fabiola Gianotti, described when speaking at a CERN/United Nations (UN) Symposium in 2015 as follows: "Decisions are taken by consensus. Consensus does not mean that everyone agrees; this is impossible. Consensus means that problems, issues, strategy and plans are discussed all together in an open manner" (CERN/United Nations, 2015). In practice it means groups being passionate and caring about their areas. The group leaders have learned that, if they are to be effective, they must articulate and defend their position with their peers and with higher management. Crucially, the prevalent organizational culture also means that they have respect for each other and know when to compromise. It is then all these groups operating to a single goal that form the reliable core engine room of these types of projects.

Meaningful purpose means different things to different people and this research has shown that their perspective is closely linked to which mini-epistemic group they are a member of. For some on the ISS, that the Intergovernmental Agreement exists at all and has survived the types of constraints we have analyzed is good enough legitimacy to justify the costs. For others, such as the astronaut corps, it is the higher meaning that matters.

While national agendas will always be present in projects of this magnitude, the driving factor that trumps these is the collective higher-level goal. Interviewees were unanimous that these are ventures which generate high emotions with one or two even suggesting that the projects have a soul of their own. One ITER executive level interviewee and veteran of the cause to bring the vision into reality stated: "there are many great science projects; but this one is mine!" The notion of high meaningfulness in the mission is also encapsulated by Maria Spiropulu, a physicist at Caltech, vice-chair of the American Physical Society Forum on International Physics and a member of an instrument collaboration at CERN:

> Being a fundamental physics lab inherently played a big role in pushing competing nations to work together ... the goal is the same, and it's very clear that it is fundamental research.... That alleviates a lot of the conflict because we're all going towards the same fundamental goal and the same dream. (Lucibella, 2014, p. 1)

The shrewd governance mechanisms, sound managerial structures, shared beliefs and meaningfulness all help the management teams in their constant striving for a collaborative approach to problem solving. However, it is the need for thoughtful, inspiring, and special leadership of the projects that is the driving factor and that we now move on to.

EMERGENCE OF THEMES OF THE SOURCE OF AGENCY AND THE CONCEPT OF LIGHT-TOUCH MANAGEMENT

Collaborative agency has emerged as an effective management means to get things done in a complex project environment. What becomes apparent in the collaborative structures of the Big Science case studies is that there are sets of mini-epistemic communities that have effective and legitimate processes within their expert areas. They are led by team leaders in the central international organization and followed by their own central team colleagues and those in the members' organizations and suppliers. These mini-epistemic communities then collaborate with similar groups to collectively form the engine room needed to deliver the project.

We contend that there are three main elements of this Big Science community culture and values that speak to leadership and followership of these groups. Together they comprise what we term a light-touch management (LTM) approach. Firstly, the top leadership carefully and skillfully nurture and promote a shared belief system and meaningfulness of purpose. Secondly, real and appropriate delegation of authority is utilized, and finally meritocracy-based decision-making is the standard practice. Here we will explain how these elements are enacted.

LTM Element 1: Promotion of a Shared Belief System and Meaningfulness

Nurturing staff to accept the principle that international collaboration is normal and fostering the right cross-cultural attitudes is essential in the international environments that the Big Science communities occupy. The four elements of the belief system (1) a shared set of normative and principled beliefs, (2) shared causal beliefs, (3) shared notions of validity and (4) a common policy enterprise, are what the successful leaders cultivate and nudge to successful outcomes for the collective. It matters who is cultivating and nudging; these leaders have to have respected standing in the communities. The top leaders, such as DGs and Directors, have many of the trappings of a regular hierarchical structure. However, the respect they command is purely meritocracy based. Every day they have to preserve that standing and be the fair and inclusive leader that their followers expect; such are the challenges, nothing else will do.

There are many examples of effective leaders on the ISS project who epitomize the triumph of achieving the four elements of the belief system over any particular cultural and/or professional background impediments that team members may bring. Dr Ellen Ochoa, the first Hispanic woman to go into space, is a shining example. Ochoa, is a veteran U.S. astronaut with over 1,000 hours in space, has a PhD from Stanford University in Electrical Engineering and became the 11th director of the Johnson Space Centre in 2012. Her consistent, collaborative leadership style has been highly appreciated resulting in numerous awards including NASA's highest, the distinguished service medal and the President's Award for outstanding leadership by a Senior Executive in a Federal Agency. Ochoa was on three ISS Missions and therefore commanded authority in the decisions she made in her later high-level management career. In a speech made at the American Association for the Advancement of Science Annual Meeting in Austin, Texas, in 2018, she points out that international collaboration is not easy:

> Maintaining that International Partnership is not easy, it requires constant cross-cultural diplomacy and negotiations at all levels, for example all parties have to agree to extend the life of the ISS ... another manifestation of the peaceful cooperation is the world-wide control network that operates continuously twenty four hours a day, seven days a week, every day of the year, coordinated by our Mission Control Centre at the Johnson

Space Centre and includes all the other parties Mission Control Centres. (American Academy for Arts and Science, 2018)

Another ISS example is Sergei Krikalev, whose early cosmonaut career included the final days of the MIR space station and was the first Russian to fly the Space Shuttle in 1994 and a member of Expedition 1 to the ISS in 2000. He was unique in straddling the two eras of space exploration when he was then selected to be the Commander of ISS Expedition 11. His calm leadership style was praised by all who served with him. His many honors include being a Hero of the Soviet Union and later the Russian Federation, a recipient of the French Legion of Honour and the NASA Distinguished Public Service Medal. As the Director of the Yuri Gagarin Cosmonaut Training Center, he has championed inter-operability with the ISS partner Space Agencies. He has an accumulated time in space of over 2 years and he provided the following insight on international space collaboration in a 2017 interview:

> There are many angles to look at what we achieved [on the ISS], engineering experience for sure, physiological lessons for sure, but the main achievement has been learning how to trust, respect and understand each other, how to collaborate in a difficult environment to achieve a common mission. (Česká televize, 2017)

This confidence in each other and sense of fulfilment in a common meaning is something the ISS community is rightly proud of and does not want to lose.

We do not agree that collaboration will inevitably win over national short-sightedness, but we contend that the binding centripetal force for collaboration gets stronger as the underlying meaningfulness develops and is woven into the fabric of the project culture. History is strewn with examples where "meaning" can be harnessed for bad reasons, however it is a powerful driving force for good when correctly stirred in the hearts of men and women. It does not need to be overdone or overstated in a heroic militaristic way to be successful. Indeed, our research has shown that the Big Science leaders evoke it sparingly and with thoughtful timing, much as with applying oil just in the right amount and frequency to a smooth-running engine.

On the confirmation of the Higgs boson, the CERN DG at the time, Professor Rolf-Dieter Heuer, commented: "The discovery marks the culmination of decades of intellectual effort by many people around the world. It is a global effort, it was a global effort, and it is a global success" (British Broadcasting Corporation, 2013). At the signature of the ITER Agreement on December 21, 2006, the host of the event, President Jacques

Chirac of France, noted that the occasion marked a memorable moment in the history of science:

> Exceptional for its scientific ambition to harness the sun´s power to take up the challenge of ecological energy, and exceptional for its international scale: the unprecedented association of seven major partners from the North to the South. It is the hand held out to future generations, in the name of solidarity and responsibility.

We contend that these examples of rousing rhetoric would seem embarrassingly out of place for endeavors of less importance. These moments matter, they help legitimize the projects, raise their profile beyond the ordinary and, as the field work revealed, are cited by the project participants to this day.

LTM Element 2: Real and Appropriate Delegation of Authority Based on Trust

James Gillies the former Head of Communications at CERN expressed in an interview that "one of the most important political lessons learned by the project governance and management regimes was that the Convention puts in place the structures that promote and allow mutual trust to be developed over time." The principle of fairness in the CERN Convention financial protocol and dispute resolution articles have allowed teams to establish workable rules and develop a project adhocracy. This has enabled expert groups of scientists and engineers (in their specific mini-epistemic community of expertise) to solve complex problems legitimately and effectively in whatever manner they see fit. This appropriate and genuine delegation of authority to the team leaders of these groups has aided the attraction and retention of the best scientific and technologist talent.

Another way of looking at this is that the DGs and their leadership teams know that they are "incomplete" as described and framed under humility by Owens and Hekman (2012) and Owens, Johnson, and Mitchell (2013). The DGs and their direct reports understand from their grasp of the complexity of the problems that no one person can or should solely influence close judgment calls. Sloman and Fernbach (2017) when examining "modern-day teamwork" find that:

> Knowledge is so sophisticated at the cutting edge of science that huge teams are required to make progress … researchers sit around a table … and each contributes bits of knowledge and ideas … hypotheses are thrown into the mix, disagreements are registered, and a consensus might build, all in a fairly chaotic series of turns and responses. A collection of expertise that, provides a group intelligence greater than the sum of its parts. (pp. 118–119)

The Big Science top leadership trust their teams and their team leaders because they must do, sure in the knowledge that delegation is not just a word but an essential way of working. The sheer number and complexity of specialist issues could not be achieved any other way. As Lawrence Walker (2017) points out when examining the moral character of heroes, heroism is not characterized by a single personality profile and that sensitivity to cultural and ethical group differences is often warranted (pp. 115–116). In our research, the requirement for these sensitivities to be met is also present in the respect and trust for the leaders of the geographically dispersed and multi-cultural mini-epistemic communities of experts that we previously charted. The DG and Director level leaders are heroic in understanding that a Big Science collaborative project is no place for solo heroes and then act accordingly.

LTM Element 3: Meritocracy Based Decision Making Built on Respect for Knowledge

Many large ventures pronounce that their organizations are a meritocracy, only those within the project structures know if it is the case. We have found that the Big Science community's leadership employ a light-touch management style with international staff and visiting external collaborators. Trust is either there or it is not in an organizational culture and must be maintained through the actions of all the players. James Gillies of CERN again:

> for the Instrument projects the spokesperson will normally reach decisions through consensus … the lead times for big decisions are also very long and this adds to the idea of the collective agreeing what is best for each instrument project.

All ideas and contributions are considered regardless of what level they have originated from, whatever nationality the person is or which member state organization or institution the person may have originated from. A meritocracy-based decision-making is not just expected but demanded at the technical and science team level by the nature of their specialist operations and the knowledge of the team members. The skilled application of the approach also helps to reduce the risk of hesitancy and inaction. It provides a means to find what Kumar and Das (2021, p. 166) identified as the right balance between temperance and actions essential for effective alliance management.

The clearest example of what this light-touch management approach means in practice is at CERN, whose leadership have had longer to develop the approach. Dr Fabiola Gianotti, speaking at a CERN/UN Symposium in 2015 as the then "CERN DG elect" fully embraced the concept and stated that in her experience, the main reasons for the success of the CERN model were that:

> These experiments have a very light, a very loose organizational structure and the leadership has no contractual power over the members of the collaborations. The Members are affiliated and report to their home institutes … authority comes from the intellectual contribution not from the hierarchy. The youngest student has a bright idea to the solution of a problem then the collaboration follows. Everyone can contribute in a significant way to shape the strategy and course of the experiment. Managerial structure is light. Some structure is needed … but it must be light and nimble, not to repress initiatives and ideas and creativity of individuals. Because the ideas and creativity are the drivers of the research. The organization is there to assist and help particularly the young people to blossom and not be impeded by bureaucracy. This would be the death of research and science.… The key element is that people are animated by a strong common passion for the scientific goals of the experiments and this passion and the realization that these goals can only be reached by working together is much stronger than the ambition and interests of the individuals, institutes and countries. Universal values like education and knowledge, transcend the political, social and economic interests of individuals and countries and as such are a very strong glue to bring mankind together and are a very strong ally of peace. (CERN/UN, 2015)

Linked with this element of meritocracy-based decision-making built on respect for knowledge comes the responsibility for the top leadership to maintain the currency of that knowledge in their workforce. Training and staying up to date have never been more important in these fields, not just for the individual but for the performance of the collective. Expert light-touch management practitioners appreciate this and build personal development requirements into their planning and resource loading modeling.

The communities are a product of complex social interdependencies and reflect ongoing relationships between their aims and the constraints of the everyday world. They comprise groups of motivated people who are highly employable in the broader science and technology sectors. It would be unfair to label them as high maintenance employees, but they are certainly a group who need special considerations with respect to working conditions and being given the freedom to work out their own solutions to complex problems as they see fit within their teams. They are given just that.

CONCLUSION

We have shown that the source of agency in Big Science organizations is mostly collective and collaborative rather than mostly about individuals. The Big Science community's management teams exercise autonomy and adapt their structures through intelligent strategies to achieve results to the level that their set-up conditions, governance and national funding regimes allow.

Both leaders and followers in the Big Science communities revel in the meaningfulness of their endeavors. They have faith in what they are doing, that helps them take on these massive challenges on behalf of society. Once established, the communities have found a way of effectively channeling their collective efforts through teams that execute open actions, share risks, and steadily build trust between each other.

We have provided evidence when considering managing constraints, that the executive leadership teams realize that fairness to all parties out-weighs any short-term political or economic gains. Dominant members have shown restraint in foregoing weighted voting wherever possible and seeking agreement by consensus on all major issues; the overriding priority being to keep the collaboration itself intact.

Power is emergent through enactment of participants' competing choices and practices rather than enacted solely through the influence of top leaders. Many Big Science governance regimes have a built-in rotation of power between the main players. The governing Councils will also act if an incumbent DG fails to perform to the high standards that are required. Delegation is not just a word but an effective way of working essential to project success. Continuous dialogue within teams and between teams is used to focus on mutual learning, deep understanding, and collaborative actions (rather than to convince the other of one's dominant point of view). Focality and legitimacy of the central teams grows as trust between them, and the dispersed members' teams mature.

We have shown that the projects have benefited from leaders who have exercised, to varying degrees, the required light-touch management approach that their environments demand. The importance of light-touch management leadership behaviors was cited by all the field work inter-viewees as the most important element in their achievements and had three main elements. Firstly, the nurturing and promotion of a shared belief system and meaningfulness grounded on the leaders' standing in the community and sincerity. Secondly, real and appropriate delegation of authority based on trust at all levels in the community and finally, an inherent culture of meritocracy-based decision-making built on respect for knowledge.

Over-dominant project leadership is rejected in the same way that over-dominance of a single research perspective is rejected. Tokenism or "non-inclusive inclusion" of team members is also not tolerated; everyone's contributions are respected. In other words, the Big Science community leaders have to exercise best practice operational management. They know that if they do not the scarce talent will either physically leave the project or even worse stay but not contribute beyond the routine.

Recommendations

We have demonstrated several ways in which Big Science organizations practice leadership and followership that can open up new perspectives for organizations and businesses with currently more traditional leadership structures. We suggest that the post-heroic, not-authoritarian view of leadership rooted in Big Science collaborations, which we term light-touch management, will inspire a wider critical and constructive debate of collective approaches to managerial practice.

We have heard strong evidence that science leaders educational background when dealing with international academic projects in their early careers helps foster the right cross-cultural attitudes. However, it does not necessarily mean that this skill of accepting other people's views will be maintained as they move into leadership positions. The fact that it generally does provides an impetus to identify the enabling features of selection that could be transferred to other domains. Here we recommend three areas for further consideration that go beyond traditional, hierarchical management.

Firstly, if we accept that high level agreements that stick are reached in the Big Science communities because those involved are members of an epistemic community of experts who have long standing personal relationships, respect each other and relish in a shared belief system, then promotion of these types of community environments and values should be encouraged. Similarly, another key supporting community factor has been the reliance on members' in-kind contributions. Although these funding arrangements have disadvantages such as the difficulty in controlling the dispersed supply chain, without the national support that they engender these projects could have been cancelled at any of several pinch-points. So, further explanation of these types of innovative contributions structures to other cross-organizational project teams should also be considered.

Secondly, the notion of rotation of decision-making roles should be further explored; this is most closely related to the ideas of shared leadership, where power must be shared between individuals over time. We recommend that this could be implemented in major project management structures based on project phase; for example, a planned change-over as the project moves from detailed design to construction and again from construction to commissioning and operation. Best leadership practice would be maintained through the rotation of decision-making capacity by the industrial members of a joint venture over the lifespan of the projects. The actual individuals fulfilling the roles could then be selected from within the joint venture pool by innovative methods such as peer voting. This idea of voting would change the dynamics between managers and non-managerial employees. Further work is needed to see what the upsides and downsides could be from an L-A-P perspective and implementation would need to be carefully managed to ascertain project continuity and implement purposeful disruptiveness.

Thirdly, long-term orientation toward keeping the collaboration intact is a notable success of Big Science collaboration. In many businesses, power games between managers are regularly played out based on the assumption that individual aspirations are valued over the collective interest. Assessment of managers could therefore be tilted with the emphasis being on the attributes that bolster the performance of the collective rather than individual feats. Many large project organizations already say that their evaluation and reward systems do this, but what we recommend here is a more radical reform to actively incentivize the light-touch-management skill set. It is the leaders that can drive the three elements that we identified (promotion of a shared belief system and meaningfulness, real and appropriate delegation of authority based on trust and meritocracy-based decision-making built on respect for knowledge) that will be needed in the future. A future faced with ever increasing scientific and technological challenges and a, quite rightly, ever demanding workforce. Those talented individuals with these light-touch-management leadership abilities need to be found, supported, and promoted.

REFERENCES

Abbott, K. W., & Hale, T. (2014). *Orchestrating global solution networks; A guide for organizational entrepreneurs*, Blavatnik School of Government, Global Solution Networks, UK. Retrieved August 12, 2017, from https://www.bsg.ox.ac.uk/sites/www.bsg.ox.ac.uk/files/documents/2014-05_Orchestrating_GlobalSolutionNetworks.pdf

Aguinis, H., & Solarino, A. M. (2019). Transparency and replicability in qualitative research: The case of interviews with elite informants. *Strategic Management Journal, 40*(8), 1291–1315.

American Association for the Advancement of Science. (2018). The International Space Station, a speech by Elle Ochoa, the then Director Johnson Space Center, NASA, at the *American Association for the Advancement of Science 2018 Annual Meeting*. Retrieved December 21, 2018, from https://www.aaas.org/node/65049

Antonakis, J. & Day, D. V. (2018). *The nature of leadership* (3rd ed.). Thousand Oaks, CA: SAGE.

Antonakis, J. (2021). Leadership to defeat COVID-19. *Group Processes & Intergroup Relations, 24*(2), 210–215.

British Broadcasting Corporation. (2013). Higgs boson scientists win Nobel prize in physics, *BBC News Article, 8 October 2013*. Retrieved October 9, 2018, from https://www.bbc.co.uk/news/science-environment-24436781

Bolden, R. (2011). Distributed leadership in organizations: A review of theory and research. *International Journal of Management Reviews, 13*(3), 251–269.

Booth, C. W., Colomb, G. G., & Williams, J. M. (2008). *The craft of research* (3rd ed.). Chicago, IL: University of Chicago Press.

Caldwell, R. (2012). Leadership and learning: A critical reexamination of Senge's learning organization. *Systemic Practice and Action Research, 25*(1), 39–55.

Cannell, C., & Kahn, R. (1968). Interviewing. In G. Lindzey and E. Aronson (Eds.), *The handbook of social psychology* (Vol. 2, pp. 526–595). Cambridge, MA: Addison-Wesley.

Conseil Européen pour la Recherche Nucléaire (CERN). (2022a). *Rules of procedure of the CERN council*. Retrieved February 5, 2022, from http://cds.cern.ch/record/2692901/files/English.pdf

CERN. (2022b). *CERN governance*. Retrieved February 5, 2022, from https://council.web.cern.ch/en

CERN/United Nations (UN). (2015). CERN/UN Symposium keynote speech by Dr. Fabiola Gianotti, CERN DG elect, *UN Web TV*. Retrieved January 12, 2018, from http://webtv.un.org/watch/panel-1-the-cern-model-science-education-and-global-public-good-cern-unog-symposium-2015/4590293913001

Česká televize. (2017). Sergei Krikalev, interview with Česká televize, the Czech Republic State TV on September 30, 2017. Retrieved January 11, 2019, from https://www.ceskatelevize.cz/porady/10441294653-hyde-park-civilizace/9271-english/29397-sergei-krikalev-former-russian-cosmonaut/

Collinson, M. (2018). What's new about leadership-as-practice? *Leadership, 14*(3), 363–370.

Dahlström, C., & Holmgrem, M. (2018). *The politics of political appointments, the quality of government institute*. Department of Political Science, University of Gothenburg. Retrieved October 3, 2018, from https://qog.pol.gu.se/digitalAssets/1517/1517594_2015_4_dahlstr--m_holmgren.pdf

Day, D. V., Gronn, P., & Salas, E. (2004). Leadership capacity in teams. *The Leadership Quarterly, 15*(6), 857–880. Retrieved March 13, 2022, from http://dx.doi.org/10.1016/j.leaqua.2004.09.

Denis, J. L., Langley, A., & Sergi, V. (2012). Leadership in the plural. *Academy of Management Annals, 6*(1), 211–283.

DeRue D. S., Nahrgang J. D., & Ashford S. J. (2015). Interpersonal perceptions and the emergence of leadership structures in groups: A network perspective. *Organization Science, 26*(4), 1192–1209.

Dooley, D. (1984). *Social research methods* (4th ed.). Hoboken, NJ: Prentice Hall.

Dunlop, C. (2012). Epistemic communities. In E. Araral, S. Fritzen, M. Howlett, M. Ramesh, & X. Wu (Eds.). *Routledge handbook of public policy* (pp. 224–238). New York, NY: Routledge.

EC. (2017). *Group of senior officials on global research infrastructures; Policy, European Commission, Research & Innovation Infrastructures Policy Unit.* Retrieved June 21, 2017, from https://ec.europa.eu/research/infrastructures/index_en.cfm?pg=gso (Accessed:).

ESFRI. (2016). *Strategy report on research infrastructures; projects and landmarks roadmap,* European Strategy Forum on Research Infrastructures. Retrieved November 11, 2017, from http://www.esfri.eu/sites/default/files/20160308_ROADMAP_single_page_LIGHT.pdf

Flyvbjerg, B. (2006). How optimism bias and strategic misrepresentation in early project development undermine implementation actions. *Oxford University Research Archive.* Retrieved May 12, 2018, from https://ora.ox.ac.uk/objects/uuid:651ebae9-dc16-4900-ad16-362d9f9dbe5e

Flyvbjerg, B. (2017). Introduction: The iron law of megaproject management. *The Oxford handbook of megaproject management.* Oxford, UK: Oxford University Press.

Flyvbjerg, B., Bruzelius, N., & Rothengatter, W. (2003). *Megaprojects and risk: An anatomy of ambition.* Cambridge, UK: Cambridge University Press.

Garan, R. (2015). *The orbital perspective.* Oakland, CA: Berrett-Koehler.

Gronn, P. (2009). Leadership configurations. *Leadership, 5*(3), 381–394.

Gronn, P. (2015). The view from inside leadership configurations. *Human Relations, 68*(4), 545–560.

Haas, P. (1992). Introduction: epistemic communities and international policy coordination, *International Organization, 46*(01), 1–35.

Holm, F., & Fairhurst, G. T. (2018). Configuring shared and hierarchical leadership through authoring. *Human Relations, 71*(5), 692–721.

International Thermonuclear Experimental Reactor Council Working Group. (2016). *International Thermonuclear Experimental Reactor (ITER) Council Working Group on the Independent Review of the Updated Long-Term Schedule and Human Resources.* Retrieved September 24, 2018, from http://www.firefusionpower.org/ITER_ICRG_Report_2016.pdf

International Thermonuclear Experimental Reactor Newsline. (2008). The MAC factor. *ITER Newsline 56.* Retrieved September 30, 2020, from https://www.iter.org/newsline/56/1180

International Thermonuclear Experimental Reactor. (2022). *ITER Governance.* Retrieved February 5, 2022, from https://www.iter.org/org/Council

Ives, M. (2005). Identifying the contextual elements of project management within organizations and their impact on project success. *Project Management Journal, 36*(1), 37–50.

Kelman, S. (2010). How political appointees undermine large IT programs—and how to turn the tide, *Harvard University and Federal Computer Week*. Retrieved October 3, 2018, from https://fcw.com/articles/2010/10/25/comment-steve-kelman-program-management-continuity.aspx

Kniffin, K. M., Narayanan, J., Anseel, F., Antonakis, J., Ashford, S. P., Bakker, A. B., Bamberger, P., Bapuji, H., Bhave, D. P., Choi, V. K., Creary, S. J., Demerouti, E., Flynn, F. J., Gelfand, M. J., Greer, L. L., Johns, G., Kesebir, S., Klein, P. G., Lee, S. Y., & Vugt, M. v. (2021). COVID-19 and the workplace: Implications, issues, and insights for future research and action. *American Psychologist, 76*(1) 63–77.

Kumar, R., & Das, T. K. (2021). National culture and legitimacy in international alliances. In T. K. Das (Ed.). *Cultural values in strategy and organization* (pp. 151–169). New York, NY: Information Age.

Lord, R. G., Gatti, P., & Chui, S. L. (2016). Social-cognitive, relational, and identity-based approaches to leadership. *Organizational Behavior and Human Decision Processes, 136*, 119–134.

Lord, R. G., Day, D. V., Zaccaro, S. J., Avolio, B. J., & Eagly, A. H. (2017). Leadership in applied psychology: Three waves of theory and research. *Journal of Applied Psychology, 102*(3), 434–451.

Lucibella, M. (2014, August/September). CERN: 60 years of collaboration, *American Physical Society News, 23,* 8. Retrieved November 27, 2017, from https://www.aps.org/publications/apsnews/201409/cern.cfm

Madia and Associates. (2013). *2013 ITER management assessment, October 18, 2013*. Retrieved September 30, 2018, from https://assets.documentcloud.org/documents/1031934/2013-iter-management-assessment.pdf

Maylor, H., & Blackmon, K. (2005). *Researching business and management*. London, UK: Palgrave Macmillan.

Miller, R., & Lessard, D. (2000). *The strategic management of large engineering projects*, Cambridge, MA: MIT Press.

NASA. (2021). *James webb space telescope, international partners and contributors*. Retrieved January 4, 2022, from https://webb.nasa.gov/content/meetTheTeam/team.html

Owens, B. P., & Hekman, D. R. (2012). Modeling how to grow: An inductive examination of humble leader behaviors, contingencies, and outcomes. *Academy of Management Journal, 55*(4), 787–818.

Owens, B. P., Johnson, M. D., & Mitchell, T. R. (2013). Expressed humility in organizations: Implications for performance, teams, and leadership. *Organization Science, 24*(5), 1517–1538.

Pearce, C. L. (2004). The future of leadership: Combining vertical and shared leadership to transform knowledge work. *Academy of Management Executive, 18*(1), 47–57.

Pearce, C. L., & Conger J. A. (Eds.). (2003). *Shared leadership. Reframing the hows and whys of leadership*. Thousand Oaks, CA: SAGE.

Pearce, C. L., & Sims H. P., Jr. (2002). Vertical versus shared leadership as predictors of the effectiveness of change management teams: An examination of aversive, directive, transactional, transformational, and empowering leader behaviors. *Group Dynamics: Theory, Research, and Practice, 6*(2), 172–197.

Petre, M., & Rugg, G. (2010). *The unwritten rules of PhD research* (2nd ed.). Berkshire, UK: Open University Press.

Raelin, J. A. (2012). The manager as facilitator of dialogue. *Organization, 20,* 818–839.

Raelin, J. A. (2016). Imagine there are no leaders: Reframing leadership as collaborative agency. *Leadership, 12*(2), 131–158.

Raelin, J. A. (2017). Leadership-as-practice: Theory and application—An editor's reflection. *Leadership, 13*(2), 215–221.

Raelin, J. A., Kempster, S., Youngs, H., Carroll, B., & Jackson, B. (2018). Practicing leadership-as-practice in content and manner. *Leadership, 14*(3), 371–383.

Robinson, M. (2021). Big science collaborations; lessons for global governance and leadership, *Global Policy, 12*(1), 66–80.

Royal Society. (2010). *New frontiers in science diplomacy.* Joint paper from the Royal Society and the American Association for the Advancement of Science. Retrieved August 12, 2017, from https://royalsociety.org/~/media/Royal_Society_Content/policy/publications/2010/4294969468.pdf

Sloman, S., & Fernbach, P. (2017). *The knowledge illusion; the myth of individual thought and the power of collective wisdom.* New York, NY: Penguin Random House.

Uhl-Bien, M., Riggio, R. E., Lowe, K. B., & Carsten, M. K. (2014). Followership theory: A review and research agenda. *Leadership Quarterly, 25*(1), 83–104.

Walker, J. L. (2017). The moral character of heroes. In S. T. Allison, G. R. Goethals, & R. M. Kramer (Eds.). *Heroism and heroic leadership* (pp. 115–116). New York, NY: Routledge.

Weinberg, A. M. (1967). *Reflections on big science.* Cambridge, MA: MIT Press.

Yukl, G. & Gardner, W. L. (2020). *Leadership in organizations* (9th global ed.). Essex, UK: Pearson.

Zhu, J., Liao, Z., Yam, K. C., & Johnson, R. E. (2018). Shared leadership: A state-of-the-art review and future research agenda. *Journal of Organizational Behavior, 39*(7), 834–852.

Zhu, J., Song, L. J., Zhu, L., & Johnson, R. E. (2018). Visualizing the landscape and evolution of leadership research. *Leadership Quarterly, 30*(2), 215–232.

CHAPTER 2

REINVENTING OPEN INNOVATION IN LARGE PHARMACEUTICAL COMPANIES

The Case of BAYER AG

**Wim Vanhaverbeke, Nadine Roijakkers,
and Dieudonnee Cobben**

ABSTRACT

This chapter examines how a pharmaceutical company has linked open innovation (OI) to the company's strategy by using a variety of innovation management techniques. This empirical research is an exploratory study that enables initial research on pharmaceutical companies integrating OI into the company's strategy, showing the importance of having a clear OI approach. The research is based on a case study on Bayer AG. The findings shed light on the innovation management techniques that a company can use to implement OI as well as how different OI modes can contribute to specific strategic objectives. We discus show it is crucial for companies in the pharmaceutical industry to develop portfolio, relationship, and project management in order to implement an OI strategy successfully.

Managerial Practice Issues in Strategy and Organization, pp. 39–64
Copyright © 2023 by Information Age Publishing
www.infoagepub.com

INTRODUCTION

Drug discovery and development in the pharmaceutical industry was historically done within the context of large in-house research and development (R&D) projects. Only selected aspects of drug discovery were outsourced to service providers. The increasing cost pressure and reduced productivity on R&D in pharmaceutical companies, and the growing pressure to provide a return on public research when making use of public funds are pushing pharmaceutical companies to join forces with different innovative players such as academic institutions, start-ups, crowds, and so forth. In order to maximize the use of both internal and external knowledge and competencies for the development of novel drugs and healing methods, pharmaceutical firms had to come up with new collaborative models (Chesbrough, 2003, 2006; Tamoschus, Hienert, & Lessl, 2015; Wellenreuther, Keppler, Mumberg, Ziegelbauer, & Lessl, 2012; Wild, Huwe, & Lessl, 2013).

Open innovation (OI) is increasingly used by organizations such as pharmaceutical firms as a way to integrate both internal and external knowledge for innovation trajectories. OI is a theoretical paradigm that captures organizations' moving beyond their firm boundaries by using internal knowledge externally and external knowledge internally to stay competitive (Chesbrough, 2006). OI partners are an important source for new strategic notions and innovative insights, therefore offering new value creation sources (Chesbrough & Appleyard, 2007; Vanhaverbeke & Roijakkers, 2013).

Traditional OI modes such as licensing and outsourcing focused on a one-way transfer of knowledge rather than on the co-creation of truly novel solutions. Joint research was usually limited to contract-research at the R&D project level. In order for pharmaceutical companies to leverage the full potential of OI, they had to create a broader portfolio of different types of collaboration modes. Contract research and fee-for-service-based outsourcing agreements are still useful, but more recently there is a trend towards more value-added collaboration models and strategic partnerships, also called network collaborations (e.g., OI ecosystems). These collaborations require strategic partnerships with significant contributions and long-term commitments of all partners involved (Hagedoorn, Roijakkers, & Van Kranenburg, 2006; Roijakkers & Hagedoorn, 2006; Vanhaverbeke & Roijakkers, 2013; West & Bogers, 2017; Wild et al., 2013).

To grasp the full potential of new collaborative models, OI has to be explicitly linked to a company's strategy, requiring a rethinking of the traditional business strategy (Chesbrough & Appleyard, 2007; Vanhaverbeke, Roijakkers, Lorenz, & Chesbrough, 2017). OI can support companies in developing emerging strategies, moving beyond limitations of closed innovation, whereas the traditional corporate strategy offers an explanation on how to create a competitive advantage and how to extract value from existing businesses. It is the combination of both that pharmaceutical companies need to survive (Vanhaverbeke & Roijakkers, 2013). As such, OI strategies have to consider both market demands and company demands (Gassman & Enkel, 2004) and need to balance exploration and exploitation strategies (Dittrich & Duysters, 2007; Vanhaverbeke & Roijakkers, 2013).

The successful linking of OI to the strategy of a pharmaceutical company depends on the use of innovation management techniques (Igartua, Albors Garrigós, & Hervas-Oliver, 2010; Vanhaverbeke & Roijakkers, 2013). These techniques increase the organization's ability to capture value from OI by creating the required preconditions and fostering knowledge application. The strategy of an organization has to be in line with portfolio management, project management, and relationship management. These techniques have a high impact on OI, as collaborative models can be risky and uncertain. As such, management of the OI strategy is crucial to successfully implement a strategy (Igartua et al., 2010). Portfolio management involves the management of innovation projects to realize the strategic goals of the company. Project management involves the use of internal institutional innovation aspects to support the specific innovation projects. Several scholars have identified important internal innovation aspects, such as *organizational culture* (Ades, Figlio, Sbragia, Porto, Plonski, & Celadon, 2013; Kratzer, Meissner, & Roud, 2017; Lopes & de Carvalho, 2018; Naqshbandi & Tabche, 2018; Pop, Leroi-Werelds, Roijakkers, & Andreassen, 2018), *processes* (Pop et al., 2018; Shah, Rust, Parasuraman, Staelin, & Day, 2006), *structure* (Pop et al., 2018; Shah et al., 2006) *motivation* (Ades et al., 2013), *performance measures* (Pop et al., 2018; Shah et al., 2006), and *capabilities* (Ades et al., 2013; Kratzer et al., 2017). In addition, relations with OI partners should be properly managed, as relational capital is a crucial element of a successful OI strategy. Alignment of partner's and the company's strategic objectives can lead to mutually beneficial situations, therefore showing the importance of relationship management (Vanhaverbeke & Roijakkers, 2013).

To date, the OI literature and the strategy literature have not been properly integrated (Vanhaverbeke et al., 2017). Strategy research is mainly empirical, practice-oriented, and focusing on open-source software development (e.g., Appleyard & Chesbrough, 2017; Chesbrough & Appleyard, 2007; Slowinski & Sagal, 2010). Attempts have been made to link both literature streams using definitions such as open strategy. Yet, research has not been able to properly (empirically) define OI strategies. Therefore, several calls for research are still valid. First, scholars call for the integration of OI into the strategy literature (Vanhaverbeke et al., 2017). Second, there is a call to understand the differentiation of OI projects according to their strategic drivers (Chesbrough & Appleyard 2007; Vanhaverbeke et al., 2017). Third, scholars call to understand how OI and strategy are linked in non-open-source software industries.

In our in-depth single case study, we seek to contribute to the OI and strategy literatures by addressing the three aforementioned calls for research. First, we will analyze how OI can be integrated in the strategy of a large pharmaceutical company to stimulate their innovation trajectories. Second, we will establish an understanding of how different OI modes can contribute to the realization of strategic objectives (portfolio management). Third, we will analyze how a company can internally support the implementation of an OI strategy via the design and implementation of project and relationship management. Therefore, we pursue the following research question: *How can OI be integrated in a multinational's global strategy to stimulate innovation trajectories?*

The results of this research show that the integration of OI into a company's strategy requires a clear OI approach. This includes proper portfolio management in which each OI mode will contribute to specific strategic objectives. In addition, this research shows that a company has to consider how to integrate the OI approach internally, by designing the management of relations and projects. Furthermore, this research also contributes to the OI literature, by showing that the integration of an OI strategy requires internal changes within an organization, for example, the consideration of management structures (e.g., relationship, portfolio, and project management). Our findings imply that, when considering the implementation of OI within an organization, the development of an OI strategy requires the development of portfolio management, and relationship and project management in order to implement it properly.

METHOD

Research Design

As this chapter aims to contribute to our understanding of how OI can be linked to a company's strategy, an exploratory single embedded case study is the most appropriate research method (Eisenhardt, 1989; Yin, 2013). It enables us to answer questions related to our research question about how the internal organization can manage projects and relations in relation to OI modes to enable the implementation of a company's OI strategy. The embedded nature of this study allows us to identify, map, and detail the understanding of several units within one specific case. The embedded units of analysis are two OI modes within Bayer's innovation program. As a result, this study aims to lay the groundwork for future, more evaluative studies (Yin, 2013).

Case Selection

The current study incorporates an in-depth single case study of Bayer, one of the world's largest pharmaceutical companies. Bayer is known for its highly innovative R&D department, resulting in many innovations introduced to the pharmaceutical sector every year. Because of changing environmental conditions, Bayer has decided to open up and started to develop new collaborative models, resulting in collaborations with a variety of partners in research and development, such as biotech companies, academic institutes, individual researchers, and contract research organizations (Tamoschus et al., 2015). The Bayer case is an interesting case for analyzing the link between OI and Bayer's strategy as the two are uniquely linked. Many pharmaceutical organizations are struggling to properly develop an OI strategy and a model including the required internal innovation management techniques. Most of the success stories on OI strategies are found in the open-source software industry (Chesbrough & Appleyard, 2007). Bayer is unique in the OI approach that they use to accomplish the strategic corporate goals. A single case study design allows us to observe and analyze in which ways OI and strategy are linked in a large pharmaceutical company (Yin, 2013).

Data Collection and Data Sources

The research underlying this chapter used qualitative semi-structured interviews and a variety of (online) sources of documentation. While the interviews with Bayer provided a basis for understanding, the details of the strategy implementation and OI modes were retrieved from both internal documents and earlier research articles that contained important details regarding the case. The use of multiple sources of evidence increased the accuracy of the research findings (Yin, 2013). The semi-structured interviews were carried out during 2017 and 2018. Data from different interviewees who were directly involved in corporate OI, R&D, and internal innovation capabilities of Bayer was collected. One interviewee was interviewed several times, to validate the findings from the other interviews and data sources. The interviews were recorded and transcribed and had an average length of 45 minutes. The interviewees held senior or middle management positions. In addition to the interview data, secondary data was collected from Bayer. We had access to a number of internal documents and to a number of research articles focusing on different embedded units. The use of a case study database and chain of evidence enhanced the reliability of this research (Gibbert, Ruigrok, & Wicki, 2008; Yin, 2013). To enhance external validity of the single case study design, theory was used to describe the link between OI and strategy and to develop an understanding of the used innovation management techniques (Yin, 2013). Hence, the chapter uses valid and reliable information regarding the linking between OI and strategy.

Data Analysis

To analyze the data, first a list of codes was developed based on theoretical findings on OI strategies, OI modes and innovation management techniques. To increase construct validity, the coding was checked by the different authors. Then, case study summaries were abstracted to show how OI and strategy are linked within Bayer and how the company internally managed the implementation of the strategy. The case study summaries aimed at condensing the meaning of the larger transcripts to identify the main themes from both the interview data and secondary data. The data was coded by using the MaxQDA software package for qualitative data analysis.

The coded data resulted in an understanding of how OI and the strategy were linked within Bayer and the internal project and relationship management that were used to manage the OI modes.

CORPORATE STRATEGY AS STARTING POINT

Pharmaceutical companies are following the example of large firms in other industries and are shifting from an approach where OI modes such as licensing and outsourcing facilitating a one-way transfer of knowledge are complemented by new ways of collaborating allowing partners to co-create truly novel solutions. In the past, OI was usually limited to contract-research at the R&D project level and was, consequently, only playing a role in the fringe of corporate R&D. Today OI is shifting to the core of pharmaceutical giants' strategy: Contract research and fee-for-service-based outsourcing agreements are still useful, but there is a trend towards more value-added collaboration models and strategic multi-partner collaborations, also called network collaborations, such as for example innovation ecosystems. These collaborations require strategic partnerships with significant contributions and long-term commitments of all partners involved (Vanhaverbeke & Roijakkers, 2013; West & Bogers, 2016; Wild et al., 2013).

This shift can only be successful if OI is explicitly linked to the corporate strategy and as it is different from a closed innovation setting, it requires a rethinking of the traditional strategy (Chesbrough & Appleyard, 2007; Vanhaverbeke et al., 2017). One of the major objectives of a company's corporate strategy is to investigate how to deploy the available resources to achieve a firm's short and long-term growth objectives. Innovations play a major role in the organic growth of companies, both in the short-term (continuous growth of the current businesses) as well as in the long-term (the development of future businesses). As OI is becoming strategically more important, OI initiatives should not be considered independently from corporate strategic objectives. Using OI strategically implies that a firm only pursues those ideas that have a clear market potential and align with the strategic goals of the organization.

Bayer has been defining its corporate strategy carefully by analyzing some major societal trends in combination with a strategic choice in which markets the company wants to be active in. Bayer's strategy starts with the observation that there are major social challenges in health and nutrition and these challenges can only be solved by continuous innovation. Crop productivity has to increase for instance 60% by 2050. Currently, 800 million people are undernourished, and 650 million suffer from obesity. By 2050, 20% of the world population will be older than 60 years. Second, the company bets on the convergence of biology (microbiome, stem cells, gene editing, cognitive science, etc.) and technology (artificial intelligence, sensors/optics, block chain, robotics), combined with the potential to leverage data in completely new dimensions. Those new technological developments have the potential to change the game in healthcare and nutrition in fundamental ways offering many new business opportunities in terms of new products (e.g., gene edited seeds to improve nutritious outcome; new modalities to treat diseases (gene therapy, RNAi, etc.), new business model (e.g., digital health, digital farming), and new processes (e.g., block chain enabled traceability; application of artificial intelligence and robotics both in farming and healthcare) (Lessl, 2014).

The business scope is essential in Bayer's corporate strategy: Bayer focusses on three mayor business areas—Pharmaceuticals (prescription drugs), Consumer Health (over-the-counter medicines, dietary supplements, dermatology products, foot care and sunscreen) and Crop Science (innovative crop protection and seeds, digital farming products, animal health). With these three business areas, the company is uniquely positioned in life sciences: It focuses on these areas, as they are based on the same research and technology bases, and they require similar business models with science-based, long, and expensive research trajectories before novel products can be introduced into the market. Innovation in general and corporate R&D in particular are crucial in realizing the ambitions to drive Bayer's business transformation and to generate new value. To achieve this transformation, Bayer's strategy focuses on building four critical *business capabilities* needed for future growth: (1). *Internal research and development* - more innovative pipeline; new insights; better decision-making; increased efficiency; (2). *OI*—early access to external expertise, technologies, and assets; (3). *Employee innovation*—new business models and concepts; agile and customer centric ways of working; and (4). *Social Innovation*—drive social progress and foster inclusive business growth; access to underserved markets (Lessl, Trill, & Birkinshaw, 2018). Bayer's innovation strategy determines which business capabilities it needs to build to ensure growth in existing and new businesses. OI is only one of the four capabilities, but the importance of these capabilities, including that of OI, is directly derived from the company's corporate strategy. At Bayer, there is no innovation without collaboration - both internal and external innovation ecosystems are crucial for future business success (Lessl, 2014). So far, we have explained the necessary link between a company's strategy and its OI activities. We did not explain yet how Bayer's strategy shaped the OI approach in the company. Bayer's strategy shapes its OI approach in four ways:

First, the strategic choice to focus on three specific business areas and to compete as a global innovation leader within these areas implies that internal technology that is not (no longer) essential to the strategy becomes a candidate for external licensing or outright sale. In contrast, external technology that complements the strategy becomes an interesting candidate for acquisition from the outside or for collaborating to co-create knowledge. Hence, the strategy determines which technologies to focus on for both outside-in and inside-out OI. The strategy determines the scope of Bayer's OI activities.

Second, the innovation strategy is also driving Bayer to extend OI from a contract research and fee-for-service-based outsourcing model, which continues to have its utility, towards more value-added collaboration models and strategic partnerships with significant contributions and long-term commitments from all partners. This trend is supported by an increasing collaboration between industry and academia, and is encouraged by governments, which are increasingly focusing on unmet medical needs and reduction of costs. Bayer has established some long-term strategic partnerships with leading academic institutes in this respect.

Third, the strategy also determines in which stage of the innovation funnel OI needs to be adopted. The company experienced that it needs to innovate with external partners from the very early step in the innovation process up until the clinical trials. The company has been very successful with its Grants4targets and Grants4Leads (an explanation follows below) to crowdsource and validate targets in very specific clinical areas the company is interested in.

Finally, Bayer recognizes the potential of digital technologies to disrupt the extant business models in the pharmaceutical industry. It therefore developed a number of initiatives to speed up the digital transformation in the firm. Grants4Apps is one example.

HOW TO OPEN UP—THE WIDE VARIETY OF OI MODES

We have seen that Bayer's strategy has shaped the OI approach of the company. The implications have resulted in the use of different collaborative innovation models that are currently used as an integral part of the OI strategy. Every collaborative innovation model (OI mode) will contribute to the realization of different strategic objectives. The management of the different OI modes is an example of portfolio management. In this section, an overview of the different OI modes that are used in the healthcare division is given, showing each OI mode's potential contribution. In the remainder of this chapter, we will explicitly focus on the healthcare section, as this section offers interesting examples and insights of how OI modes can contribute to different strategic objectives. An overview of the OI modes of Bayer can be found in Figure 2.1.

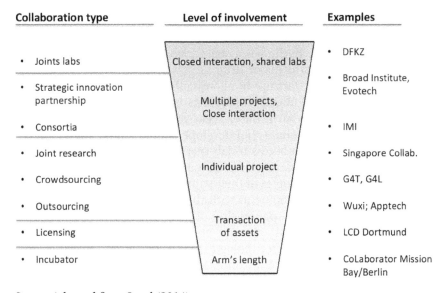

Source: Adapted from Lessl (2014).

Figure 2.1.   Flexible partnership models at Bayer Healthcare.

Inbound OI Modes

In order to tap into the fast growing scientific and technological developments, pharmaceutical companies have to rely on different OI modes to access different types of knowledge to ensure collaboration along the value chain. A variety of new collaboration models have been developed, such as strategic alliances, innovation incubators and industry-on-campus models, crowdsourcing, and pre-completive consortia.

In contrast to collaboration between partners in a specific R&D project, *strategic alliances* are long term oriented, risk-and-reward sharing agreements based on substantial contributions of partners in terms of content, resources, and financial contributions (Lessl & Douglas, 2010; Wild et al., 2013). They are called strategic because these partners play an important role in the strategy development of Bayer Healthcare. These partnerships are built to benefit from partners' complementary expertise which is not available in the pharma company, and which would be difficult to obtain in a cost-efficient and timely manner. We will describe the strategic alliance between Bayer Healthcare and the German Cancer Research Center (DKFZ) directed at joint drug discovery and development in cancer therapy as a notable example (Remneland Wikhamn & Wikhamn, 2013).

Innovation incubators and *industry-on campus-models* are other recently developed collaboration modes (Lessl & Asadullah, 2014; Robaczewska & Vanhaverbeke, & Lorenz, 2019). They promote interactions between academia and industry by providing access to funding, lab space, and drug-discovery technologies. The CoLaborator of Bayer Healthcare—both in San Francisco and in Berlin—is a shared lab for start-ups in life science whose technology platforms or drug targets align with Bayer's strategy. The goal is to support start-ups by allowing them to use the firm's research labs. In addition, CoLaborator scientists have access to Bayer's global research network. In return, Bayer seeks preferred access to collaborate with the emerging companies. J&J developed a similar approach in Beerse (Belgium): Start-ups get access to lab space and to J&J's global research network. For the pharmaceutical companies it is a way to learn early on about promising technologies in their strategic therapeutic areas and they fully nurture these developments with the assets and infrastructure they have. Pharmaceutical companies do not claim any intellectual property rights (IP) agreements with start-ups at this stage, as it is an early-stage learning process about new technologies or possible targets. Binding agreements are only signed once a technology proved to be valuable for the company (Lessl & Asadullah, 2014).

Next, Bayer Healthcare also makes use of *crowdsourcing*: Through which the company is leveraging the expertise of the larger scientific community, often using an online platform. Crowdsourcing can only be successful if the company can precisely define the problems, expectations, offerings, and intellectual property arrangements. Success of crowdsourcing also depends on quick response times and a flexible (low bureaucratic) approach. Bayer Healthcare has been championing this approach in the pharma industry with the development of the Grants4Targets initiative and later the Grants4Leads and Grants4Apps. In essence, this initiative brings together drug-discovery and development expertise and novel target ideas, supported by a one-year grant. In addition, here, IP rights remain entirely with the applicant and promising targets are pursued later by means of separate collaboration agreements. Grants4Leads are grants offered to groups that have chemical molecules, which can act as lead compounds. Grants4Apps helps Bayer to prepare for the digital era. Digitalization is a major element of the future in healthcare. This OI mode is focusing on software. In Grants4Apps Bayer uses an accelerator approach where the apps developers stay for four months in Bayer's premises in Berlin. The company offers intense coaching, with senior executives and people from different disciplines helping the apps developers to grow and develop their ideas (Lessl et al., 2011).

Finally, Bayer Healthcare also collaborated—just as many other pharmaceutical companies—in so-called *precompetitive consortia*. These consortia have been successful in other industries such as the semiconductor industry and parties from industry, academia, patient organizations, and regulatory agencies who have the common ambition to advance drug discovery and development-addressing problems that are too complex to be solved by any individual institution alone form them. As the technical issues are early stage—and solutions still need years to be introduced successfully in the market—partners have no issues in collaborating in this precompetitive stage, even with parties they traditionally consider as competitors. Bayer HealthCare is participating for instance in the Innovative Medicines Initiative, a joint initiative of the European Union and the European Federation of Pharmaceutical Industries and Associations (EFPIA). It is the world's largest public-private partnership in healthcare research and development, with the goal to speed up the development of safer and more effective drugs (Remneland Wikhamn & Wikhamn, 2013).

These new collaboration modes form, in combination with the more traditional ones, a varied set of collaboration instruments that allow Bayer to tap into different external sources of knowledge and technology at different stages in the development process.

Outbound OI Modes

As with inbound OI, Bayer also developed new ways of collaborating to recoup some of the earlier R&D investments. These additional channels to develop and commercialize existing in-house technology are out collaborating, out-licensing and spin-offs.

Collaborating of development projects that were originally developed in the company is an interesting way for expanding markets for the external use of internal innovations. In this case, the company is looking for partners, ideally with complementary expertise and market access. The company can look for a partner to introduce the new product jointly in the market. Bayer HealthCare's oral, direct factor Xa inhibitor rivaroxaban (Xarelto) was for instance co-developed and is co-marketed with Johnson & Johnson.

Out-licensing of projects can be used for several reasons. Several patents may no longer be interesting for Bayer (change in strategy, difficulties in clinical trials, or success of competing drugs) but the company can license patents to other firms. Out-licensing is also an interesting way to balance overall portfolio risk: A particular lead or drug candidate can be too risky to continue its development—especially in the expensive clinical trials. In this case, the firm will out-license the technology to a partner, most likely with the option to and back-license it after success has been guaranteed in the next development stages.

Spin-offs are used to generate value from de-emphasized research and business areas. Often, the ideas that spin off have no direct strategic value or fit with the organization and therefore others are allowed to commercialize the research ideas. As an example, at Bayer HealthCare a dedicated group within Global Drug Discovery aims at creating value from de-prioritized pre-Proof-of-Concept (pre-PoC) assets and to progress them through partnerships employing flexible deal models, while licensing transactions for later assets (post-PoC) and marketed drugs are managed by a Global Business Development and Licensing group (Remneland Wikhamn & Wikhamn, 2013).

These collaboration models allow Bayer to extract value from innovations and patents that have no direct internal value and are therefore potentially valuable for external partners.

HOW TO MANAGE THE PROJECT?—INSIGHTS FROM DKFZ-BHC AND GRANT4TARGETS PROGRAM

In the previous section, the OI approach of Bayer has been explained, by showing how different OI modes contribute to the realization of strategic objectives. Each of the OI modes needs to be managed to increase the organization's ability to capture value from OI. Project management and relationship management is important to create the required preconditions for OI. In this section, we will explain Bayer's project management approach, as can be seen in Figure 2.2 (Lessl, 2014) and will briefly explain its implementation in two collaborative models (DKFZ-BHC and Grant4Targets (G4T Program).

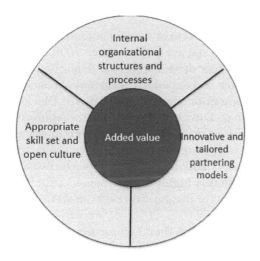

1. **Internal Organization and processes:**
We focus on excellence in alliance and partnership management.

2. **Tailored and innovative partnering models:**
We focus 'on-eye-level' partnerships and explore new avenues to offer customized and innovative partnering tools.

3. **Appropriate skill set and open culture:**
We foster an open culture and skills by trainings and open innovation concepts

Source: Adapted from Lessl (2014).

Figure 2.2.   Project management within Bayer.

Bayer's Project Management Approach

When Bayer manages OI modes in their healthcare section, they first develop internal organizational structures and processes to do so, for example by specifying which departments take part. Then, Bayer strategically determines to which extent and which areas they share knowledge with others to stimulate the OI process to decide upon which OI modes fit. In addition, each collaboration is unique and customized partnering tools can be required. Last, but definitely not least, Bayer considers the required skills and open culture. Employees and partners need to have a pattern of shared values and beliefs that help to understand how the OI strategy functions (Pop et al., 2018). By combining these three elements, Bayer creates internal and external benefits.

DKFZ-BHC and Grant4Targets Program

The following examples are two modes where Bayer had to invest considerably in terms of funding and management time and where collaboration requires new ways to manage the partnerships beyond the traditional, project-based partnerships.

DKFZ-BHC—The Strategic Alliance

The strategic alliance between the German Cancer research Center (DKFZ) and Bayer Healthcare (BHC) started in November 2008. It is a strategic alliance in the field of oncologic drug discovery and development and the cooperation intends to foster and expedite translation of research findings into therapeutic development or medical applications. DKFZ is the largest cancer research center in Europe with over 3,000 employees. BHC has a long-standing expertise in drug discovery and development. The objective of the partnership is to translate research output into new drugs and treatments by joint discovery and development projects. By joining forces, the two partners bring together highly complementary expertise leading to highly innovative treatment for patients and they can set up joint projects along the value chain.

The benefit for both partners is based on their complementary expertise. BHC does not have a lot of expertise on very specific disease areas on the molecular level. BHC is for instance collaborating with a clinic (NCT) because BHC has insufficient expertise in clinical studies. This is for BHC a very good partnership: BHC has the expertise how to develop and test drugs, but it does not have the clinical expertise. Thus, bringing together complementary expertise in joint projects is what creates value.

As the collaboration involves an academic-industrial partnership, Bayer had to use customized and innovative partnering tools, to enable the building of mutual trust. In the following two paragraphs, we will explain how the collaboration was developed concerning the internal structure, processes, and culture.

Internal structure and processes: The governance of academic-industrial partnerships has to be designed carefully given the opportunities and challenges of such collaboration. The structure should reflect equal partnership with joint decision making. To meet these goals two joint committees were established with equal representation of DKFZ and Bayer members: the Joint Steering Committee (JSC) as a decision-making body with budget responsibility and the Joint Research Review Committee (JRRC) as an operating body identifying and managing the joint projects. The role of the JRRC is to select and manage projects and it recommends those projects to the JSC. The JSC decides which projects are selected and funded. JRRC's management of joint projects has proved to be efficient and provides a platform of intensive, in-depth scientific dialogue and continuous review of ideas and ongoing projects (Wellenreuther et al., 2012). Joint decision-making ensures that only those projects are funded that include scientific challenges and are promising for pharmaceutical development. This double criterion guarantees the commitment of both sides to follow-up. The joint decision-making helps to identify those projects that have the strongest potential for both organizations.

Financial terms, confidentiality issues, management of intellectual property rights and the commercial exploitation of joint findings are covered by a detailed framework agreement. Consequently, scientists on both sides do not have to worry about these issues, which leaves them free to concentrate on their scientific work. Furthermore, novel project ideas can be picked-up quickly to start a joint project. The collaboration between BHC and the German Cancer Research Center is based on a *risk and reward sharing approach*. That implies that there is joint decision making along the entire process: So there are joint project teams and steering committee. It is a nice example where the partners started with the certain framework and extended it over time. It took time to set up this type of collaboration, but it has been proven so successful that Bayer has copied it also for number of different partnerships with other institutions.

The risk and reward sharing approach is also reflected in the way the project is funded. The joint decision-making and the equal funding of the projects reflect the joint responsibility between BHC and DFKZ. Both partners contribute about 1 million Euros per year to a joint budget and only when the defined milestones are achieved; the academic partners are financially rewarded. The fact that both partners have high stakes in the strategic alliance leads to high level of engagement and commitment on both sides. Both partners are investing time to discuss which projects should be selected and they take full responsibility for their success and failure.

Moreover, joint projects have to meet the same criteria as any internal project at Bayer. Thus, projects done internally or done with partners undergo the same evaluation and have to meet the same criteria. Bayer also communicates these decision criteria to its partners; because the company wants to be transparent, and work jointly towards meeting these decision criteria. Attaining these criteria is also how the firm measures success. Working with these criteria for projects is a learning process from both sides. Bayer communicates very early that milestone payments are linked to these criteria. If there is, no agreement about this Bayer will not continue the partnership. It is very important to bring it up very early on, be very clear what do you want to achieve. So far, the experience is that partners appreciate that the company is clear about the goals they aim to achieve, because then they can decide whether to join forces to achieve these goals.

To ensure alignment of the committees and foster the steering of the overall partnership, alliance management has been implemented on both sides. Two project leaders, one from each partner, which again reflects joint responsibility, lead joint projects. Professional alliance management is crucial to run join projects in an efficient and non-bureaucratic way. They also resolve problems and potential conflict hands-on. Alliance management is not a part of business development, but of the research organization. This choice has been very successful, because earlier collaborations in research are part of the research organization. We also see it as a way of talent development when people from research can go into alliance management: They learn different capabilities and how to manage partnerships before they move on to the next level.

In addition, fee-for-service projects, exclusively funded by Bayer, may be initiated. In 2013, the alliance partners extended their collaboration by a joint laboratory. In this lab, partners work on more advanced projects in the area of immune-oncology, and they jointly invest up to 2.5 million Euros per year (DKFZ, n.d.).

Culture and skills: For large pharmaceutical companies it is challenging how to generate value from their collaboration with academic institutes. At the time when Bayer was setting up this partnership with German Cancer Research Institute, most employees and managers in the company were skeptical. Would it make sense? Can such partnership generate value? The academics were also afraid: They were questioning the benefits of the collaboration for academia and feared that the Bayer would only steal their ideas, without properly contributing.

When the first successes became visible, resistance dropped, and both the employees of Bayer and the academics became much more positive towards the alliance. The feeling of positivity was reached with ideas such as the possibility to initiate and stimulate joint translational projects. To do so, the partnership supports the exchange of ideas and promotes personal contacts between DKFZ and Bayer scientists. Scientific exchange and dialogue are fostered by mutual visits and joint organization of scientific events. Once a joint project has been started, the mixed, interdisciplinary teams intensively cooperate in the form of project meetings and joint completion of the project plan. DFKZ scientists can also sign up for a temporary research stay at Bayer.

The fact that BHC works only with few strategic partners in the academic world besides DFKZ (such as Johns Hopkins) also increased positivity at the side of the academics. Bayer selects new partners in the light of strategic priorities, within strategic therapeutic areas. The number is limited because this type of collaboration is intense and time consuming, and a company only want to invest in such relationship when it is instrumental in realizing its innovation strategy.

Today, DKFZ and BHC organize calls for proposals. In addition, people from Bayer are proposing new projects, but they always have to do it in partnership with the German Cancer Research Center. The cooperation involves shared financing of joint projects up to 6 million Euros in total per year. Up to now, 46 joint projects have been initiated, of which 23 have already reached first milestones in early pharmaceutical development. Some projects entered clinical testing.

Grant4Target Program—Crowdsourcing

In the case of strategic alliances with academic institutes, it is relatively easy for BHC to shortlist the potential partners as only a dozen of institutes have excellent expertise in the disease areas BHC is interested in. The situation completely changes when the company is looking for interesting targets identified by researchers around the world. The knowledge in the world about targets is many times larger than the knowledge inside BHC: There are numerous targets identified, but they stay invisible to Bayer. To capture the potential value of novel targets, BHC developed a new OI approach, that is, G4T. With G4T BHC wants to join forces with academia and biotech firms to translate innovative targets into drugs, and BHC provides a grant to evaluate and validate these targets.

G4T is a novel type of collaborative model focusing on the identification of new drug targets at the very beginning of the drug discovery process. On the one hand, this identification process is a major challenge for pharma companies in their drug discovery process. On the other hand, many scientists are engaged in understanding molecules that represent potentially innovative targets. In other words, academia may have several ideas about targets while pharmaceutical companies have the expertise to validate potential drug targets (Medina-Franco, Giulianotti, Welmaker, & Houghten, 2013). The question for pharmaceutical companies is thus, how to tap into the wealth of externally developed knowledge about drug targets in an effective and cost-efficient way. Bayer developed the G4T as an organizational experiment, providing small grants and drug discovery expertise to support the evaluation and validation of new drug targets.

The academic-industrial partnership as presented in the section above, showed the specific implications for this unique partnership. In the upcoming paragraphs, we will explain how Bayer customized the partnership with the crowd and its specific implications.

Internal structure and processes: How does the G4T approach looks like? GT4 is a kind of crowdsourcing. The challenges to be solved are clearly communicated by BHC to find novel targets for known assets. An internet portal is used to allow easy access to the initiative from all over the world. Bayer also announces the GT4 in selected journals, at conferences and via emails to specific groups. Scientists can submit a proposal and after a review by a group of BHC senior experts, the G4T committee makes grant decisions. The project may start after the grant approval letter is sent out and an internal expert has been nominated as project partner and contact.

Targets are the important starting points for developments of a novel treatment. If done correctly the company can be quite successful. When the wrong target is chosen then in the end the firm invests a lot of money in molecules, which are not really linked to the disease. Identifying and validating targets is based on a lot of basic research. The pharmaceutical company needs to understand how the tumor or disease is developing. Grants4Targets allow BHC to tap into huge amounts of basic research that have been leading to the targets and bringing the targets together. However, this is done in many ways: BHC scientists go to the conferences, read literature etc. The G4T it the additional source that allows the company to get access to insights based on a lot of basic research. The G4T tries to evaluate and validate novel targets there. G4T offers some funding to validate whether or not a target has potential, and thus useful to for continued investments to advance it and to come up with a lead. For example, if the target would be the enzyme, you would develop the inhibitor but first you want to know that this enzyme is critical for the disease and that requires a lot of research.

By 2018, more than 1,000 applications and more than 100 grants that we have approved. GT4 is organized two times per year. The G4T initiative is processing the proposals very fast: Approval letters are sent out only 8 weeks after the submission deadline. It is further characterized by a minimum of bureaucracy. In addition, a detailed list of the disease areas, the indications as well as the therapeutic principles BHC is interested in are communicated. This is done to keep the number of proposals manageable, and to ascertain that proposals fit the need of the company and to ensure a strategic fit on both sides. There are three types of grants (see Table 2.1).

Culture and skills: G4T is a typical OI mode that combines the specific expertise of the academia and industry to bring forward innovative target ideas and while guaranteeing that it generates value for both partners. These benefits are summarized in Table 2.2.

In G4T, applicants apply to get support, and BHC gets the reports, but the IP remains with the owner. The program is based on the trust between the partners and therefore it is important that an internal scientist act as a champion to help develop the project plan, develop proper questions, and sometimes help with some compounds or models. Similarly, BHC encourages publications of interesting result, as the company is not interested at that stage in IP protection but in getting information earlier: This is what is leading to a competitive advantage. Publishing is possible because it is such an early stage in the drug development process: For BHC IP becomes

Table 2.1

Grant Types Grants4Target Program

Support Grants (5,000–10,000 Euro) to further advance research on targets that are at a very early stage of discovery; fixed grant approval letter; IP rights remain with the applicant.

Focus Grants (10,000–125,000 Euro) for more mature ideas, for example, to address specific aspects of a target as a first step towards transferring it to the drug-discovery process; fixed grant approval letter; IP rights remain with the applicant.

Collaborative Grants (50,000–250,000 Euro) to move the target into the drug discovery process in a substantial joint effort; terms have to be negotiated.

Source: Lessl et al. (2011).

Table 2.2

G4T Program Benefits for Industry and Academia

Academia	Industry
• Gain access to bridging funds to field-test novel target ideas and take the next step to translate discoveries into therapeutics	• Gain access to novel drug target ideas and leading academic groups
• Gain access to specific tools such as compounds and modern in silico, in vitro or in vivo drug discovery methodologies to validate novel targets	• Gain access to specific tools, assays, and animal models supporting target validation and compound characterization
• Obtain specific know-how about drug discovery such as target validation criteria, plans and screening	• Get information on disease-specific know-how
• Possibility to further advance target in a joint collaborative project after successful target validation	• Clear communication ensures high strategic fit of applications
• Target definition and criteria for G4T submissions	• Clear communication ensures high strategic fit of applications

important once the compound is developed. At that time, the company applies for patents. It is very rare that targets are patented.

RELATIONSHIP MANAGEMENT—THE RESOLVE MODEL

Most interorganizational collaborations fail not because of technological difficulties or business problems, but because of lack of professional relationship management (Dyer, Kale, & Singh, 2001; Wittmann, 2007). Bayer experienced that more than half of their collaborative projects failed because of problems in the relationship between the partners. To reduce the number of failing partnerships Bayer's management came up with the model to foster the establishment and management of successful relationships with its R&D and innovation partners. Successful interorganizational collaborations are relationships that deliver value to all organizations involved relative to alternative investments. The Bayer management identified six key success factors for successful collaborations and consolidated that in the so-called RESOLVE model (see Figure 2.3) (Lessl & Douglas, 2010). Bayer has developed several initiatives to meet these critical success factors. Bayer's model shows the importance of relationship management when implementing an OI strategy within an organization. Below we briefly discuss how Bayer tries to meet the factors.

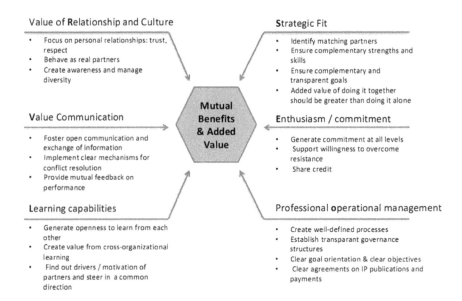

Source: Adapted Lessl and Douglas (2010).

Figure 2.2.   RESOLVE Model—Key success factors for professional alliance management at Bayer.

First, the establishment of a *trusting relationship* between partners is considered as the most important success factor in collaboration. Partnering companies have to ask: "Do we fit together? Do we have the same values and is there a cultural fit? Is there willingness to respect and support each other?" Therefore, it is crucial to invest in the establishment of a solid relationship, especially at the start of the collaboration. Teambuilding efforts as well as regular meetings are options to meet this challenge.

Second, evaluating the *strategic fit* between the partners is vital. Drivers and goals for academia and industry are often different. It is important to check what the expectations and goals are of the different partners. What do the partners want to get out of the collaboration? Do the goals fit together? Do the partners provide the required complementary skills and expertise? Therefore, being transparent about each other's goals is an essential prerequisite for value-generating relationships. In order to create benefit the skills and expertise also have to be complementary: The need for complementarity is often underestimated, as the selection of partners is frequently based on purely scientific criteria.

Third, successful partnerships require *professional operational management*. Answers on the following questions should be formulated to make a partnership a success: Who is in the driver seat for the collaboration, both on a management level and on an operational level? Is there an alliance manager on both sides to make collaboration management effective? Have clear agreements been made before the start of the collaboration regarding objectives, timelines, publication strategy, IP rights, budget, decision processes, and conflict management? Have all stakeholders been involved in the agreement, and do they support it? Lack of professional operational management can be a challenge mainly for academic institutions, but it can be alleviated by introducing project management training for group leaders and senior scientists.

Fourth, partners should be open to *learn from each other*. As the goal of partnerships is to come up with highly innovative projects and success depends on the willingness to learn from partners that have complementarity skills: Academic partners can learn a lot about drug discovery and required standards, while industry partners should learn from new ideas scientific areas that have not been pursued so far. In other words, partners have to be open-minded to overcome established paradigms and beliefs and specific training and programs for cross-organizational learning should be provided to the alliance members.

The fifth success factor relies on *open and timely communication* with the partners. For a communication strategy to be effective, the following questions have to be answered: How is the communication culture of the partner? How can timely communication and efficient exchange of information be ensured (e.g., regular meetings, communication platforms)? Are conflict management conflict escalation measurements in place? If conflicts appear, clear mechanisms for conflict resolution (e.g., mediation by project leader, steering committees) must be in place. Innovation partners are involved in strategic, long-term collaboration and should therefore be informed about a firm's strategic changes beforehand. In addition, internal communication in both partners is required to align all the stakeholders involved.

Finally, the five previously mentioned success factors would not result in partnership success if it were not combined with *real commitment and enthusiasm*. Commitment to build a value generating partnerships is required at all levels involved—from the scientists to top management. Organizational changes always lead to resistance: What can be done to overcome resistance and to motivate the people involved? Furthermore, will the benefits of the collaboration be shared equitably? What is in it for each partner? To keep the level of enthusiasm and engagement high in the partner organizations, active stakeholder management is crucial. In the past, it has often been overlooked that the projects need internal supporters and champions to be moved further along the value chain. As a result, projects, even if the results were promising, were stuck. Furthermore, collaborative projects compete with projects generated within the company as well as with projects performed with other partners within a pharmaceutical company. Therefore, it is important to connect the collaborative projects to the internal evaluation processes and see them as a part of the firm's overall project portfolio. This helps to create awareness in the organization and readiness to support them further on. The same is true for the academic organization. Here, the projects compete with other ongoing research activities and public grants. One key incentive to create commitment is to focus on common interests based on complementary expertise. Furthermore, as scientists in academia need to publish, a balance has to be found between publication of findings and maintaining confidentiality. A joint publication strategy has to be figured out: The academic partner needs to consider the impact of publications on the patenting in a joint project, whereas the industrial partner has to take into account the importance of publications for academic collaborators (Lessl & Douglas, 2010).

DISCUSSION AND CONCLUSIONS

This research shows how OI can be integrated in the strategy of a large pharmaceutical company. We have illustrated that to integrate OI into a corporate strategy, a company has to develop and implement innovation management techniques. Portfolio management results in a specific OI approach, to manage different OI modes. In addition, we have found that an organization has to develop project and relationship management techniques, in order to specify how to implement the OI approach. Certain internal innovation aspects such as culture, processes, and structures, need to be explicitly defined and implemented, in order to provide the required institutional dimensions for innovation trajectories. Crowdsourcing for example has a more explorative character that enables companies to identify interesting future research directions. In addition, a variety of OI modes is required as each of these modes represents different strategic drivers. Each internal innovation aspect need to be properly managed. In the case of Bayer, a number of internal aspects received attention, but also some aspects have not been considered in Bayer's project management, such as performance measurement. To enable a company to fully benefit from OI, both exploration and exploitation strategies have to be considered. Based on our findings, we conclude that the linking of OI and strategy requires a company to consider the use of different OI modes and a variety of project and relationship management techniques.

Based on our research findings, we have discovered that OI should be explicitly linked to a company's strategy, and we found that innovation management techniques have to be considered when implementing an OI strategy. It is important for managers to consider the importance of portfolio, project, and relationship management, when considering using OI within their organization. We therefore formulated several recommendations for managers.

First, we recommend managers to clearly define what their organization aims to reach with the implementation of OI. It is important to understand that OI can be used along the innovation spectrum and to define the implications of the OI strategy. Each OI mode can contribute to different strategic drivers, when properly managed. When linking OI to the company's strategy, a manager should clearly understand the company's strategic goals and then choose the appropriate OI modes that can be used for the realization of the goals. In other words, managers should use clear portfolio management to understand which OI projects aim to achieve which strategic objectives.

Second, managers should consider providing the required institutional environment needed for the implementation of OI strategies. In order to be successfully implemented, project management techniques that provide the required internal innovation aspects such as culture, processes, structures and metrics have to be considered and implemented. When one of these aspects fails to be present, the implementation of the OI strategy becomes much more difficult for the firm. In addition, performance measurement needs attention; it is important for management to know whether the strategic goals have been accomplished or not in order to adjust the innovation aspects or the strategic goals.

Third, science-industry collaborations should be stimulated and supported by both academics and the companies. As seen in the example of Bayer, the synergy between academics and can lead to interesting research and innovation opportunities. Managers should understand the differences between both sectors and should try to bridge the gap, for example by understanding each other's language, interests, and motivations. In addition, it is important that both partners be treated as equally important, by for example sharing the decision-making power.

This study has a number of limitations that in turn provide interesting future research directions. *First*, limitations exist related to the research design and sample. Our single case study provides information on only one specific case study in the pharmaceutical industry, restricting the generalizability of the research findings towards other organizations and industries. The pharmaceutical sector has a number of distinct characteristics, for example, the extremely high costs and risks involved in the production of medicines, therefore resulting in specific strategic objectives. In addition, we only investigated one company within the pharmaceutical sector, and it is not known whether their competitors take similar or different approaches towards (open) innovation. Future research could focus on understanding how OI and strategy are linked within other pharmaceutical firms. In addition, future research could also focus on understanding how strategy and OI are linked within other industries, such as the automotive or manufacturing industry. The question is whether the dynamics of the Bayer case are unique or industry specific. *Second*, limitations exist related to the data collection. The limited amount of interviewees lacks the generalizability of the research, as it is not known how other employees of Bayer, but also how the collaboration partners experience the link between OI and strategy. Future research could focus on integrating a more diverse range of interviewees, such as more general staff, OI managers, collaboration partners, politicians, and so forth.

ACKNOWLEDGMENTS

We would like to thank Monika Lessl, PhD, from Bayer for her support and valuable feedback throughout the process. Without her support, this chapter would not have been possible. We thank attendees of the World Open Innovation Conference 2019 in Rome for their feedback on the earlier version of this chapter.

REFERENCES

Ades, C., Figlioli. A., Sbragia, R., Porto, G., Plonski, G. A., & Celadon, K. (2013). Implementing open innovation: The case of Natura, IBM and Siemens. *Journal of Technology Management & Innovation, 8*(May), 12–25.

Appleyard, M. M., & Chesbrough, H. W. (2017). The dynamics of open strategy: From adoption to reversion. *Long Range Planning, 50*(3), 310–321.

Chesbrough, H. (2003). *Open innovation: The new imperative for creating and profiting from technology.* Boston, MA: Harvard Business School Press.

Chesbrough, H. (2006). *Open business models: How to thrive in the new innovation landscape*. Boston, MA: Harvard Business School Press.

Chesbrough, H. W., & Appleyard, M. M., (2007). OI and strategy. *California Management Review, 50*(1), 57–76.

Dittrich, K., & Duysters, G. (2007). Networking as a means to strategy change: The case of open innovation in mobile telephony. *Journal of Product Innovation Management, 24*(6), 510–521.

DKFZ (n.d.). *DKFZ and Bayer: A partnership in drug discovery and development.* Retrieved July 28, 2019, from https://www.dkfz.de/en/dkfz-bayer-allianz/index.html

Dyer, J., Kale, P., & Singh, H. (2001). How to make strategic alliances work? *MIT Sloan Management Review, 42*(2), 37–43.

Eisenhardt, K. M. (1989). Building theories from case study research. *Academy of Management Review, 14*(4), 532–550.

Gassman, O., & Enkel, E. (2004). Towards a theory of open innovation: Three core process archetypes. *Proceedings of the R&D Management Conference (RADMA).* Lissabon, Portugal, 2004.

Gibbert, M., Ruigrok, W., & Wicki, B. (2008). What passes a rigorous case study? *Strategic Management Journal, 29*(13), 1465–1474.

Hagedoorn, J., Roijakkers, N., & Van Kranenburg, H. (2006). Inter-firm R&D networks: The importance of strategic network capabilities for high-tech partnership formation. *British Journal of Management, 17*(1), 39–53.

Igartua, J., Albors Garrigós, J., & Hervas-Oliver, J. L. (2010). How innovation management techniques support an open innovation strategy. *Research Technology Management, 23*(3), 41–52.

Kratzer, J., Meissner, D., & Roud, V. (2017). Open innovation and company culture: Internal openness makes the difference. *Technological Forecasting & Social Change, 119*(C), 128–138.

Lessl, M. (2014). *Open Innovation @ Bayer HealthCare*. Presentation at the European Innovation Forum, January 16–17, 2014.

Lessl, M., & Asadullah, K. (2014). Collaborative innovation in pharmaceutical industry: Approaches and requirements. In R. Chaguturu (Ed.), *Collaborative innovation in drug discovery: Strategies for public and private partnerships* (pp. 255–266). Hoboken, NJ: Wiley.

Lessl, M., & Douglas, F. (2010). From technology-transfer to know-how interchange. *Wissenschaftsmanagement, 2010*(2), 34–41.

Lessl, M., Schoepe, S., Sommer, A., Schneider, M., & Asadullah, K. (2011). Grant4Targets – An innovative approach to translate ideas from basic research into novel drugs. *Drug Discovery Today, 16*(7/8), 288–292.

Lessl, M., Trill, H., & Birkinshaw, J. (2018, December 17). Fostering employee innovation at a 150-year-old company. *Harvard Business Review Online*.

Lopes, A. O. V. B. V., & de Carvalho, M. M. (2018). Evolution of the open innovation paradigm: Towards a contingent conceptual model. *Technological Forecasting & Social Change, 132*, 284–298.

Medina-Franco, J., Giulianotti, M., Welmaker, G., & Houghten, R. (2013). Shifting from the single to the multitarget paradigm in drug discovery. *Drug Discovery Today, 18*(9/10), 495–501.

Naqshbandi, M. M., & Tabche, I. (2018). The interplay of leadership, absorptive capacity, and organizational learning culture in open innovation: Testing a moderated mediation model. *Technological Forecasting & Social Change, 133*(C), 156–167

Pop, O. A., Leroi-Werelds, S., Roijakkers, N., & Andreassen, T. W. (2018). Institutional types and institutional change in healthcare ecosystems. *Journal of Service Management, 29*(4), 593–614.

Remneland Wikhamn, B., & Wikhamn, W. (2013). Structuring of the open innovation field. *Journal of Technology Management & Innovation, 8*(3), 173–85.

Robaczewska, J., Vanhaverbeke, W., & Lorenz, A. (2019). Applying open innovation strategies in the context of a regional innovation ecosystem: The case of Janssen Pharmaceuticals. *Global Transitions, 1*(2019), 120–131.

Roijakkers, N., & Hagedoorn, J. (2006). Inter-firm R&D partnering in pharmaceutical biotechnology since 1975: Trends, patterns, and networks. *Research Policy, 35*(3), 431–446.

Shah, D., Rust, R. T., Parasuraman, A., Staelin, R., & Day, G. S. (2006). The path to customer centricity. *Journal of Service Research, 9*(2), 113–124.

Slowinski, G., & Sagal, M. W. (2010). Good practices in open innovation. Research *Technology Management, 53*(5), 38–45.

Tamoschus, D., Hienert, C., & Lessl, M. (2015). *Developing a framework to manage a pharmaceutical innovation ecosystem,* Paper presented at the 2nd World Open Innovation Conference, November 19–20, 2015, Santa Clara, CA.

Vanhaverbeke, W., & Roijakkers, N. (2013). Enriching open innovation theory and practice by strengthening the relationship with strategic thinking. In N. Pfeffermann, T. Minshall, & L. Mortara (Eds.), *Strategy and communication for innovation* (pp. 15–26). Cham, Switzerland: Springer.

Vanhaverbeke, W., Roijakkers, N., Lorenz, A., & Chesbrough H. (2017). The Importance of Connecting Open Innovation to Strategy. In N. Pfeffermann & J. Gould (Eds.), *Strategy and communication for innovation: Integrative perspectives on innovation in the digital economy* (pp. 3–15). Cham, Switzerland: Springer.

Wellenreuther, R., Keppler, D., Mumberg, D., Ziegelbauer, K., & Lessl, M. (2012). Promoting drug discovery by collaborative innovation: A novel risk- and reward-sharing partnership between the German Cancer Research Center and Bayer Healthcare. *Drug Discovery Today, 17* (21/22), 1242–1248.

West, J., & Bogers, M. (2017). Open innovation: Current status and research opportunities. Innovation: Management. *Policy and Practice, 19*(1), 43–50.

Wild, H., Huwe, C., & Lessl, L. (2013), "Collaborative innovation"—Regaining the edge in drug discovery. *Angewandte Chemie (international edition), 52*(10), 2684–2687.

Wittmann, M. (2007). Strategic alliances: What can we learn when they fail? *Journal of Business-to-Business Marketing, 14*(3), 1–19.

Yin, R. K. (2013). *Case study research: Design and methods.* Thousand Oaks, CA: SAGE.

CHAPTER 3

IT TAKES TWO TO TANGO

Exploring the Complementary Roles of CEO and Chairperson of the Board

Gabriella Padilla, Johan Bruneel, and Frédéric Dufays

ABSTRACT

In the field of corporate governance, literature on board dynamics has primarily investigated the relationship between the top management and the board of directors, failing to take into account the pivotal relationship between the two top leaders in an organization, namely the CEO and the Chairperson of the board. Despite this relationship playing a crucial role in several organizational processes, there has been limited knowledge to date on the key contributing factors to the success in this relationship. Through an extensive analysis of conceptual and empirical studies, this chapter explores the current dimensions of the CEO-Chair relationship comparing current theoretical approaches and building a comprehensive model on how the relationship impacts different organizational outcomes. We complement our conceptual development with insights from interviews with Chairs and CEOs. By doing so, we seek to further our understanding on leadership in organizations, strategic management, and board dynamics.

Managerial Practice Issues in Strategy and Organization, pp. 65–104
Copyright © 2023 by Information Age Publishing
www.infoagepub.com

INTRODUCTION

In corporate governance, the board of directors is commonly considered as the most powerful decision-making body in the organization consisting of three units: (1) the board of non-executive directors, (2) the Chairperson responsible for leading the board, and (3) the Chief Executive Officer (CEO) (Forbes & Milliken, 1999). Literature that has looked at the relationship between these three constituents has primarily focused on the relationship between board members as a group in relation to the top management, without looking at the individual relationship between CEO and Chairperson of the board (Boyd, Haynes, & Zona, 2011). Despite this relationship playing a crucial role in several organizational processes such as the development of firm-level capabilities (Srour, Shefer, & Carmeli, in press), board effectiveness (Kakabadse, Kakabadse, & Barrat, 2006) and decision making (Sievinen, Ikäheimonen, & Pihkala, 2021), knowledge on the key contributing factors to the success of this partnership remains limited to date. Some scholars have recently begun to identify the interrelated field conditions that have played part on this overlook (e.g., Cornforth & Macmillan, 2016; Kakabadse et al., 2006; Kakabadse, Kakabadse, & Knyght, 2010).

First and foremost, studying the CEO-Chair relationship involves by definition two different individuals, each one occupying one of these roles. Kakabadse et al. (2006) explain the overlook on CEO-Chair relationships by the dominance of governance empirical studies relying on U.S. or U.K. sample, where CEO duality—the practice of the same person holding both the CEO and Chair positions in a firm—remained common practice until recently. Studies on this subject mainly deal with the effect of CEO duality on performance (Boyd, 1995; Elsayed, 2010), executive turnover (Harrison, Torres, & Kukalis, 1988; Krause, Semadeni, & Cannella, 2014), and board monitoring (Finkelstein & D'aveni, 1994; Finkelstein & Hambrick, 1989). However, according to recent data from ISS ESG, as for the year 2021 nearly 60% of S&P 500 companies have now separate CEO and Chair positions compared to 37% in 2011 (Sun, 2021). This trend suggests a reconfiguration of what we currently know on board dynamics and the relationship between the board and chief executives. Accordingly, the present work seeks to explore the key contributing factors to the success of the CEO-Chair relationship, as well as the mechanisms through which this relationship influences board dynamics and organizational performance.

The chapter is organized as follows. The first section provides a brief overview on the dominant perspectives surrounding the board-CEO relationship, and the conditions that have shaped what we currently know on board dynamics. The second section is two-fold; it first explores the role and leadership styles associated with both effective CEO and Chairpersons of the board, it then examines the nature, dimensions and characteristics of the CEO-Chair relationship and their potential complementarity. Finally, the third section presents a comprehensive model on how the relationship impacts different organizational outcomes in practice, in particular how the CEO-Chair relationship influences key board processes, namely psychological safety, cohesiveness as well as cognitive, and relationship conflict. We complement the conceptual development with insights from interviews with 8 CEO-Chair dyads from different industries and organizational structures.

DOMINANT PERSPECTIVES ON BOARD DYNAMICS

Two main research streams structure the traditional literature on corporate governance. One stream has primarily investigated the impact of board composition, board characteristics, and board structure on firm performance (Zahra & Pearce, 1989). The other stream has been concerned with what constitutes an effective board and examined the tasks boards fulfill in relation to management, with particular attention to their control, service and resource dependence roles (Johnson, Daily, & Ellstrand, 1996). However, recent content analyses on governance uncovered particular biases that have limited our understanding on board processes and dynamics. For instance, Boyd and colleagues (2011) find that prior research on board-CEO dynamics has a skewed focus in terms of samples, topics and theoretical perspectives. First, similarly to the studies conducted by Huse (1993) and Kakabadse et al. (2006) on board relations, the authors identified an Anglo-Saxon bias as nearly all studies on board-CEO dynamics are based on U.S. samples, leaving us with very little knowledge outside the domain of American boardrooms. Second, the authors point that only a handful of topics dominate the conversation, with most studies exploring boards' effect on executive compensation (Boyd, 1995; Chhaochharia & Grinstein, 2009), tenure (Zajac & Westphal, 1996), and turnover (Weisbach, 1988). And third, despite the multiple roles that board performs, the focus on the Anglo-American context has contributed to the emphasis on agency theory (Boyd et al., 2011). Agency theory remains the central theoretical framework to explain governance issues despite the concerns raised due to its principally U.S.-centered development, limiting its applicability to other institutional and geographic settings (Aguilera, Filatotchev, Gospel, & Jackson, 2008).

In reality, what Lawrence (1997) and Pettigrew (1992) once called the "black box" of managerial elites, has only recently gradually begun to open to research. This includes studies that have been able to actually observe what happens inside the black box of the boardroom and analyze the processes, dynamics and interactions between board members (cf. Bezemer, Nicholson, & Pugliese, 2014; Garg & Eisenhardt, 2017; Veltrop, Bezemer, Nicholson, & Pugliese, 2021). The present section provides a brief overview on the current dominant perspectives regarding the board-CEO relationship to later build on the specific and critical relationship between the CEO and Chair.

Agency Theory: The Board as Monitor

Although recent academic research on the ideal settings and what constitutes a productive CEO-board relationships has started to gain traction (Garg & Eisenhardt, 2017), most empirical literature examining this relationship remains focused on the board's involvement in corporate strategy and performance through monitoring management which is rooted in agency theory (Westphal, 1999). According to Fama and Jensen (1983), a central premise of agency theory is that the separation of ownership from control leads to conflict between managers and shareholders. This conflict is accentuated by a combination of information asymmetry, difference in risk profiles, uncertainty, and managerial opportunism (Boyd et al., 2011). According to agency theorists, the system behind corporate governance and the overseeing role of the board are important mechanisms to harmonize agency conflicts and limit potential managers' self-serving behavior (Deutsch, 2005; Eisenhardt, 1989; Roberts & Stiles, 1999). In this view, the primary task of the board consists in monitoring and controlling management to secure that they are carrying out their managerial responsibilities in the best interests of shareholders and minimize agency costs (Fama & Jensen, 1983).

Despite the different roles boards play in relation to management, most empirical studies consider monitoring management the primary mechanism by which effective boards influence corporate strategy and performance (Shen, 2003; Westphal, 1999), and consequently, agency theory as the base theoretical lens to analyze the board-CEO relationship (Boyd et al., 2011). For instance, Weisbach's (1988) early study on corporate governance underlines boards' crucial role of securing stakeholders' interest and examines the difference between outside and inside directors on effectively performing their monitoring and control tasks and its effect on CEO turnover. Similarly, Hermalin and Weisbach (1998) examine board effectiveness as a function of its independence and unravel the negotiation process between existing directors and the CEO over board succession. They find board independence to be crucial as it increases their willingness to monitor the CEO. On a similar vein, Tosi and Gomez-Mejia (1989) explore the extent to which monitoring and CEO compensation vary depending on firm structure, and find supportive evidence that boards have more influence on the level of CEO compensation in owner-controlled firms than in management-controlled ones. These results are consistent with recent evidence of Graham, Kim, and Leary (2020), who conducted one of the few longitudinal studies on board dynamics. They show how within-firm dynamics of corporate boards impact tenure, turnover, and performance from the CEO and vice-versa. One of the main contributions from their study lies in the interdependence between boards and management, as in particular, the authors show how on average one-third of the board is replaced with CEOs' new designation or how higher CEO performance increases CEO compensation, reducing the board's needs for excessive monitoring over time.

However, some scholars have suggested that agency conflict between management and direction sheds light only on one aspect of the different tasks performed by boards and ignores the potential collaborative relation between them (Cornforth & Macmillan, 2016). As pointed out by Boyd et al. (2011), given the complexity of corporate governance, expecting a single theoretical framework to explain all properties of governance dynamics would posit an oversimplification of the underlying processes, relations and mechanisms that play part inside the board.

Stewardship Theory: The Board as Advisor

Stewardship theory challenges the presumption of managerial opportunism of agency theory and assumes agents to work in the best interest of the principal. Despite presenting a complete opposite view to agency theory, stewardship theory offers an alternative approach by presenting managers in a more positive light, one where they share common interests with owners and identifying them as stewards motivated to act in the best interests of stakeholders and the firm, as opposed to opportunistic (Davis, Schoorman, & Donaldson, 1997; Donaldson & Davis, 1991). In this view, managers' behaviors are driven by intrinsic meaningful rewards rather than extrinsic ones, and strongly lean towards cooperation (Boyd et al., 2011). Meanwhile, the main role of the board consists in working together with management in the best interest of the organization and improving performance by supporting the CEO's decision-making and providing advice and counsel (Cornforth & Macmillan, 2016), thus replacing control with empowerment and autonomy (Boyd et al., 2011). According to Davis et al. (1997), this can only be achieved through a collaborative alliance where counsel, mentoring and training are provided as opposed to a controlling relationship that can have a negative effect on steward managers who might feel over-constrained and therefore hinders the development of 'effective and collaborative working relationships with principals' (Shen, 2003,

p. 466). Moreover, stewardship theorists have suggested some ways for organizations to encourage pro-organizational behavior as opposed to self-interest, including rearrangements in the work culture such as supporting a collective environment, lower power distance and involvement-oriented conditions to help increase identification with the organization (Davis et al., 1997; Etzioni, 1975; Tosi, Brownlee, Silva, & Katz, 2003).

Empirical research focusing exclusively on stewardship theory remains limited, as most researchers use the two leading theoretical lenses (agency and stewardship) as complementary rather than disconnected, and investigate the effects of both control and compensation between board and management, and performance (Shen, 2003; Westphal, 1999). This has particularly been done regarding the impact of board independence, offering mixed results (Bhagat & Bolton, 2008). While previous studies on board independence predicted higher company performance via agency's theory monitoring (Shleifer & Vishny, 1997; Tosi & Gomez-Mejia, 1994), Muth and Donaldson's (1998) study on board structure reframes the relation of CEO duality and board performance through stewardship theory and notes that highly independent boards surprisingly have a negative effect on shareholder wealth and share growth. Stewardship theory explains this result by external directors' potential lower identification levels with the organizational compared to their ownership interests, and therefore their failure to support and empower management, thus reducing company performance. Westphal (1999) finds similar support to these claims in his investigation of the impact of social ties on board tasks, and reports that close connections between board and management has a positive impact on independent directors providing advice and counsel to the CEO.

Resource Dependence: The Board as Resource Provider

According to resource dependence theory (RDT), organizations' survival depends on their ability to secure vital resources from the external environment and the board of directors is a key mechanism to procure them (Boyd et al., 2011). RDT is rooted in the seminal work of Pfeffer and Salancik (1978) who proposed fours main contributions from boards: (1) advice and counsel; (2) legitimacy; (3) communication channels between external organizations and the firm; and (4) preferential access to resources. Similar to stewardship theory, RDT emphasizes a collaborative board-CEO relationship where the board assists management by acting as boundary spanners that support firms to minimize dependence by gaining resources and providing information (Muth & Donaldson, 1998). In this view, board's relationship with management does not play a unilateral correspondence, but according to Pfeffer and Salancik (1978), new members appointed to the board are expected to concern themselves with the organization's problems and contribute through different means such as offering advice, expanding the social network by establishing crucial contacts, and raising capital, which ultimately supports organizational performance and increase shareholders' return.

Empirical studies on resource dependence have examined the impact of board capital and resource provision in terms of the board providing advice and counsel, legitimacy, communication channels, and tangible resources such as M&As (Hillman & Dalziel, 2003; Hillman, Withers, & Collins, 2009). In one of the first empirical studies focusing on the firm's capacity to manage its relationship with its environment via the board, Pfeffer (1972) took a random sample of nonfinancial corporations and showed how board size and board composition are interrelated to an organization's response to conditions in the external environment, and can be used as instruments to manage environmental contingencies, in particular by board co-optation and securing an adequate resource supply for the future. In turn, such resource provision has been linked to organizational performance (Hillman & Dalziel, 2003), although reviews present little support evidence on the direct impact of board composition on financial gains, suggesting the need to explore multiple theoretical perspective to better understand this relationship (Dalton, Daily, Ellstrand, & Johnson, 1998).

In this line, others like Pugliese, Minichilli, and Zattoni (2014) examine whether past firm performance and industry regulation affect board's monitoring and advice tasks, and find a negative association between past firm performance and board performance, while greater industry regulation has a positive effect. Interestingly, the authors also find evidence that while board monitoring and advice tasks come from different theoretical backgrounds, in practice boards tend to engage in both tasks at the same time. In their study on the effect of board interlocks on firm performance, Zona, Gomez-Mejia, and Withers (2018) come to a similar conclusion that combining agency and resource dependence theory in terms of boards' tasks provides a more complete interpretation of the impact of boards on firm performance. Table 3.1 summarizes the dynamics in the CEO-Chair relationship and the role of the board in the three key theoretical perspectives.

While these perspectives have advanced our knowledge on tasks boards perform as a decision-making group, surprisingly little is known on the interactions between members and their implications for decision-making processes. Despite calls for more than 30 years to go beyond the direct link of board composition on board performance, literature remains concentrated on the effects of board characteristics on firm performance (García-Ramos & Díaz, in press; Guest, 2009), executive turnover (Harrison et al., 1988), and board control (Berger & Bonaccorsi di Patti, 2006).

Table 3.1

CEO-Board Relationship Dynamics

Theoretical Perspective	CEO–Board Relationship Dynamic	Board Role
Agency Theory	Control and managerial opportunism	Oversee and monitor
Stewardship Theory	Management Empowerment	Advice and counsel
Resource Dependence Theory	Collaboration	Provide resources and information

Without considering the processes and mechanisms that affect board behaviors, our understanding of the board as a strategic decision-group will remain limited (Forbes & Milliken, 1999; Pettigrew, 1992). In a context where "interpersonal boardroom dynamics and the ecological context of relationships remains as virgin territory" (Kakabadse et al., 2006, p. 135), new research on governance dynamics has been pointing out the importance of the CEO-Chair relationship on board dynamics and subsequently firm performance (Kakabadse et al., 2006; Srour et al., in press; Stewart, 1991; Zheng & Zhu, 2021). There a number of factors why we propose the CEO-Chair relationship would contribute to influence on board behaviors. First, while the Chair functions as the leader of the board, he/she also maintains a direct relationship with the CEO. This often involves meeting with the CEO outside the boardroom, as well as organizing the agenda together prior official meetings, thus influencing the board conversation before directors can even be involved. Second, the Chair not only mediates the dialogue during board meetings, but also serve as overall intermediary between management and non-executive directors. Moreover, the Chair represents the first line of communication between the CEO and the board; not only their relationship will influence how the board perceive the CEO, but a negative relationship has the potential to increase conflict levels, therefore affecting performance.

Given the key role of the CEO-Chair relationship on different board dynamics, we seek to contribute to the governance literature by exploring the core elements and success factors of this dyad, and subsequent impact on the board and firm performance. Consequently, we propose a conceptual development on the CEO-Chair relationship based on an extensive literature review that we complement with insights from in-depth interviews with 8 CEO-Chair dyads. The overall model is illustrated in Figure 3.1 and it is divided in four levels of analysis (individual, dyad, boardroom and organization), each of them constituting a building block of the model.

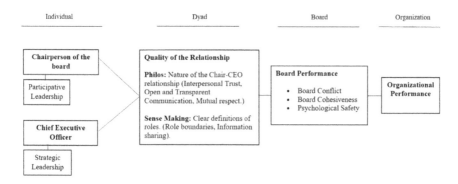

Figure 3.1.   Inpact of the CEO-Chair relationship model.

To maximize the representativeness of the CEO-Chair relationship in different contexts, we conducted 14 interviews from different types of organizations: Organization 1 (ORG1), is a non-profit social enterprise. Organization 2 (ORG2) and Organization 3 (ORG3) represent hybrid organizations as they combine multiple and sometimes opposite logics, by pursuing a social mission through the use of market mechanisms (Battilana & Dorado, 2010; Ebrahim, Battilana, & Mair, 2014). More specifically, ORG2 constitutes an agricultural cooperative enterprise, while ORG3 stands for a public company in the health sector. The rest are for for-profit companies with different organizational structures. Organization 4 (ORG4) represents a family business, Organization 5 (ORG5) a for-profit construction company and Organization 6 (ORG6) an investment fund. Organizations 7 (ORG7) and 8 (ORG8) are venture capital backed companies: ORG7 an information technology start-up and ORG8 a medical device company. These eight organizations were selected as they represent different organizational structures with various levels of centralization and decision-making processes. Table 3.2 provides an overview of some key characteristics of the interviewees and their organizations. Their combination of diverse industry sectors, institutional contexts, and mixed levels of hierarchical authority suited the cases to investigate the CEO-Chair relationship as rather uniform or a context-driven phenomenon. The duration from the interviews ranged from 1 hour to 1 hour 50 minutes.

RELATIONSHIP BETWEEN THE CEO— CHAIRPERSON OF THE BOARD

As previously presented, most of what we know on governance dynamics relies on the interaction between the board of directors as a group and top management. However, at the dyad level, the bilateral interaction between

Table 3.2

Interviews Overview

Organiza-tion	Type of Or-ganization	Founding Year	Industry	Age (years) CEO	Age (years) Chair	Tenure (years) CEO	Tenure (years) Chair	Dyad Tenure
ORG1	Non-for-profit	2008	Social	55	55	10	6.5	6.5
ORG2	Cooperative	2004	Agriculture	70	/	6	6	4
ORG3	Public	1997	Healthcare	60	74	3	9	3
ORG4	Family Business	1997	Textiles	58	63	6	10	6
ORG5	For-Profit	2011	Construction	41	56	10	10	10
ORG6	For-Profit	2020	Investment Fund	41	47	2	2	2
ORG7	VC Backed Company	2015	Information Technology	54	50	~ 2	6	~ 2
ORG8	VC Backed Company	2011	Medical device specialties	54	/	7	7	7

CEO and Chair has only been studied to a limited extent, giving us to date little empirical evidence on the idiosyncrasies of this relationship and the elements that determine the success of this partnership.

In practice, it has not been until the past decade that the practice to split the CEO and Chair roles became common practice. Following the increasing scrutiny in past decades on the boards of directors due to the number of serious corporate frauds and failures (Stiles, 2001), in 1992 the Government of the United Kingdom appointed the Cadbury Committee to report a set of recommendations regarding the structure and responsibilities of the board of directors in order to mitigate corporate risk. This report resulted in The Code of Best Practices and comprised two key recommendations: (1) to include at least three nonexecutive (i.e., outside) directors to the board, and (2) the positions of chief executive officer (CEO) and Chairperson of the board to be held by two different individuals (Cadbury, 1992). The suggestions were set to limit the CEO's concentration of power and improve board oversight through the addition of independent directors. Despite these early recommendations, only board independence quickly became adopted, and it has not been until recently that companies started to split the CEO and Chair roles (Sun, 2021).

This new configuration calls for the need to further explore this dyad, to better understand the nature and dynamics of their relationship, as well as their impact on the board and overall organization. Therefore, this section focuses on exploring the conditions of the CEO-Chair relationship and identifying the key characteristics that support a high-quality work relationship between this dyad. First, we address the settings of the CEO-Chair relationship through role theory, and examine their specific roles, boundaries, as how they affect each other's tasks. Second, we look into leadership theory and investigate the type of leadership style strongest associated with each position, as well as the type traits, skills and behaviors linked with high perception of effectiveness. Next, we investigate complementarity fit between CEO and Chair in terms of both leadership style and role expectations they have from each other. Finally, we distinguish the key elements that characterize a high-quality work relationship based on leader-member-exchange theory. We complement the conceptual development with our interview findings.

Role Theory: Role Delimitation and Negotiated Social Order

According to role theory, roles are an interpersonal phenomenon formed by the expectations of everyone involved with the performance of the focal person (Katz & Kahn, 1978). Because each individual has their own perspective of what a given role entails, roles transcend job descriptions and eventually become a mutual understanding about what an individual's role involves (Roberts & Stiles, 1999). This mutual understanding is achieved through a number of feedback loops, where in addition to the job holder's own expectations of their role and activities, the job holder also adapts depending on others' expectations based on their reactions and behaviors (Katz & Kahn, 1978).

Based on role theory, our exploration of the CEO and Chair's roles comes also three-folded. First, we explore the CEO and Chair roles based on institutional prescriptions and their own understanding of what their position entails. Second, we examine the expectations they have on each other's responsibilities and third, we examine how they experience role delimitation and the areas in which they perceive those lines at times to be somewhat blurred.

First, based on the set of good practices introduced by the Cadbury (1992) report, the positions of CEO and Chair should not only be separate, but count with a clear distinction between their roles and responsibilities. According to their recommendations, the role of CEO is considered a full-time post, where the holder is primarily responsible for the daily management of the organization, helps in the formulation and implementation of corporate strategy, and is ultimately accountable for the performance of the company (Kakabadse et al., 2006; Weir & Laing, 2001).

The Chair on the other hand, is considered a part-time and independent position, mostly responsible for ensuring that the board works effectively (Gabrielsson, Huse, & Minichilli, 2007), and occasionally serves as the external face of the company, particularly in relation to stakeholders and investors (Cadbury, 1992). This division of responsibilities was consistent during our interviews where most interviewees divided the roles of CEO and Chair as operations versus boardroom; both in terms of the perception of their own role, as well as by identifying the roles and responsibilities of their peer.

In terms of role delimitation, most interviewees highlighted the importance of respecting each other's tasks and not crossing each other domains, although these were more frequently cited by the CEO. For example, the CEO from ORG8 stressed the importance of each leader having their own domain, being management the domain of the CEO. According to the executive, "my role is to run the company, [the Chair's] role is to challenge me but not to manage the company." Similarly, the CEO from ORG3 also highlighted the importance of the Chair to respect such boundaries: "the truth is [the Chair] never chooses to deal with operational matters, and you sometimes have Chairmen who tend to want to deal with operational matters, he doesn't do that." Also, the Chair from ORG8 emphasized the importance of respecting the CEOs rank: "I would definitely be careful calling on his staff directly without either warning him before or CC'ing him on all correspondence, that's a bit of a golden rule for me."

Despite this emphasis on having clear role delimitations, scholars have also noted the intertwined relationship between both actors, for instance, while the boardroom represents the playing field of the Chair, a key role of him/her is to act as a bridge and moderator between the CEO and the other non-executive directors (Roberts & Stiles, 1999). According to Chair ORG2 "the role of the Chairman is to build a bridge between management and the board of directors that build bridges." Similarly, while the domain of the CEO takes place on the day-to-day management, their role consists in communicating their team the vision of the board and jointly take action. The execution of this role was found to also be valued by the Chair: "as CEO it is important that he can easily translate the wishes of the board to his management, and that he can translate the expectations and the aspirations of his management into the management of expectations of his board" (Interview with Chair ORG6).

Additionally, empirical studies have discovered that these roles are not always as black and white as governance codes portray, and that in fact, often these two roles overlap and thus can be better understood as dependent (Roberts & Stiles, 1999; Stewart, 1991). The first exploration on CEO-Chair role dependency can be found in the work by Stewart (1991) who examined this relationship in various districts of the U.K.'s National

Health Service and found the CEO to be dependent on the Chair for advice or support, while the Chair depends on the CEO for briefing and information. Similarly, Roberts and Stiles's (1999) study on the relationship between CEO-Chair in U.K. corporations found that the conventional approach "the Chair runs the board while the chief executive runs the business" (p. 46) is rather simplistic as it ignores the areas where capacities overlap and might create ambiguity, particularly in the domains of strategy and external relations, thus requiring the holders to negotiate their respective role responsibilities. This negotiation was particularly noted in terms of strategy formulation and on organizing the board's agenda. First, in terms of the board's agenda, most dyads reported organizing the agenda prior the board meetings together: "leading the meeting means that, of course, the Chair also puts together the agenda. I do that together with the director, making sure that all the points that need to be raised are addressed" (Interview with Chair from ORG3). However, in terms of strategy formulation some reported the board to be in charge, while others reported the top management to be in charge and the role of the board to supervise. To exemplify, according to ORG4 "[the] executive committee makes the vision and strategy of the company," while ORG7 reported the CEO's responsibility to be "making sure that the strategy which is laid down by the board of directors is executed."

Therefore, based on previous studies and insights obtained during the interviews conducted, having a good understanding on their own roles and responsibilities as well as a clear role delimitation constitute key elements of the CEO-Chair relationship. However, as a simple division between Chairs and CEOs tasks does not provide for the full picture regarding their dynamic (Cornforth & Macmillan, 2016), we further explore their function inside the organization through leadership theory.

Leadership Theory

Given that the CEO and the Chair of the board are two leaders who perform different tasks in the organization, their roles demand them to engage in different type of behaviors and leadership styles to achieve their specific tasks (Kakabadse et al., 2006). We distinguish leadership from the role theory, as leadership is not restricted to an individual holding a specific position inside the organization. As stated by Selznick (1957/1984) "Leadership is not equivalent to office-holding or high prestige or authority or decision-making. It is not helpful to identify leadership with whatever is done by people in high places" (p. 24). In this sense, someone in a formal high-rank position does not per definition exhibit leadership behaviors.

Although many definitions for leadership exist, we follow Stogdill (1950) who claims: 'Leadership may be considered as the process (act) of influencing the activities of an organized group in its efforts toward goal setting and goal achievement' (p. 3). This conceptualization highlights the dynamic nature of leadership in organizations through four key elements. First, this approach identifies leadership as a process and an interactive affair that occurs between the leader and the followers, as opposed to a trait or individual attribute (Northouse, 2021). Second, leadership is concerned with how leaders influence the organization's or group's vision, strategies and objectives (Ruben & Gigliotti, 2017). Third, leadership requires "others" to occur, be it in a small group, community or large organizations (Northouse, 2021). Lastly, the focal point of the leaders efforts involves achieving common goals jointly with the group (Rauch & Behling, 1984). In this account, leadership involves action rather than an inborn characteristic, as it requires interaction between the leader and others to occur.

In the context of corporate governance, the Chair is generally only leader inside the boardroom and it is through their relationships with key actors, that the Chair exerts influence and has an impact on board effectiveness (Harrison & Murray, 2012). Thus, some scholars have suggested that the Chair requires specific skills to fulfill their role and ensure that the board performs well, such as promoting broad and open discussion, facilitating interaction, considering others' opinions, and assisting on boards' engagement through participative decision-making processes (Gabrielsson et al., 2007; Roberts, McNulty, & Stiles, 2005). Empirical studies such as the one conducted by Leblanc and Gillies (2005) suggest that effective Chairs provide control around the board's agenda but also engage in deeper instrumental behaviors such as bringing relevant issues forward, creating a culture that allows for differences of opinion as well as being inclusive and freely sharing information (p. 202–203). Similarly, Kakabadse and colleagues (2006) find that although the role of the Chair can vary among organizations, those who were considered to be most effective act as "boundary spanners," are "sensitive to contextual demands," provide a "platform for participation," "respect role delineation," and "manage board room dynamics" (p. 141). Moreover, Harrison and Murray's (2012) study on Chair leadership highlights that Chairs who were perceived as effective were also seen as having an impact on board's leadership, CEO effectiveness, and on the organization's capacity to achieve its objectives.

Regarding leadership theory, these behaviors are consistent with participative leadership which reflects the degree to which leaders involve others in the making and implementation of decisions (Dorfman, 2004). According to this approach, participative leaders consult with employees, ask for their suggestions, and employ team members' information input in order to make decisions (Arnold, Arad, Rhoades, & Drasgow,

2000; Chen & Tjosvold, 2006). Drawing from participatory management, this type of leadership balances the involvement of both managers and followers in different organizational procedures such as information-processing, decision-making, or problem-solving (Wagner, 1994). Leaders who exhibit participative leadership engage in a specific set of behaviors such as encouraging team members to express their ideas and opinions, actively considering their suggestions and solving problems through consultation and joint discussion (Arnold et al., 2000; Buengeler, Homan, & Voelpel, 2016; Veltrop et al., 2021). As the CEO from ORG4 noted: "[The Chair] makes sure that everybody in the meeting has their say, and that they can do this saying in the meeting." Likewise, the CEO from ORG8 pointed out the importance of the Chair's leadership and management style for decision-making, particularly in order to reach consensus:

> The leadership style for the Chair ideally needs to be the one that aligns everyone without being confrontational.... So, it is diplomacy, negotiation skills, but at the same time a lot of listening and respect for people around the table.... That is important because then everyone feels that the decision made is the right one and they favor it rather than being opposed.

The CEO on the other hand, being a full-time position, is regarded to exercise leadership on a continuous basis as their primarily responsibilities involve not only the implementation of the organization's strategy but also leading employees in everyday company settings and promoting a healthy work environment (Gabrielsson et al., 2007). Given the high-rank position of the CEO in the top management team and its key role on strategy, leadership scholars have suggested strategic leadership as means to better understand the impact of top executives' leadership in the organization (Jansen, Vera, & Crossan, 2009; Vera & Crossan, 2004). Strategic leadership is rooted in the work of upper echelons theory (UET) (Hambrick & Mason, 1984) which argues that organizations are reflections of the top managers team's characteristics. According to UET, executives' characteristics and experiences shape their perceptions, choices, and actions in ways that ultimately impact a variety of firm outcomes (Cannella & Monroe, 1997).

Building from UET, strategic leadership similarly focuses on the effect of individuals at the top of the organization, but expands by considering the interpersonal relationship between leader and followers in addition to the leaders' responsibility to design a vision that englobes the objectives and purpose of the organization (Abuzaid, 2016; Carter & Greer, 2013). Similarly, the Chair from ORG1 described the leadership of the CEO as strategic:

> [The CEO] is strategically very strong, he listens very well to people, he is also very sensitive to problems. He is a problem solver, he really goes for it

and takes people into account as well, and is a very good communicator ...
he is very long-term planning.

Moreover, in their review on strategic leadership, Boal and Hooijberg's (2000) identify some activities often associated with this type of leadership including "making strategic decisions; creating and communicating a vision of the future; developing key competencies and capabilities; developing organizational structures, processes, and controls; and managing multiple constituencies" (p. 516). This understanding on the role of the CEO as both leader of operations and vision articulation were corroborated during our interviews: "CEO is responsible for the operations and he also has an executive committee ... that executive committee makes the vision and strategy of the company, so regarding the markets and the products we're going into" (Interview with Chair from ORG4).

Based on our interviews and consistent with previous findings, effective Chairs are those perceived to carry out participative leadership behaviors and promote organized dialogue inside the board by encouraging participation, ensuring everyone inside the board has their say and effectively handle disagreements between board members (Bernstein, Buse, & Bilimoria, 2016). The CEOs on the other hand, are encouraged to focus on operations and the implementation of strategy, being responsible for running the day-to-day business, as well as leading and encouraging their the top management team (Carter & Greer, 2013; Interview with Chair from ORG7). Furthermore, while the role tasks and leadership style of these two key actors might appear as opposite, some scholars have drawn attention to the overlapping domains between CEO and Chair and proposed that role delimitation is only successful if these two actors can arrive at a complementarity of roles (Roberts & Stiles, 1999). The following section therefore explores the CEO-Chair complementarity.

Complementarity Fit

Complementarity between CEO and Chair has been previously suggested to be beneficial for the organization but has been limited assessed (Roberts & Stiles, 1999; Stewart, 1991). Hodgson et al. (1965) for example, initially examined the interrelations surrounding executive teams and coined the concept of "role constellations." Role constellations are formed by people with interrelated roles and suggest a "complementarity of functions," where the different members offer some specialization and balance each other. One type of executive constellation is the dyad where "one of the pairs looks after the boundary processes of the organization, while the other looks after its internal dynamics" (p. 486).

Similarly, Stewart's (1991) study acknowledges CEO-Chair complementarity as desirable and calls future research to examine what each party brings to the table in terms of particular skills and behaviors to advance their partnership and ensure the best outcomes. Following this call, Roberts and Stiles (1999) identify two main types of CEO-Chair relationships namely competitive and complementary, and find that "complementarity" is often cited in terms of skills and experience, in addition to less evident qualities such as interests, temperament, and instinct. Moreover, Kakabadse et al. (2010) find support for the need of functional complementarity between CEO-Chair but point out the need to assess its impact on both board and organizational performance. Therefore, to further investigate complementarity and its effect on the different aspects of the organization, we draw from the organizational studies literature.

Building from Person-Environment (P-E) fit, interactionist behavioral theorists have explored complementarity in terms of the relationship between individuals and situations regarding matching values (Edwards & Shipp, 2007). In general terms, PE-fit refers to the degree of congruence or match between the attributes of two sets of variables, namely the person and the environment, in producing significant positive (or negative) outcomes (Muchinsky & Monahan, 1987). Within this paradigm, two traditions can be distinguished: supplementary and complementary fit. Supplementary fit focuses on the similarity or matching characteristics between the person and other individuals in the environment. This tradition is typically represented by research examining the matching of values between employees and organizations (e.g., when both the employee and the organization value diversity) (Kristof, 1996). Complementary fit occurs when, despite both parts being different, they possess characteristics that the other part finds valuable (Edwards & Shipp, 2007). According to Muchinsky and Monahan (1987), this type of complementarity occurs when "the weaknesses or needs of the environment are offset by the strength of the individual, and vice-versa." Thus, complementary fit suggests that an individual has certain skills that an organization requires, or that an organization offers the rewards that an individual wants (Cable & Edwards, 2004).

However, when looking at dyad relationships, most PE-fit research has focused on supplementary fit, meaning that ideally people have the same values or leadership styles (Kristof, 1996). Moreover, PE-fit has highly investigated the relationships between person-job, person-organization, person-group, and person-supervisor fit, but not person-person (peer) fit (Kristof-Brown, Zimmerman, & Johnson, 2005). This lets a gap in the field as complementarity on horizontal relationships (person-person) remain to be explored, let alone on leadership complementarity. Therefore, expanding the scope of dyad relations to horizontal ones and including complementarity fit in leadership styles opens the possibility to explore complementarity between two key leaders inside an organization, and examine to what degree differences in terms of roles, skills, behaviors or leadership styles, can positively impact different organizational outcomes, which are discussed in Section 3.

Quality of the CEO-Chair Relationship

Leader-member-exchange theory (LMX) offers a special framework to understand dyadic relationships as it conceptualizes leadership as a process that is centered on the interaction between leader and follower, making the quality of the dyad's relationship the focal point of the leadership process (Northouse, 2021). In this framework, the quality between leader-follower exchanges is based on key elements such as mutual trust, respect, and commitment and relates to key organizational outcomes related to performance, innovation, or organizational citizenship behavior among others (Graen & Uhl-Bien, 1995). In their examination of LXM, Liden and Maslyn (1998) find that high-quality work relationships, which are characterized by trust, liking, professional respect, and loyalty, are linked to increasing performance; whereas low-quality relations translate into limited trust and support lowering the positive outcomes of their interaction.

In the same manner, Kakabadse et al. (2010) argue that the quality of the relationship between CEO and Chair plays an increasingly important role in several organizational processes such as "decision making, information sharing, resource mobilization, and employee well-being" (p. 286). Based on their framework, the nature of the CEO-Chair relationship can be understood by two key "chemistry" elements: *sense-making* and *philos*. *Sense-making* refers to the cognitive and analytical capacity of both individuals to process their environment, while *philos* refers to the social bonding that is created through mutual trust, affinity, open communication and respect. Similarly, Hiland (2008) propose that the strongest CEO-Chair relationships are characterized by mutual trust, respect, open communication, and a balance between the domains of governance and management. In line, we use the LMX framework to conceptualize the key characteristics of a high-quality relationship between CEO and Chair in terms of trust, mutual respect, open and transparent communication.

Interpersonal Trust

Interpersonal trust is a complex phenomenon and has developed in two main theoretical traditions (Lewicki, Tomlinson, & Gillespie, 2006). On one hand, the behavioral tradition understands trust as rational-choice behavior that can be expressed between cooperative or competition choices in a game (Hardin, 1993; Williamson, 1993). On the other hand, the psychological tradition seeks to understand the complex conditions that involve intrapersonal trust such as expectations, intentions, affect, and dispositions. One of the earliest and most influential conceptualizations of interpersonal trust entails the one developed by Rotter in 1967. Drawing from several fields of psychology, Rotter introduced the construct of interpersonal trust as one of the most important factors for the success of social organizations. Indeed, Rotter (1967) defines trust as the "generalized expectancy that the verbal statements of others can be relied upon" (p. 651) and maintains it has a direct impact on the efficiency, adaptation and even survival of social groups. This generalized expectancy has led most empirical studies to similarly conceptualize and measure trust as an expectation that the actions or words of another person can be relied on, with the addition that there can also be an underlying belief or expectation that the other person has good intentions toward oneself (Cummings & Bromiley, 1996; Dirks, 1999).

In the context of the CEO-Chair relationship, scholars have highlighted the importance of trust for the success of this dyad (cf. Kakabadse et al., 2010; Koskinen & Lämsä, 2017; Roberts & Stiles, 1999; Zheng & Zhu, 2021). As claimed by Kakabadse et al. (2010), trust is a fundamental characteristic of the CEO-Chair relationship as it promotes mutual self-disclosure and facilitates information sharing. Moreover, according to McAllister (1995), trust is particularly important given that complexity and uncertainty are inherent in managerial work, thus managers are embedded with the critical task of developing and maintaining trust with their different social ties, as effective horizontal working relationships are particularly vital for the organization. In particular under conditions of uncertainty and complexity, mutual confidence and trust play an important role to sustain effective coordinated action (Thompson, 1967).

Empirical studies have examined the impact of trust on organizational outcomes such as team performance (Dirks, 1999), interpersonal cooperation (McAllister, 1995), and employees' organizational citizenship behavior (Mayer & Gavin, 2005). Others have examined the inter-relationships between trust, control, and risk in strategic alliances (Das & Teng, 2001). At the dyad level, as reviewed by Scandura and Pellegrini (2008), studies on trust have found a positive and significant relation with vertical work relationships (cf. Dulebohn, Bommer, Liden, Brouer, & Ferris, 2012; Gomez & Rosen, 2001; Wat & Shaffer, 2005) event though previous research on LMX presents certain limitations as the scope focuses on vertical dyad structures (e.g., leader-follower, supervisor-subordinate), evaluates trust from only one member, or takes a snap of trust at a single point in time, therefore overlooking the multilevel, bilateral, and multidimensional nature of trust.

In this line, Zaheer, McEvily, and Perrone (1998) present a more interactive view on trust, as the authors argue that while dispositional trust reflects the willingness to trust others in general (Rotter, 1971), relational forms of trust specifically refers to the extent that one agent trusts their counterpart in the dyad. Given that dyads are composed by two agents, relational trust is based on the exchanges between both actors as trust is set to be based and developed through the encounters and experiences with each other (Ring & Van de Ven, 1992; Zaheer et al., 1998). However, and as pointed out by Koskinen and Lämsä (2017), while these type of studies acknowledge the reciprocal nature of trust, only a few studies have actually examined trust considering both points of view (Das & Teng, 2001; Yakovleva, Reilly, & Werko, 2010). As noted by one of the CEOs:

> I need to trust, it's very important the word *trust* ... the board has to trust that the CEO is doing the right things in his operational role, and the CEO needs to trust his Chair but also his board ... are backing him up in the decisions that they take. So, it's a two-way trust. (Interview with CEO from ORG7)

Other scholars have noted that trust is most consequential when other elements such as risk and vulnerability are involved (Mayer, Davis, & Schoorman, 1995; Rousseau, Sitkin, Burt, & Camerer, 1998). As signalized by Cruz, Gómez-Mejia, and Becerra (2010), "a party who enjoys little immunity will likely perceive more peril in trusting another party on whom he/she depends, and hence will be less inclined to believe in that party's good intentions" (p. 73). In a governance context, the CEO has been noted to be dependent on the board, since one of the primary tasks involving the board consists in replacing poorly performing CEOs (for evidence of the negative relationship between firm performance and the likelihood of CEO turnover, see: Brunello, Graziano, & Parigi, 2003; Denis & Denis, 1995; Haleblian & Rajagopalan, 2006). However, Koskinen, and Lämsä (2017) also identify that the vulnerability of Chairpersons increases as they are highly dependent on the information provided by the CEO. Therefore, vulnerability in this relationship is argued to be present bilateral. On one hand, the Chair is dependent on the CEO for keeping he/she updated on operations and relevant events on the work floor, while the CEO depends on the Chair for advice and maintaining an open channel between the board and management.

This emphasis on trust as a necessary platform for open interaction has equally been addressed on previous CEO-Chair studies (Kakabadse et al., 2010). Given that open communication is particularly important as both the CEO and Chair depend on each other for sharing knowledge and information, we further explore how these actors perceive open and transparent communication.

Open and Transparent Communication

The second most cited element during the interviews was good communication which was framed as a mix between frequent, open and transparent. As discussed by Norman, Avolio, and Luthans (2010), open and transparent communication has largely been associated as a key element in effective organizations. First, open communication can be generally understood as being receptive and responsive to the information of others (Rogers, 1987, p. 60), and specifically in the context of leadership, it involves how leader and followers exchanging information with each other, as well as the quality of their relationship (Norman et al., 2010). Second, transparency communication refers to exchanges that are characterized by "sharing relevant information, being open to giving and receiving feedback, being forthcoming regarding motives and the reasoning behind decisions, and displaying alignment between words and actions" (Vogelgesang, 2008, p. 43). During our interviews, we identified two main outcomes regarding open and transparent communication, namely the quality of the relation and information sharing.

First, regarding the quality of the CEO-Chair relationship, both open and transparent communication were often quoted as good indicators, as when asked about the type of relationship with the CEO, the Chair from ORG1 recalled: "good, open, transparent, and if something doesn't go well, we will say it." Similarly, Chair from ORG6 identified open and transparent communication as a key element in its relationship with the CEO:

> [the CEO] is always very transparent too. If there is sometimes a point of criticism from the directors, I can also discuss it openly with him.... If everything can be said and there can be open communication, if something is not going well, you can just talk about it and I think that the most important thing is that there are no matters that cannot be discussed.

Secondly, and aligned with Vogelgesang's (2008) framework of transparency as sharing relevant information and being forthcoming, the Chair from ORG7 quoted:

> I live by a very simple rule ...: *"good news is no news, no news is bad news and bad news is good news."* It means that if we don't get news, it is possibly bad news. Why is the CEO hiding something? ... If the CEO brings bad news, it is actually good news. It means that the CEO is not shy about sharing this and he is confident enough for sharing this. It means that if something went wrong, he wants to tell it to the board.... Good news is actually no news, as we all expect it to be good.

Therefore, regardless whether the news is subjectively categorized as good or bad, Chairs particularly value when the CEO shares relevant information and keep them informed. Open communication, Rogers (1987) highlights, constitutes the first step towards problem solving as it enables the identification of problems and opportunities, and is thus associated to organizational performance. Moreover, the Chair from ORG2 stressed the importance of full transparency and openness with the CEO prior board meetings: "There has to be an awfully large openness between the CEO and the Chair, apart from not going on each other's terrain, actually a complete openness of all files that will pass through the boardroom table." And highlighted: "There [at the board], the CEO must be able to provide 100% transparency to the Chairman."

Interesting to note, while Chairs stressed the importance of CEOs to be transparent and sharing relevant information, CEOs on the other hand, highlighted the need to engage in communication topics beyond work-related issues. To exemplify, CEO from ORG4, recalls:

> Important is also that you can talk about more than only business together. Talk about your family, your children, vice-versa, or your sports.... So that you go much broader than only the business to business because then it becomes a very more cold relationship because behind every manager, there's a human being with their human being personal problems, and so on. So, to have this openness to talk about this, and then that creates a totally different relationship.

In a similar vein, CEO from ORG1 mentioned having a good relationship based on a softer type of open communication and supportive behavior from the Chair:

> open, good, encouraging ..., I think we professionally have no secrets from each other.... The things we are working on are actually not all that easy and in fact it is sometimes terribly difficult.... Being a CEO is a lonely job ... [the Chair would sometimes ask:] *how is it, does it work? Is everything alright?* And just listen and say, *I know it's hard*.

Finally, although having good communication was highlighted on both sides, Chairs particularly stressed the expectation of executives to be initiators. As Chair from ORG7 explained: "What I expect from my CEO is transparency ... I think transparency is a key word there." "Also, fairly frequent contacts are necessarily. So, I expect from my CEO that he regularly reaches out."

Mutual Respect

Another dimension of high quality relationships suggested by LMX theory concerns the presence of high levels of mutual respect regarding the capabilities of the other (Graen & Uhl-Bien, 1995). Similar work relationship theories suggest mutual respect as a key element to the development of high-quality interactions, such as the virtuous circle proposed by Roberts and Stiles (1999) which includes trust, confidence and respect for relationship building. Likewise, relational coordination theory proposes mutual respect as an important element on high quality work relationships, particularly as it is suggested to promote high-quality communication thus enabling effective work coordination (Gittell, 2006, and 2003 as cited in Carmeli & Gittell, 2009).

While respect can be found in many theoretical backgrounds, in organizational studies mutual respect is rooted in the psychology field, which in turn recognizes two main forms of respect: recognition and appraisal respect (Wiedner & Mantere, 2019). The first involves consideration and recognizing what someone else's cares about as important; while the second refers to showing appreciation to an individual or group's competence or their efforts towards achieving competence (Darwall, 1977). This competence appraisal was particularly noted by the Chairs from ORG4 and ORG6. The Chair from ORG4 interpreted mutual respect in their dyad as trusting each other's capabilities and giving space to each other to act:

> We are a very good working tandem ... the mutual respect we have for each other is very important. We both appreciate the way we do that.... He also respects me for the chances he gets because he says *"yes, you did take a step back for me."* And he continues to appreciate that too.

Chair from ORG6 on the other hand perceives the CEO's respect and appreciation towards the board's competence by sharing information:

> I think the way in which they prepare the files is done with great respect for the skills of the directors. They are very detailed with the information they provide which does indicate that they have respect for the board.

Mutual respect has also been noted to a key element to mediate conflict and differences in working relationships (Gittell, 2006) as its behaviors include listening and paying attention to other's needs as well as emphatic behaviors such as acknowledging and understating the other party's position (Dutton, 2003, as cited in Srour et al., in press). According to Carmeli and Gittell (2009), work relationships that are connected by mutual respect allow them to perform their roles in an open environment and will be less likely to blame each other for failures and embrace the occasion as a learning experience. This mediation effect of mutual respect was also stressed by the CEO from ORG4:

> We respect each other's way of thinking. Sometimes, we don't agree on certain things, but it's not because you don't agree on certain things that you cannot deal with it in a respectful way in that sense. That even though we choose for left/right decision, that doesn't change our relationship and how we see each other as persons.

Therefore, trust and open and transparent communication, along with mutual respect, appear to be three crucial elements for a high-quality CEO-Chair relationship. Based on our findings, both trust and open and transparent communication enable crucial information sharing by maintaining open channels of communication, while mutual respect enhances the quality of their relationship by taking into consideration each other's views and acknowledging their respective positions. Given the direct impact of their relationship in several board processes, such as board conflict, psychological safety and board cohesiveness, we further explore these on the next section.

CEO-CHAIR IMPACT ON BOARD PERFORMANCE

Research on organizational and board performance has mainly focused on the influence of the upper echelons' characteristics, with special attention to the influence of the CEO (Withers & Fitza, 2017). As pointed out by Liu, Fisher, and Chen (2018), most of the research on the "CEO effect" has concentrated on the CEO's background and personality (Hambrick & Mason, 1984; Zhu & Chen, 2015), behavioral characteristics and leadership styles (Conger, 1999; Waldman, Ramirez, House, & Puranam, 2001; Yukl, 2012), identity (Lord & Hall, 2005), cognitions (Eggers & Kaplan, 2009), and demographics (Buyl, Boone, Hendriks, & Matthyssens, 2011), without taking into account the social dynamics within the board beyond executives characteristics and board composition. It was Pettigrew's (1992) call for research on the actual behaviors that started to broaden our knowledge on what actual boards look like and their processes. Similarly, Nadler (2004) claims that "the key to better corporate governance lies in the working relationships between boards and managers, in the social dynamics of board interaction, and in the competence, integrity and constructive involvement of individual directors" (p. 102).

As shown in the past two sections, research suggests that a good relationship between CEO-Chair has the potential to benefit both board and organizational performance (Kakabadse et al., 2010). According to Morais, Kakabadse, and Kakabadse (2018), the costs of a bad CEO-Chair relationship can translate in a decline of board effectiveness, increased intragroup conflict, time loss and deviation from core tasks; thereby making a good relationship between the CEO and Chair essential to the proper functioning of the board and the overall organization. Therefore, in this section we dive into these two arguments and propose a model for the mechanisms through which the quality of the CEO-Chair relationship influences board dynamics and affect salient organizational outcomes such as board performance and organizational performance.

Board Performance

The governance literature frames board effectiveness in multiple ways. Forbes and Milliken (1999) for example, frame board performance in terms of its fulfillment of its control and service tasks, which refer to the duty of overseeing and monitoring management in the best interest and expectations of the stakeholders, as well as providing guidance by advice and counsel. Others like Stiles (2001) and Zhang (2010) identify a third board task involving strategy which includes 'controlling and evaluating strategic decisions, ratification of these decisions through advice and counsel, as well as initiating strategic decision proposals (Kanadlı, Zhang, & Kakabadse, 2020, p. 584).

Despite evidence that role separation improves board performance by increasing board's independent action (Coombes & Wong, 2004), only few studies have explored the mechanisms though which the CEO-Chair relationship actually influence social dynamics inside the board. Guerrero, Lapalme, and Séguin (2015) for example, finds evidence that both a strong CEO-Chair relationship and Chair' leadership style, increases board members' motivation and commitment to do their tasks by facilitating a participative environment. However, to fill the gap in other noted key mechanisms through which the CEO-Chair relationship impacts board performance and strategic-decision processes, we propose that a high-quality CEO-Chair relationship will positively contribute to board effectiveness by influencing the levels of psychological safety and cohesiveness of the board, as well as the degree of cognitive and relationship conflict at the board level.

Board Dynamics

"it's what happens around the table—how people talk to each other, how they interact"

—Jay Lorsch (Bernhut, 2004, as cited in Leblanc, 2005).

Psychological Safety

According to Forbes and Milliken (1999), unlike the top management team which focuses on strategy implementation, the board of directors can be better understood as a critical decision-making group that is given the complex task of strategic-issue processing. Given that board members are highly interdependent and their output cognitive in nature, their effectiveness is conditional to social-psychological processes like group discussion, group participation and information exchange (Forbes & Milliken, 1999; Milliken & Vollrath, 1991). Psychological safety is one key element that is positively linked to high levels of group discussion and participation in organizational work teams. Edmondson's (1999) seminal work on psychological safety, refers to the concept as a team's climate where members believing that they can speak out without the fear of being penalized for sharing their opinion. When the group feels safe to take interpersonal risks, it promotes vulnerable behaviors such as asking for help, seeking feedback and admitting mistakes, which in turn benefit the team's capacity for problem-solving (Dutton, 2003; Edmondson, 1999).

Previous studies have started to investigate the role of the Chair's leadership style on the board psychological safety. According to Veltrop et al. (2021), participative leadership from the Chairs goes beyond moderating board discussions and cues board members that the boardroom is a safe and respectful environment where they can speak openly. Our interviews supported this argument. For example, CEO from ORG7 described the role of the Chair as critical to create a safe and respectful board atmosphere:

> The Chair should take care of that there is a good atmosphere in the board based on respect and that's not always the case. I've also had board meetings in which people were scared to talk ... and where when you were asked to give a presentation, you saw the board members not really listening to what you were saying but more to ask you a question to crash you. Of course [board members] are there to ask critical questions, that's no problem, but it should not be a management by fear mentality where you might get punished or get laid off.

Therefore, while the Chair's role is to enable board members to challenge management and moderate critical discussion, to create an atmosphere where this is conducted respectfully towards others opinions and positions is equally important. This is in line with Edmonson's (1999) framework of psychological safety which describes it as an outcome of interpersonal trust and mutual respect.

In addition to this direct effect, we propose in our model that the quality in the relationship between CEO-Chair will also influence the boardroom environment and signal to board members whether it is safe to speak up.

This argument goes in line with Carmeli and Gittell's (2009) proposal on the positive effect of high-quality relationships in creating work environments where team members become more active in the organization and share their honest opinions due to experiencing low-risk by feeling valued and appreciated (Kahn, 2007). This influence of the CEO-Chair relationship on the board's environment was noted by the CEO of ORG4: "If there's a tension or many tensions between the CEO and the Chair, I think the other members of the board will feel less comfortable.... There are no subjects that could not be tackled because we are there." According to this CEO, having a good CEO-Chair relationship creates a safe environment inside the board where members can freely discuss difficult subjects without repercussions which makes it for effective board meetings.

> **Proposition 1:** *A high-quality CEO-Chair relationship; which is based on interpersonal trust, open and transparent communication, and mutual respect, will positively influence the level of psychological safety experienced by the board.*

Cohesiveness

Board cohesiveness refers to the level of interpersonal attraction between board members and their level of motivation to stay on the board (Forbes & Milliken, 1999; Summers, Coffelt, & Horton, 1988). According to work-group studies, there is a positive link between group members attraction and high levels of members satisfaction and commitment to the group (Katz & Kahn, 1978; Summers et al., 1988; Zaccaro & Dobbins, 1989). To reach high levels of positive exchanges at the governance level, it has been suggested that a greater board-management interactions will further facilitate shared understandings (Sundaramurthy & Lewis, 2003). Given that the first contact between the CEO and the board remains the Chairperson of the board, a good understanding between these two actors is a particularly important basis for further boardroom interactions. As previously argued, trust is a key element in the CEO-Chair relationship as it enables transparency and information sharing. Indeed, trust facilitates collaboration at the board level by increasing CEO's advice-seeking behavior (Westphal, 1999). However, while trust eases the cohesive and secure environment necessary for open interactions, strong social ties and mutual trust inside the board can also lead towards excessive cohesion (Sundaramurthy & Lewis, 2003). One mechanism to achieve cohesiveness that we observed throughout the interviews was joint CEO-Chair preparation of the board agenda (Interviews with ORG1, ORG3, ORG4, ORG5):

> We see each other a lot and we talk to each other a lot ... in a meeting we will never go in confrontation with each other or go into different points of view. So that rarely or never happens ... when we go to board meetings we already know what will be said. (Interview with Chair from ORG4)

In addition to this understanding between the dyad, the same Chair stressed that is was also important that the board felt that there was still room for discussion (Interview with Chair from ORG4): "[Board members] do feel that we are well attuned to each other and that there is trust.... We come to board meetings with the same view so that there is no discussion." However "there is also sufficient demand on the board of directors of whether [the decision] is good or not and often advice is requested ... there is sufficient room for discussion and questioning, it is not dictatorial." Therefore, while a high-quality CEO-Chair relationship might increase levels of board cohesiveness, it is key that seeking consensus does not harm critical discussion-making and team's processing efforts (Sundaramurthy & Lewis, 2003). On the other hand, it has been suggested that a negative CEO-Chair relationship can fraction the CEO-board relationship and engage in a "partisan struggle for support" (Roberts & Stiles, 1999, p. 47).

Proposition 2: *A high-quality CEO-Chair relationship will positively influence the level of cohesiveness experienced by the board.*

Board Conflict

Given the level of complexity and interdependence of the board, conflict eventually arises and can have either beneficial or harmful effects on strategic decision (Amason & Sapienza, 1997; Jehn, 1995). Jehn (1995) distinguishes between two types of conflict. First, task conflict, also known as cognitive conflict, refers to the perception of disagreement between group members concerning decision-making due to disparity of opinions, viewpoints or ideas. Second, relationship or emotional conflict concerns the perception of interpersonal incompatibility due to the presence of friction or dislike between the parties (Simons & Peterson, 2000). Task conflict has been suggested to benefit effective decision-making in working teams (Jehn & Mannix, 2001). In particular, in the face of complex cognitive tasks, working teams can reap benefits from task conflict as it improves strategic decision making and information exchange through the combination of different perspectives, the challenging of ideas, as well as by carefully considering and evaluating alternative options (Amason & Sapienza, 1997; Forbes & Milliken, 1999; Jehn, 1995; Schwenk, 1990). Similarly, Simons and Peterson (2000) point to a dual benefit of task conflict: it increases group decision quality due to the greater cognitive understanding derived from discussion and it promotes affective acceptance of group decisions given that team members have the opportunity to let themselves be heard and share their own opinion (p. 102). In this sense, the role of the Chair becomes particularly important in moderating board meetings in a way that facilitates debate, yet does not lead to a hostile atmosphere:

> The Chair has to make sure that everybody has time to give their opinion.... You ask the questions, you challenge the CEO, you ask the opinion of your fellow board members and at the end of the time, you decide yes or no when a proposition was presented, or you decide about the actions. The Chair is important that he ask all the board members to say okay, do you agree or not, do you have any comments and afterwards he's closing that topic and that's very formal.... To make that process very firm is the role of the Chair and respect everybody and that everybody is given the chance to voice their opinion or veto, that everybody is included in the discussion. (Interview with CEO from ORG7)

Relationship conflict, on the other hand, can be detrimental to strategic decision as it can produce distrust and friction between group members (Brehmer, 1976). According to Amason and Sapienza (1997), relationship conflict can hinder teams' effectiveness by reducing information exchange, as well as inhibit group's commitment towards one another and their decisions. As CEO from ORG7 illustrated:

> it is very difficult for a CEO if there is a bad relationship because every time he has to take a decision, he has to go to the board and might be shot, and then has to go back to the team and the budget has to be changed.... Also, the management team, they get insecure because there is a wall: they make a budget, they do their best and the board declines. People starts questioning the management team and the management team starts questioning the board.

Therefore, if not managed correctly, board conflict can produce a dysfunctional strategic decision making process that eventually translates into significant resource, time and effort losses (Amason & Sapienza, 1997); thus making the teams' success highly dependent on their capacity to "recognize, confront, and constructively manage the range of conflict that is inherent—and often necessary" for their processes (Raben & Spencer, 1998, p. 171, as cited in Liu, Fu, & Liu, 2009).

Recent studies have suggested the participative leadership style of the Chair to moderate board-CEO cognitive conflict and board's monitoring tasks (Veltrop et al., 2021). The interview with the Chair from ORG6 also indicated their moderating role between the board and the CEO: "there will be some conflicts or disagreements between the directors and management. I do think that the most important role of the Chair should be to mediate and seek consensus in this regard."

However, if there is not a good CEO-Chair relationship to begin with, the CEO can see themselves isolated without the support from the Chair to either bring difficult subjects to the table or to get the board's support in strategic decision issues. To exemplify:

> The Chair will support me and he will say, *"I agree and this is why I agree"* and it is important. So instead of me alone facing the investors on the board level, he is going to be on my side ... I think his role is to challenge me outside, to prepare me and then support me during the debate. (Interview with CEO from ORG8).

Similarly, another CEO confirmed that it was important to discuss key points with the Chair in advance so there would be no surprise inside the boardroom that could create tension:

> We have already prepared the meeting and [the Chair] knows my position. usually we also already know that there is a risk that he or she [a board member] will not agree with that ... [the Chair] will never tell me in the meeting "that is not correct." I've never come across that. (Interview with CEO from ORG3)

Along these lines, we propose:

> **Proposition 3:** *A high-quality CEO-Chair relationship will reduce relationship conflict and moderate cognitive conflict at the board level.*

DISCUSSION AND CONCLUSIONS

Starting from the premise that boards of directors and their dynamics have a strong influence on organizational performance, we developed in this chapter a model shedding light on the relationship between CEO and Chair and its influence on different board processes. We first provided an overview on dominant perspectives on board dynamics and highlighted that studies on the relation between the board as a whole and the management (or the CEO) are prominent in the literature on governance and disregard the specific role of the Chair. Then, drawing from extant literature and multiple theoretical frameworks, and complementing with evidence from semi-structured interviews with CEO-Chair dyads, we described the relationship between the CEO and the Board.

We contribute to the literature on governance and the strategic management field in two ways. First, we clarify the roles and profiles of the CEO and Chair of the board when these are two distinct persons, and how they relate to one another. Consistently, the division of responsibilities is considered by the actors as clear: CEOs deal with operations, while the Chair has a role in the boardroom. We also show that effective CEOs are associated with a strategic leadership style, while effective Chairs would rather adopt a participative leadership style. However, we highlight that there are areas where capacities overlap, potentially leading to role ambiguity. Strategy formulation and agenda setting for the board were specifically identified as responsibilities requiring the CEO and Chair to enter negotiation. This translated among others into vast informal contacts prior board meetings between CEO and Chair, which can be seen as a way of anticipating and preventing potential conflicts. Hence, we show the importance to consider the CEO-Chair role dependency and the interrelationship between these two persons in studying governance.

Our second contribution focuses on this interdependency as we address the impacts at the board and organization levels of a high-quality relationship between the CEO and the Chairperson of the board. In particular, we propose that a good CEO-Chair relationship contributes to board effectiveness by positively impacting three key dynamics at the board level: (1) it creates psychological safety for the CEO and for other board members in the boardroom, (2) it reduces board conflict, and (3) it increases board cohesiveness. In addition, we uncover that this high-quality relationship can have positive individual effects on CEOs, as they reflect on the way the Chairperson, by engaging in conversations that go beyond word issues, endorses a "comforting role" on top of their role as a sounding board, countering thereby a feeling of loneliness and increasing their well-being.

The theoretical and exploratory character of this chapter reveal the importance of the relationship between the CEO and the Chairperson of the board in organizations, regardless of their legal status (for-profit corporation, co-operative, non-profit, etc.). Although multiple theories touch upon it, we offer an integrating model on this relationship, that needs to be tested. We hope that the model and propositions we have developed will open the floor for future empirical studies informing the role of the dyad CEO-Chair on board dynamics, organizational performance, and more broadly on governance.

REFERENCES

Abuzaid, A. N. (2016). Testing the impact of strategic leadership on organizational ambidexterity: A field study on the jordanian chemical manufacturing companies. *International Journal of Business and Management*, *11*(5), 328–339.

Aguilera, R. V., Filatotchev, I., Gospel, H., & Jackson, G. (2008). An organizational approach to comparative corporate governance: Costs, contingencies, and complementarities. *Organization Science, 19*(3), 475–492.

Amason, A. C., & Sapienza, H. J. (1997). The effects of top management team size and interaction norms on cognitive and affective conflict. *Journal of Management, 23*(4), 495–516.

Arnold, J. A., Arad, S., Rhoades, J. A., & Drasgow, F. (2000). The empowering leadership questionnaire: The construction and validation of a new scale for measuring leader behaviors. *Journal of Organizational Behavior, 21*(3), 249–269.

Battilana, J., & Dorado, S. (2010). Building sustainable hybrid organizations: The case of commercial microfinance organizations. *Academy of Management Journal, 53*(6), 1419–1440.

Berger, A. N., & Bonaccorsi di Patti, E. (2006). Capital structure and firm performance: A new approach to testing agency theory and an application to the banking industry. *Journal of Banking & Finance, 30*(4), 1065–1102.

Bernhut, S. (2004) Leader's edge: an interview with Professor Jay Lorsch, Harvard Business School. *Ivey Business Journal, 65*(4), 1–5.

Bernstein, R., Buse, K., & Bilimoria, D. (2016). Revisiting agency and stewardship theories: Perspectives from nonprofit board chairs and CEOs. *Nonprofit Management and Leadership, 26*(4), 489–498.

Bezemer, P. J., Nicholson, G., & Pugliese, A. (2014). Inside the boardroom: Exploring board member interactions. *Qualitative Research in Accounting and Management, 11*(3), 238–259.

Bhagat, S., & Bolton, B. (2008). Corporate governance and firm performance. *Journal of Corporate Finance, 14*(3), 257–273.

Boal, K. B., & Hooijberg, R. (2000). Strategic leadership research: Moving on. *Leadership Quarterly, 11*(4), 515–549.

Boyd, B. K. (1995). CEO duality and firm performance: A contingency model. *Strategic Management Journal, 16*(4), 301–312.

Boyd, B. K., Haynes, K. T., & Zona, F. (2011). Dimensions of CEO-board relations. *Journal of Management Studies, 48*(8), 1892–1923.

Brehmer, B. (1976). Social judgment theory and the analysis of interpersonal conflict. *Psychological Bulletin, 83*(6), 985–1003.

Brunello, G., Graziano, C., & Parigi, B. M. (2003). CEO turnover in insider-dominated boards: The Italian case. *Journal of Banking & Finance, 27*(6), 1027–1051.

Buengeler, C., Homan, A. C., & Voelpel, S. C. (2016). The challenge of being a young manager: The effects of contingent reward and participative leadership on team-level turnover depend on leader age. *Journal of Organizational Behavior, 37*(8), 1224–1245.

Buyl, T., Boone, C., Hendriks, W., & Matthyssens, P. (2011). Top management team functional diversity and firm performance: The moderating role of CEO characteristics. *Journal of Management Studies, 48*(1), 151–177.

Cable, D. M., & Edwards, J. R. (2004). Complementary and supplementary fit: A theoretical and empirical integration. *Journal of Applied Psychology, 89*(5), 822–834.

Cadbury, A. (1992). *Report of the committee on the financial aspects of corporate governance*. London, UK: Gee & Co.

Cannella, A. A., & Monroe, M. J. (1997). Contrasting perspectives on strategic leaders: Toward a more realistic view of top managers. *Journal of Management, 23*(3), 213–237.

Carmeli, A., & Gittell, J. H. (2009). High-quality relationships, psychological safety, and learning from failures in work organizations. *Journal of Organizational Behavior, 30*(6), 709–729.

Carter, S. M., & Greer, C. R. (2013). Strategic leadership. *Journal of Leadership & Organizational Studies, 20*(4), 375–393.

Chen, Y. F., & Tjosvold, D. (2006). Participative leadership by American and Chinese managers in China: The role of relationships. *Journal of Management Studies, 43*(8), 1727–1752.

Chhaochharia, V., & Grinstein, Y. (2009). CEO Compensation and board structure. *The Journal of Finance, 64*(1), 231–261.

Conger, J. A. (1999). Charismatic and transformational leadership in organizations: An insider's perspective on these developing streams of research. *Leadership Quarterly, 10*(2), 145–179.

Coombes, P., & Wong, S. C. Y. (2004). Chairman and CEO—one job or two? *The McKinsey Quarterly, 2*, 42–47.

Cornforth, C., & Macmillan, R. (2016). Evolution in board chair–CEO relationships: A negotiated order perspective. *Nonprofit and Voluntary Sector Quarterly, 45*(5), 949–970.

Cruz, C. C., Gómez-Mejia, L. R., & Becerra, M. (2010). Perceptions of benevolence and the design of agency contracts: CEO-TMT relationships in family firms. *Academy of Management Journal, 53*(1), 69–89.

Cummings, L. L., & Bromiley, P. (1996). The organizational trust inventory (OTI). *Trust in Organizations: Frontiers of Theory and Research, 302*(330), 39–52.

Dalton, D. R., Daily, C. M., Ellstrand, A. E., & Johnson, J. L. (1998). Meta-analytic reviews of board composition, leadership structure, and financial performance. *Strategic Management Journal, 19*(3), 269–290.

Darwall, S. L. (1977). Two kinds of respect. *Ethics, 88*(1), 36–49.

Das, T. K., & Teng, B. S. (2001). Trust, control, and risk in strategic alliances: An integrated framework. *Organization Studies, 22*(2), 251–283.

Davis, J. H., Schoorman, F. D., & Donaldson, L. (1997). Toward a stewardship theory of management. *Academy of Management Review, 22*(1), 20–47.

Denis, D. J., & Denis, D. K. (1995). Performance changes following top management dismissals. *Journal of Finance, 50*(4), 1029.

Deutsch, Y. (2005). The impact of board composition on firms' critical decisions: A meta-analytic review. *Journal of Management, 31*(3), 424–444.

Dirks, K. T. (1999). The effects of interpersonal trust on work group performance. *Journal of Applied Psychology, 84*(3), 445–455.

Donaldson, L., & Davis, J. H. (1991). Stewardship theory or agency theory: CEO governance and shareholder returns. *Australian Journal of Management, 16*(1), 49–64.

Dorfman, P. W. (2004). International and cross-cultural leadership research. In B. J. Punnett & O. Shenkar (Eds.), *Handbook for international management research* (pp. 267–349). Ann Arbor, MI: University of Michigan Press

Dulebohn, J. H., Bommer, W. H., Liden, R. C., Brouer, R. L., & Ferris, G. R. (2012). A meta-analysis of antecedents and consequences of leader-member exchange: Integrating the past with an eye toward the future. *Journal of Management, 38*(6), 1715–1759.

Dutton, J. E. (2003). *Energize your workplace: How to create and sustain high-quality connections at work.* San Francisco, CA: Jossey-Bass.

Ebrahim, A., Battilana, J., & Mair, J. (2014). The governance of social enterprises: Mission drift and accountability challenges in hybrid organizations. *Research in Organizational Behavior, 34*, 81–100.

Edmondson, A. (1999). Psychological safety and learning behavior in work teams. *Administrative Science Quarterly, 44*(2), 350–383.

Edwards, J. R., & Shipp, A. J. (2007). The relationship between person-environment fit and outcomes: An integrative theoretical framework. In C. Ostroff & T. A. Judge (Eds.), *Perspectives on organizational fit* (pp. 209–258). New York, NY: Lawrence Erlbaum.

Eggers, J. P., & Kaplan, S. (2009). Cognition and renewal: Comparing CEO and organizational effects on incumbent adaptation to technical change. *Organization Science, 20*(2), 461–477.

Eisenhardt, K. M. (1989). Agency theory: An assessment and review. *The Academy of Management Review, 14*(1), 57.

Elsayed, K. (2010). A multi-theory perspective of board leadership structure: What does the Egyptian corporate governance context tell us? *British Journal of Management, 21*(1), 80–99.

Etzioni, A. (1975). *A comparative analysis of complex organizations.* New York, NY: The Free Press.

Fama, E. F., & Jensen, M. C. (1983). Separation of ownership and control. *The Journal of Law and Economics, 26*(2), 301–325.

Finkelstein, S., & D'aveni, R. A. (1994). CEO duality as a double-edged sword: How boards of directors balance entrenchment avoidance and unity of command. *Academy of Management Journal, 37*(5), 1079–1108.

Finkelstein, S., & Hambrick, D. C. (1989). Chief executive compensation: A study of the intersection of markets and political processes. *Strategic Management Journal, 10*(2), 121–134.

Forbes, D. P., & Milliken, F. J. (1999). Cognition and corporate governance: Understanding boards of directors as strategic decision-making groups. *Academy of Management Review, 24*(3), 489–505.

Gabrielsson, J., Huse, M., & Minichilli, A. (2007). Understanding the leadership role of the board Chairperson through a team production approach. *International Journal of Leadership Studies, 3*(1), 21–39.

García-Ramos, R., & Díaz, B. D. (in press). Board of directors structure and firm financial performance: A qualitative comparative analysis. *Long Range Planning, 54*(6). https://doi.org/10.1016/j.lrp.2020.102017

Garg, S., & Eisenhardt, K. M. (2017). Unpacking the CEO-board relationship: How strategy making happens in entrepreneurial firms. *Academy of Management Journal, 60*(5), 1828–1858.

Gittell, J. H. (2006). Relational coordination: Coordinating work through relationships of shared goals, shared knowledge and mutual respect. In O. Kyriakidou & M. Özbilgin (Eds.), *Relational perspectives in organizational studies* (pp. 74–94). Cheltenham, UK: Edward Elgar.

Gomez, C., & Rosen, B. (2001). The leader–member exchange as a link between managerial trust and employee empowerment. *Group & Organization Management, 26*(1), 53–69.

Graen, G. B., & Uhl-Bien, M. (1995). Relationship-based approach to leadership: Development of leader-member exchange (LMX) theory of leadership over 25 years: Applying a multi-level multi-domain perspective. *The Leadership Quarterly, 6*(2), 219–247.

Graham, J. R., Kim, H., & Leary, M. (2020). CEO-board dynamics. *Journal of Financial Economics, 137*(3), 612–636.

Guerrero, S., Lapalme, M. È., & Séguin, M. (2015). Board chair authentic leadership and nonexecutives' motivation and commitment. *Journal of Leadership and Organizational Studies, 22*(1), 88–101.

Guest, P. M. (2009). The impact of board size on firm performance: evidence from the UK. *The European Journal of Finance, 15*(4), 385–404.

Haleblian, J., & Rajagopalan, N. (2006). A cognitive model of CEO dismissal: Understanding the influence of board perceptions, attributions and efficacy beliefs. *Journal of Management Studies, 43*(5), 1009–1026.

Hambrick, D. C., & Mason, P. A. (1984). Upper echelons: The organization as a reflection of its top managers. *Academy of Management Review, 9*(2), 193–206.

Hardin, R. (1993). The street-level epistemology of trust. *Politics & Society, 21*(4), 505–529.

Harrison, Y. D., & Murray, V. (2012). Perspectives on the leadership of chairs of nonprofit organization boards of directors: A grounded theory mixed-method study. *Nonprofit Management and Leadership, 22*(4), 411–437.

Harrison, J. R., Torres, D. L., & Kukalis, S. (1988). The changing of the guard: Turnover and structural change in the top-management positions. *Administrative Science Quarterly, 33*(2), 211–232.

Hermalin, B. E., & Weisbach, M. S. (1998). Endogenously chosen boards of directors and their monitoring of the CEO. *The American Economic Review, 88*(1), 96–118.

Hiland, M. (2008). The board chair-executive director relationship: Dynamics that create value for nonprofit organizations. *Journal for Nonprofit Management, 1*(12) 1–10.

Hillman, A. J., & Dalziel, T. (2003). Boards of directors and firm performance: Integrating agency and resource dependence perspectives. *Academy of Management Review, 28*(3), 383–396.

Hillman, A. J., Withers, M. C., & Collins, B. J. (2009). Resource dependence theory: A review. *Journal of Management, 35*(6), 1404–1427.

Hodgson, R. C., Levinson, D. J., & Zaleznik, A. (1965). *The executive role constellation: An analysis of personality and role relations in management*. Boston, MA: Harvard University.

Huse, M. (1993). Relational norms as a supplement to neo-classical understanding of directorates: An empirical study of boards of directors. *Journal of Socio-Economics, 22*(3), 219–240.

Jansen, J. J. P., Vera, D., & Crossan, M. (2009). Strategic leadership for exploration and exploitation: The moderating role of environmental dynamism. *Leadership Quarterly, 20*(1), 5–18.

Jehn, K. A. (1995). A multimethod examination of the benefits and detriments of intragroup conflict. *Administrative Science Quarterly, 40*(2), 256.

Jehn, K. A., & Mannix, E. A. (2001). The dynamic nature of conflict: A longitudinal study of intragroup conflict and group performance. *Academy of Management Journal, 44*(2), 238–251.

Johnson, J. L., Daily, C. M., & Ellstrand, A. E. (1996). Boards of directors: A review and research agenda. *Journal of Management, 22*(3), 409–438.

Kahn, W. A. (2007). Meaningful connections: Positive relationships and attachments at work. In J. E. Dutton, & B. R. Ragins (Eds.), *Exploring positive relationships at work: Building a theoretical and research foundation* (pp. 189–206). Mahwah, NJ: Lawrence Erlbaum Associates.

Kakabadse, A., Kakabadse, N. K., & Barratt, R. (2006). Chairman and chief executive officer (CEO): That sacred and secret relationship. *Journal of Management Development, 25*(2), 134–150.

Kakabadse, A. P., Kakabadse, N. K., & Knyght, R. (2010). The chemistry factor in the Chairman/CEO relationship. *European Management Journal, 28*(4), 285–296.

Kanadlı, S. B., Zhang, P., & Kakabadse, N. K. (2020). How job-related diversity affects boards' strategic tasks performance: the role of Chairperson. *Corporate Governance: The International Journal of Business in Society, 20*(4), 583–599.

Katz, D., & Kahn, R. L. (1978). *The social psychology of organizations*. New York, NY: Wiley.

Koskinen, S., & Lämsä, A. M. (2017). Development of trust in the CEO-chair relationship. *Baltic Journal of Management, 12*(3), 274–291.

Krause, R., Semadeni, M., & Cannella, A. A. (2014). CEO duality: A review and research agenda. *Journal of Management, 40*(1), 256–286.

Kristof, A. L. (1996). Person-organization fit: An integrative review of its conceptualizations, measurement, and implications. *Personnel Psychology, 49*(1), 1–49.

Kristof-Brown, A. L., Zimmerman, R. D., & Johnson, E. C. (2005). Consequences of individuals' fit at work: A meta-analysis of person-job, person-organization, person-group, and person-supervisor fit. *Personnel Psychology, 58*(2), 281–342.

Lawrence, B. S. (1997). The black box of organizational demography. *Organization Science, 8*(1), 1–22.

Leblanc, R. (2005). Assessing board leadership. *Corporate Governance: An International Review, 13*(5), 654–666.

Leblanc, R., & Gillies, J. (2005). *Inside the boardroom: How boards really work and the coming revolution in corporate governance*. Mississauga, Canada: John Wiley & Sons.

Lewicki, R. J., Tomlinson, E. C., & Gillespie, N. (2006). Models of interpersonal trust development: Theoretical approaches, empirical evidence, and future directions. *Journal of Management, 32*(6), 991–1022.

Liden, R.C., & Maslyn, J.M. (1998). Multidimensionafity of leader-member exchange: An empirical assessment through scale development. *Journal of Management, 24*(1), 43-72.

Liu, D., Fisher, G., & Chen, G. (2018). CEO attributes and firm performance: A sequential mediation process model. *Academy of Management Annals, 12*(2), 789–816.

Liu, J., Fu, P., & Liu, S. (2009). Conflicts in top management teams and team/firm outcomes. *International Journal of Conflict Management, 20*(3), 228–250.

Lord, R. G., & Hall, R. J. (2005). Identity, deep structure and the development of leadership skill. *Leadership Quarterly, 16*(4), 591–615.

Mayer, R. C., & Gavin, M. B. (2005). Trust in management and performance: Who minds the shop while the employees watch the boss? *Academy of Management Journal, 48*(5), 874–888.

Mayer, R. C., Davis, J. H., & Schoorman, F. D. (1995). An integrative model of organizational trust. *Academy of Management Review, 20*(3), 709–734.

McAllister, D. J. (1995). Affect- and cognition-based trust as foundations for interpersonal cooperation in organizations. *Academy of Management Journal, 38*(1), 24–59.

Milliken, F. J., & Vollrath, D. A. (1991). Strategic decision-making tasks and group effectiveness: Insights from theory and research on small group performance. *Human Relations, 44*(12), 1229–1253.

Morais, F., Kakabadse, A., & Kakabadse, N. (2018). The chairperson and CEO roles interaction and responses to strategic tensions. *Corporate Governance: The International Journal of Business in Society, 18*(1), 143–164.

Muchinsky, P. M., & Monahan, C. J. (1987). What is person-environment congruence? Supplementary versus complementary models of fit. *Journal of Vocational Behavior, 31*(3), 268–277.

Muth, M. M., & Donaldson, L. (1998). Stewardship theory and board structure: A contingency approach. *Corporate Governance: An International Review, 6*(1), 5–28.

Nadler, D. A. (2004). Building better boards. *Harvard Business Review, 82*(5), 102–105.

Norman, S. M., Avolio, B. J., & Luthans, F. (2010). The impact of positivity and transparency on trust in leaders and their perceived effectiveness. *The Leadership Quarterly, 21*(3), 350–364.

Northouse, P. G. (2021). *Leadership: Theory and Practice*. Thousand Oaks, CA: SAGE.

Pettigrew, A. M. (1992). On studying managerial elites. *Strategic Management Journal, 13*(S2), 163–182.

Pfeffer, J. (1972). Size and composition of corporate boards of directors: The organization and its environment. *Administrative Science Quarterly, 17*(2), 218.

Pfeffer, J., & Salancik, G. R. (1978). *The external control of organizations: A resource dependence perspective*. New York, NY: Harper & Row.

Pugliese, A., Minichilli, A., & Zattoni, A. (2014). Integrating agency and resource dependence theory: Firm profitability, industry regulation, and board task performance. *Journal of Business Research*, *67*(6), 1189–1200.

Raben, C.S. and Spencer, J. (1998), Confronting senior team conflict: CEO choices. In D. C. Hambrick, D. A. Nadler, & M. L. Tushman (Eds.), *Navigating change: How CEOs, top teams, and boards steer transformation* (pp. 170–190). Boston, MA: Harvard Business School Press.

Rauch, C. F., & Behling, O. (1984). Functionalism: Basis for an alternate approach to the study of leadership. In J. G. Hunt, D. M. Hosking, C. A. Schriesheim, & R. Stewart (Eds.), *Leaders and managers: International perspectives on managerial behavior and leadership* (pp. 45–62). New York, NY: Pergamon Press.

Ring, P. S., & Van de Ven, A. H. (1992). Structuring cooperative relationships between organizations. *Strategic Management Journal*, *13*(7), 483–498.

Roberts, J., & Stiles, P. (1999). The relationship between chairmen and chief executives: Competitive or complementary roles? *Long Range Planning*, *32*(1), 36–48.

Roberts, J., McNulty, T., & Stiles, P. (2005). Beyond agency conceptions of the work of the non-executive director: Creating accountability in the boardroom. *British Journal of Management*, *16*(S1), S5–S26.

Rogers, D. P. (1987). Openness. *The Journal of Business Communication*, *24*(4), 53–61.

Rotter, J. B. (1967). A new scale for the measurement of interpersonal trust. *Journal of Personality*, *35*(4), 651–665.

Rotter, J. B. (1971). Generalized expectancies for interpersonal trust. *American Psychologist*, *26*(5), 443–452.

Rousseau, D. M., Sitkin, S. B., Burt, R. S., & Camerer, C. (1998). Not so different after all: A cross-discipline view of trust. *Academy of Management Review*, *23*(3), 393–404.

Ruben, B. D., & Gigliotti, R. A. (2017). Communication: Sine qua non of organizational leadership theory and practice. *International Journal of Business Communication*, *54*(1), 12–30.

Scandura, T. A., & Pellegrini, E. K. (2008). Trust and leader-member exchange: A closer look at relational vulnerability. *Journal of Leadership and Organizational Studies*, *15*(2), 101–110.

Schwenk, C. R. (1990). Conflict in organizational decision making: An exploratory study of its effects in for-profit and not-for-profit organizations. *Management Science*, *36*(4), 436–448.

Selznick, P. (1984). *Leadership in administration: A sociological interpretation*. Evanston, IL: Row, Peterson. (Original work published 1957)

Shen, W. (2003). The dynamics of the CEO-board relationship: An evolutionary perspective. *Academy of Management Review*, *28*(3), 466–476.

Shleifer, A., & Vishny, R. W. (1997). A survey of corporate governance. *Journal of Finance*, *52*(2), 737–783.

Sievinen, H. M., Ikäheimonen, T., & Pihkala, T. (2021). The role of dyadic interactions between CEOs, Chairs and owners in family firm governance.

Journal of Management and Governance. https://doi.org/10.1007/s10997-020-09561-7

Simons, T. L., & Peterson, R. S. (2000). Task conflict and relationship conflict in top management teams: The pivotal role of intragroup trust. *Journal of Applied Psychology, 85*(1), 102–111.

Srour, Y., Shefer, N., & Carmeli, A. (in press). Positive chair-CEO work relationships: Micro-relational foundations of organizational capabilities. *Long Range Planning*, Article No. 102124. https://doi.org/10.1016/j.lrp.2021.102124

Stewart, R. (1991). Chairmen and chief executives: An exploration. *Journal of Management Studies, 28*(5), 511–528.

Stiles, P. (2001). The impact of the board on strategy: An empirical examination. *Journal of Management Studies, 38*(5), 627–650.

Stogdill, R. M. (1950). Leadership, membership and organization. *Psychological Bulletin, 47*(1), 1–14.

Summers, I., Coffelt, T., & Horton, R. E. (1988). Work-group cohesion. *Psychological Reports, 63*(2), 627–636.

Sun, M. (2021). *Microsoft's combination of CEO and chairman roles goes against trend*. Retrieved November 9, 2021, from https://www.wsj.com/articles/microsofts-combination-of-ceo-and-chairman-roles-goes-against-trend-11623970653

Sundaramurthy, C., & Lewis, M. (2003). Control and collaboration: Paradoxes of governance. *Academy of Management Review, 28*(3), 397–415.

Thompson, J. D. (1967) *Organizations in action: Social science bases of administrative theory*. New York, NY: McGraw-Hill.

Tosi, H. L., Brownlee, A. L., Silva, P., & Katz, J. P. (2003). An empirical exploration of decision-making under agency controls and stewardship structure. *Journal of Management Studies, 40*(8), 2053–2071.

Tosi, H. L., & Gomez-Mejia, L. R. (1989). The decoupling of CEO pay and performance: An agency theory perspective. *Administrative Science Quarterly, 34*(2), 169.

Tosi, H. L., & Gomez-Mejia, L. R. (1994). CEO compensation monitoring and firm performance. *Academy of Management Journal, 37*(4), 1002–1016.

Veltrop, D. B., Bezemer, P. J., Nicholson, G., & Pugliese, A. (2021). Too unsafe to monitor? How board-CEO cognitive conflict and chair leadership shape outside director monitoring. *Academy of Management Journal, 64*(1), 207–234.

Vera, D., & Crossan, M. (2004). Strategic leadership and organizational learning. *Academy of Management Review, 29*(2), 222–240.

Vogelgesang, G. R. (2008). *How leader interactional transparency can impact follower psychological safety and role engagement*. [Unpublished PhD dissertation, The University of Nebraska]. Lincoln, Nebraska, United States.

Wagner, J. A. 1994. Participation's effect on performance and satisfaction: A reconsideration of research evidence. *Academy of Management Review, 19*(2), 312–330.

Waldman, D. A., Ramirez, G. G., House, R. J., & Puranam, P. (2001). Does leadership matter? CEO leadership attributes and profitability under conditions of perceived environmental uncertainty. *Academy of Management Journal, 44*(1), 134–143.

Wat, D., & Shaffer, M. A. (2005). Equity and relationship quality influences on organizational citizenship behaviors: The mediating role of trust in the supervisor and empowerment. *Personnel Review, 34*(4), 406–422.

Weir, C., & Laing, D. (2001). Governance structures, director independence and corporate performance in the UK. *European Business Review, 13*(2), 86–95.

Weisbach, M. S. (1988). Outside directors and CEO turnover. *Journal of Financial Economics, 20*(3), 431–460.

Westphal, J. D. (1999). Collaboration in the boardroom: Behavioral and performance consequences of ceoboard social ties. *Academy of Management Journal, 42*(1), 7–24.

Wiedner, R., & Mantere, S. (2019). Cutting the Cord: Mutual respect, organizational autonomy, and independence in organizational separation processes. *Administrative Science Quarterly, 64*(3), 659–693.

Williamson, O. E. (1993). Calculativeness, trust, and economic organization. *The Journal of Law and Economics, 36*(1), 453–486.

Withers, M. C., & Fitza, M. A. (2017). Do board chairs matter? The influence of board chairs on firm performance. *Strategic Management Journal, 38*(6), 1343–1355.

Yakovleva, M., Reilly, R. R., & Werko, R. (2010). Why do we trust? Moving beyond individual to dyadic perceptions. *Journal of Applied Psychology, 95*(1), 79–91.

Yukl, G. (2012). Effective leadership behavior: What we know and what questions need more attention. *Academy of Management Perspectives, 26*(4), 66–85.

Zaccaro, S. J., & Dobbins, G. H. (1989). Contrasting group and organizational commitment: Evidence for differences among multilevel attachments. *Journal of Organizational Behavior, 10*(3), 267–273.

Zaheer, A., McEvily, B., & Perrone, V. (1998). Does trust matter? Exploring the effects of interorganizational and interpersonal trust on performance. *Organization Science, 9*(2), 141–159.

Zahra, S. A., & Pearce, J. A. (1989). Boards of directors and corporate financial performance: A review and integrative model. *Journal of Management, 15*(2), 291–334.

Zajac, E. J., & Westphal, J. D. (1996). Director reputation, CEO-board power, and the dynamics of board interlocks. *Administrative Science Quarterly, 41*(3), 507–529.

Zhang, P. (2010). Board information and strategic tasks performance. *Corporate Governance: An International Review, 18*(5), 473–487.

Zheng, J., & Zhu, Y. (2021). Chair–CEO trust and firm performance. *Australian Journal of Management, 47*(1), 163–198.

Zhu, D. H., & Chen, G. (2015). CEO narcissism and the impact of prior board experience on corporate strategy. *Administrative Science Quarterly, 60*(1), 31–65.

Zona, F., Gomez-Mejia, L. R., & Withers, M. C. (2018). Board interlocks and firm performance: Toward a combined agency–resource dependence perspective. *Journal of Management, 44*(2), 589–618.

CHAPTER 4

CEO-CFO RELATIVE OPTIMISM AND FIRM MERGERS AND ACQUISITIONS

Wei Shi and Guoli Chen

ABSTRACT

Our chapter examines two critical members in the top management "sub-team"—CEO and CFO—in firms' merger and acquisition (M&A) decision. We propose a concept of CEO–CFO relative optimism, measured by CEO's optimism relative to CFO's pessimism, to capture the subteam's collective cognitive schema in attentional focus and information processing, and study their conjoined influence on corporate decisions. We posit that firms with high CEO-CFO relative optimism will undertake more acquisitions than firms with low CEO-CFO relative optimism because optimistic CEOs are less attentive to risk associated with acquisitions in the absence of CFOs high in pessimism. In addition, the role of CEO-CFO relative optimism in affecting M&A intensity is more pronounced when CFOs are board members at focal firms and firms face a dynamic external environment, because CFO's opinions are more salient in these situations. Furthermore, acquisitions by firms with high CEO-CFO relative optimism will have a more negative influence on firm operating performance than those with low CEO-CFO relative optimism. Using a sample of U.S. public firms over the period of 2002–2013, we find empirical support for our arguments.

Managerial Practice Issues in Strategy and Organization, pp. 105–143
Copyright © 2023 by Information Age Publishing
www.infoagepub.com

INTRODUCTION

Upper echelons theory suggests that top managers can significantly shape strategies and performance of the firms that they lead (Finkelstein, Hambrick, & Cannella, 2009; Hambrick & Mason, 1984). One stream of upper echelons research has focused on CEOs and examined how CEOs' backgrounds, experiences, values, and psychological orientations influence a wide range of strategic decisions and firm performance (for a review, see Finkelstein et al., 2009; Wang, Holmes, Oh, & Zhu, 2016). Yet, CEOs share power and make decisions jointly with other top executives and studying only CEOs may not provide a full insight into the role of top executives in strategic decisions (Hambrick & Mason, 1984). Another stream of upper echelons research evolves around top management teams (TMTs) (Carpenter, Geletkanycz, & Sanders, 2004). Although such research is conceptually clear about the definition of a TMT, it is empirically challenging to define who should be included in a TMT and the relevance of the TMT as a meaningful unit of analysis has been questioned (Arendt, Priem, & Ndofor, 2005; Hambrick, 2007; Jackson, 1992).

Hambrick (2007) suggests that the focus on "subteams" of TMTs who are relevant decision makers for given strategic decisions can improve the predictive strength of upper echelons theory. Our study responds to such a call by examining CEO–CFO relative optimism, captured by *CEO optimism* relative to *CFO pessimism*, in shaping firm merger and acquisition (M&A) decisions. We examine CEO-CFO dyads because CEOs often make final M&A decisions and CFOs play a critical role in identifying acquisition targets, conducting due diligence, arranging financing, and engaging in post-deal execution (Altman, 2002; Huyett & Koller, 2011), thus CEO and CFO are critical "subteam" members. We focus on optimism and pessimism, not only because they are "cognitive characteristics" that can shape individuals' attentional focus and information processing (Peterson, 2000), but also they are consistent with the CEO's and CFO's respective role expectations.

Specifically, optimism refers to positive outcome expectancies (Segerstrom, 2001), and optimists tend to discount unwanted facts and information (Geers & Lassiter, 1999). The CEO is often depicted as the "eternal optimist pushing ahead at full speed, sometimes with rose-colored glasses" (Tulimieri & Banai, 2010), the executive whose main task is to frame a positive view of the future and to sustain inspiration for organizational members (Mintzberg, 1973). In contrast, pessimism pertains to an inclination to emphasize adverse aspects, conditions, and possibilities, and pessimists are thus more sensitive to contradictory and negative information (Segerstrom, 2001; Smith, Ruiz, Cundiff, Baron, & Nealey-Moore, 2013). The CFO is often seen as the proverbial "Dr. No" who seeks to minimize risks and ensure an adequate return on future capital allocations and investments (Cockrell & Kambil, 2015). Thus, optimism and pessimism are well aligned with the CEO's article and the CFO's role expectations (Um et al., in press).

We first posit that firms with higher CEO-CFO relative optimism (i.e., high CEO optimism but low CFO pessimism) will undertake a larger number of acquisitions than firms with low CEO-CFO relative optimism (i.e., low CEO optimism and high CFO pessimism). In the former scenario, because CFOs low in pessimism are less prone to point out risk associated with acquisition targets, optimistic CEOs will perceive low risk in M&As in the absence of "naysayers" CFOs. Yet, when firms have low CEO-CFO relative optimism, they are more likely to perceive high risk in M&As and will refrain from a large number of M&As. We then posit that the positive relationship between CEO–CFO relative optimism and M&A intensity is more pronounced when CFOs are board members at focal firms because the directorships enable such CFOs to impose a greater influence on CEOs. Furthermore, when firms face a dynamic external environment, CEOs are more likely to seek the input of CFOs when making strategic decisions (Arendt et al., 2005). As a result, the positive relationship between CEO-CFO relative optimism and firm M&A intensity becomes stronger in a dynamic environment. Because firms with low CEO-CFO relative optimism tend to show great caution when making M&A decisions than those with high CEO-CFO relative optimism, the former have a smaller chance of adversely selecting acquisition targets than the latter. Accordingly, M&As conducted by the former will have a more positive influence on firm performance than those by the latter.

Using a sample of 2,357 firms in the period of 2002–2013, we find support for our arguments. Our findings first can contribute to upper echelon research (Finkelstein et al., 2009; Hambrick & Mason, 1984) by examining the influence of an important top management subteam's collective cognitive schema—CEO-CFO relative optimism—on firm M&A decisions. Our focus on the CEO-CFO subteam differs from prior research that has either focused on the individual level of CEOs or the team level of TMTs, enriching our understanding of the role of TMT subteams in strategic decisions. Building on the assumption that CEOs and CFOs have different role expectations, we focus on CEO optimism and CFO pessimism and develop a concept of CEO-CFO relative optimism to capture the subteam's collective cognitive schema in information attending, screening, and processing which subsequently can influence organization decisions. Second, our findings highlight the important role of CFOs in M&A decisions. Although the role of CEOs in shaping M&A decisions has been extensively documented in M&A research (e.g., Gamache, McNamara, Mannor, & Johnson, 2015; Hayward & Hambrick, 1997), scholars have not paid much attention to the role of CFOs in M&A decisions. Our findings can contribute to M&A

research by highlighting the joint influence of CEOs and CFOs on firm M&A decisions.

THEORY AND HYPOTHESES

Upper Echelons Research

Built on the premise of bounded rationality (Cyert & March, 1963; March & Simon, 1958), upper echelons theory suggests that top executives' cognitive biases and personality characteristics can affect their fields of vision, perception and interpretation, and this in turn can influence strategic choices and firm performance (Hambrick & Mason, 1984). One stream of upper echelons theory research focuses on how CEOs' backgrounds, experiences, values, and psychological orientations can shape a wide range of strategic decisions and firm performance (for a review, see Finkelstein et al., 2009; Wang et al., 2016). The reason for a focus on CEOs is self-evident given that CEOs are the executives who have "overall responsibility for the conduct and performance of an entire organization" (Finkelstein et al., 2009, p. 9). This stream of research implicitly assumes that CEOs are solely responsible for firm outcomes.

Another stream of upper echelons research has revolved around TMTs which include the CEO and other executives who report directly to the CEO. Hambrick and Mason (1984) argue that the CEO shares task and power with other non-CEO executives and TMTs can be perceived as dominant coalitions that collectively shape strategic decisions and firm performance (Carpenter et al., 2004). Although it is conceptually clear about the definition of a TMT, it is empirically challenging to define who should be included in a TMT. Meanwhile, the relevance of the TMT as a meaningful unit of analysis has also been questioned by scholars (Arendt et al., 2005; Hambrick, 2007; Jackson, 1992). This is because not all the top executive positions are created equal, and if all top executives do not "collectively engage in information processing or decision making, then what is the point in trying to use their collective characteristics ... to predict company strategy or performance?" (Hambrick, 2007). Hambrick (2007) proposes that the next frontier of upper echelons research should be TMT subteams because examining interactions and dynamics within the subteams who are relevant in certain decision making can improve the predictive strength of upper echelons theory. Our study responds to such a call by focusing on an important top management subteam, CEO and CFO, and examines how their collective cognitive framework in information attending and processing, captured by CEO-CFO relative optimism, shapes firm M&A decisions.

Cognitive Style of Optimists and Pessimists

Upper echelons research has paid increasing attention to the influence of CEOs' psychological attributes and cognitive frameworks on firm strategic decisions (Chatterjee & Hambrick, 2007; Gamache et al., 2015; Hayward & Hambrick, 1997; Hiller & Hambrick, 2005; Nadkarni & Herrmann, 2010). Unlike prior research that focuses solely on CEOs, we attempt to explore how CEOs' and CFOs' attributes together shape firm strategic decisions. For that purpose, we examine the role of CEO-CFO relative optimism—a comparison of CEO optimism with CFO pessimism—in firm M&A decisions. We choose to investigate CEO optimism and CFO pessimism instead of other psychological attributes (e.g., overconfidence, hubris, big-five personality traits) because compared with previously studied CEO psychological attributes, optimism and pessimism are more directly related to cognitive processes (Peterson, 2000) and can capture how CEO-CFO dyads collectively process information. Optimism refers to "positive outcome expectancies" (Segerstrom, 2001), whereas pessimism refers to an inclination to emphasize adverse aspects, conditions, and possibilities or to expect the worst possible outcomes (Smith et al., 2013). Optimism and pessimism are polar opposites (Smith et al., 2013) pertaining to the degree to which a person has favorable or unfavorable expectancies of attaining a desired end-state (Carver, Reynolds, & Scheier, 1994). Peterson (2000) suggests that optimism (and thus also pessimism) is often treated as a "a cognitive characteristic—a goal, an expectation, or a causal attribution—which is sensible so long as we remember that the belief in question concerns future occurrences about which individuals have strong feelings" (pp. 44–45).

More important, optimism and pessimism are aligned with CEOs' and CFOs' respective role expectations. Role theory suggests that individuals behave according to their social roles in a given setting (Biddle, 1986, 2013; Linton, 1936; Mead, 1925; Zurcher, 1983), often as a means of avoiding role conflicts which may lead to higher social interaction costs or even interaction failure (Biddle, 1986; Merton, 1957; Sarbin & Allen, 1968). Social roles can be defined by the situations in which actors are embedded. In the corporate setting, the CEO, as a link between the internal organization and the external environment, plays the role of a leader who aggressively seeks new business opportunities, sees the upside of potential threats, and sets the agenda and direction for the growth of the organization (Mintzberg, 1973). CEOs are expected to be optimistic and seize the next growth opportunity fast; thus, optimism is consistent with CEOs' role expectations. In contrast, the CFO needs to be "the face of a realist, urging caution and wary of risk" (Tulimieri & Banai, 2010, p. 240). In this sense, CFOs' roles call for them to be defensively pessimistic. Thus, being optimistic is consistent with the expectations of the CEO position whereas being more conservative and pessimistic is aligned with the expectations of the CFO position.

Early psychology research generally treats optimism and pessimism as dispositional traits in that such research focuses on their respective physical and psychological benefits and costs (Kluemper, Little, & Degroot, 2009). For instance, people with trait optimism recover faster from surgery and report a higher quality of life (Trunzo & Pinto, 2003). Recent study suggests that optimism and pessimism can be considered as stable states (Peterson, 2000; Seligman, 1998) that relate more strongly to proximal, context-related outcomes (Kluemper et al., 2009). Given that we focus on how CEO optimism and CFO pessimism together affect firm M&A decisions (which are proximal and context-related outcomes), we posit that optimism and pessimism is more malleable than dispositional traits yet more stable than transient states (e.g., positive and negative moods).

Social psychology research has shown that optimists and pessimists differ from each other cognitively in terms of how they attend to environmental stimuli, and process and interpret information (Segerstrom, 2001; Spirrison & Gordy, 1993). Optimism can lead to positive modes of thinking (Akhtar, 1996; Epstein & Meier, 1989; Scheier, Carver, & Bridges, 1994). When faced with what is plainly negative information, optimists are inclined to reframe it in a positive way (Seligman, 1998). As a result, optimists tend to discount unwanted facts when making evaluations, and mentally reconstruct experiences to avoid contradictions (Taylor & Gollwitzer, 1995). Indeed, their attention to positive stimuli and reframing negative situations may lead to the "blind pursuit" of their ideas (Gibson & Sanbonmatsu, 2004).

In contrast, pessimists often eschew the rose-tinted glasses and are more likely to heed contradictory information and evaluate it critically (Gibson & Sanbonmatsu, 2004; Spencer & Norem, 1996). In other words, they are less easily persuaded by positive information and more sensitive to negative information (Geers, Handley, & McLarney, 2003; Spirrison & Gordy, 1993). Spirrison and Gordy (1993) find that pessimistic individuals can catch a greater number of errors while performing a proofreading task, being less likely to ignore imperfections than their optimistic counterparts. In essence, pessimists are vigilant in their efforts to avoid potential disasters and strategically insure against errors of commission (Norem & Cantor, 1986; Norem & Illingworth, 1993). In sum, optimists and pessimists have distinct cognitive styles and attend to stimuli and information differently: optimists exhibit an attentional bias for positive information, tending to neglect inconsistent information and focus on goal-facilitating information, whereas pessimists demonstrate an attentional bias for information that is negative, inconsistent, and goal inhibiting.

CEO-CFO Relative Optimism and Number of M&As

Although M&As help top managers increase their compensation (Harford & Li, 2007) and social standing (Palmer & Barber, 2001), top managers exhibit great caution in making M&A decisions given high risk associated with M&As (Pablo, Sitkin, & Jemison, 1996). M&As require substantial commitment of corporate resources, the integration of the target can be very challenging, and most M&As fail to achieve organizational and strategic fit (King, Dalton, Daily, & Covin, 2004). If an M&A yields poor shareholder returns, it can result in top manager turnover (Lehn & Zhao, 2006). When top managers perceive high risk in potential targets, they will refrain from acquiring such targets (Pablo et al., 1996). Our study examines how firm's M&A decisions are influenced by CEO-CFO collective cognitive scheme in terms of optimism and pessimism.

Each CEO or CFO could be placed on the optimism-pessimism continuum. To be consistent with their role expectations, we focus on CEO optimism and CFO pessimism. More specifically, since optimistic CEOs tend to demonstrate an attentional bias for positive information and reframe clearly negative information in positive ways (Davis, Nolen-Hoeksema, & Larson, 1998; Park, 1998), such CEOs are less likely to perceive high risk in potential M&A targets and are more prone to make more M&As than less optimistic CEOs. In contrast, pessimistic CFOs who have more realistic expectations and focus their attention on negative or inconsistent information tend to perceive high risk in potential target firms. Accordingly, these CFOs will devote great effort to scrutinize target firms, conduct in-depth due diligence investigations, and pinpoint potential risks of undertaking M&As. Thus, CFOs high in pessimism are less likely to espouse a large number of M&As than those low in pessimism.

Given that our study focuses on the CEO-CFO subteam, we propose a concept of CEO-CFO relative optimism—a comparison of CEO optimism with CFO pessimism, which captures the top management subteam's cognitive schema in screening, processing, and interpreting information and responding to environmental stimuli. We argue that firms with high CEO-CFO relative optimism (i.e., high CEO optimism paired with low CFO pessimism) will undertake a large number of M&As because CFOs low in pessimism are inattentive to negative information and may not play an effective "naysayer" role and help optimistic CEOs identify risk associated with potential M&A targets. As a result, CEO-CFO subteams will collectively perceive low risk in target firms and make a large number of M&A decisions. However, when CEOs are matched more pessimistic CFOs (i.e., a medium level of CEO-CFO relative optimism), such CEOs will devote more effort to scrutinizing target firms, conducting in-depth due diligence investigations, and pinpointing the potential risks of acquiring target firms because the pessimistic CFOs may insist that the optimistic CEOs reevaluate all the detailed information about target firms. When CEO optimism is low and CFO pessimism is high, firms have low CEO-CFO relative optimism. In such a case, because both CEOs and CFOs are inclined to evaluate M&A target firms carefully and perceive high risk in engaging in intensive M&A activities, firms lead by such a CEO-CFO subteam will exhibit a low level of acquisitiveness.

Hypothesis 1: *When the level of CEO-CFO relative optimism increases, the number of M&As conducted by a firm will increase.*

Moderating Effects of CFO Director and Environmental Dynamism

Hypothesis 1 implies that CEO-CFO relative optimism can influence firm M&A intensity. If our theory holds, the role of CEO-CFO relative optimism in shaping M&A decisions will be more pronounced when the CFO (and his/her pessimism orientation) has more means to influence the CEO (i.e., a board member at the focal firm) and when the CEO is more likely to seek the CFO's inputs.

Although CEOs are oftentimes board members of their firms, CFOs are less frequently granted board seats in the firms that they serve (Bedard, Hoitash, & Hoitash, 2014). We contend that CFOs who are board members at focal firms can have a stronger influence on corporate strategic decisions than those whose are not board members. Board seats provide top managers with additional power and influence (Finkelstein, 1992). When CFOs sit on their firms' boards, they can directly participate in key strategic decision-making and vote on important strategic issues. In addition, CFOs sitting in their boardrooms can have convenient access to and form coalitions with other board members to counterbalance the influence of CEOs on strategic decisions. Thus, CFOs who are board members at focal firms can exert a stronger influence on M&A decisions than those who are not board members.

In addition, CEOs may need to actively engage in CFOs who are board members in the M&A decision process to ensure that those CFOs will be on their side in the boardrooms. Thus, board-member CFOs can play a more effective "naysayer" role and their cognitive style can have a more pronounced influence on firm strategies than CFOs who are not board members at focal firms. In contrast, when CFOs are not board members, they may find it challenging to shape firm acquisition decisions because they may have limited means to influence CEOs, and CEOs may not be attentive to their viewpoints. Thus, the role of CFO pessimism in shaping

CEO-CFO collective cognitive schema will be more pronounced when CFOs are board members at focal firms than they are not board members.

Hypothesis 2: *The relationship proposed in Hypothesis 1 will be stronger when CFOs are board members at focal firms than when CFOs are not board members at focal firms.*

CEOs' decisions are subject to the influence of other top managers (Chattopadhyay, Glick, Miller, & Huber, 1999; Hambrick & Mason, 1984), and this is particularly true when firms are faced with high ambiguity and complexity because CEOs are more likely to seek input and advice from other top managers including CFOs under such a scenario (Arendt et al., 2005). Dynamic environments are characterized by unpredictable and rapid change (Dess & Beard, 1984), whether related to new technologies, uncertain demands, or variations in customer preferences. In a highly dynamic environment, firm performance is subject to factors beyond the control of top executives (Li & Simerly, 1998; Shi, Connelly, & Sanders, 2016). Therefore, CEOs are more likely to consult CFOs in strategic decision making, and CFO pessimism should have a more salient influence on containing CEO optimism in the presence of dynamically changing external environments than in the presence of stable external environments.

Conversely, CEOs face less decision uncertainty in stable external environments (Kotter, 1982). CEOs may place less weight on the role of CFOs in M&A decisions, and the role of CFO pessimism in shaping CEO-CFO relative optimism is likely to be weaker. Even if CEOs may seek pessimistic CFOs' inputs, such CFOs may not necessarily raise red flags as, faced with stable environments, they may pay less attention to negative information cues and risk associated with target firms. In sum, the level of CEO-CFO relative optimism will have a more profound influence on shaping M&A intensity when firms are faced with dynamic external environments than with stable external environments.

Hypothesis 3: *The relationship proposed in Hypothesis 1 will be stronger when firms face high environmental dynamism than when firms face low environmental dynamism.*

M&A Performance Implications

Having noted that optimists and pessimists have different cognitive styles when processing information, we posit that M&As by firms with high CEO-CFO relative optimism have a more negative influence on firm performance than those by firms with low CEO-CFO relative optimism. In the presence of high CEO-CFO relative optimism, firms may undertake M&As without nailing down as many details as possible about target firms because CEOs high in optimism and CFOs low in pessimism are both tolerant with ambiguous information, and CFOs will not engage in constructive debates and express dissent to CEOs. As a result, such a CEO-CFO subteam may not utilize an extensive decision process to analyze opportunities and threats associated with target firms and conduct detailed analyses (Fredrickson & Mitchell, 1984). The expression of dissent is crucial to the quality of decisions (Dooley & Fryxell, 1999) because exposure to minority dissent produces higher cognitive conflict (Amason, 1996; Gruenfeld, Thomas-Hunt, & Kim, 1998). As CFOs low in pessimism may not play an effective role of devil's advocate, CEO-CFO subteams are unlikely to have high cognitive conflicts and thorough discussion. As a result, firms with high CEO-CFO relative optimism will have a high chance of adversely selecting M&A targets, and M&As made by such firms may experience strategic and organizational misfit, exerting a negative influence on firm operating performance.

When CEO optimism is similar to CFO pessimism (i.e., a medium level of CEO-CFO relative optimism), such CEO-CFO combinations may experience higher cognitive conflicts because such CEOs and CFOs hold different expectations about M&A targets. As pessimistic CFOs tend to adopt a negative outlook and expect the worst (Norem & Cantor, 1986), they are more likely to urge caution and make optimistic CEOs wary of potential risk associated with acquisition targets and play the role of "naysayer" by engaging in active and intense debates about M&A targets (Schweiger, Sandberg, & Ragan, 1986). As a result, such CEO-CFO dyads will resort to comprehensive strategic decision processes and engage in extensive discussions of strategic options (Lant, Milliken, & Batra, 1992), reducing the likelihood of adversely selecting M&A targets.

In the presence of low CEO-CFO relative optimism (i.e., low CEO optimism and high CFO pessimism), CEO-CFO dyads are least likely to adversely select M&A targets because both CEOs and CFOs are prone to pinpoint as many details as possible about M&A targets before making final M&A decisions. Such CEO-CFO dyads will not acquire a target firm unless they possess substantial information about the target and have conducted in-depth due diligence analysis to ensure strategic and organizational fit, reducing the probability of adversely selecting M&A targets. In other words, M&As made by firms with low CEO-CFO relative optimism have the lowest likelihood of harming firm performance.

Hypothesis 4: *The relationship between a firm's M&A activities and its subsequent performance is negatively moderated by CEO-CFO relative optimism.*

METHOD

Sample and Data

Our sample selection starts with quarterly conference call transcript data obtained from the Thomson Reuters's *StreetEvents* database over the period of 2002–2013. *StreetEvents* offers the largest available archive of global transcripts, briefs, events, guidance, and filings. We focus on companies listed in the United States. The type of transcripts included in this study covers quarterly earnings conference calls, corporate conference calls, conference presentations, and analyst conference calls, as these events are all related to corporate disclosure. From this sample, we culled conference calls where both CEOs and CFOs were present. We obtained financial data from Compustat and the Center for Research in Security Prices (CRSP). We obtained CEO and CFO characteristic data from Capital IQ People Intelligence, MorningStar Governance, and BoardEx.

The study of top executives' characteristics is a challenging endeavor. Prior research (Fanelli, Misangyi, & Tosi, 2009; Gamache et al., 2015; Kaplan, 2008) has used letters to shareholders in annual reports to capture CEO attributes, values, and cognition. This study uses conference calls to measure CEO optimism and CFO pessimism, which are further used to measure CEO-CFO relative optimism. Compared with letters to shareholders, CEOs' and CFOs' speeches during conference calls can capture personalized CEO and CFO communication (Bowen, Davis, & Matsumoto, 2002; Francis, Hanna, & Philbrick, 1997). In particular, research suggests that the language used during speeches yields important clues to individuals' thinking styles, psychological states, and personalities (Pennebaker & King, 1999; Slatcher, Chung, Pennebaker, & Stone, 2007). The use of language is representative of an individual's cognitive processes and personality (Pennebaker & Graybeal, 2001).

Measures

Dependent Variables

We count *the number of M&As* that a firm has announced and eventually completed in a year to measure our first dependent variable (Sanders, 2001; Shi, Hoskisson, & Zhang, 2017; Shi, Zhang, & Hoskisson, 2017).[1] We obtain all the completed M&As listed in the SDC Mergers and Acquisitions Database as a "merger," "acquisition of majority interest," "acquisition of asset," or "acquisition of certain assets." To ensure that the sample included only meaningful transactions from the acquirer's perspective, we limited it to deals with a transaction value over $1 million (Moeller, Schlingemann, & Stulz, 2005).

Our second dependent variable is *firm operating performance*. We use return on assets (ROA) to measure firm operating performance. We focus on operating performance instead of market performance because market performance reflects investors' perceptions and may not capture the true performance implications of M&As. ROA is the mostly commonly used measure of operating performance (Cannella, Park, & Lee, 2008; Carpenter, 2002; He & Huang, 2011), and measured as operating income before depreciation over book value of total assets. We also use return on equity (ROE) as an alternative measure of firm operating performance.

Independent Variable

Our independent variable is *CEO-CFO relative optimism*—the ratio of CEO optimism to CFO pessimism. To measure our independent variable, we need to measure CEO optimism and CFO pessimism first. As argued before, although each individual executive can be placed on the optimism-pessimism continuum, we focus on CEO optimism and CFO pessimism because they are more consistent with respective roles in the organization (and our data later also show CEOs tend to be more optimistic and CFOs tend to be more pessimistic). Our measure of CEO optimism and CFO pessimism draws from research on cognitive linguistics, which holds that a person's cognitive styles can be reflected in their use of words (Pennebaker, Mehl, & Niederhoffer, 2003). We use the dictionaries of *positive words* and *negative words* developed by Loughran and McDonald (2011) to capture CEO optimism and CFO pessimism. Loughran and McDonald (2011) developed dictionaries of positive and negative words by adapting the General Inquirer Harvard IV-4 dictionary, and addressed the issue that words generally classified as negative, such as "cost" or "liability," do not carry negative connotations in a business setting. To measure CEO optimism and CFO pessimism, we extract CEOs' and CFOs' speeches from conference call transcripts, and then calculate the percentage of positive and negative words used by CEOs and CFOs in each conference call.

Following Davis, Ge, Matsumoto, and Zhang (2015), we use the difference between the average percent of positive words and negative words spoken by a CEO during all the conference calls in a year to measure CEO optimism. Since optimism and pessimism are two ends of a bipolar dimension (Smith et al., 2013), the difference score can better capture CEO optimism. Similarly, we use the difference between the average percent of negative words and positive words spoken by a CFO during all the conference calls in a year to measure CFO pessimism. The average of CEO positive words across our 2,356 sample firms is 1.9% and the average CFO of positive words is 1.1%, suggesting that CEOs generally use more positive words (and more optimistic) than CFOs. The average of CEO negative words is 0.87% and the average of CFO negative words is 0.91%, suggesting that CFOs generally use more negative words (and more pessimistic) than CEOs.

Our measure of CEO-CFO relative optimism is constructed as:

$$CEO\text{-}CFO\ relative\ optimism = ln(\frac{1+CEO\ optimism\ score}{1+CFO\ pessimism\ score})\quad (1)$$

We use the natural logarithm to account for skewness and add "1" to both nominator and denominator to avoid negative value and division by "0." This measure suggests that a firm has high CEO-CFO relative optimism when the CEO optimism score is higher than the CFO pessimism score. In contrast, when the CFO pessimism score is higher than the CEO optimism score, our measure will produce a low CEO-CFO relative optimism score.

CEOs (CFOs) may use more positive words and fewer negative words when firms are performing well or have good performance prospects. In this sense, our measure of CEO-CFO relative optimism can reflect firm fundamentals instead of CEO-CFO collective cognitive schemas. Therefore, we break down CEO-CFO relative optimism into a normal component that is related to firm fundamentals and a residual component that cannot be explained by firm fundamentals and may better reflect CEO-CFO collective cognitive schema.[2]

To measure residual CEO-CFO relative optimism, we first run an OLS regression with the following variables as predictors: CEO age, CEO gender, CFO age, CFO gender, ROA, the natural logarithm of total assets, market-to-book ratio, debt ratio, cash holding ratio, Fama-French 48 industry fixed-effects (Fama & French, 1997), and year fixed-effects. *Market-to-book ratio* is measured as the ratio of market capitalization of a firm to its book value. *Debt ratio* is measured as the ratio of the sum of long-term debt and short-term debt to book value of total assets, and *cash holding ratio* is measured as the ratio of cash and short-term investments to book value of assets. We use residuals from this OLS regression to measure CEO-CFO relative optimism and test our hypotheses. Our results are similar if we use raw values of CEO-CFO relative optimism to conduct our analyses. Consistent with prior research (Gamache et al., 2015), we annually update our measure of CEO-CFO relative optimism in the analysis.[3]

Due to CEO or CFO turnover, we can have multiple CEO-CFO dyads in a year firm. Given that our dependent variables are measured at the firm year, we calculate firm-year CEO-CFO relative optimism using the average of all the CEO-CFO dyads in a firm year. We control for *CEO-CFO turnover* in a firm year to partial out the influence of top manager turnover on our dependent variables. Our results are similar if we drop firm-years associated with CEO or CFO turnover.

Moderators

Our study proposes two moderators. The first moderator is *CFO director*, which receives a value of "1" if a CFO is a board member at the focal firm and "0" otherwise. The second moderator is *environmental dynamism*. We follow the procedures outlined by Boyd (1995) to measure *environmental dynamism*. To do so, we run a regression with total industry sales (based on four-digit SIC codes) as the dependent variable and time as a predictor, based on the five years' data immediately preceding the focal year of analysis. Environmental dynamism is the standard error of the slope of the regression coefficient of time divided by the mean value of total industry sales over the five preceding years. This is an annual, industry-level variable.

Control Variables

We draw on the M&A literature and include the following firm-level, CEO-level, and board-level variables that may affect firm M&A intensity: At the firm level, we first control for *firm size* by taking the natural log of total assets because size affects a firm's ability to undertake acquisitions (Haleblian, Devers, McNamara, Carpenter, & Davison, 2009). Second, we control for firm performance using *ROA*, as firms with better financial performance may have more resources to undertake M&As (Carper, 1990). Third, we control for firm *cash holding ratio* and *debt ratio* because these two variables influence the level of financial resources available for M&As (Duchin, 2010).

We control for *institutional ownership concentration* using a Herfindahl-Hirschman index because institutional investors are more likely to monitor managers in the presence of high ownership concentration (Demsetz & Lehn, 1985). Data on institutional ownership are obtained from the *Thomson Reuters 13F* database. Because financial analysts play an important external governance role (Chen, Harford, & Lin, 2015), we control for *analyst coverage* using the number of analysts following a firm in a year.

In addition to firm-level control variables, we include the following CEO-level and board-level control variables. We first control for *CEO duality* because CEOs holding chair positions can have higher levels of discretion in influencing their firms' strategic decisions (Finkelstein, 1992). CEO duality is coded as "1" if CEOs hold board chair positions and "0" otherwise. *Board independence ratio* is controlled because a board with a high percent of outside directors may be more willing to exert a monitoring role (Dalton, Hitt, Certo, & Dalton, 2007). We control for *CEO option pay ratio* and *CEO equity ownership* because these two variables may influence firm acquisition decisions (Sanders, 2001; Sanders & Hambrick, 2007). CEO option pay ratio is measured as the ratio of the total value of annual option awards to the total value of compensation, and CEO equity ownership is measured as the ratio of the number of shares owned by the CEO to the total number of shares outstanding. Following the same measurement procedures, we control for *CFO option pay ratio* and *CFO equity ownership* because CFOs' compensation structure also influences corporate policies and decisions (Chava & Purnanandam, 2010).

We include three CEO-CFO dyadic-level variables relating to CEO-CFO demographic backgrounds because they can influence the nature of social dynamics between CEOs and CFOs, which in turn affect our dependent variables. The first variable is *CEO-CFO tenure overlap*, which is measured as shared tenure between CEOs and CFOs. The second variable refers to *CEO-CFO same gender*, which receives a value of "1" if the CEO and CFO have the same gender and "0" otherwise. The third variable captures whether the CEO and CFO have the *same education level*. We classify education backgrounds into three levels: undergraduate degrees, master's degrees, and doctoral degrees. If the CEO and CFO have the same education level, a CEO-CFO dyad receives a value of "1," and "0" otherwise.

Estimation Method

The first dependent variable of Hypotheses 1–3 is the number of M&As, which is a count variable. Two methods commonly used to analyze count data are negative binomial regressions and Poisson regressions. To control for biases arising from time-invariant firm heterogeneity, we choose firm fixed-effects regressions. We choose firm fixed-effects Poisson regressions over fixed-effects negative binomial regressions because the latter do not provide a true fixed-effects analysis (Allison & Waterman, 2002). Fixed-effects Poisson regressions can only model firms that have time-variant dependent variables (Allison, 2005) and around one third of our final sample firms do not have any M&As announcement during the sample frame. Therefore, we also use firm fixed-effects OLS regressions to test Hypotheses 1–3 and find similar results.

The dependent variable of Hypothesis 4 is firm performance, and we use firm fixed-effects OLS regressions to test this hypothesis. We measure our dependent variables at $t+1$ and all the other variables at t to deal with possible causality issues.

RESULTS

Table 4.1 shows descriptive statistics for variables used in this study. Table 4.2 is used to test Hypothesis 1. Model 1 includes all the control variables and CEO optimism (residual measure)[4] and CFO pessimism (residual measure) as predictors. The coefficient estimate of *CEO optimism* is positive

($\beta = 0.06, p < .05$) and the coefficient estimate of *CFO pessimism* is negative ($\beta = -0.07, p < .05$), suggesting that optimistic CEOs are positively associated, and pessimistic CFOs are negatively associated, with the number of M&As, indicating that CEOs high in optimism generally undertake more M&As than those low in optimism, whereas CFOs high in pessimism undertake fewer than those low in pessimism.

Hypothesis 1 argues that high CEO-CFO relative optimism is positively associated with the number of M&As. In Model 2, the coefficient estimate of *CEO–CFO relative optimism* is positive and statistically significant ($\beta = 7.92, p < .01$), supporting Hypothesis 1. In terms of economic magnitude, one standard deviation increase in CEO-CFO relative optimism will give rise to an 8.2% increase in the number of M&As. In Model 2, we report results from a firm fixed-effects OLS regression, and we take the natural logarithm of the number of M&As. The coefficient estimate of *CEO-CFO relative optimism* is positive and statistically significant ($\beta = 0.94, p < .01$), supporting Hypothesis 1. Model 3 report results from a firm fixed-effects OLS regression with the natural logarithm of the transaction value of all the M&As conducted in a year as the dependent variable. The coefficient estimate of *CEO-CFO relative optimism* is positive and statistically significant ($\beta = 3.95, p < .05$).

Table 4.3 is used to test the moderating effects of CFO director and environmental dynamism. Hypothesis 2 proposes that the relationship between CEO-CFO relative optimism and the number of M&As will be stronger when CFOs are board members at the focal firms. In Model 1, we examine the interaction effect between CEO-CFO relative optimism and CFO director. The coefficient estimate of the interaction term is positive but statistically not significant. Such a non-finding may be due to the fact that we use firm fixed-effects regressions and CFO director is time-invariant for half of our sample firms. As an alternative way to test the moderating effect, we conduct subgroup analyses based on whether a CFO is a board member at the focal firm. Model 2 shows that the coefficient estimate of *CEO-CFO relative optimism* is positive and statistically significant ($\beta = 10.31, p < .01$) for the CFO director subgroup. However, for the non-CFO director subgroup in Model 3, the coefficient estimate of *CEO-CFO relative optimism* is positive but statistically not significant ($\beta = 4.89$, n.s.). Results in Models 2–3 provide support for Hypothesis 2. The coefficient in Model 2 suggests that, when a CFO is a board member, one standard deviation increase in CEO-CFO relative optimism will lead to a 10.8% increase in the number of M&As. This represents about 31.7% increase compared to the whole sample (i.e., 10.8%/8.2% = 1.317).

Hypothesis 3 proposes that the positive relationship between CEO-CFO relative optimism and the number of M&As is stronger when firms face high environmental dynamism. In Model 4, the coefficient of *CEO-CFO*

Table 4.1
Descriptive Statistics

Variable	Mean	S.D.	1	2	3	4	5	6	7	8	9	10	11	12	13	14	15	16	17	18	19	20
1 Number of acquisitions	0.29	0.75	1.00																			
2 CEO-CFO relative optimism	0.00	0.01	0.03	1.00																		
3 CFO director	0.47	0.50	0.06	0.01	1.00																	
4 Environmental dynamism	2.44	4.75	0.04	-0.02	-0.03	1.00																
5 Firm size	7.13	1.93	0.12	0.00	0.43	0.13	1.00															
6 ROA	0.06	0.14	0.07	0.00	0.18	-0.13	0.28	1.00														
7 Debt ratio	2.04	3.96	-0.01	-0.01	0.06	0.20	0.31	-0.04	1.00													
8 Cash holding ratio	0.18	0.21	-0.07	0.00	-0.16	-0.03	-0.44	-0.32	-0.19	1.00												
9 Institutional ownership concentration	0.08	0.09	-0.08	-0.02	-0.26	0.01	-0.42	-0.27	-0.01	0.09	1.00											
10 Analyst coverage	9.37	7.46	0.10	0.01	0.35	0.09	0.66	0.20	0.04	-0.06	-0.36	1.00										
11 CEO-CFO turnover	0.22	0.42	0.05	0.00	0.08	-0.01	0.13	0.01	0.03	-0.03	-0.03	0.10	1.00									
12 CEO duality	0.32	0.50	0.04	0.01	0.12	0.00	0.14	0.09	0.03	-0.11	-0.07	0.08	-0.02	1.00								
13 Board independence	0.71	0.13	-0.06	0.03	-0.69	0.06	-0.21	-0.17	0.04	0.06	0.17	-0.23	-0.03	-0.11	1.00							
14 CEO option pay ratio	0.16	0.24	-0.03	-0.01	0.07	-0.03	0.10	-0.07	-0.03	0.17	-0.08	0.22	0.05	-0.04	0.00	1.00						
15 CEO equity ownership	0.01	0.03	-0.03	0.00	-0.12	-0.01	-0.20	0.01	-0.04	0.06	0.09	-0.13	-0.04	0.17	0.01	-0.07	1.00					
16 CFO option pay ratio	0.12	0.17	-0.03	-0.01	-0.02	-0.03	-0.02	-0.10	-0.07	0.23	-0.04	0.14	-0.06	-0.05	0.04	0.65	-0.04	1.00				
17 CFO equity ownership	0.00	0.00	-0.02	-0.03	-0.13	-0.01	-0.23	0.00	-0.02	0.01	0.07	-0.18	0.01	0.01	0.10	-0.11	0.13	-0.10	1.00			
18 CEO-CFO tenure overlap	3.73	4.32	-0.02	-0.03	-0.20	0.00	-0.09	0.02	-0.01	-0.02	0.01	-0.08	-0.14	0.16	0.08	-0.07	0.15	-0.04	0.13	1.00		
19 CEO-CFO same gender	0.70	0.46	0.04	0.00	0.36	-0.02	0.14	0.03	0.01	-0.03	-0.09	0.12	0.08	0.03	-0.22	0.02	-0.02	-0.01	-0.05	-0.28	1.00	
20 CEO-CFO same education level	0.38	0.49	0.01	-0.01	0.11	0.00	0.07	0.04	0.02	-0.04	-0.04	0.07	0.03	0.02	-0.06	0.00	-0.03	-0.01	-0.03	-0.05	0.17	1.00

Note: Absolute value of correlations greater than .03 statistically significant at $p < .05$.

121

Table 4.2
CEO-CFO Cognitive Style and Firm M&As

Variable	Model 1OLS	Model 2 Poisson	Model 3 OLS	Model 4 OLS
CEO relative optimism		7.92***	0.94***	3.95**
		[2.35]	[0.32]	[1.83]
CEO optimism	0.06**			
	[0.03]			
CFO pessimism	−0.07**			
	[0.03]			
Firm size	−0.29***	−0.29***	−0.09***	−0.49***
	[0.07]	[0.07]	[0.01]	[0.07]
ROA	2.00***	2.00***	0.23***	1.50***
	[0.41]	[0.41]	[0.04]	[0.21]
Debt ratio	−0.01*	−0.01*	−0.00*	−0.01**
	[0.01]	[0.01]	[0.00]	[0.01]
Cash holding ratio	1.27***	1.27***	0.22***	1.31***
	[0.38]	[0.38]	[0.04]	[0.21]
Institutional ownership concentration	−3.76***	−3.76***	−0.36***	−1.75***
	[0.76]	[0.76]	[0.06]	[0.34]
Analyst coverage	−0.00	−0.00	0.00	0.01
	[0.01]	[0.01]	[0.00]	[0.01]
CEO–CFO turnover	0.02	0.02	0.00	0.05
	[0.05]	[0.05]	[0.01]	[0.05]
CEO duality	−0.01	−0.01	−0.01	−0.02
	[0.06]	[0.06]	[0.01]	[0.06]
Board independence	0.23	0.23	0.03	0.22
	[0.32]	[0.32]	[0.05]	[0.27]
CEO option pay ratio	0.04	0.03	−0.00	−0.04
	[0.11]	[0.11]	[0.02]	[0.13]
CEO equity ownership	−1.25	−1.26	−0.19	−1.60**
	[1.08]	[1.09]	[0.12]	[0.68]
CFO option pay ratio	0.17	0.19	0.02	−0.01
	[0.16]	[0.16]	[0.03]	[0.15]

(Table continued on next page)

Table 4.2 (Continued)
CEO-CFO Cognitive Style and Firm M&As

Variable	Model 1OLS	Model 2 Poisson	Model 3 OLS	Model 4 OLS
	[15.15]	[15.13]	[2.22]	[10.84]
CEO-CFO tenure overlap	0.00	0.00	0.00	0.01
	[0.01]	[0.01]	[0.00]	[0.01]
CEO-CFO same gender	0.03	0.03	0.01	0.06
	[0.07]	[0.07]	[0.01]	[0.05]
CEO-CFO same education level	–0.01	–0.01	–0.00	–0.03
	[0.06]	[0.06]	[0.01]	[0.06]
Constant			0.80***	4.04***
			[0.10]	[0.50]
Observations	10,148	10,148	15,800	15,800
Firm fixed-effects	YES	YES	YES	YES
Year fixed-effects	YES	YES	YES	YES
Adjusted R-squared	.	.	0.246	0.210
Chi–squared	629.9	628.2	.	.
Log–likelihood	–5732	–5733	–2886	–30952

Notes: Standard errors clustered by firms in brackets. *** $p < 0.01$, ** $p < 0.05$, * $p < 0.1$. Two-tailed tests.

Table 4.3
Moderating Effect of CFO Director and Environmental Dynamism

Variable	Model 1	Model 2 CFO director	Model 3 Non-FO director	Model 4
CEO relative optimism	5.01	10.31***	4.89	5.67**
	[3.41]	[3.26]	[3.75]	[2.66]
CEO relative optimism	4.82			
x CFO director	[4.48]			
CEO relative optimism				0.69**
x Environmental dynamism				[0.30]
CFO director	0.03			
	[0.10]			
Environmental dynamism				0.01
				[0.01]

(Table continued on next page)

Table 4.3 (Continued)
Moderating Effect of CFO Director and Environmental Dynamism

Variable	Model 1	Model 2 CFO director	Model 3 Non-FO director	Model 4
Firm size	−0.29***	−0.28***	−0.42***	−0.29***
	[0.07]	[0.11]	[0.11]	[0.07]
ROA	2.00***	1.86**	2.06***	2.10***
	[0.41]	[0.82]	[0.48]	[0.41]
Debt ratio	−0.01*	−0.01	−0.01	−0.01*
	[0.01]	[0.01]	[0.01]	[0.01]
Cash holding ratio	1.27***	1.11**	2.08***	1.27***
	[0.38]	[0.49]	[0.37]	[0.38]
Institutional ownership concentration	−3.78***	−7.06***	−2.81***	−3.78***
	[0.76]	[1.84]	[0.85]	[0.76]
Analyst coverage	−0.00	−0.01	0.01	−0.00
	[0.01]	[0.01]	[0.01]	[0.01]
CEO–CFO turnover	0.02	0.09	−0.14*	0.02
	[0.05]	[0.07]	[0.08]	[0.05]
CEO duality	−0.01	−0.03	−0.07	−0.01
	[0.06]	[0.08]	[0.13]	[0.06]
Board independence	0.30	0.07	−0.29	0.23
	[0.42]	[0.61]	[0.54]	[0.32]
CEO option pay ratio	0.03	−0.07	0.13	0.02
	[0.11]	[0.13]	[0.21]	[0.11]
CEO equity ownership	−1.28	−3.01	−0.39	−1.25
	[1.09]	[1.96]	[1.46]	[1.08]
CFO option pay ratio	0.19	0.12	0.38	0.19
	[0.16]	[0.23]	[0.26]	[0.16]
CFO equity ownership	2.69	4.13	8.91	1.96
	[15.07]	[25.98]	[20.62]	[15.20]
CEO-CFO tenure overlap	0.00	0.01	−0.01	0.00
	[0.01]	[0.01]	[0.01]	[0.01]
CEO-CFO same gender	0.02	−0.31	0.15*	0.03
	[0.07]	[0.19]	[0.08]	[0.07]
CEO-CFO same education level	−0.01	0.16*	−0.19**	−0.01
	[0.06]	[0.09]	[0.09]	[0.06]

(Table continued on next page)

Table 4.3 (Continued)
Moderating Effect of CFO Director and Environmental Dynamism

Variable	Model 1	Model 2 CFO director	Model 3 Non-FO director	Model 4
Observations	10,148	5,031	4,130	10,148
Firm fixed-effects	YES	YES	YES	YES
Year fixed-effects	YES	YES	YES	YES
Chi-squared	631.9	423.8	308.8	628.1
Log-likelihood	–5732	–2934	–2155	–5730

Notes: Standard errors clustered by firms in brackets. *** p <0.01, ** p <0.05, * p <0.1. Two-tailed tests.

relative optimism × *Environmental dynamism* is positive and statistically significant ($\beta = 0.69$, $p < .05$), supporting Hypothesis 3. In terms of economic magnitude, when environmental dynamism takes its high value (mean + 1 S.D.), the number of M&As increases by 22% when CEO-CFO relative optimism moves from its low value (mean – 1 S.D.) to its high value (mean + 1 S.D.). However, when environmental dynamism takes its low value, the number of M&As will increase by 8.9% for the same increase in CEO-CFO relative optimism. Figure 4.1 graphs the interaction between CEO-CFO relative optimism and environmental dynamism. We find a stronger positive relationship between CEO-CFO relative optimism and the number of M&As in the presence of high dynamism (the dotted line) than low dynamism (the solid line).

Hypothesis 4 suggests that the relationship between M&A intensity and firm performance is negatively moderated by CEO-CFO relative optimism. Table 4.4 is used to test Hypothesis 4. The dependent variables of Models 1–2 is ROA. In Model 1, the coefficient estimate of *CEO-CFO relative optimism* × *Number of M&As* is negative and statistically significant ($\beta = -0.35$, $p < 0.05$). In Model 2, the coefficient of *CEO-CFO relative optimism* × *Value of M&As* is negative and statistically significant ($\beta = -0.09$, $p < 0.01$). Results in Models 1–2 support Hypothesis 4. Based on results in Model 1, when CEO–CFO relative optimism takes its low value, ROA will *increase* by 4.7% when the number of M&As increases from its low value to high value; however, when CEO-CFO relative optimism takes its high value, ROA will *decrease* by 1.4% for the same increase in the number of M&As. We graph the interaction effect in Figure 4.2. Figure 4.2 shows a positive relationship between the number of M&As and ROA when CEO-CFO relative optimism (the solid line) is low, but a negative relationship when CEO-CFO relative optimism (the dotted line) is high.

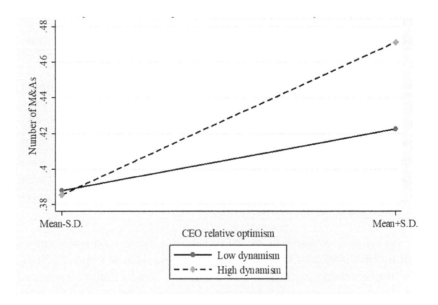

Figure 4.1.   Moderating effect of environmental dynamism.

Table 4.4

Firm Performance as Dependent Variables

Variable	Model 1 ROA	Model 2 ROA	Model 3 ROE	Model 4 ROE
CEO relative optimism	−0.35**		−2.06**	
x Number of M&As	[0.16]		[1.02]	
CEO relative optimism		−0.09***		−0.43**
x Value of M&As		[0.03]		[0.17]
CEO relative optimism	0.79***	0.81***	2.29***	2.34***
	[0.10]	[0.10]	[0.62]	[0.62]
Number of M&As	0.00		0.01	
	[0.00]		[0.01]	
Value of M&As		0.00		0.00
		[0.00]		[0.00]
Firm size	−0.01	−0.01	−0.01	−0.01
	[0.00]	[0.00]	[0.02]	[0.02]
Debt ratio	−0.00	−0.00	0.02***	0.02***
	[0.00]	[0.00]	[0.01]	[0.01]

(Table continued on next page)

Table 4.4 (Continued)

Firm Performance as Dependent Variables

Variable	Model 1 ROA	Model 2 ROA	Model 3 ROE	Model 4 ROE
Cash holding ratio	-0.06***	-0.06***	-0.19**	-0.19**
	[0.02]	[0.02]	[0.08]	[0.08]
Institutional ownership concentration	-0.04	-0.04	0.22	0.21
	[0.03]	[0.03]	[0.28]	[0.28]
Analyst coverage	0.00	0.00	0.00	0.00
	[0.00]	[0.00]	[0.00]	[0.00]
CEO-CFO turnover	-0.00	-0.00	0.01	0.01
	[0.00]	[0.00]	[0.01]	[0.01]
CEO-CFO tenure overlap	-0.00	-0.00	-0.00	-0.00
	[0.00]	[0.00]	[0.00]	[0.00]
CEO-CFO same gender	-0.00	-0.00	-0.00	-0.00
	[0.00]	[0.00]	[0.01]	[0.01]
CEO-CFO same education level	-0.00	-0.00	0.02	0.02
	[0.00]	[0.00]	[0.02]	[0.02]
CEO duality	-0.00	0.00	0.00	0.00
	[0.00]	[0.00]	[0.02]	[0.02]
Board independence	-0.02	-0.02	-0.09	-0.09
	[0.01]	[0.01]	[0.06]	[0.06]
CEO option pay ratio	-0.01	-0.01	0.04	0.05
	[0.01]	[0.01]	[0.04]	[0.04]
CEO equity ownership	-0.02	-0.02	-0.09	-0.09
	[0.04]	[0.04]	[0.18]	[0.18]
CFO option pay ratio	-0.00	-0.00	-0.02	-0.02
	[0.01]	[0.01]	[0.05]	[0.05]
CFO equity ownership	0.80	0.81	-3.43	-3.42
	[0.68]	[0.68]	[2.98]	[2.98]
Constant	0.17***	0.17***	0.32**	0.32**
	[0.03]	[0.03]	[0.15]	[0.15]
Observations	14,842	14,842	14,841	14,841
Firm fixed-effects	YES	YES	YES	YES
Year fixed-effects	YES	YES	YES	YES
Within R-squared	0.0311	0.0313	0.0214	0.0215
Between R-squared	0.0483	0.0477	0.101	0.100
Overall R-squared	0.0399	0.0396	0.0635	0.0633

Notes: Standard errors clustered by firms in brackets. *** $p < 0.01$, ** $p < 0.05$, * $p < 0.1$. Two-tailed tests.

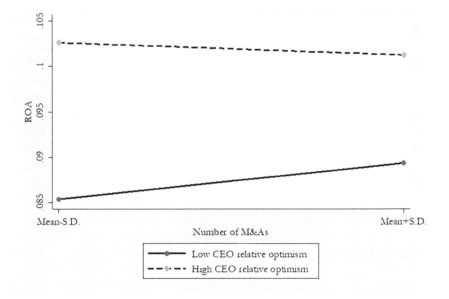

Figure 4.2.   Interaction between CEO relative optimism and number of M&As.

Models 3–4 present results with ROE as the dependent variable. The coefficient estimates of the two interaction terms are both negative and statistically significant, consistent with Hypothesis 4.

Supplementary Analyses

Propensity-Score Reweighting Regressions

One may argue that the relationship between CEO-CFO relative optimism and M&A intensity/ROA can be driven by boards' selection of CEOs and CFOs. To mitigate bias from the non-random assignment of CEOs and CFOs, we conduct propensity-score reweighting regressions (Nichols, 2007). This reweighting approach is similar to simulating what would occur if all firms had both high and low levels of CEO-CFO relative optimism, addressing the possibility that specific types of firms have a high level of CEO-CFO relative optimism. To implement the reweighting regressions, we first estimate a probit model predicting the probability of a firm having a high or low level of CEO-CFO relative optimism. Following Almandoz and Tilcsik (2016), we use the median value of CEO-CFO relative optimism to code whether a CEO-CFO dyad has a high or low level of relative optimism. We include all the variables used in predicting the number of

M&As in the first-stage probit regression. In addition, we use the average of CEO-CFO relative optimism for all the CEOs in the same state (excluding focal CEO) as an instrument. Research shows that geography plays a critical role in the managerial labor market and firms are more likely to tap managers from other geographically close firms (Yonker, 2017). Therefore, state-level CEO-CFO relative optimism can predict focal firm's CEO-CFO relative optimism, but the CEO-CFO relative optimism of other firms in the same state should not exert a direct influence on the focal firm M&As and performance. In unreported first-stage regression, the coefficient estimate of our instrument is positive and statistically significant ($\beta = 17.37$, $p < .05$). Based on the probit regression results, we calculate the odds of a firm belonging to the high or low CEO-CFO relative optimism group, and then use the odds as a weight in the second-stage regressions. Results from the reweighting regressions are reported in Table 4.5.

Table 4.5
Propensity Score Reweighting Regressions

Variable	Model 1 Number	Model 2 CFO director Number	Model 3 Non-CFO director Number	Model 4 Number	Model 5 ROA	Model 6 ROA
CEO relative optimism	0.95***	1.18**	0.67	0.66*	0.81***	0.83***
	[0.33]	[0.52]	[0.55]	[0.37]	[0.11]	[0.11]
CEO relative optimism				0.12**		
x Environmental dynamism				[0.06]		
CEO relative optimism					−0.34*	
x Number of M&As					[0.17]	
CEO relative optimism						−0.09***
x Value of M&As						[0.03]
Environmental dynamism				0.00		
				[0.00]		
Number of M&As					0.00	
					[0.00]	
Value of M&As						0.00
						[0.00]

(Table continued on next page)

Table 4.5 (Continued)
Propensity Score Reweighting Regressions

Variable	Model 1 Number	Model 2 CFO director Number	Model 3 Non-CFO director Number	Model 4 Number	Model 5 ROA	Model 6 ROA
Firm size	-0.09***	-0.12***	-0.10***	-0.09***	-0.01	-0.01
	[0.01]	[0.02]	[0.02]	[0.01]	[0.00]	[0.00]
ROA	0.23***	0.31***	0.18***	0.23***		
	[0.04]	[0.08]	[0.05]	[0.04]		
Debt ratio	-0.00*	-0.00	-0.00	-0.00*	-0.00	-0.00
	[0.00]	[0.00]	[0.00]	[0.00]	[0.00]	[0.00]
Cash holding ratio	0.22***	0.25***	0.24***	0.22***	-0.06***	-0.06***
	[0.04]	[0.08]	[0.05]	[0.04]	[0.02]	[0.02]
Institutional ownership concentration	-0.35***	-0.80***	-0.23***	-0.35***	-0.04	-0.04
	[0.07]	[0.18]	[0.08]	[0.07]	[0.03]	[0.03]
Analyst coverage	0.00	-0.00	0.00	0.00	-0.00	-0.00
	[0.00]	[0.00]	[0.00]	[0.00]	[0.00]	[0.00]
CEO–CFO turnover	0.01	0.02*	-0.02*	0.01	-0.00	-0.00
	[0.01]	[0.01]	[0.01]	[0.01]	[0.00]	[0.00]
CEO duality	-0.01	-0.00	-0.01	-0.01	0.00	0.00
	[0.01]	[0.02]	[0.02]	[0.01]	[0.00]	[0.00]
Board independence	0.04	0.02	-0.02	0.04	-0.02	-0.02
	[0.05]	[0.12]	[0.09]	[0.05]	[0.01]	[0.01]
CEO option pay ratio	-0.00	-0.01	0.01	-0.00	-0.01	-0.01
	[0.02]	[0.03]	[0.03]	[0.02]	[0.01]	[0.01]
CEO equity ownership	-0.20	-0.35	-0.06	-0.19	-0.02	-0.02
	[0.12]	[0.23]	[0.17]	[0.12]	[0.04]	[0.04]
CFO option pay ratio	0.02	0.03	0.03	0.02	0.00	0.00
	[0.02]	[0.05]	[0.03]	[0.03]	[0.01]	[0.01]
CFO equity ownership	-0.75	2.56	-1.64	-0.78	0.75	0.76
	[2.23]	[4.50]	[2.81]	[2.23]	[0.75]	[0.75]
CEO-CFO tenure overlap	0.00	0.00	-0.00	0.00	-0.00	-0.00
	[0.00]	[0.00]	[0.00]	[0.00]	[0.00]	[0.00]

(Table continued on next page)

Table 4.5 (Continued)
Propensity Score Reweighting Regressions

Variable	Model 1 Number	Model 2 CFO director Number	Model 3 Non-CFO director Number	Model 4 Number	Model 5 ROA	Model 6 ROA
CEO-CFO same gender	0.00	–0.03	0.02	0.00	–0.00	–0.00
	[0.01]	[0.03]	[0.01]	[0.01]	[0.00]	[0.00]
CEO-CFO same education level	–0.00	0.02	–0.02	–0.00	–0.00	–0.00
	[0.01]	[0.02]	[0.01]	[0.01]	[0.00]	[0.00]
Constant	0.80***	1.13***	0.76***	0.80***	0.17***	0.17***
	[0.10]	[0.20]	[0.14]	[0.10]	[0.03]	[0.03]
Observations	15,800	7,365	8,435	15,800	14,842	14,842
Firm fixed-effects	YES	YES	YES	YES	YES	YES
Year fixed-effects	YES	YES	YES	YES	YES	YES
Adjusted R-squared	0.245	0.233	0.278	0.245	0.763	0.763

Notes: Standard errors clustered by firms in brackets. *** $p < 0.01$, ** $p < 0.05$, * $p < 0.1$. Two-tailed tests.

Because fixed-effects Poisson cannot implement reweighting regressions, we conduct all the analyses using firm-fixed effects OLS regressions. The dependent variable of Model 1 is the logged number of M&As, and the coefficient estimate of *CEO-CFO relative optimism* is positive and statistically significant ($\beta = 0.95$, $p < .01$), consistent with Hypothesis 1. Models 2–3 conduct subgroup analyses based on whether a CFO is a director at the focal firm. The coefficient estimate of *CEO-CFO relative optimism* is positive and statistically significant ($\beta = 1.18$, $p < .05$) for the CFO director subgroup (Model 2), consistent with Hypothesis 2. In Model 4, the coefficient estimate of *CEO-CFO relative optimism* × *Environmental dynamism* is positive and statistically significant ($\beta = 0.12$, $p < .05$), consistent with Hypothesis 3. In Models 5–6 with firm performance (ROA) as the dependent variable, the coefficient estimates of the interaction terms are both negative and statistically significant, supporting Hypothesis 4.

Alternative Dictionaries of Optimism and Pessimism

In addition to using the list of positive and negative words compiled by Loughran and McDonald (2011) to measure optimism and pessimism, we also measure them using another word list from DICTION 5.0 (Hart,

2000). DICTION has been mostly used to analyze narrative disclosure of politicians (Bligh, Kohles, & Meindl, 2004; Hart & Jarvis, 1997), and recently used to analyze business disclosure (Davis, Piger, & Sedor, 2012; Davis & Tama-Sweet, 2012). Following Davis et al. (2012), we use the sum of praise words, satisfaction words, and inspiration words to measure optimism, and use blame words, hardship words, and denial words to measure pessimism. CEO optimism score is measured as the difference between CEO optimism and CEO pessimism, and CFO pessimism score is measured as the difference between CFO pessimism and CFO optimism. We then calculate residual CEO-CFO relative optimism. Results from this alternative dictionary are reported in Models 1–5 of Table 4.6.

Results are largely consistent with our main analyses reported on Tables 4.2–4.4. The coefficient estimate of *CEO-CFO relative optimism* is positive and statistically significant ($\beta = 0.87$, $p < .05$) in Model 1. In Model 2 (the CFO director subgroup), the coefficient estimate of *CEO-CFO relative optimism* is positive and statistically significant ($\beta = 1.18$, $p < .05$). In Model 4, the coefficient estimate of *CEO-CFO relative optimism* × *Environmental dynamism* is positive and statistically significant ($\beta = 0.15$, $p < .10$, two-tailed test). In Model 5, the coefficient estimate of *CEO-CFO relative optimism* × *Number of M&As* is negative and statistically significant ($\beta = -0.07$, $p < .10$, two-tailed test).

Using Q&A Transcripts

Some may be concerned that CEOs' and CFOs' prepared speeches during conference calls are highly polished and may not reflect their true psychological orientations. During the question and answer (Q&A) sections, the CEO and CFO spontaneously address questions raised by financial analysts and investors. Thus, the Q&A sections of transcripts may capture CEOs' and CFOs' psychological states more effectively. We check the robustness of our findings by measuring CEO optimism and CFO pessimism based only on the Q&A sections of transcripts. We find the correlations between the CEO optimism measure based on the presentation section and the CEO optimism measure based on the Q&A section is 0.24 ($p < .01$) and the same correlation for the CFO pessimism is 0.12 ($p < .01$). Detailed results using Q&A transcripts to measure CEO optimism and CFO pessimism are presented in Models 6–10 of Table 4.6. The estimated coefficients are generally consistent with our main analyses reported in Tables 4.2–4.4, except for the interaction between CEO-CFO relative optimism and number of M&As in Model 10. Our findings are generally consistent with Davis et al. (2015) who find similar results by measuring managerial tone based on the prepared-remarks section versus improvisational comments made by the manager during the Q&A section.

Table 4.6
Supplementary Analyses

Variable	Model 1	Model 2	Model 3	Model 4	Model 5	Model 6	Model 7	Model 8	Model 9	Model 10
	DICTION measure					Q&A transcript				
	Number	Number (CFO director)	Number (Non-CFO director)	Number	ROA	Number	Number (CFO director)	Number (Non-CFO director)	Number	ROA
CEO relative optimism	0.87**	1.18**	0.55	0.51	0.08***	4.61**	7.480***	0.487	2.388	0.159
	[0.39]	[0.51]	[0.61]	[0.44]	[0.02]	[1.92]	[1.637]	[3.751]	[2.645]	[0.106]
CEO relative optimism x Environmental dynamism				0.15*					0.168*	
				[0.08]					[0.093]	
CEO relative optimism x Number of M&As					−0.07**					0.017
					[0.03]					[0.200]
Environmental dynamism				0.01					0.008	
				[0.01]					[0.007]	
Number of M&As					0.00					0.004**
					[0.00]					[0.002]

(Table continued on next page)

133

Table 4.6 (Continued)
Supplementary Analyses

Variable	Model 1	Model 2	Model 3	Model 4	Model 5	Model 6	Model 7	Model 8	Model 9	Model 10
		DICTION measure					Q&A transcript			
	Number	Number (CFO director)	Number (Non-CFO director)	Number	ROA	Number	Number (CFO director)	Number (Non-CFO director)	Number	ROA
Firm fixed-effects	YES	YES	YES	YES	YES	YES	YES	YES	YES	YES
Year fixed-effects	YES	YES	YES	YES	YES	YES	YES	YES	YES	YES
Chi-squared	619.3	418.5	308.7	617.2		570.0	374.0	277.9	657.6	
Log-likelihood	−5737	−2938	−2155	−5735		−5109	−2652	−1905	−5107	
Within R-squared					0.0248					0.0246
Between R-squared					0.0447					0.100
Overall R-squared					0.0379					0.0710

Notes: Standard errors clustered by firms in brackets. *** $p < 0.01$, ** $p < 0.05$, * $p < 0.1$. Two-tailed tests.

DISCUSSION

This study examines the influence of CEO-CFO relative optimism on firm M&A decisions. We find evidence that firms with high CEO-CFO relative optimism undertake more M&As than those with low CEO-CFO relative optimism. Such an effect is particularly strong when CFOs are board members at focal firms or when firms face a dynamic external environment. We also find that acquisition activities have a negative relationship with firm performance when CEO-CFO relative optimism is high but a positive relationship when CEO-CFO relative optimism is low. These results not only show that the CEO and CFO's collective cognitive schema captured by their optimism and pessimism matters in strategic decision making, but also highlight the important role of CFOs in shaping both firm M&A intensity and the quality of M&A decisions.

Our results have implications for several streams of strategic management research. First, different from prior research that has either focused on the individual level of CEOs or the team level of TMTs, this study takes a mid-way approach and focuses on an important top management subteam, namely CEOs and CFOs, and examine the influence of their collective cognitive schema on M&A decisions. Taking such a mid-way approach is important because not all positions within a TMT are created equal and not all executives within a TMT play the same role in different strategic decisions. Building on prior research, we have argued that optimists and pessimists exhibit different cognitive styles in terms of attentional focus and information processing. This study extends prior upper echelons research by proposing that CEO-CFO relative optimism that captures the collective cognitive schema of an important TMT subteam can provide new insights into how top managers influence firm strategic decisions.

Related, an increasing number of studies have focused on the influence of CEO psychological orientations such as narcissism (Chatterjee & Hambrick, 2007) and overconfidence (Chen, Crossland, & Luo, 2015) on firm strategic decisions. Our study moves beyond study of individual CEOs by also considering other non-CEO executives' psychological orientations (i.e., CFOs in our chapter) and investigating their joint influence (captured by CEO-CFO relative optimism) on strategic decisions. Although the importance of CFOs in TMTs has witnessed a sharp increase since the enactment of the Sarbanes-Oxley Act, strategy research has been silent on the role of CFOs in corporate decision making. Our study documents that CFOs exert an influence on acquisition decisions as well. In the presence of pessimistic CFOs, optimistic CEOs not only undertake fewer acquisitions, but are also less likely to undertake value-destructive acquisitions. Thus, our findings enrich the M&A literature by highlighting the role of CFOs in firm acquisition decisions.

As with any empirical study, this study has limitations that may provide avenues for future research. We focus on CEO optimism and CFO pessimism because optimism and pessimism, as two related constructs, are nicely aligned with CEOs' and CFOs' respective role expectations and can directly influence cognitive processes (Peterson, 2000). Yet, differences and similarity between CEOs and CFOs in terms of other psychological orientations (e.g., temporal focus and big-five personality characteristics) may also impact firm strategic decisions. For instance, when both CEOs and CFOs have a high level of future temporal focus, firms may devote greater attention to long-term-oriented investments and pay less attention to short-term investments. More research is needed to examine the implications of differences and similarities between CEOs and CFOs in terms of other psychological orientations.

Second, our chapter proposes two moderators—CFO board directorship and external environmental dynamism—strengthen the role of CEO-CFO relative optimism in M&A decisions. Future research can examine other boundary conditions. For instance, we do not consider the nature of social relationships between CEOs and CFOs. When CEOs and CFOs have high social cohesion, on the one hand, pessimistic CFOs may feel more comfortable raising different opinions and thus play a more significant role in reducing optimistic CEOs' acquisitiveness. On the other hand, cohesion can give rise to group thinking (Janis, 1982). To safeguard their harmony with CEOs, pessimistic CFOs may be unwilling to point out negative and contradictory information for optimistic CEOs. As a result, the influence of CEO-CFO relative optimism in M&A activities will be weaker.

Relatedly, future research can examine the contingency effect of CEO-CFO behavioral integration (Hambrick, 1994). Behavioral integration refers to the level of collaborative behavior, quantity and quality of information exchanged, with an emphasis on joint decision making (Hambrick, 1994; Simsek, Veiga, Lubatkin, & Dino, 2005). We posit that the role of CEO-CFO relative optimism in M&A decisions will be more pronounced when CEOs and CFOs demonstrate a high level of behavioral integration in that the high social integration enables CFOs to play the role of "naysayer" more effectively (Smith, Smith, Olian, Sims Jr, O'Bannon, & Scully, 1994).

Finally, our focus is the CEO-CFO dyad, and we do not explore the conjoint influence of CEOs and other non-CEO top managers (such as COOs) on firm strategic decisions. Future research can compare which subteams have the strongest predictive power on firm strategic decisions. Another related idea is to explore how differences in optimism and pessimism between CEOs and independent board chairs affect board effectiveness. A large number of studies have examined whether having an independent board chair improves firm governance quality, but empirical evidence is inconclusive (Krause, Semadeni, & Cannella, 2014). We posit that an optimistic board chair may not be an effective monitor for an optimistic CEO because the former is less likely to pinpoint potential risks associated with strategic decisions being made by the latter. Examining CEOs' and independent board chairmen's collective cognitive schema can provide new insights into when splitting the positions of CEO and chair might improve the quality of corporate governance.

NOTES

1. We obtain similar results by using total acquisition transaction value as a dependent variable in testing Hypotheses 1–3.
2. Our results are stronger if we use the raw values of CEO optimism and CFO pessimism to measure CEO-CFO relative optimism that captures their collective cognitive schema.
3. Using annually updated measure suggest optimism-pessimism is malleable than dispositional traits. However, CEO-CFO relative optimism does not have substantial variance for the same CEO-CFO pair firm-years in our data, suggesting that it is more stable than transient states.
4. To calculate CEO optimism (residual), we run an OLS regression with CEO optimism as a dependent variable and CEO age, CEO gender, ROA, log assets, market-to-book ratio, debt ratio, cash holding ratio, Fama-French 48 industry fixed-effects, and year fixed-effects as predictors. We follow the same procedure to calculate CFO pessimism (residual).

REFERENCES

Akhtar, S. (1996). "Someday..." and "If only..." fantasies: Pathological optimism and inordinate nostalgia as related forms of idealization. *Journal of the American Psychoanalytic Association, 44*, 723–753.

Allison, P. (2005). *Fixed effects regression methods for longitudinal data using SAS*. Cary, NC: SAS.

Allison, P. D., & Waterman, R. P. (2002). Fixed-effects negative binomial regression models. *Sociological Methodology, 32*, 247–265.

Almandoz, J., & Tilcsik, A. (2016). When experts become liabilities: Domain experts on boards and organizational failure. *Academy of Management Journal, 59*, 1124–1149.

Altman, D. (2002). The taming of the finance officers. *The New York Times*. April 14, B1.

Amason, A. C. (1996). Distinguishing the effects of functional and dysfunctional conflict on strategic decision making: Resolving a paradox for top management teams. *Academy of Management Journal, 39*, 123–148.

Arendt, L. A., Priem, R. L., & Ndofor, H. A. (2005). A CEO-adviser model of strategic decision making. *Journal of Management, 31*, 680–699.

Bedard, J. C., Hoitash, R., & Hoitash, U. (2014). Chief financial officers as inside directors. *Contemporary Accounting Research, 31*, 787–817.

Biddle, B. J. (1986). Recent development in role theory. *Annual Review of Sociology, 12*, 67–92.

Biddle, B. J. (2013). *Role theory: Expectations, identities, and behaviors.* Cambridge, MA: Academic Press.

Bligh, M. C., Kohles, J. C., & Meindl, J. R. (2004). Charisma under crisis: Presidential leadership, rhetoric, and media responses before and after the September 11th terrorist attacks. *Leadership Quarterly, 15*, 211–239.

Bowen, R. M., Davis, A. K., & Matsumoto, D. A. (2002). Do conference calls affect analysts' forecasts? *Accounting Review, 77*, 285–316.

Boyd, B. (1995). CEO duality and firm performance: A contingency model. *Strategic Management Journal, 16*, 301–312.

Cannella, A. A., Jr., Park, J.-H., & Lee, H.-U. (2008). Top management team functional background diversity and firm performance: Examining the roles of team member colocation and environmental uncertainty. *Academy of Management Journal, 51*, 768–784.

Carpenter, M. A. (2002). The implications of strategy and social context for the relationship between top management team heterogeneity and firm performance. *Strategic Management Journal, 23*, 275–284.

Carpenter, M. A., Geletkanycz, M. A., & Sanders, W. G. (2004). Upper echelons research revisited: Antecedents, elements, and consequences of top management team composition. *Journal of Management, 30*, 749–778.

Carper, W. B. (1990). Corporate acquisitions and shareholder wealth: A review and exploratory analysis. *Journal of Management, 16*, 807–823.

Carver, C. S., Reynolds, S. L., & Scheier, M. F. (1994). The possible selves of optimists and pessimists. *Journal of Research in Personality, 28*, 133–141.

Chatterjee, A., & Hambrick, D. C. (2007). It's all about me: Narcissistic chief executive officers and their effects on company strategy and performance. *Administrative Science Quarterly, 52*, 351–386.

Chattopadhyay, P., Glick, W. H., Miller, C. C., & Huber, G. P. (1999). Determinants of executive beliefs: Comparing functional conditioning and social influence. *Strategic Management Journal, 20*, 763–789.

Chava, S., & Purnanandam, A. (2010). CEOs versus CFOs: Incentives and corporate policies. *Journal of Financial Economics, 97*, 263–278.

Chen, G., Crossland, C., & Luo, S. (2015). Making the same mistake all over again: CEO overconfidence and corporate resistance to corrective feedback. *Strategic Management Journal, 36*, 1513–1535.

Chen, T., Harford, J., & Lin, C. (2015). Do analysts matter for governance? Evidence from natural experiments. *Journal of Financial Economics, 115*, 383–410.

Cockrell, S. A., & Kambil, A. (2015, December 24). Rethinking the CFO's role as strategist. *Wall Street Journal.* https://deloitte.wsj.com/articles/rethinking-the-cfos-role-as-strategist-1450933339?tesla=y.

Cyert, R., & March, J. (1963). *A behavioral theory of the firm.* Englewood Cliffs, NJ: Prentice Hall.

Dalton, D. R., Hitt, M. A., Certo, S. T., & Dalton, C. M. (2007). The fundamental agency problem and its mitigation: Independence, equity, and the market for corporate control. *Academy of Management Annals, 1*, 1–64.

Davis, A. K., Ge, W., Matsumoto, D., & Zhang, J. L. (2015). The effect of manager-specific optimism on the tone of earnings conference calls. *Review of Accounting Studies, 20*, 639–673.

Davis, A. K., Piger, J. M., & Sedor, L. M. (2012). Beyond the numbers: Measuring the information content of earnings press release language. *Contemporary Accounting Research, 29*, 845–868.

Davis, A. K., & Tama-Sweet, I. (2012). Managers' use of language across alternative disclosure outlets: Earnings press releases versus MD&A. *Contemporary Accounting Research, 29*, 804–837.

Davis, C. G., Nolen-Hoeksema, S., & Larson, J. (1998). Making sense of loss and benefiting from the experience: Two construals of meaning. *Journal of Personality and Social Psychology, 75*, 561.

Demsetz, H., & Lehn, K. (1985). The structure of corporate ownership: Causes and consequences. *Journal of Political Economy, 93*, 1155–1177.

Dess, G. G., & Beard, D. W. (1984). Dimensions of organizational task environments. *Administrative Science Quarterly, 29*, 52–73.

Dooley, R. S., & Fryxell, G. E. (1999). Attaining decision quality and commitment from dissent: The moderating effects of loyalty and competence in strategic decision-making teams. *Academy of Management Journal, 42*, 389–402.

Duchin, R. (2010). Cash holdings and corporate diversification. *Journal of Finance, 65*, 955–992.

Epstein, S., & Meier, P. (1989). Constructive thinking: A broad coping variable with specific components. *Journal of Personality and Social Psychology, 57*, 332–350.

Fama, E. F., & French, K. R. (1997). Industry costs of equity. *Journal of Financial Economics, 43*, 153–193.

Fanelli, A., Misangyi, V. F., & Tosi, H. L. (2009). In charisma we trust: The effects of CEO charismatic visions on securities analysts. *Organization Science, 20*, 1011–1033.

Finkelstein, S. (1992). Power in top management teams: Dimensions, measurement, and validation. *Academy of Management Journal, 35*, 505–538.

Finkelstein, S., Hambrick, D. C., & Cannella, A. A. (2009). *Strategic leadership: Theory and research on executives, top management teams, and boards.* New York City, NY: Oxford University Press.

Francis, J., Hanna, J. D., & Philbrick, D. R. (1997). Management communications with securities analysts. *Journal of Accounting and Economics, 24*, 363–394.

Fredrickson, J. W., & Mitchell, T. R. (1984). Strategic decision processes: Comprehensiveness and performance in an industry with an unstable environment. *Academy of Management Journal, 27*, 399–423.

Gamache, D., McNamara, G., Mannor, M. J., & Johnson, R. E. (2015). Motivated to acquire? The impact of CEO regulatory focus on firm acquisitions. *Academy of Management Journal, 58*, 1261–1282.

Geers, A. L., Handley, I. M., & McLarney, A. R. (2003). Discerning the role of optimism in persuasion: The valence-enhancement hypothesis. *Journal of Personality and Social Psychology, 85*, 554.

Geers, A. L., & Lassiter, G. D. (1999). Affective expectations and information gain: Evidence for assimilation and contrast effects in affective experience. *Journal of Experimental Social Psychology, 35*, 394–413.

Gibson, B., & Sanbonmatsu, D. M. (2004). Optimism, pessimism, and gambling: The downside of optimism. *Personality and Social Psychology Bulletin, 30*, 149–160.

Gruenfeld, D. H., Thomas-Hunt, M. C., & Kim, P. H. (1998). Cognitive flexibility, communication strategy, and integrative complexity in groups: Public versus private reactions to majority and minority status. *Journal of Experimental Social Psychology, 34*, 202–226.

Haleblian, J., Devers, C. E., McNamara, G., Carpenter, M. A., & Davison, R. B. (2009). Taking stock of what we know about mergers and acquisitions: A review and research agenda. *Journal of Management, 35*, 469–502.

Hambrick, D. C. (1994). Top management groups: A conceptual integration and reconsideration of the team label. *Research in Organizational Behavior, 16*, 171–213.

Hambrick, D. C. (2007). Upper echelons theory: An update. *Academy of Management Review, 32*, 334–343.

Hambrick, D. C., & Mason, P. A. (1984). Upper echelons: The organization as a reflection of its top managers. *Academy of Management Review, 9*, 193–206.

Harford, J., & Li, K. (2007). Decoupling CEO wealth and firm performance: The case of acquiring CEOs. *Journal of Finance, 62*, 917–949.

Hart, R. (2000). *DICTION 5.0: The text-analysis program.* Thousand Oaks, CA: SAGE.

Hart, R. P., & Jarvis, S. E. (1997). Political debate forms, styles, and media. *American Behavioral Scientist, 40*, 1095–1122.

Hayward, M. L. A., & Hambrick, D. C. (1997). Explaining the premiums paid for large acquisitions: Evidence of CEO hubris. *Administrative Science Quarterly, 42*, 103–127.

He, J. Y., & Huang, Z. (2011). Board informal hierarchy and firm financial performance: Exploring a tacit structure guiding boardroom interactions. *Academy of Management Journal, 54*, 1119–1139.

Hiller, N. J., & Hambrick, D. C. (2005). Conceptualizing executive hubris: The role of (hyper-)core self-evaluations in strategic decision-making. *Strategic Management Journal, 26*, 297–319.

Huyett, B., & Koller, T. (2011). How CFOs can keep strategic decisions on track. *McKinsey on Finance, 38*, 10–15.

Jackson, S. E. (1992). Consequences of group composition for the interpersonal dynamics of strategic issue processing. *Advances in Strategic Management, 8*, 345–382.

Janis, I. L. (1982). *Groupthink: Psychological studies of policy decisions and fiascos.* Boston, MA: Houghton Mifflin.

Kaplan, S. (2008). Cognition, capabilities, and incentives: Assessing firm response to the fiber-optic revolution. *Academy of Management Journal, 51*, 672–695.

King, D. R., Dalton, D. R., Daily, C. M., & Covin, J. G. (2004). Meta-analyses of post-acquisition performance: Indications of unidentified moderators. *Strategic Management Journal, 25*, 187–200.

Kluemper, D. H., Little, L. M., & Degroot, T. (2009). State or trait: effects of state optimism on job-related outcomes. *Journal of Organizational Behavior, 30*, 209–231.

Kotter, J. (1982). *The general managers*. New York, NY: Free Press.

Krause, R., Semadeni, M., & Cannella, A. A. (2014). CEO duality: A review and research agenda. *Journal of Management, 40*, 256–286.

Lant, T. K., Milliken, F. J., & Batra, B. (1992). The role of managerial learning and interpretation in strategic persistence and reorientation: An empirical exploration. *Strategic Management Journal, 13*, 585–608.

Lehn, K. M., & Zhao, M. X. (2006). CEO turnover after acquisitions: Are bad bidders fired? *Journal of Finance, 61*, 1759–1811.

Li, M. F., & Simerly, R. L. (1998). The moderating effect of environmental dynamism on the ownership and performance relationship. *Strategic Management Journal, 19*, 169–179.

Linton, R. (1936). *The study of man: An introduction*. Oxford, UK: Appleton-Century.

Loughran, T. I. M., & McDonald, B. (2011). When is a liability not a liability? Textual analysis, dictionaries, and 10-Ks. *Journal of Finance, 66*, 35–65.

March, J. G., & Simon, H. A. (1958). *Organizations*. New York, NY: Wiley.

Mead, G. H. (1925). The genesis of the self and social control. *International Journal of Ethics, 35*, 251–277.

Merton, R. K. (1957). The role-set: Problems in sociological theory. *British Journal of Sociology, 8*, 106–120.

Mintzberg, H. (1973). A new look at the Chief Executive's job. *Organizational Dynamics, 1*, 21–30.

Moeller, S. B., Schlingemann, F. P., & Stulz, R. M. (2005). Wealth destruction on a massive scale? A study of acquiring-firm returns in the recent merger wave. *Journal of Finance, 60*, 757–782.

Nadkarni, S., & Herrmann, P. (2010). CEO personality, strategic flexibility, and firm performance: The case of the Indian business process outsourcing industry. *Academy of Management Journal, 53*, 1050–1073.

Nichols, A. (2007). Causal inference with observational data. *Stata Journal, 7*, 507–541.

Norem, J. K., & Cantor, N. (1986). Anticipatory and post hoc cushioning strategies: Optimism and defensive pessimism in "risky" situations. *Cognitive Therapy and Research, 10*, 347–362.

Norem, J. K., & Cantor, N. (1986). Defensive pessimism: Harnessing anxiety as motivation. *Journal of Personality and Social Psychology, 51*, 1208–1217.

Norem, J. K., & Illingworth, K. (1993). Strategy-dependent effects of reflecting on self and tasks: Some implications of optimism and defensive pessimism. *Journal of Personality and Social Psychology, 65*, 822.

Pablo, A. L., Sitkin, S. B., & Jemison, D. B. (1996). Acquisition decision-making processes: The central role of risk. *Journal of Management, 22*, 723–746.

Palmer, D., & Barber, B. M. (2001). Challengers, elites, and owning families: A social class theory of corporate acquisitions in the 1960s. *Administrative Science Quarterly, 46*, 87–120.

Park, C. L. (1998). Stress-related growth and thriving through coping: The roles of personality and cognitive processes. *Journal of Social Issues, 54*, 267–277.

Pennebaker, J. W., & Graybeal, A. (2001). Patterns of natural language use: Disclosure, personality, and social integration. *Current Directions in Psychological Science, 10*, 90–93.

Pennebaker, J. W., & King, L. A. (1999). Linguistic styles: Language use as an individual difference. *Journal of Personality and Social Psychology, 77*, 1296–1312.

Pennebaker, J. W., Mehl, M. R., & Niederhoffer, K. G. (2003). Psychological aspects of natural language use: Our words, our selves. *Annual Review of Psychology, 54*, 547–577.

Peterson, C. (2000). The future of optimism. *American Psychologist, 55*, 44–55.

Sanders, W. G. (2001). Behavioral responses of CEOs to stock ownership and stock option pay. *Academy of Management Journal, 44*, 477–492.

Sanders, W. M. G., & Hambrick, D. C. (2007). Swinging for the fences: The effects of CEO stock options on company risk taking and performance. *Academy of Management Journal, 50*, 1055–1078.

Sarbin, T. R., & Allen, V. L. (1968). Role theory. In G. Lindzey (Ed.), *Handbook of social psychology* (3rd ed., Vol. 1, pp. 488–567). Reading, MA: Addison-Wesley.

Scheier, M. F., Carver, C. S., & Bridges, M. W. (1994). Distinguishing optimism from neuroticism (and trait anxiety, self-mastery, and self-esteem): A reevaluation of the Life Orientation Test. *Journal of Personality and Social Psychology, 67*, 1063–1078.

Schweiger, D. M., Sandberg, W. R., & Ragan, J. W. (1986). Group approaches for improving strategic decision making: A comparative analysis of dialectical inquiry, devil's advocacy, and consensus. *Academy of Management Journal, 29*, 51–71.

Segerstrom, S. C. (2001). Optimism and attentional bias for negative and positive stimuli. *Personality and Social Psychology Bulletin, 27*, 1334–1343.

Seligman, M. (1998). *Learned optimism.* New York, NY: Pocket Books.

Shi, W., Connelly, B. L., & Sanders, W. G. (2016). Buying bad behavior: Tournament incentives and securities class action lawsuits. *Strategic Management Journal, 37*, 1354–1378.

Shi, W., Hoskisson, R. E., & Zhang, Y. A. (2017). Independent director death and CEO acquisitiveness: Build an empire or pursue a quiet life? *Strategic Management Journal, 38*, 780–792.

Shi, W., Zhang, Y., & Hoskisson, R. E. (2017). Ripple effects of CEO awards: Investigating the acquisition activities of superstar CEOs' competitors. *Strategic Management Journal, 38*, 2080–2102.

Simsek, Z., Veiga, J. F., Lubatkin, M. H., & Dino, R. N. (2005). Modeling the multilevel determinants of top management team behavioral integration. *Academy of Management Journal, 48*, 69–84.

Slatcher, R. B., Chung, C. K., Pennebaker, J. W., & Stone, L. D. (2007). Winning words: Individual differences in linguistic style among US presidential and vice-presidential candidates. *Journal of Research in Personality, 41*, 63–75.

Smith, K. G., Smith, K. A., Olian, J. D., Sims H. P., Jr., O'Bannon, D. P., & Scully, J. A. (1994). Top management team demography and process: The role of social integration and communication. *Administrative Science Quarterly, 39*, 412–438.

Smith, T. W., Ruiz, J. M., Cundiff, J. M., Baron, K. G., & Nealey-Moore, J. B. (2013). Optimism and pessimism in social context: An interpersonal perspective on resilience and risk. *Journal of Research in Personality, 47*, 553–562.

Spencer, S. M., & Norem, J. K. (1996). Reflection and distraction: Defensive pessimism, strategic optimism, and performance. *Personality and Social Psychology Bulletin, 22*, 354–365.

Spirrison, C. L., & Gordy, C. C. (1993). The constructive thinking inventory and detecting errors in proofreading. *Perceptual and Motor Skills, 76*, 631–634.

Taylor, S. E., & Gollwitzer, P. M. (1995). Effects of mindset on positive illusions. *Journal of Personality and Social Psychology, 69*, 213–226.

Trunzo, J. J., & Pinto, B. M. (2003). Social support as a mediator of optimism and distress in breast cancer survivors. *Journal of Consulting and Clinical Psychology, 71*, 805.

Tulimieri, P., & Banai, M. (2010). A new corporate paradigm: The CEO and CFO – A partnership of equals. *Organizational Dynamics, 39*, 240–247.

Wang, G., Holmes Jr, R. M., Oh, I. S., & Zhu, W. (2016). Do CEOs matter to firm strategic actions and firm performance? A meta-analytic investigation based on upper echelons theory. *Personnel Psychology, 69*, 775–862.

Yonker, S. E. (2017). Geography and the market for CEOs. *Management Science, 63*, 609–630.

Um, C. T., Guo, S.-L., Lumineau, F., Shi, W., Song, R. (in press). The downside of CFO function-based language incongruity. *Academy of Management Journal*.

Zurcher, L. A. (1983). *Social roles: Conformity, conflict, and creativity*. Beverly Hills, CA: SAGE.

CHAPTER 5

A PRACTICE-BASED VIEW OF BUSINESS MODELING

Cognition and Knowledge in Action

Arash Najmaei, Jo Rhodes, and Peter Lok

ABSTRACT

In this chapter, we situate the strategic management of business models within the strategy-as-practice view to create a more-nuanced view of how managers manage business models. We introduce the notion of business modeling as the practice of managing business models and posit that managers are actively involved in actions guided by their cognition and knowledge structures that shape their practice of business modeling. More specifically, this chapter builds on practice theory, activity theory and socio-cognitive view and develops an argument for why the practice of business modeling is essential to understand how business models work. This practice involves various actions that span organizational boundaries and cut across levels of analysis. Our view is premised on the assumption that practice of business modeling represents a form of dyadic reciprocal causation in which business model of the firm guides managerial actions, which in turn lead to adjustments in the business model through learning practices. Theoretical and practical implications of this view will be discussed and several directions for research will be presented.

Managerial Practice Issues in Strategy and Organization, pp. 145–174
Copyright © 2023 by Information Age Publishing
www.infoagepub.com

INTRODUCTION

Strategy is supposed to lead the firm to a sustainable success (Carter, Clegg, & Kornberger, 2008). Success of any business however lies in its business model. Any firm has implicitly or explicitly a business model which delineates how it does its business (Teece, 2010). The business model is a set of assumptions about the business and the corresponding set of activities that define how a firm creates value for its customers and captures this value by transforming it into profit and wealth (Zott & Amit, 2010). More specifically, business models help managers enact opportunities by structuring resources into multilevel activities span boundaries of the firm (George & Bock, 2011).

Business models lack agency. They are not self-propelling entities, are not available in the strategic factor markets, and thus cannot be traded and are not protected by property rights. Enterprising individuals or teams with entrepreneurial capacity and strategic mindset develop and manage business model for specific commercial purposes (Amit & Zott, 2001, 2012; Chesbrough & Rosenbloom, 2002). This is the managerial agency that makes a business mode a business model. That is why similar firms, serving similar markets have business models that enable them to produce differential value offerings.

That said, a business model—as a mental model representing the business of the firm in the mind of executives or a full-scale model of realized organizational activities that shows how a firm does its business—needs development and constantly adjusted or remodeled. We call this process business modeling and consider it a strategic phenomenon initiated at the managerial level and that directly influences a firm and its path to success.

The emerging perspective of behavioral strategy is a suitable theoretical lens through which to examine this phenomenon. Behavioral strategy concerns the psychological and cognitive contexts through which strategic phenomena are crafted and executed by strategists (Gavetti, Greve, Levinthal, & Ocasio, 2012). The practice turn (Golsorkhi, Rouleau, Seidl, & Vaara, 2010; Johnson, Langley, Melin, & Whittington, 2007; Vaara & Whittington, 2012) within this domain pays a closer attention to the actual actions undertaken during these phenomena. According to this view, strategy is something people do (Jarzabkowski & Spee, 2009). Therefore, the practice turn concerns the way psychological and cognitive factors are enacted or translated into strategic actions (Orlikowski, 2000). Being about the action, the practice of behavioral strategy is informed by at least three closely related theoretical frameworks: the practice theory (PT), the activity-system view or interchangeably the activity-theory (AT), and the socio-cognitive theory (SCT).

The practice theory builds on three core themes (Whittington, 2006). These three are: (1) the social context in which practice (i.e., doing or something) takes place; (2) the actual act of doing something (i.e., how the practice is performed or how the activities are conducted); and finally (3) the actor who performs the practice (the human side of practice or the human action and the knowledge, skills and other factors that form the foundation of one's actions). The activity-theory (Jarzabkowski, 2005), on the other hand, suggests that, any activity is to fulfil a specific goal and involved human action. It further argues that all actions that contribute to the fulfilment of the goal are part of the activity. Thus, activities differ in terms of their constituent actions; finally, the socio-cognitive theory (Bandura, 1989, 2001) argues that human action is based on human agency. Further, human agency is regulated by cognitive capabilities that are developed partly through the personal experience and partly through the observation and environmental factors.

Research on the practice of strategic behaviors has received considerable attention (Jarzabkowski & Spee, 2009) and has begun to go beyond strategy and permeate other branches of management such as information systems (Whittington, 2014). However, very little, if any, attention has been paid to the practice of developing and adjusting the business model of the firm (BM) as a fundamental strategic undertaking of the firm (Eckhardt, 2013). Business models are living entities that co-evolve with markets to enable organizational adaptation (Najmaei, 2013). Managing this co-evolution is a strategic undertaking involving actions that influence value creation and value capturing activities of the firm. Drawing on the practice view, business modeling encompasses managerial actions that shape the actual act of managing business model of the firm in evolving markets. This perspective situates strategic management of business models within the practice view and offers new insights into a more practical view of business models.

We argue that not only such a view is lacking but also it strongly resonates with the theory and practice of behavioral strategy and particularly its practice view. In particular, not only this view extends the boundaries of strategy-as-practice into the realm of business model literature but also it directly addresses the call for a deeper understanding of the micro-foundation of business models (Demil, Lecocq, Ricart, & Zott, 2013). We believe our view advances scholars understanding of some new avenues though which strategic management theories can interact with and inform the business model literature to enhance cumulative progress in this field of inquiry.

Towards this end, the remaining of this chapter is organized as follows. The next section reviews the theoretical evolution of the practice view in the behavioral strategy. The second section extends the view of the behavioral strategy and its practice to the business model literature by illuminating how business models differ from strategies and how business modeling is a complex adaptive strategic phenomenon represented by a set of strategic activities practiced my managers. Drawing upon the first two sections the third section outlines a practice-based view of business modeling and illustrates its potential dimensions and aspects. In particular, it delineates boundaries of this view relative to the cognitive and organizational view of business models and shows how this view adds original value to the current body of knowledge on the practice of strategies. Finally, the fourth section sheds light on various implications of this view for theory, practice and management education and proposes a set of research directions for future inspiring further research in this field.

ACTIONS, ACTIVITY SYSTEMS, AND PRACTICE OF STRATEGY

An Overview of Strategy as Practice

The traditional conception of firms or business organizations in economics and management has been based on the neoclassical economics that follows assumptions of full rationality (Augier, 2004). This view offers incomplete and misleading accounts for behaviors of business enterprises in the changing and industrialized world, for a number of reasons (Kaplan, 2011). It assumes that: (1) a firm enjoys perfect information and certainty about environmental outcomes, (2) it suffers no control or adaptability problems and hence can maximize profit, and (3) its strategies and performance are predictable. Hence, this view fails to provide a clear abstraction and explanation for firms' heterogeneities in a real business environment in which risk and uncertainty are undeniable (Knight, 1921, 1965). In this view, "there is no room for strategy of any kind on the part of decision makers" (Cyert & Williams 1993, p. 5) and literature fails to provide explanations for firm behaviors from the perspective of internal mechanisms such as attributes of executives and their actions (Hambrick, 2007; Hambrick & Mason, 1984).

The stream of strategic leadership relaxes these assumptions by focusing on "the people who have overall responsibility for an organization-the characteristics of those people, what they do, and how they do it" (Hambrick, 1989, p. 6). This view builds on the behavioral theory of the firm (Cyert & March, 1963) and suggests that personality, cognition and behaviors of executives shape the foundation of strategies and their distal, organizational and proximal, performance consequences (Gavetti et al., 2012; Powell, Lovallo, & Fox, 2011). As this branch has started to mature and accumulate a body of coherent knowledge, scholars have shaped a sub-specialization known as the strategy as practice (hereafter SAP). SAP provides a more-specific and view of activities and actions undertaken during the formulation and execution of strategies (Chia, 2004; Jarzabkowski, 2003, 2004).

SAP shifts the attention from strategy as a property of organization, that is, something that on organization has to a strategy as a practice, that is, something that people do (Whittington, 2006). Hence, it attends to a more micro-level view by specifying detailed day-to-day processes and practices also known as micro-strategies that constitute organizational strategies and their consequences (Johnson et al., 2003). In SAP strategies are viewed as situated, socially accomplished activities (Jarzabkowski & Spee, 2009). This perspective not only enables SAP to offer insightful accounts for both theorists and practitioners that are closer to the reality of the business (i.e., business in action) but also helps scholars better understand micro-level phenomena that link resources and institutional logics to macro level strategies and firm-level outcomes (Johnson et al., 2003).

The notion of practice in SAP germinates from the bridge between individualism and societism in the social theory. The former overemphasizes the role of individual human actions while the latter overemphasizes the significance of social forces in shaping the dynamics of social systems (Whittington, 2006). Three pillars of this view are social systems, individuality and actors who perform the practice (Whittington, 2006). Social systems refers to shared understandings, meanings, cultural rules, procedures, and norms that guide and enable human action. Individuality concerns "how" actions are actually carried out by capturing their practical sense in the context and "actors" refer to those whose skills and initiative activities shape the practice (Carter et al., 2008; Jarzabkowski & Spee, 2009; Whittington, 2006). By focusing on actual actions in their social contexts, SAP becomes distinct from other micro-level frameworks of behavioral strategy such as strategic cognition (Narayanan, Zane, & Kemmerer, 2011) and micro-foundation view (Felin, Foss, Heimeriks, & Madsen, 2012). To understand this distinction better, we distinguish among practice, actions and activities.

From the Practice View to Activities and Actions

In the language of SAP, practice in singular form is conceptually different from practices in the plural form. A practice is the actual activity while practices are norms, rules, traditions and procedures or any form of social, symbolic and materials by which a practice is constructed (Jarzabkowski, 2004; Jarzabkowski & Spee, 2009). More specifically, a practice is composed of activities. It resembles recurrent activities while practices resemble formal procedures or structure of activities (Carter et al., 2008). Therefore, a practice is akin to a self-reinforcing recurrent learning activity (Carter et al., 2008).

An activity, itself, involves several actions which are done synchronously or asynchronously to achieve certain objectives. Following this logic, a practice becomes vaguely synonymous with routines and rules (Carter et al., 2008) and in its plural form become responsible for reinforcing stability and efficiency or an agent for adaptation and changes, depending on its objective. Having said that, it is useful to know that practices are in fact, "what is inside processes" (Johnson et al., 2003, p. 11) and collectively form organizational processes.

The flow of activity through which the strategic goal of the practice is accomplished becomes the praxis, defined as "as a stream of activity that interconnects the micro actions of individuals and groups with the wider institutions in which those actions are located and to which they contribute" (Jarzabkowski & Spee, 2009, p. 73). The conceptual distinction between practice (Praxis) and practices in SAP is consistent with the practice theory in sociology. Reckwitz (2002) defines them aptly as follows:

> "Practice" (Praxis) in the singular represents merely an emphatic term to describe the whole of human action. "Practices" in the sense of the theory of social practices, however, is something else. A "practice" (Praktik) is a routinized type of behavior which consists of several elements, interconnected to one other: forms of bodily activities, forms of mental activities, "things" and their use, a background knowledge in the form of understanding, know-how, states of emotion and motivational knowledge.... A Practice-a way of cooking, working, etc.... Likewise, a practice represents a pattern which can be filled out by a multitude of single and often unique actions reproducing the practice (a certain way of consuming goods can be filled out by plenty of actual acts of consumption). The single individual—as a bodily and mental agent—then acts as the "carrier" (Träger) of a practice—and, in fact, of many different practices which need not be coordinated with one another. (pp. 249–250)

An actor or practitioner performs practices in a manner that forms an identifiable process. A practitioner can be an individual actor such as a CEO or an aggregate actor such as the top management team (TMT) of a firm (Jarzabkowski & Spee, 2009). Therefore, when studying strategies as practice it is important to attend to the actual doing of a practice, the activities that constitute it and specify whether they have been undertaken by an individual or an aggregate actor (Vaara & Whittington, 2012).

The activity theory in sociology (Vygotsky, 1978) helps clarify this issue. According to Vygotsky, an activity involves human action and interaction. All actions and interactions that contribute towards the fulfilment of a specified goal are part of an activity (Zott & Amit, 2010, p. 225). To conclude, one could conclude that actions of actors form activities and a stream of activities shape practice of doing strategies. Figure 5.1 offers a schematic representation of this argument.

Figure 5.1.   From actions to practice.

It is important to discriminate between two views of activity systems in SAP. As we will show in the next section, this distinction is central to a practice-based view of business modeling. In general, activities when coordinated form activity-systems. In strategy, there are at least two activity-system perspectives. The economic-oriented activity system view emphasizes productive activities of the firm as a unit of production (Stigler, 1951). In this view, a firm

> engages in a series of distinct operations: purchasing and storing materials; transforming materials into semifinished products and semifinished products into finished products; storing and selling the output; extending credit to buyers; etc. ... therefore it is partitioned among the functions or processes which constitute the scope of its activity. (Stigler, 1951, p. 157)

The second view takes a strategic flavor and emphasizes activities that shape strategic behavior of the firm. This view builds on the Porter's "value chain" view (Porter, 1985) which he later called "the activity-based view" (Porter, 1998). Porter defines an activity as a discrete economic process within the firm (Porter, 1985) and argues that the essence of strategy is differentiation and all differences among firms derive from activities they perform. Therefore, "differentiation arises from both the choice of activities and how they are performed" (Porter, 1996, p. 62). Accordingly, competitive advantage is created when firms do different activities or do similar activities differently (Porter, 1996). This argument puts activity-systems at the center of strategy analysis. Further, the way individual activities are performed is instrumental in the strategic performance of the firm because the value of individual activities depends on the configuration of other activity choices of a firm and fit among all activities it performs (Porter & Siggelkow, 2008).

Activities at the firm level differ from activities at the individual level in the sociological view of activity-system described before. Our contention is that, even though a firm-level activity system view is a useful framework for strategy analysis but it loses its utility and collapses when applied at the individuals' level. Building on the activity-theory (Vygotsky, 1978) firm level activities can be seen as goal oriented, collective actions carried out by individuals through a social process that both shapes the context and is shaped by the context of the activity (Zott & Amit, 2010). Therefore, since, individuals perform firm level activities; the activity-system discussed here should be viewed as an individual level activity-system composed of human actions that collectively construct the firm level activity-systems (Figure 5.2).

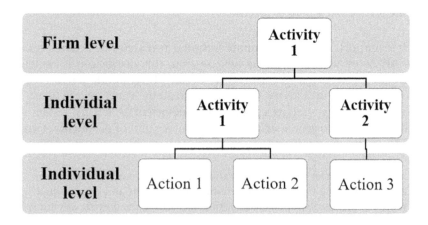

Figure 5.2.   A schematic view of actions and activities at individual and firm level.

Building on this argument, human action is the cornerstone of the activity-system view and is the pivotal unit of analysis in the practice of strategy. Perhaps the Austrian economist Von Mises (1949) has offered the most famous account for the human action. He describes action as purposeful behavior, real things not planned but unrealized acts. Further, he eloquently argues that, human action theory concerns real actions not psychological events that result in actions. In this view,

> action is will put into operation and transformed into an agency, is aiming at ends and goals, is the ego's meaningful response to stimuli and to the conditions of its environment, is a person's conscious adjustment to the state of the universe that determines his life. (p. 11)

The notion of consciousness implies that human actions are those actions that individuals choose to perform for a reason (Greve, 2001). As put by Von Mises (1949, p. 14), the main reason for the acting man is "to substitute a more satisfactory state of affairs for a less satisfactory." Therefore, the actor knows why she/he has done this particular action not something else and has a certain level of control over the sequence of movements that constitute the action (Greve, 2001).

We do not intend to engage in an in-depth analysis of the psychology of action. However, it should suffice to say that, the SAP view concerns the actions of strategic elites, executives or top managers whose behaviors are driven by strategic goals and define how strategies courses of action are formulated and executed to achieve those goals (Carter et al., 2008; Johnson et al., 2007; Suddaby, Seidl, & Le, 2013).

The essence of SAP is to explain factors and mechanisms that enhance or hinder executives from acting strategically. In this view, executives' actions as publicly observable movements in contrast to their mental representations (Rouse, 2006) which implies the primacy of individual choice and factors that are instrumental in executives' choice making. In the next section; we will further elaborate this argument by synthesizing insights from knowledge-based view, strategic cognition and particularly the theory of social cognition.

Knowledge, Cognition, and a Social-Cognitive View of Strategic Actions

Acting means using agency intentionally to make things happen (Bandura, 2001). Therefore, action is based on the capacity to exercise control over thoughts and motivation (Bandura, 1989; Von Mises, 1949). Individuals through their actions change themselves and their situations (Bandura, 1989). Before we delve further into the mechanism of action, it seems reasonable to discriminate action from behavior. Behavior refers to "doing of any sort," however action is "behavior imbued with meaning" (Cook & Brown, 1999) or as we see, actions are meaningful behaviors.

Individuals use symbolic structures of knowledge to interpret the surrounding world and ascribe meaning to their behavior (Reckwitz, 2002). These representational structures in the mind are cognitive entities used in computational algorithms for interpretation of the world (Gavetti & Rivkin, 2007). Knowledge structures are developed through learning along life trajectories (Nooteboom, 2009) and their existence implies both the possession of knowledge and engaging in the act of knowing (i.e., acquiring knowledge). Therefore, different individual have different cognitive structures to the extent that their learning along their life trajectories differ (Nooteboom, 2009).

The social cognitive theory (Bandura, 1989) explains these differences via an emergent interactive perspective according to which actions are taken through reciprocal interactions among cognitive and environmental events (Bandura, 1989). More specifically, actions involves knowledge and cognitive mechanism of knowing in the form of reasoning and information processing (Bandura, 2001; Reckwitz, 2002). Knowledge structures contain general and specific information about an action that are mobilized through the process of "knowing" to guide and inform actions. This phenomenon involves "knowing what" and "knowing how" that are linked to each other within an action (Reckwitz, 2002). Thus, the capacity to act improves as knowledge structures and cognitive capabilities driving the capacity of knowing advance. In other words, the interactions between cognition and knowledge represent inward mechanisms that help individuals cope with this uncertainty and generate conditions for outward human action (Reckwitz, 2002). This line of thinking is consistent with the view of Cook and Brown (1999) in which, existing knowledge possessed by individuals represents something they use in their actions whereas their act of "knowing" represents a cognitive process that is done as a part of an action.

Since actions occur over time and future is unknown, actions are inherently associated with uncertainty (Mcmullen & Shepherd, 2006). Social cognitive theory suggests that people judge the correctness of their action in face of uncertainty using predictive and operative thinking drawing on the state of knowledge that is constantly evolving through these interactions (Bandura, 1989). Because of the uncertain nature of actions, people evaluate their actions through constant learning about: (1) the outcomes of their actions in terms of its contribution to the purpose of the action, (2) the effects that other people's actions produce, and (3) deductions from established knowledge structures and what necessarily results from them (Bandura, 2001). Effective actions are then used in formulation of predictive rules for future actions (Bandura, 1989).

These interactions underpin various evaluative mechanisms such as "observational learning, inferences from exploratory experiences, information conveyed by verbal instruction, and innovative cognitive syntheses of preexisting knowledge" (Bandura, 1989, p. 1181) which collectively guide the production of appropriate behavior and provide the internal standards for corrective adjustments to future actions (Bandura, 1989). Consequently, in acting as agents people draw on their existing knowledge and cognitive skills to produce desired actions and assess outcome of their actions (Bandura, 2001; Cook & Brown, 1999; Gavetti & Rivkin, 2007). Therefore, we posit that the actor and his actions are held together and linked to cognitive processes that constantly relate knowledge structures to the act of knowing. Building on this view, in the next section we propose an action-centered view of how executives manage their business models through a set of actions collectively known as the practice of business modeling.

STRATEGIZING BUSINESS MODEL CHANGE: THE PRACTICE OF BUSINESS MODELING

Whenever a firm is established, it adopts a business model (Teece, 2010). There appears to be two schools of thought in the adoption of business models. The cognitive school sees business models as cognitive representation of the business in the mind of managers. According to this view a business model, makes implicit assumptions about customers, competitors, revenue and cost structures and nature of changes in the market in the mind of managers (Teece, 2010). These assumptions are then reflected in managers' hypotheses about how to make and deliver market offerings and convert revenue into profit (Teece, 2010). The business model becomes a part of firm's dominant logic (Obloj, Obloj, & Pratt, 2010) and represent managers' mental models or mindsets about markets (Tollin, 2008). The cognitive school can be best summarized as a perspective in which business models are conceptualized as mental models about the business or simplified representations of the reality of business, alternatively knowledge structures about dimensions of the business and markets in the mind of managers that help them to ascribe meaning to their business and its position in the marketplace.

As previously noted, knowledge structures inform and guide actions. Therefore, business models serve as filters that helps managers sift through information, ascribe meaning to them, picture their business and make choices with regard to customers, value offerings, cost and profit formulas, competitors, and the behavior of their business in the business ecosystem (Teece, 2010). For instance, a business model enables managers to describe their business, tell stories about it and attract customers and investors (Magretta, 2002).

On the other hand, the organizational school conceptualizes business models as structures of resources for exploiting opportunities (George

& Bock, 2011), a reflection of the firm's realized strategies (Casadesus-Masanell & Ricart, 2010) or a carefully designed set of interrelated activities involving human, technological and capital resources for creating value (Zott & Amit, 2010). Alternatively, business model has also been viewed as "a complex set of interdependent routines that is discovered, adjusted, and fine-tuned by doing" (Winter & Szulanski, 2001, p. 731). According to this organizational view, a business model entails boundary-spanning structures that convert resources into value creating and capturing activities (Zott, Amit, & Massa, 2011). Drawing on this view, Casadesus-Masanell and Ricart (2010) posit that strategy is the choice of business model and all other organizational choices are to implement, refine, and adjust the business model of the firm. In this view, business models are built on industry value chains and represent various constellations of activities that define competitive spots in an industry (Magretta, 2002).

Both views converge on the fact that business models are dynamic entities, they need to adjust to market changes and successful managers and by implication firms continuously adjust their business models (Aspara, Lamberg, Laukia, & Tikkanen, 2011, 2013; Katkalo, Pitelis, & Teece, 2010; Teece, 2007). Despite this notion, the existing business model literature is surprisingly silent about how these cognitive and organizational views relate to each other. The main contention of this chapter, as noted earlier, is that a practice-based view would link these two schools by offering a theoretical conversation that connects managers' actions and practices with the firm's activity-systems to create a better picture of how business models are developed and adjusted to co-evolve with markets.

Drawing on this premise, we define business models as "knowledge structures held my managers about their business that are transformed into multilevel and boundary-spanning organizational activities for creating and capturing value." We suspect that the emphasis on only cognitive or organizational activity views rather than synthesizing them would add to the complexity surrounding the concept of business models. Accordingly, by defining business modeling as the process of adopting, implementing, and adjusting business models we imply that business models are dynamic living entities that are managed through activities of managers. Subsequently, we posit that business modeling involves managerial actions, activities and practices building on changes in their mental models and converted into changes in the organizational models of activities.

The practice of business modeling is a strategic practice. Such practices are defined as an identifiable context-specific process commonly performed by managers from a variety of firms (Bromiley & Rau, 2014). Some examples are the practice of business model reinvention or business model transformation performed by executives of firms such as Apple, Nokia, HP, and so forth, or the practice of business model replication in which a business model is replicated in new geographical locations (Winter & Szulanski, 2001). This practice is frequently performed by retailers, banks, etc.

Table 5.1 illustrates a summary of key terms and their definitions used in this line of thinking. As we will outline in the remaining part of this section, managers vary in their capacity to perform actions, coordinate them in activities and lead organizations towards business model changes. Following the definition of business modeling we distinguish between actions involved in the adoption of a business model and those involved in the process of changing/adjusting a business model.

Table 5.1

Key Terms and Their Definitions in the Practice-Based View of Business Modeling

Key term	Definition
Business model	Knowledge structures held my managers about their business that are transformed into multilevel and boundary-spanning organizational activities for creating and capturing value.
Business modeling	The process of adopting, implementing, and adjusting business models.
Business modeling action	Managerial actions that underpin their business modeling process
Business modeling activities	Coordinated business modeling actions aimed for achieving specific goals.
Business modeling practices	Repeated routinized patterns of business modeling activities.
The practice of business modeling	Identifiable context-specific business modeling process commonly performed by managers of different firms such as the practice of business model reinvention, the practice of business model replication, and so forth.
Cognition	The process of developing and adjusting knowledge structures though cognitive actions such as learning (knowing).
Knowledge	Knowledge structures used to ascribe meaning to the world.

Strategizing Actions and Genesis of Business Models

A business model is developed to exploit an opportunity. An opportunity here refers to an "economic circumstance where if the correct good or service were to be properly organized and offered for sale that the result would be profitable" (Eckhardt & Shane, 2010, p. 48). Existence of an opportunity implies that a market has not reached its full potential and thus there is room for action to take it closer to its potential (Dimov, 2011).

Opportunities are recognized based on perceptions of market relationships, and simply reflect ideas about what can be done given the existing knowledge and resources (Dimov, 2011). These ideas can emerge through searches based on prior experience or knowledge (Shane, 2000) or by serendipitous discovery and fortuitous circumstances (Vaghely & Julien, 2010).

To enact an opportunity, the individual needs to form a mental picture of the business and then develop some structures to increase the viability of the opportunity and reduce its uncertainty as well as its sensitivity to the environment (Dimov, 2011). This mental picture and corresponding structures form the origin of the business model of the firm.

Structures within the business model may include different components of a business such as financial and non-financial resources, employees, and necessary relationships with customers, suppliers, regulatory bodies, and other institutions (Teece, 2010) within the social context, such as markets and industries in which the business is situated (Dimov, 2011). Individuals may employ a variety of techniques to develop these structures and acquire necessary resources for their business model to enact opportunities. For instance, some may use symbolic actions to acquire necessary resources (Zott & Huy, 2007), whereas others may rely on bricolage to gain necessary resources (Baker & Nelson, 2005). Some also acquire resources by developing ties (formal and informal relationships) with different resource holders (Zhang, Soh, & Wong, 2010, 2011). These structures enable the founder to carve out a space in the market, and secure and sustain this space to run the business (Dimov, 2011). Through its business model, the venture gains legitimacy (Lounsbury & Glynn, 2001) and becomes a new part of the market (Dimov, 2011).

Therefore, adoption and development of a business model is a praxis, an unfolding phenomenon composed of strategic activities embedded in the marketplace. It is composed of numerous actions of an enterprising individual, an actor, a practitioner who recognizes opportunity, assesses its feasibility and desirability, acquires necessary resources, and structures them in some productive ways to take advantage of the opportunity.

These microstrategies or strategizing actions precede development of a business model. A practice-based view of the genesis of a business model involves actions germinating from the interactions between existing knowledge about the business and ongoing knowledge acquired though learning about the business and its dynamics as they unfold in the market to carve the position of the firm. These socially constructed and embedded actions explain (1) how enterprising individuals actually recognize, and evaluate opportunities that can be exploited by a new business model, (2) obtain and use various tools or means to develop this cognitive capacity and (3) tools and means they use to acquire and allocate resources to exploit the recognized opportunity.

The practice of developing a business model is based on the capacity to develop and adjust knowledge structures or mental models about the market. Hence, it involves two sets of actions: the "business model ideation" that encompasses cognitive processes of sensing and evaluating conditions in the market using existing knowledge and experience. This could be a single venturing idea or a series of modified ideas (Dimov, 2011), and "business model structuring" which includes knowing and learning to know how to acquire and allocate resources to turn the idea into tangible outcomes and engaging in actual acquisition and structuring of resources.

It is important to discriminate between business model "ideation" and "structuring." This classification is at the heart of our argument because it enables scholars to better understand specific actions, activities and practices involved in the formation of business models across serial (those who establish multiple ventures in sequence), portfolio (those who establish multiple ventures in parallel) and nascent (those who have established only one venture so far) entrepreneurs (Parker, 2014).

Strategizing Post-Development Business Model Changes

As noted earlier, when a business model is developed it becomes a part of the market. Thus, business models are to coevolve with markets, if businesses based on them are to survive. This coevolution is carried out when managers adjust their knowledge structures about the position of their firms in the markets and change their resource structures accordingly. Failure to do so will result in the loss of the capacity to compete and adapt. Business model changes take various forms depending on the nature of changes in the market place. In rapidly changing markets, managers need to constantly emphasize radical changes and develop new business models whereas in less dynamic markets, business models are more likely to go through episodes of incremental changes. In either scenario, managers' ability to initiate and manage necessary business model changes is instrumental in continued success of the firm.

Prior research suggests that managers tend to develop enduring beliefs about the correctness of their business model and protect it especially when it has been successful for a period of time (Hambrick et al., 1993). Therefore, to become able to adjust their business models managers need to overcome cognitive barriers and become free of nostalgia, denial and arrogance (Hamel & Välikangas, 2003). Actions that managers undertake to achieve this goal are central part of their business modeling. For instance, an executive could be committed to the current business model without emphasizing business model changes, perhaps because "it is all he or she knows, unaware of other options" (Hambrick, Geletkanycz, & Fredrickson, 1993, p. 404). Another explanation could be that executives may know the value of a specific change in the business model but they tend to reject or discount it because they don't have enough market and technological knowledge to assess the uncertainty involved in pursuing it (Mosakowski, 2002).

Several activities could help managers tackle these obstacles. For example, metacognitive trainings has been argued to help managers recognize the value of cognitive resiliency (Haynie, Shepherd, & Patzelt, 2012). In addition, constant involvement in various knowledge-acquiring activities such as experimentation, vicarious learning, grafting, and scanning have been proven effective for enabling managers change their knowledge structures (Chandler & Lyon, 2009). Therefore, a practice-based view of this phenomenon suggests that there is to a plethora of possible actions and activities undertaken by managers to reduce cognitive inertia that is associated with their resistance to initiate business modeling activities. Mangers can use various tools, techniques and polices ranging from cognitive trainings to advice-seeking practices in order to initiate and manage incremental and radical changes to their business model.

Structural barriers stemming from complex configurations of resources represent another side of business modeling. In some cases, managers are cognizant of the value and urgency of business model changes; they have also obtained necessary knowledge to implement required changes. However, the existing business model of the firm is associated with complex configurations of resources, capabilities and bundle of inter-dependent activities that any change would leads to unmanageable internal complexity. Under these circumstances, business modeling involves actions and activities to reduce internal complexity, simplify resource structures and reconfigure complex activities.

The practice of business modeling becomes about the ability to divert resources from the existing structures to new ones in a less complicated fashion. This diversion involves reconfiguring, rebounding and re-arranging resources across boundary-spanning activities that may need to be strategized, and executed separately concurrently or sequentially over an extended period of time (Achtenhagen Melin, & Naldi, 2013; Aspara et al., 2011, 2013).

Prior research on dynamic capabilities (Eisenhardt & Martin, 2000; Teece, Pisano, & Shuen, 1997) suggests that reconfiguring resource structures is based partly on knowing resources and their versatility and partly on managerial creativity and imagination in using resources differently in different conditions. Managers develop dynamic managerial capabilities using their cognitive and social capabilities (Adner & Helfat, 2003) to examine benefits and opportunity costs associated with changes in the activity-system of the firm. Then they decide which activities should to be maintained, modified or discarded. These undertakings can take various forms such as developing new product lines, changing delivery systems, discontinuing a service, etc. and indicate numerous business modeling possibilities. Through these business modeling practices, managers enable the firm to adjust its business model in order to achieve an evolutionary fit (Helfat et al., 2007).

Therefore, managers' actions to restructure resources and reconfigure activities lie at the heart of the practice-based view of business modeling. numerous research avenues to explore and examine tools, techniques, and policies that managers employ to perform these activities. These may include different types and number of analogies (Lovallo, Clarke, & Camerer, 2012), or a business model canvas (Osterwalder & Pigneur, 2009) that maps out different scopes of a firm's activity-system.

Because managers vary in their ability to overcome cognitive inertia and reconfigure their resource structures, firms vary in their business modeling, some adjust their business models timely by reconfiguring their activity systems while others fall behind and lose their competitive spot in the marketplace. Therefore, a practice-based view of business modeling supersedes both the cognitive view and organizational view of business modeling (Table 5.2) by creating a more realistic and practical view of various business-modeling actions that take place in the context of the firm and its business landscape.

DISCUSSION

The view developed in this chapter indicates that a practice-based view of business modeling has both theoretical and practical appeal. Not only would it provides a set of theoretically-grounded insights into the behavioral foundation of management of business models as a key strategic action but it would also facilitates the understanding of how actually executives engage in the practice of business modeling. It offers a sound theoretical ground for delving into real actions involved in developing and adjusting business models. It is also scalable, meaning that it can be applied in small as well as large firms. In the following subsections, we outline some of the implications of this view.

Table 5.2

Theoretical Positioning of a Practice-Based View of Business Modeling

	Practice-based view of business modeling	Cognitive view of business modeling	Organizational view of business modeling
Conceptualization of business modeling	Evolution of a business model from the perspective of actions and practices of managers who have the responsibility for the business model of the firm	Evolution of a business model from the perspective of cognitive structures of managers who have the responsibility for the business model of the firm	Evolution of a business model from the perspective of organization wide activities involving resources, and capabilities
Unit of analysis	Managerial practices and actions involved in the management of business models.	Changes or rigidity in managers' mindset, logic, cognitive structures, hypothesis, assumptions that enhance or constrain business model adjustments	Organizational strategies, activities, and initiatives involving various human, technological and financial resources that transform, reinforce, or create business models
Level of analysis	Both micro and macro	Micro	Macro
Key assumption	Managerial actions are building blocks of how business models are adopted and change.	Understanding managerial cognition is the key to understand how business models are adopted change.	Firm-level activities, routines, and capabilities form building blocks of business model evolution.
Theoretical roots	Action theory, practice theory, SAP, socio-cognitive theory	Strategic cognition, behavioral view	Dynamic capabilities, organizational activity-system view, resource-based theories

Theoretical Implications

The practice-based view of business modeling outlined here sheds new light and further extends current research on the management of business models in several ways. First, it adds to the activity-based view of business models (Achtenhagen et al., 2013; Zott & Amit, 2010) by outlining a behavioral foundation for executives' actions that inform and configure firm level activity-systems. Particularly, the departure point of this chapter from the recent works of Zott and Amit (2010) and Achtenhagen et al. (2013) is its focus on the individual-level actions that shape both organizational level activity-systems (Zott & Amit, 2010) and strategizing activities (e.g., quality and cost-structure policies, product line and customer segment expansions) (Achtenhagen et al., 2013). It suggests that managers intentional actions embedded in the social practice of managing their business could account for mechanisms that enable or constrain business model changes.

More specifically, our behavioral accounts offer a theoretical foundation for actions and activities that construct the organizational-level activity-based view of business models. This departure may seem at first a subtle point, however, we believe, at least for two reasons it is a substantial one. First, the activity-system view sees the business model as a system of inter-related organizational activities. This neglects the role of business models as cognitive structures that influence managerial actions. As a result, our practice-based view offers a complementary view offering a more complete understanding of what business models are, how they function and how they are managed though actions of managers.

Second, we outlined business modeling as a socially constructed process involving a dyadic reciprocal causation in which business model of the firm as a mental model guides managerial actions. Learning and evolution of these actions would, in turn, lead to adjustments in the business model of their firms. This reciprocity is an important mechanism though which strategic practices are institutionalized. It hence offers novel insights into the micro-foundations of business model institutionalization and helps scholars gain a deeper understanding of how strategic practices of managers and business model of the firm interact in forming multilevel boundary-spanning intuitional activities (Zott et al., 2011).

In addition, the practice-based view of business modeling has potential to advance the current body of knowledge on the neo-institutional dimension of strategy-as-practice (Suddaby et al., 2013). As noted, business models represent cognitive structures encompassing assumptions about customers, markets and broader business ecosystem. The neo-institutional view pays specific attention to institutional logics or beliefs about external words that shape institutional practices of managers (Friedland & Alford, 1991).

Practices of business modeling builds on these structures. It, hence, suggests that business models change through interactions between actors' (i.e., managers) cognition and knowledge of the external intuitional setting of the business. That is cause-and-effect relationships in markets and industries where the business is situated. Studying these practices using our framework offers new insights into how business model serve as intuitional logics in guiding strategic actions of managers and how managers' actions in return can lead to adjustments in intuitional logics shared by members of an organization. Further, since business models become part of markets. Business model changes can lead to macro institutional changes. These changes have been evidenced by the evolution off social networking business model from Yahoo360® to Facebook® or the evolution of airline industry. Therefore, a practice-based view of business modeling as outlined here can offer a more nuanced understanding of some mechanisms through which conversations between SAP and neo-intuitionalism theory yield theoretical and practical insights into the nature of managerial work and its implications at both micro and macro levels.

Managerial Implications

Since every business has a business model that influences and is influenced by actions of its managers, our view can yield very important and timely implications for managers of all businesses regardless of their size, form and scope of operation. First, effective business modeling has become a priority for managers in order to reinforce business adaptability, survival and growth. Studying managerial actions at the core of business models may help them to better recognize their own ability to engage in distinct but related activities that shape value creation and capturing capacities of their business. Our study suggests that this ability stem from learning and cognitive flexibility. The capacity to learn trends and patterns in the marketplace and technological landscape of the business can be expanded through consultations, and external advice-seeking actions that in return leads to an improved cognitive capacity for business modeling.

Secondly, understanding actions and practices in context offers important insights for training of effective managers capable of initiating and leading strategic changes such as redirecting and reinventing business models. This is a key premise of SAP view (Vaara & Whittington, 2012; Wright, Paroutis, & Blettner, 2013). Accordingly, managers should be aware of this and try to instill such training in their personal development agenda.

Implications for Management Education

Managing business models has become an important topic for MBAs. Hence we believe our study has also implications for management education. Our study posits that business models go beyond simple conceptual models, schematic activity-systems and organizational structures, they are instead multilevel complex systems of managerial cognition and action transformed into organizational activities. This conception has wider implications for management education in our business schools. It is clear that, if this is the case, management educators need to spend more time cultivating this view in business schools' learning environment and deliver this view effectively to the students of organizational change, entrepreneurship and strategic management. Teaching this view would make study of business models and business modeling of exemplar executives such as Steve Jobs more practical and relevant to broader audience. Therefore, "if one of the key goals of business schools is to better qualify our students for the real world" (Wright et al., 2013, p. 119). Then, using the model proposed in this chapter, we can equip the next generation of management students with the needed knowledge required for the effective management of business models in the competitive realities of today's business world.

Directions for Future Research

As a research area, a practice-based view of business modeling is a fertile ground for future study. We are convinced that future work might benefit from conversations between business models and SAP literatures as two growing domains of inquiry. These links help to build a stronger theoretical and empirical foundation for the study of managerial actions and practices with regard to business models, how they come into existence, how they change, and why they change.

Insofar as research directions in managerial practice of business modeling is concerned, we believe that clustering these actions in two categories of business model development and post-development changes highlight compelling avenues for future research. This approach is consistent with our model and maintains conceptualization of business models (Zott et al., 2011) and current research trend in this field (Demil et al., 2013).

Capturing actions and practices in context requires context-specific qualitative approaches. Therefore, we build on existing reviews of research on SAP (Suddaby et al., 2013; Vaara & Whittington, 2012; Wright et al., 2013) and particularly qualitative research methods to offer a series of directions, specific areas within these directions, key possible research questions and useful research methods. Table 5.3 offers a summary of these directions.

Addressing the above research questions help scholars gain an expanded understanding of why and how executives engage in the practice of managing their business models and what they usually do to develop and change their business models. It is also important to mention that, given the centrality of business models in organizing resources, and initiating and commercializing innovations, such attempts would give life and power to more robust, fine-grained research on the role of managerial actions and practices in dynamic capabilities, initiating and responding to disruptive business model innovations, and corporate venturing among others.

Table 5.3

A Summary of Research Directions for a Practice-Based View of Business Modeling

Research direction	Key dimensions	Corresponding research areas	Some research questions	Some research methods
Development of new business models	Initial business modeling opportunity recognition activities.	Actions undertaken to detect opportunities Actions undertaken to Assess its feasibility	How do actually managers recognize opportunities for new business models?	Ethnographic observation In-depth interviews Document analysis such as minutes of meetings and managers' diaries
	Initial resource structuring (acquiring and allocating necessary resources to exploit the opportunity) activities.	Actions undertaken to acquire resources to exploit it Tools and techniques used toward achievement of these goals	What strategic tools, techniques, do they use? What actions do managers take to acquire necessary resources to enact business model opportunities? Are there any common practices among managers of firms in an industry with regard to these actions? What contextual factors constrain or enhance these actions?	Shadowing Analysis of video and audio recordings

(Table continued on next page)

Table 5.3 (Continued)

A Summary of Research Directions for a Practice-Based View of Business Modeling

Research direction	Key dimensions	Corresponding research areas	Some research questions	Some research methods
Post-development business model changes	Tackling the cognitive inertia and turning it into a cognitive resiliency for initiating and managing business model changes	Actions undertaken to change and adjust assumptions about the current and new business models	What actions do really mangers perform to adjust their cognitive structures?	Ethnographic observation In-depth interviews
	Reconfiguring organizational activities, changing existing resource structures, developing and managing new structures	Actions undertaken to choose activities and configuration of resources that are needed to change, maintained, or discarded	What strategic tools, methods and policies do help managers to change their assumptions about the correctness of their business models?	Document analysis such as minutes of meetings and managers' diaries Shadowing
		Actions undertaken during strategic activities of changing old and creating new structures	What conditions are more/less conducive to these cognitive changes?	Analysis of video and audio recordings
		Heterogeneous and homogenous actions across radical or incremental restructuration of resources	Are there common areas of practice among managers of similar firms in terms of involvement in these cognitive activities?	

(Table continued on next page)

Table 5.3 (Continued)

A Summary of Research Directions for a Practice-Based View of Business Modeling

Research direction	Key dimensions	Corresponding research areas	Some research questions	Some research methods
Post-development business model changes			What actions do really mangers perform to adjust their resource structures?	
			What strategic tools, methods and policies help managers change their existing resource structures?	
			What sort of actions are performed concurrently or sequentially during restructuring of resources?	
			What conditions are more/less conducive to these resource-based changes?	
			Are there common areas of practice among managers of similar firms in terms of involvement in these resource-management activities?	

CONCLUSION

Organizational scholars have argued that strategic management of business models is key to success of the firm. This chapter has helped to develop a behavioral account for some of the specific mechanisms through which executives manage their business models. In this chapter, we drew on the theory of practice and its branch in the strategic management, the strategy-as-practice view (SAP) to develop a dynamic behavioral view of business models labelled as "a practice-based view of business modeling". It suggested that successful executives constantly adjust their business models through the practice of business modeling. This practice involves strategic actions that are informed and guided though the interaction between executives' cognition –act of knowing- and knowledge structures. Both knowledge as a cognitive resource and knowing as a process of learning are particularly important because they represent complementary structures that jointly build the capacity to manage business models. This chapter is perhaps the first step towards a practice-oriented, action-focused understanding of business models. Given the paucity of empirical work on this field, we believe there is a growing need for empirical research that focuses on specific business modeling actions situated in practices of ordinary daily work of executives. This is a productive inquiry essential to ongoing research on the behavioral and micro-foundation of strategy and strategic work. It is our hope that this chapter inspires further research to connect notions from behavioral theories with more fine-grained and specific perspectives of business models to shed new light on how the business literature capture the essence of differences and similarities among managers' actions in adopting and adjusting business models.

ACKNOWLEDGMENT

This chapter, save some minor changes, was earlier published as Najmaei, Arash, Rhodes, Jo, and Lok, Peter. (2015). A practice-based view of business modeling: Cognition and knowledge in action. In T. K. Das (Ed.), *The practice of behavioral strategy* (pp. 77–104). Charlotte, NC: Information Age Publishing.

REFERENCES

Achtenhagen, L., Melin, L., & Naldi, L. (2013). Dynamics of business models—strategizing, critical capabilities and activities for sustained value creation. *Long Range Planning, 46*, 427–442.

Adner, R., & Helfat, C. E. (2003). Corporate effects and dynamic managerial capabilities. *Strategic Management Journal, 24*, 1011–1025.

Amit, R., & Zott, C. (2001). Value creation in e-business. *Strategic Management Journal, 22*, 493–520.

Amit, R., & Zott, C. (2012). Creating value through business model innovation. *MIT Sloan Management Review, 53*(3), 41–49.

Aspara, J., Lamberg, J.-A., Laukia, A., & Tikkanen, H. (2011). Strategic management of business model transformation: Lessons from Nokia. *Management Decision, 49*, 622–647.

Aspara, J., Lamberg, J.-A., Laukia, A., & Tikkanen, H. (2013). Corporate business model transformation and inter-organizational cognition: The case of nokia. *Long Range Planning, 46*, 459–474.

Augier, M. (2004). March'ing towards "a behavioral theory of the firm": James G. March and the early evolution of behavioral organization theory. *Management Decision, 42*, 1257–1268.

Baker, T., & Nelson, R. E. (2005). Creating something from nothing: Resource construction through entrepreneurial bricolage. *Administrative Science Quarterly, 50*, 329–366.

Bandura, A. (1989). Human agency in social cognitive theory. *American Psychologist, 44*, 1175–1184.

Bandura, A. (2001). Social cognitive theory: An agentic perspective. *Annual Review of Psychology, 52*, 1–26.

Bromiley, P., & Rau, D. (2014). Towards a practice-based view of strategy. *Strategic Management Journal, 35*, 1249–1256.

Carter, C., Clegg, S. R., & Kornberger, M. (2008). So!apbox: Editorial essays: Strategy as practice? *Strategic Organization, 6*, 83-99.

Casadesus-Masanell, R., & Ricart, J. E. (2010). From strategy to business models and onto tactics. *Long Range Planning, 43*, 195–215.

Chandler, G. N., & Lyon, D. W. (2009). Involvement in knowledge-acquisition activities by venture team members and venture performance. *Entrepreneurship: Theory & Practice, 33*, 571–592.

Chesbrough, H., & Rosenbloom, R. S. (2002). The role of the business model in capturing value from innovation: Evidence from Xerox Corporation's technology spin-off companies. *Industrial and Corporate Change, 11*, 529–555.

Chia, R. (2004). S-as-p: Reflections on the research agenda. *European Management Review, 1*(1), 29–34.

Cook, S. D. N., & Brown, J. S. (1999). Bridging epistemologies: The generative dance between organizational knowledge and organizational knowing. *Organization Science, 10*, 381-400.

Cyert, R. M., & March, J. G. (1963). *A behavioral theory of the firm.* Englewood Cliffs, NJ: Prentice Hall.

Cyert, R. M., & Williams, J. R. (1993). Organizations, decision making and strategy: Overview and comment. *Strategic Management Journal, 14*, 5–10.

Demil, B., Lecocq, X., Ricart, J. E., & Zott, C. (2013). Business models: Call for papers for a special issue. *Strategic Entrepreneurship Journal.*

Dimov, D. (2011). Grappling with the unbearable elusiveness of entrepreneurial opportunities. *Entrepreneurship: Theory & Practice, 35*, 57–81.

Eckhardt, J. T. (2013). Opportunities in business model research. *Strategic Organization, 11*, 412–417.

Eckhardt, J. T., & Shane, S. (2010). An update to the individual-opportunity nexus. In Z. J. Acs & D. B. Audretsch (Eds.), *Handbook of entrepreneurship research: An interdisciplinary survey and introduction* (Vol. 5, pp. 47–77). New York, NY: Springer.

Eisenhardt, K. M., & Martin, J. A. (2000). Dynamic capabilities: What are they? *Strategic Management Journal, 21*, 1105–1121.

Felin, T., Foss, N. J., Heimeriks, K. H., & Madsen, T. L. (2012). Microfoundations of routines and capabilities: Individuals, processes, and structure. *Journal of Management Studies, 49*, 1351–1374.

Friedland, R., & Alford, R. R. (1991). Bringing society back in: Symbols, practices, and institutional contradictions. In W. W. Powell & P. J. DiMaggio (Eds.), *The new institutionalism in organizational analysis* (pp. 232–266). Chicago, IL: University of Chicago Press.

Gavetti, G., Greve, H. R., Levinthal, D. A., & Ocasio, W. (2012). The behavioral theory of the firm: Assessment and prospects. *Academy of Management Annals, 6*, 1–40.

Gavetti, G., & Rivkin, J. W. (2007). On the origin of strategy: Action and cognition over time. *Organization Science, 18*, 420–439.

George, G., & Bock, A. J. (2011). The business model in practice and its implications for entrepreneurship research. *Entrepreneurship: Theory & Practice, 35*, 83–111.

Golsorkhi, D., Rouleau, L., Seidl, D., & Vaara, E. (Eds.). (2010). *Cambridge handbook of strategy as practice*. Cambridge, UK: Cambridge University Press.

Greve, W. (2001). Traps and gaps in action explanation: Theoretical problems of a psychology of human action. *Psychological Review, 108*, 435–451.

Hambrick, D. C. (1989). Guest editor's introduction: Putting top managers back in the strategy picture. *Strategic Management Journal, 10*, 5–15.

Hambrick, D. C. (2007). Upper echelons theory: An update. *Academy of Management Review, 32*, 334–343.

Hambrick, D. C., Geletkanycz, M. A., & Fredrickson, J. W. (1993). Top executive commitment to the status quo: Some tests of its determinants. *Strategic Management Journal, 14*, 401–418.

Hambrick, D. C., & Mason, P. A. (1984). Upper echelons: The organization as a reflection of its top managers. *Academy of Management Review, 9*, 193–206.

Hamel, G., & Välikangas, L. (2003). The quest for resilience. *Harvard Business Review, 81*(9), 52–63.

Haynie, J. M., Shepherd, D. A., & Patzelt, H. (2012). Cognitive adaptability and an entrepreneurial task: The role of metacognitive ability and feedback. *Entrepreneurship: Theory & Practice, 36*, 237–265.

Helfat, C. E., Finkelstein, S., Mitchell, W., Peteraf, M. A., Singh, H., Teece, D. J., & Winter, S. G. (2007). *Dynamic capabilities: Understanding strategic change in organizations*. Malden, MA: Blackwell.

Jarzabkowski, P. (2003). Strategic practices: An activity theory perspective on continuity and change. *Journal of Management Studies, 40*, 23–55.

Jarzabkowski, P. (2004). Strategy as practice: Recursiveness, adaptation, and practices-in-use. *Organization Studies, 25*, 529–560.

Jarzabkowski, P. (2005). *Strategy as practice: An activity based approach*. London, UK: SAGE.

Jarzabkowski, P., & Spee, A. P. (2009). Strategy-as-practice: A review and future directions for the field. *International Journal of Management Reviews, 11*, 69–95.

Johnson, G., Langley, A., Melin, L., & Whittington, R. (2007). *Strategy as practice: Research directions and resources*. Cambridge, UK: Cambridge University Press.

Johnson, G., Melin, L., & Whittington, R. (2003). Guest editors' introduction micro strategy and strategizing: Towards an activity-based view. *Journal of Management Studies, 40*, 3–22.

Kaplan, S. (2011). Research in cognition and strategy: Reflections on two decades of progress and a look to the future. *Journal of Management Studies, 48*, 665–695.

Katkalo, V. S., Pitelis, C. N., & Teece, D. J. (2010). On the nature and scope of dynamic capabilities. *Industrial and Corporate Change, 19*, 1175–1186.

Knight, F. H. (1921). *Risk, uncertainty and profit*. New York, NY: Harper & Row.

Knight, F. H. (1965). *Risk, uncertainty and profit* (Reprint and Extension). New York, NY: Harper & Row.

Lounsbury, M., & Glynn, M. A. (2001). Cultural entrepreneurship: Stories, legitimacy, and the acquisition of resources. *Strategic Management Journal, 22*, 545–564.

Lovallo, D., Clarke, C., & Camerer, C. (2012). Robust analogizing and the outside view: Two empirical tests of case-based decision making. *Strategic Management Journal, 33*, 496–512.

Magretta, J. (2002). Why business models matter. *Harvard Business Review, 80*(5), 86–92.

Mcmullen, J. S., & Shepherd, D. A. (2006). Entrepreneurial action and the role of uncertainty in the theory of the entrepreneur. *Academy of Management Review, 31*, 132–152.

Mosakowski, E. (2002). Overcoming resource disadvantages in entrepreneurial firms: When less is more. In M. A. Hitt, R. D. Ireland, S. M. Camp, & D. L. Sexton (Eds.), *Strategic entrepreneurship: Creating a new mindset* (pp. 107–130). New York, NY: Wiley-Blackwell.

Najmaei, A. (2013). *Leading growth: CEO's cognition, knowledge acquisition and business model innovation in face of dynamism—a mixed-methods study of Australian SMEs*. Unpublishd doctoral thesis, Macquarie University, Sydney, Australia.

Narayanan, V. K., Zane, L. J., & Kemmerer, B. (2011). The cognitive perspective in strategy: An integrative review. *Journal of Management, 37*, 305–351.

Nooteboom, B. (2009). *A cognitive theory of the firm: Learning, governance and dynamic capabilities*. Cheltenham, UK: Edward Elgar.

Obloj, T., Obloj, K., & Pratt, M. G. (2010). Dominant logic and entrepreneurial firms' performance in a transition economy. *Entrepreneurship: Theory & Practice, 34*, 151–170.

Orlikowski, W. J. (2000). Using technology and constituting structures: A practice lens for studying technology in organizations. *Organization Science, 11*, 404–428.

Osterwalder, A., & Pigneur, Y. (2009). *Business model generation*. Hoboken, NJ: Wiley.

Parker, S. C. (2014). Who become serial and portfolio entrepreneurs? *Small Business Economics. 43*, 887–898

Porter, M. E. (1985). *Competitive advantage*. New York, NY: Free Press.

Porter, M. E. (1996). What is strategy? *Harvard Business Review, 74*(6), 61–78.

Porter, M. E. (1998). Introduction. In M. E. Porter (Ed.), *Competitive advantage*. New York, NY: Free Press.

Porter, M., & Siggelkow, N. (2008). Contextuality within activity systems and sustainability of competitive advantage. *Academy of Management Perspectives, 22*(2), 34–56.

Powell, T. C., Lovallo, D., & Fox, C. R. (2011). Behavioral strategy. *Strategic Management Journal, 32*, 1369–1386.

Reckwitz, A. (2002). Toward a theory of social practices: A development in culturalist theorizing. *European Journal of Social Theory, 5*, 243–263.

Rouse, J. (2006). Practice Theory. In D. M. Gabbay, P. Thagard, & J. Woods (Eds.), *Philosophy of anthropology and sociology: Handbook of the philosophy of science* (Vol. 15, pp. 499–540). London, UK: Elsevier.

Shane, S. (2000). Prior knowledge and the discovery of entrepreneurial opportunities. *Organization Science, 11*, 448–469.

Stigler, G. J. (1951). The division of labor is limited by the extent of the market. *Journal of Political Economy, 59*, 185–193.

Suddaby, R., Seidl, D., & Le, J. K. (2013). Strategy-as-practice meets neo-institutional theory. *Strategic Organization, 11*, 329–344.

Teece, D. J. (2007). Explicating dynamic capabilities: The nature and microfoundations of (sustainable) enterprise performance. *Strategic Management Journal, 28*, 1319–1350.

Teece, D. J. (2010). Business models, business strategy and innovation. *Long Range Planning, 43*, 172–194.

Teece, D. J., Pisano, G., & Shuen, A. (1997). Dynamic capabilities and strategic management. *Strategic Management Journal, 18*, 509–533.

Tollin, K. (2008). Mindsets in marketing for product innovation: An explorative analysis of chief marketing executives' ideas and beliefs about how to increase their firms' innovation capability. *Journal of Strategic Marketing, 16*, 363–390.

Vaara, E., & Whittington, R. (2012). Strategy-as-practice: Taking social practices seriously. *Academy of Management Annals, 6*, 285–336.

Vaghely, I. P., & Julien, P.-A. (2010). Are opportunities recognized or constructed? An information perspective on entrepreneurial opportunity identification. *Journal of Business Venturing, 25*, 73–86.

Von Mises, L. (1949). *Human action* (4 ed.). New Haven, CT: Yale University Press.

Vygotsky, L. (1978). *Mind and society*. Cambridge, MA: Harvard University Press.

Whittington, R. (2006). Completing the practice turn in strategy research. *Organization Studies, 27*, 613–634.

Whittington, R. (2014). Information systems strategy and strategy-as-practice: A joint agenda. *Journal of Strategic Information Systems, 23*, 87–91.

Winter, S. G., & Szulanski, G. (2001). Replication as strategy. *Organization Science, 12*, 730–743.

Wright, R. P., Paroutis, S. E., & Blettner, D. P. (2013). How useful are the strategic tools we teach in business schools? *Journal of Management Studies, 50*, 92–125.

Zhang, J., Soh, P.-H., & Wong, P.-K. (2010). Entrepreneurial resource acquisition through indirect ties: Compensatory effects of prior knowledge. *Journal of Management, 36*, 511–536.

Zhang, J., Soh, P.-H., & Wong, P.-K. (2011). Direct ties, prior knowledge, and entrepreneurial resource acquisitions in China and Singapore. *International Small Business Journal, 29*, 170–189.

Zott, C., & Amit, R. (2010). Business model design: An activity system perspective. *Long Range Planning, 43*, 216–226.

Zott, C., Amit, R., & Massa, L. (2011). The business model: Recent developments and future research. *Journal of Management, 37*, 1019–1042.

Zott, C., & Huy, Q. N. (2007). How entrepreneurs use symbolic management to acquire resources. *Administrative Science Quarterly, 52*, 70–105.

CHAPTER 6

DYNAMIC CAPABILITIES AND FIRM PERFORMANCE UNDER ENVIRONMENTAL AND FIRM-SPECIFIC UNCERTAINTY

Evidence From the Venture Capital Industry

Sohvi Heaton and Alex Makarevich

ABSTRACT

We address one of the core issues in managerial practice, the allocation of firm resources. Managers need to frequently adjust firms' resource allocation in order to sustain competitive advantage in today's dynamic and volatile business environment. However, this agile approach can create disruption and not provide enough time for new investments to pay off. Drawing from the literature on dynamic capabilities, we clarify the conditions under which a firm's capability to reallocate resources positively affects its performance. Analyzing the U.S. venture capital industry from 1970 to 2015, we find that dynamic capabilities are associated with higher firm performance as the environmental uncertainty increases. However, in firms facing firm-specific uncertainty, dynamic capabilities are associated with lower performance, especially at higher levels of such uncertainty. This research suggests that the relationship between dynamic capabilities and uncertainty is more nuanced than the current literature suggests and highlights the trade-off between the cost of maintaining dynamic capabilities and achieving evolutionary fitness with the environment. These findings have implications for the managerial practice of resource allocation.

Managerial Practice Issues in Strategy and Organization, pp. 175–194
Copyright © 2023 by Information Age Publishing
www.infoagepub.com
175

INTRODUCTION

Allocation of firm resources is one of the core issues in managerial practice. In particular, managers must find the right balance between allocating resources toward a firm's ability to deal with the dynamism of its environment, that is, an ability to cope with often unexpected or hard-to-predict but consequential environmental challenges and allocating resources toward achieving greater efficiency in a firm's existing areas of competence. Neglecting either area may spell disaster. Especially in today's dynamic and volatile business environment managers need not only to find the right balance between these two competing demands on a firm's resources, but also adjust the resource allocation in order to sustain competitive advantage.

In this chapter we consider the issue of resource allocation through the prism of the concept of dynamic capabilities. This concept has been developed in managerial literature in order to better understand how firms tackle the need to constantly adapt to their changing environments. While the concept has helped elucidate the question of why some firms success-fully deal with changes in their environment while others fail, gaps in our understanding of how dynamic capabilities affect firms remain. In par-ticular, while prior research has focused on understanding what dynamics capabilities are and how firms create them, relatively less attention has been paid to the question of trade-offs that developing dynamic capabili-ties may necessitate. In particular, the question of resource allocation to the development of dynamic capabilities under different conditions which firms face is underexplored. In this chapter, drawing from the literature on dynamic capabilities, we clarify the conditions under which the managerial practice of resource reallocation positively affects its performance.

This chapter is organized as follows. In the next section, we briefly review the literature on dynamic capabilities. Based on that, we then build argu-ments about the trade-offs that the development of dynamics capabilities necessitates in firms and about the conditions under which allocation of resources to developing dynamic capabilities improves firms' performance vs. when it hinders it. We then proceed with an overview of our data and empirical analyses conducted to test our hypotheses, present the results of our analyses, and discuss theoretical and practical implications of our work. We conclude with an overview of the study's contributions and avenues for future research.

DYNAMIC CAPABILITIES AND ORDINARY CAPABILITIES

Dynamic capabilities have been defined as the firm's ability to integrate, build, and reconfigure internal and external competences to address rapidly changing environments in which there is deep uncertainty (Teece, Pisano, & Shuen, 1997). Dynamic capabilities are higher-level capabilities to integrate, build, and reconfigure internal and external resources/ competences to address, and possibly shape, rapidly changing business environments (Teece & Leih, 2016; Teece et al., 1997). Dynamic capabilities involve higher-level activities that can enable an enterprise to direct its ordinary activities toward high-payoff endeavors. This requires managing, or "orchestrating," the firm's resources to address and shape rapidly changing business environments (Teece, 2014). Dynamic capabilities can be thought of as consisting of three clusters of activities: (1) identification and assessment of an opportunity (sensing), (2) mobilization of resources to address an opportunity and to capture value from doing so (seizing), and (3) continued renewal to execute and sustain the innovation at scale (transforming). These activities must be performed expertly if the firm is to remain relevant as markets and technologies change, although some firms will be stronger than others in performing some or all of these tasks (Teece, 2012).

Whereas ordinary capabilities are about doing things right, dynamic capabilities are about doing the right things, at the right time, based on new product (and process) development, unique managerial orchestration processes, a strong and change-oriented organizational culture, and a prescient assessment of the business environment and technological opportunities (Teece, 2014, p. 331). Dynamic capabilities are higher-level activities that enable an enterprise to direct its activities towards producing goods and services in high demand (or likely to be in high demand soon). Ordinary capabilities involve the performance of those administrative-, operational-, or governance-related functions that are necessary to complete tasks. Dynamic capabilities enable the firm to integrate, build, and reconfigure internal and external resources to address and shape rapidly changing business environments.

The concept of dynamic capabilities has contributed to the understanding of organizational adaptation by analyzing how firms not only sense important developments but also adapt to environments and emerging technologies, and where possible shape them too (Teece, 2007, 2014).

Trade-Offs of Dynamic Capabilities

Dynamic capabilities can have a positive influence on firm performance through various mechanisms. For example, dynamic capabilities enhance the effectiveness and speed of firm responses to environmental turbulence, which eventually improves performance (Hitt, Bierman, Shimizu, & Kochhar, 2001). Dynamic capabilities allow the firm to take advantage of revenue enhancing opportunities and adjust its operations to reduce

costs (Drnevich & Kriauciunas, 2011, p. 258). Through sensing opportunities and reconfiguration, dynamic capabilities provide the firm with a new
set of decision options, which may result in improved firm performance
(Teece, 2007).

Maintaining dynamic capabilities, however, typically involves continuous change that may be disruptive to firms. It also can involve long-term
commitments to specialized resources. The more pervasive and detailed
the patterning of the activity involved, the higher the costs of the commitments tend to be (Winter, 2003, p. 992). For instance, when altering their
resource base, transaction and coordination costs (e.g., hiring consultants
who facilitate the change) usually occur (Chakrabarti, Vidal, & Mitchell,
2011; Karim, 2006). In addition, firms incur unlearning costs when re-
moving existing processes to reduce friction from implementing changes
(Lavie, 2006).

The costs of creating and sustaining dynamic capabilities sometimes
exceed their benefits (Schilke, 2014; Drnevich & Kriauciunas, 2010; Zollo
& Winter, 2002). It is costly to have a dynamic capability when there is
no occasion for change. An aggressive search for such occasions is also a
mistake. Sensing capability requires managerial effort and attention to out-
ward-looking activities (Helfat & Peteraf, 2015). Winter (2003, p. 993) notes
that "attempting too much change … can impose additional costs when the
frequent disruption of the underlying capability outweighs the competitive
value of the novelty achieved." Thus firms must make a trade-off between
the cost of maintaining dynamic capabilities and the ability to adapt to the
environment effectively. This trade-off is contingent on conditions in which
firms operate and, more specifically, the type of uncertainty they face.

Role of Context in the Utility of Dynamic Capabilities

The relevance of the dynamic capabilities is context dependent (Teece,
Pisano, & Shuen, 1997; Winter, 2003). Scholars have characterized business
environments and examined the interplay between dynamic capabilities and
different types of business markets, such as moderately dynamic markets,
high-velocity markets (Eisenhardt & Martin, 2000), and VUCA worlds
(Schoemaker, Heaton, & Teece, 2018). Many studies indicate that the value
of dynamic capabilities is likely to be high in fast-moving (high-uncertainty)
competitive environments where semi-continuous modification of what
the enterprise is doing is required to maintain a good fit with the business
ecosystem (Helfat, Finkelstein, Mitchell, Peteraf, Singh, Teece, & Winter,
2009; Helfat & Winter, 2011; Teece, 2012, p. 1397).

Highly dynamic environments with uncertain outcomes and demand
for novel actions pose unique challenges to management (Schilke, 2014,

p. 182). Schoemaker, Heaton, and Teece (2018) explain that VUCA (volatile, uncertain, complex, and ambiguous) conditions call for strong dynamic capabilities to drive sensemaking and stimulate the generation of innovative offerings, new business models, and fast action.

Although scholars have highlighted the importance of uncertainty as a key moderator for the effectiveness of dynamic capabilities, they have not examined the nature of uncertainty involved. The framework we use differentiates firm-specific uncertainty from environmental uncertainty. This distinction lies at the core of our argument.

Boundary Conditions of Dynamic Capabilities

As discussed, there are trade-offs of having dynamic capabilities, and thus the extent to which dynamic capabilities contribute to competitive advantage is context specific. Increasingly, researchers have identified boundary conditions of dynamic capabilities. Scholars often focus on environmental dynamism as a key contingency (Teece et al., 1997) because dynamic environments require that firms change more frequently, which offers more opportunity to exercise dynamic capabilities and recuperate the costs of developing them (Drnevich & Kriauciunas, 2011; Wilden & Gudergan, 2015). Indeed, studies show a positive relationship between dynamic capabilities and competitive advantage in dynamic environments although Schilke (2014) found that this relationship becomes weaker at very high levels of environmental dynamism.

Other authors argue that environmental munificence can shape access to resources and thus affects the value of dynamic capabilities (Aragon-Correa & Sharma, 2003; Zott, 2003). Schoemaker et al. (2016) suggest that dynamic capabilities are helpful particularly as the world becomes more volatile, uncertain, complex, and ambiguous (VUCA). Strong dynamic capabilities improve the likelihood that an organization can adjust to the unexpected ("the unknown unknowns"). Under deep uncertainty, managers should make informed decisions about the path ahead, and update them as new evidence emerges, which points to the need for dynamic managerial capabilities (Adner & Helfat, 2003).

Although these insights into the boundary conditions of dynamic capabilities have been helpful, there has been a call for a more nuanced approach to the role of context in affecting the value of dynamic capabilities (e.g., Ambrosini & Bowman, 2009; Peteraf, Di Stefano, & Verona, 2013; Wilden, Gudergan, Nielsen, & Lings, 2013; Wilden, Devinney, & Dowling, 2016). The relationship between dynamic capabilities and competitive advantage is complex and focusing on environmental dynamism without attention to other relevant factors may describe an incomplete picture of the value of dynamic capabilities (Fainshmidt, Pezeshkan, Frazier, Nair, & Markowski, 2016; Grant & Bakhru, 2016; Peteraf et al., 2013; Ringov, 2017). Hence, to better understand the effect of dynamic capabilities on competitive advantage, below we discuss how the nature of uncertainty might shape the value of dynamic capabilities.

Environmental Uncertainty, Firm-Specific Uncertainty, and Dynamic Capabilities

A firm's environment is considered uncertain if managers responsible for the future development of the firm are unable to accurately predict how the market environment will change (Milliken, 1987). Environmental uncertainty often results from changes in the environment that are difficult to predict, such as regulatory changes (Sutcliffe & Zaheer, 1998) and volatility in the product market (Wholey & Brittain, 1989). Williamson (1985, p. 57) refers to environmental uncertainty as "innocent" and "non-strategic." Environmental uncertainty requires timely decisions from alliance partners (Huber et al., 1990) about appropriate responses to environmental changes.

Prior research has indicated that dynamic capabilities are conducive to firm performance under environmental uncertainty (e.g., Teece & Leih, 2016). Dynamic capabilities allow firms to sense, recognize, assess, and pursue opportunities in firms' environment (Teece, 2007). Strong dynamic capabilities are necessary to address uncertainty that stems from firms' environment and are entrepreneurial in nature (Teece, Peteraf, & Leih, 2016). The greater the uncertainty in the business environment, the more critical strong dynamic capabilities become for the firm's performance (Teece et al., 2016).

Under low environmental uncertainty, on the other hand, firms are not likely to significantly benefit from dynamic capabilities, as the ability to sense, recognize, assess, and pursue opportunities is relatively less valuable in more predictable environments where ordinary capabilities may suffice (Schoemaker et al., 2018). This leads us to formulate:

Hypothesis 1: *At high levels of environmental uncertainty, dynamic capabilities have a positive effect on firm performance.*

Some firms may also face stronger firm-specific uncertainty than environmental uncertainty (Beckman, Haunschild, & Phillips, 2004). Firm-specific uncertainty is loosely analogous to unique risk or nonsystematic risk in the finance literature (Beckman et al., 2004). Teece et al. (2016) posit that, while mere risk, such as the possibility that a rival will launch a next-generation product earlier than expected, doesn't require dynamic capabilities, uncertainty does. Managers facing greater uncertainty require greater information-processing capabilities than managers facing standard risks (Duncan, 1972; Pennings, 1975; Tung, 1979). As nonsystematic risk can be controlled, firm-specific uncertainty is often more controllable than market uncertainty (Beckman et al., 2004). Knight (1921) who first introduced the distinction between risk and uncertainty defined a risky setting when those making decisions in the setting did not know, for sure, how a decision would turn out, but knew the possible outcomes associated with a decision and the probability of those different outcomes occurring. An uncertain setting is where the decision maker cannot know the possible outcomes nor the probability of these outcomes occurring.

Firm-specific uncertainty needs to be managed differently from environmental uncertainty. It can be managed by firms through traditional tools, such as contractual arrangements (Teece et al., 2016, p. 27). In the venture capital (VC) industry, for instance, where firm-specific uncertainty stems from the nature of their investments (e.g., the information asymmetry between the entrepreneur and the VC (e.g., Matusik & Fitza, 2012) and the inherent investment risk), VC firms can structure equity allocation and compensation arrangements of entrepreneurial teams in a way that adjusts for the level of risk VCs are exposed to (e.g., Norton & Tenenbaum, 1993). VCs can also closely monitor their portfolio companies by being actively involved in the ventures' strategy making process and operations (Gompers & Lerner, 2004; MacMillan, Kulow, & Khoylian, 1989).

These control mechanisms, however, require traditional tools and methods that firms can utilize relying on ordinary capabilities rather than dynamic capabilities. Change and resource commitments necessary for maintaining dynamic capabilities become costly for firms when they do not need dynamic capabilities, and investment in dynamic capabilities may detract from resources that would have otherwise been spent on ordinary capabilities. This effect is likely to increase with higher firm-specific uncertainty and higher need for ordinary capabilities. Therefore, we put forward:

Hypothesis 2: *The higher the firm-specific uncertainty, the weaker the effect of dynamic capabilities on firm performance.*

DATA AND METHODS

Data

Data for this analysis come from the VentureXpert (SDC Platinum) database compiled by Thompson Reuters. The dataset (along with the

VentureOne database) is one of the most comprehensive sources of data on venture investments in the U.S. and worldwide. The data include detailed information on VC firms' investments, such as the date of each investment round, round amount invested, recipient company name and location, as well as the names and locations of all investors. For sample homogeneity, we use data on investments made by VC firms located in the U.S. Since some of the entries in the VentureExpert dataset were backlogged, data prior to 1970s may be less accurate. Accordingly, we use data from 1970 till 2015 for greatest possible reliability. The 45 year period ensures that our data cover a variety of market conditions so that our analysis is not likely to suffer from a bias related to a specific time period.

Organizations making venture capital investments include different types, such as private equity firms, investment banks, corporations, and private individuals. For simplicity, we refer to all types of venture investors as "firms" in this analysis. We refer to organizations receiving investments as "companies."

Dependent Variable

In the VC industry, like other types of investment industries, a good measure of firm performance would be the rate of return on investment. However, most VC firms are organized as partnerships that do not have to publicly disclose their investment performance. In fact, a firm's rate of return is probably the most closely guarded secret in the VC industry. For this reason, prior research has come to rely on other indicators of VC firm performance. In particular, a clear indicator of success for any VC firm is the initial public offering (IPO) of a company in its portfolio. Because an IPO usually provides a greater return on investment than other ways of capitalizing on an investment, an IPO undoubtedly represents investment success in the VC industry. Besides, an IPO event of a portfolio company raises a VC firm's prominence in the industry, increases its status (Pollock, Lee, Jin, & Lashley, 2015), and facilitates its deal flow (e.g., Makarevich, 2018). Similarly, an acquisition of a VC firm's portfolio company likewise represents success as it clearly indicates interest of another company in a VC firm's investment. Based on these considerations, we follow Matusik and Fitza's (2012) approach and operationalize VC firm performance with a binary variable that captures whether or not a VC firm invested in a given year in a company that (eventually) underwent an IPO event or was acquired in an M&A deal. This variable captures a VC firm's ability to select companies for investment with a high success potential.

Independent Variable

Following the approach of Drnevich and Kriauciunas (2011), we operationalize *dynamic capabilities* by the ratio of new market segments to all market segments in a firm's portfolio over the prior five year. Entering new market segments on the one hand allows firms to take advantage of newly emerging market opportunities and to diversify their investments, which is crucial for sustained success in the investment industry. At the same time, entering a new market requires an ability to muster or acquire capabilities that will allow firms to succeed in that market. Thus this variable allows us to capture VC firms' ability to reconfigure or build their internal competencies in order to address changing environments. Such ability is what indicates the presence of dynamic capabilities (Heaton, Teece, & Agronin, in press; Teece et al., 1997; Teece et al., 2016). We use a five-year moving window for this and other variables in our analysis as most appropriate based on the nature of the industry: a five-year period roughly corresponds to the average duration of a VC investment and thus allows us to continuously gauge firms' presence in new market segments.

Moderating Variables

We operationalize *firm-specific uncertainty* by the ratio of early-stage investments to all investments in a firm's portfolio over the prior five years. In VC investing, early-stage investments are riskier than late-stage investments because little information is available about the company at initial stages. As a company develops and obtains a track record, investors are better able to make investment decisions as they have more information. Early stage investors thus experience more uncertainty compared to later stage investors. Therefore, a VC firm that has a high percentage of its portfolio invested at early stages faces relatively more uncertainty. Because this type of uncertainty is dependent on individual firms' investment decisions, it is firm-specific.

We operationalize *environmental uncertainty* by the ratio of VC firms exiting the VC industry to all firms in the industry over the prior five years. Exit of VC firms from the industry whether due to failure or ceasing of operations indicates adverse industry conditions. This variable allows us to capture the risk of firm failure and, therefore, uncertainty that firms experience. Because it is calculated at the level of the entire VC industry, this variable is not specific to particular firms and applies to all firms in the industry. It, therefore, captures environmental uncertainty that VC firms face.

Control Variables

We include variables that capture key firm characteristics, their investment history, their industry network characteristics, and time period effects to account for potential alternative explanations. Our control variables include firm age, size (measured by the total amount of prior investments), geographical location, network centrality (number of co-investment partners), network closure (i.e., the amount of structural holes in firms' industry networks), history of firms' performance (number of IPOed companies in the prior 5 years), experience (the total number of companies invested in), and diversification across market segments (measured by Herfindahl-Hirschman Index). We also break down the entire period of our analysis (1970–2015) into five decades and include dummy variables for the decades in order to account for time period effects in our analysis.

Model

Our data consist of observations of VC firms across a 45 year period with firms leaving and joining the pool. We thus have an unbalanced longitudinal panel data. Testing our hypotheses involves estimating a binary dependent variable. Given these modeling conditions, we chose the generalized linear models (GLM) with logit link and random intercept as the most appropriate model. The model takes the following form:

$$\text{logit}(\pi_i) = \log(\frac{\pi_i}{1-\pi_i}) = \beta_0 + \beta_1 x + e,$$

where π_i is the probability that firm i invested in a company that eventually underwent either and IPO or an acquisition, β_0 is a vector of intercepts, β_1 is a vector of coefficients on independent, moderating, and control variables, and e is the error term. The model is fit by maximum likelihood method and numerical integration via Gauss-Hermite quadrature.

RESULTS

Table 6.1 presents descriptive statistics and correlations for all variables in the analysis. None of the variables are correlated to the extent that would result in a multicollinearity problem. Even though the correlation between Amount invested in the prior 5 years and Firm size (total amount of prior investment) is moderate to high (0.86), this may inflate standard errors of point estimates, but will not bias the estimates (Kennedy, 2008). Since both of these are control variables, even if their points estimates are inflated, it is not a significant cause for concern.

Table 6.1
Variables in the Analysis: Descriptive Statistics and Correlation Matrix

	Variable	Mean	Std. Dev	1	2	3	4	5	6	7	8	9	10	11	12
1	Firm performance	0.74	0.44												
2	Firm age	12.97	8.07	0.02											
3	Silicon Valley location	0.22	0.41	0.09	0.05										
4	Amount invested in prior 5 years (adj.)	2.59	0.71	0.11	0.27	0.01									
5	Firm size (total amount of prior investment, adj.)	5.54	1.57	0.08	0.41	0.01	0.86								
6	Number of IPOed companies in prior 5 years	2.43	4.67	0.22	0.31	0.18	0.31	0.28							
7	Experience (total # of companies invested in)	54.01	76.08	0.16	0.66	0.18	0.47	0.59	0.59						
8	Co-investment network centrality	59.27	68.67	0.29	0.28	0.30	0.30	0.25	0.65	0.66					
9	Co-investment network closure	0.10	0.18	-0.24	-0.07	-0.16	-0.09	-0.09	-0.21	-0.22	-0.38				
10	Diversification across market segments	9.71	6.62	0.32	0.36	0.18	0.39	0.37	0.64	0.70	0.80	-0.38			
11	Environmental uncertainty	0.27	0.11	-0.36	0.13	-0.03	0.05	0.10	-0.25	0.07	-0.06	0.08	-0.10		
12	Firm-specific uncertainty	0.33	0.26	0.10	-0.18	0.18	-0.13	-0.15	0.08	-0.01	0.21	-0.28	0.13	-0.11	
13	Dynamic capabilities	0.48	0.32	-0.17	-0.49	-0.12	-0.20	-0.25	-0.35	-0.48	-0.40	0.31	-0.52	-0.02	0.03

Table 6.2 reports the results from generalized linear models of VC firms' performance. We use Akaike's Information Criterion (AIC) to compare nested and non-nested models. AIC indicates the loss of precision when the maximum likelihood estimate is substituted for the true parametric estimate in the likelihood function, with smaller AIC values indicating better fitting models.

Table 6.2

GLM Models of Effects of VC Firms' Dynamic Capabilities and Environmental and Firm-Specific Uncertainty on Firm Performance

	Model 1		Model 2		Model 3		Model 4		Model 5	
Intercept	2.700	***	2.612	***	2.536	***	3.254	***	3.190	***
	(0.086)		(0.106)		(0.110)		(0.127)		(0.132)	
Decade dummies	Incl.		Incl.		Incl.		Incl.		Incl.	
Firm age	−0.030	***	−0.026	***	−0.025	***	−0.026	***	−0.026	***
	(0.004)		(0.005)		(0.005)		(0.005)		(0.005)	
Silicon Valley location	0.190	**	0.160	*	0.158	*	0.170	***	0.168	***
	(0.076)		(0.079)		(0.080)		(0.080)		(0.080)	
Amount invested in prior 5 years	0.000		0.000		0.000		0.000		0.000	
	(0.000)		(0.000)		(0.000)		(0.000)		(0.000)	
Firm size (total amount of prior investment)	0.001	***	0.001	***	0.001	**	0.001	***	0.001	***
	(0.000)		(0.000)		(0.000)		(0.000)		(0.000)	
Number of IPOed portfolio companies in prior 5 years	−0.029	*	−0.029	*	−0.029	**	−0.046	***	−0.046	***
	(0.014)		(0.014)		(0.014)		(0.014)		(0.014)	
Experience (total # of companies invested in)	−0.003	***	−0.004	***	−0.004	**	−0.003	**	−0.003	**
	(0.001)		(0.001)		(0.001)		(0.001)		(0.001)	
Co–investment network centrality (# of partners in prior 5 years)	0.013	***	0.013	***	0.013	***	0.014	***	0.014	***
	(0.001)		(0.001)		(0.001)		(0.001)		(0.001)	

(Table continued on next page)

Table 6.2 (Continued)
GLM Models of Effects of VC Firms' Dynamic Capabilities and Environmental and Firm-Specific Uncertainty on Firm Performance

	Model 1		Model 2		Model 3		Model 4		Model 5	
Co–investment network closure	−0.542	***	−0.640	***	−0.644	***	−0.589	***	−0.594	***
	(0.095)		(0.108)		(0.108)		(0.108)		(0.108)	
Diversification across market segments	0.117	***	0.123	***	0.122	***	0.121	***	0.120	***
	(0.008)		(0.008)		(0.008)		(0.008)		(0.008)	
Environmental uncertainty	−9.410	***	−9.431	***	−9.436	***	−11.810	***	−11.790	***
	(0.224)		(0.234)		(0.234)		(0.353)		(0.354)	
Firm–specific uncertainty	0.151	**	0.048	*	0.338	**	0.068		0.280	**
	(0.074)		(0.027)		(0.142)		(0.083)		(0.144)	
Dynamic capabilities			0.085	**	0.218	**	−1.315	***	−1.204	***
			(0.066)		(0.085)		(0.159)		(0.171)	
Dynamic capabilities x Environmental uncertainty					5.085	***			5.024	***
					(0.525)				(0.527)	
Dynamic capabilities x Firm–specific uncertainty							−0.449	**	−0.322	*
							(0.179)		(0.179)	
Observations	16071		16071		16071		16071		16071	
AIC	21650		19860		19850		19770		19710	

$* p < .10; ** p < .05; *** p < .01$ Standard errors are in parentheses

Model 1 presents a baseline specification that only includes control variables. Model 1 indicates that performance is higher in VC firms located in Silicon Valley, larger firms (measured by the total amount of prior investment), more central firm in the co-investment network, firms with more open networks, and more diversified firms. These findings correspond to expectations regarding VC firms' performance. At the same time, older firms, firms with greater number of prior investments, and firms that had a greater number of IPOs of portfolio companies in the past 5 years show lower performance. These finding indicate that there may be complex relationships between VC firm performance and its age, experience, and prior history of success. Model 1 also indicates that firms facing firm-specific uncertainty show higher performance than those facing low firm-specific uncertainty and the reverse is true with regard to environmental uncertainty.

Model 2 introduces our independent variable, Dynamic capabilities. The positive and highly statistically significant coefficient (at the $p < 0.05$ level) on this variable indicates that, overall, in line with prior literature on the subject dynamic capabilities increase firm performance.

In Models 3 and 4 we introduce interactions between variables capturing dynamic capabilities and environmental and firm-specific uncertainty, respectively. The positive and highly statistically significant (at the $p < 0.01$ level) coefficient (5.085) on the interaction term between dynamic capabilities and environmental uncertainty indicates that dynamic capabilities enhance performance in VC firms facing high environmental uncertainty. The negative and highly statistically significant (at the $p < 0.05$ level) coefficient (–0.449) on the (Dynamic capabilities x Firm-specific uncertainty) term indicates that dynamic capabilities are associated with lower performance in firms facing high firm-specific uncertainty. In Model 5 we include all main effects and interaction terms simultaneously. Model 5 indicates that the interaction terms between dynamic capabilities and environmental and firm-specific uncertainty retain both their direction and statistical significance confirming the resulting of Models 3 and 4.

To facilitate the interpretation of these results we include Figures 6.1 and 6.2. In Figure 6.1, the dashed line shows estimated VC firm performance when environmental uncertainty is high (mean + 2SD). The upward slope of the line indicates that the greater a firm's dynamic capabilities, the higher its performance when a firm faces high environmental uncertainty. This lends support to Hypothesis 1. The solid black line in Figure 6.1 corresponds to estimated VC firm performance when environmental uncertainty is low (mean – 2SD). The downward slope of the line indicates that in firms facing low levels of environmental uncertainty, dynamic capabilities are associated with lower performance.

Figure 6.2 shows that in VC firms facing both high firm-specific uncertainty (the dashed line corresponding to mean + 2SD) and low firm-specific uncertainty (solid black line corresponding to mean – 2SD), dynamic capabilities are associated with reduced firm performance. This lends support to Hypothesis 2. The steeper downward slope of the line corresponding to high firm-specific uncertainty indicates that dynamic capabilities are especially associated with lower performance when the levels of firm-specific uncertainty are higher.

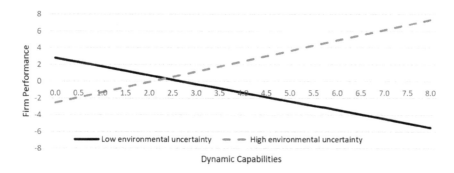

Figure 6.1.   The interaction of dynamic capabilities and environmental uncertainty on VC firm performance.

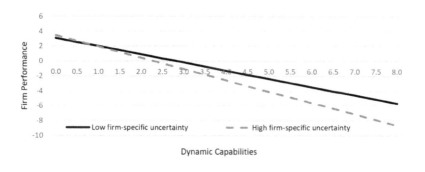

Figure 6.2.   The interaction of dynamic capabilities and firm-specific uncertainty on VC firm performance.

DISCUSSION AND CONCLUSION

In this study, we set out to examine how firms' dynamic capabilities affect performance under different types of uncertainty. Our study was inspired partly by the observation that a lack of conceptual clarity regarding the role of contingencies, such as dynamism, in effects of dynamic capabilities has been 'particularly striking' over the years (Ringov, 2017, p. 654; see also, Di Stefano et al., 2014). We found that the nature of uncertainty alters the effectiveness of dynamic capabilities. When firms face high environmental uncertainty, their dynamic capabilities help them achieve superior performance—the ability to deal with challenging environment that dynamic capabilities provide enhances firm performance. However, when environmental uncertainty that firms face is low or when they face firm-specific rather than environmental uncertainty, dynamic capabilities are associated with lower performance—under these conditions firms require a different kind of capabilities in order to achieve superior performance. This finding illustrates a fundamental trade-off that firms encounter when developing dynamic capabilities.

Conceptually, this study contributes to the debate on the relevance of dynamic capabilities in different contexts (Arend & Bromiley, 2009; Girod & Whittington, 2017; Helfat & Winter, 2011) by identifying boundary conditions that impact the effectiveness of dynamic capabilities. It shows that the value of dynamic capabilities is contingent on the type of uncertainty firms face and the trade-off between the cost of maintaining dynamic capabilities and adaptability to the environment.

We contribute to the literature on dynamic capabilities by theorizing about and empirically testing the specific types of uncertainty and dynamic capabilities that lead to a competitive advantage. Some scholars have identified environmental uncertainty as a key contingency (Schoemaker et al., 2018). Extending this line of thinking, we show that the type of uncertainty is an overlooked factor that affects the effectiveness of dynamic capabilities. That is, dynamic capabilities are conducive to fit in uncertain environments that are also munificent, but may have limited ability to do so in dealing with firm-specific uncertainty, so there are reduced benefits from deploying dynamic capabilities. This finding is consistent with Eisenhardt and Martin's (2000) assertion that dynamic capabilities are a necessary, but insufficient, condition for competitive advantage. In such contexts, ordinary capabilities may allow firms to deal with firm-specific uncertainties as they occur, reducing the need for routinized change activities in the form of dynamic capabilities (Winter, 2003, p. 992). Little uncertainty in the environment means recouping costs associated with dynamic capabilities would be difficult. On the other hand, an uncertain environment is likely to help firms recover the costs of dynamic capabilities. In sum, this study contributes to producing a more nuanced understanding of dynamic capabilities and has implications for firm strategy under different types of uncertainty.

We also contribute to the literature investigating organizational responses to uncertainty. Organizational and strategy research has examined how organizations respond to environmental uncertainty, highlighting either responses that avoid uncertainty (López-Gamero, Molina-Azorín, & Claver-Cortés, 2011; Yang, Burns, & Backhouse, 2004) or those that are proactive (Aragon-Correa & Sharma, 2003; Hoffmann, Trautmann, & Hamprecht, 2009). However, prior studies have paid less attention to the mechanisms that underlie divergent responses (Dutt & Joseph, 2019). Our results imply that dynamic capabilities are a key contingency that drive variation in outcome of corporate responses to uncertainty.

Our research was conducted in the context of U.S. venture capital firms only. The venture capital industry is shaped by its institutional context such as regulations and labor practices. Future research should examine the impact of different institutional contexts allowing for broader conclusions to be made about the type of uncertainty and the effectiveness of dynamic capabilities in achieving superior performance. The present research is best considered as a stepping stone in the pursuit of the larger endeavor.

Managerial Implications

Our study provides several implications for managers seeking to best allocate resources. Managers should consider the specific types of uncertainty their firms are facing when contemplating the deployment of change-oriented routines. For instance, our results suggest that dynamic capabilities should not be deployed when firms face low environmental uncertainty, as the costs incurred by such change-oriented routines may not be recoverable in settings that require just ordinary capabilities. In dealing with firm-specific uncertainty, managers should carefully consider whether the potential benefits of deploying dynamic capabilities are worth the costs. In such settings, managers might consider allocating resources to improving ordinary capabilities rather than attempting to develop dynamic capabilities.

A firm can make continuous improvements to its operational capabilities and thus become a pioneer in efficiency. In sum, there are multiple ways to change and even in dynamic environments managers should carefully consider whether routinized change in the form of dynamic capabilities is the best means of change depending on whether they face environmental uncertainty or firm-specific uncertainty.

REFERENCES

Adner, R., & Helfat, C. E. (2003). Corporate effects and dynamic managerial capabilities. *Strategic Management Journal, 24*(10), 1011–1025.

Ambrosini, V., & Bowman, C. (2009). What are dynamic capabilities and are they a useful construct in strategic management? *International Journal of Management Reviews, 11*(1), 29–49.

Aragon-Correa, J. A., & Sharma, S. (2003). A contingent resource-based view of proactive corporate environmental strategy. *Academy of Management Review, 28*(1), 71–88.

Arend R., Bromiley P. (2009). Assessing the dynamic capabilities view: Spare change, everyone? *Strategic Organization, 7*(1), 75–90.

Beckman, C., Haunschild, P., & Phillips, D. (2004). Friends or strangers? Firm-specific uncertainty, market uncertainty, and network partner selection. *Organization Science, 15*(3), 259–275.

Chakrabarti, A., Vidal, E., & Mitchell, W. (2011). Business transformation in heterogeneous environments: The impact of market development and firm strength on retrenchment and growth reconfiguration. *Global Strategy Journal, 1*(1-2), 6–26.

Di Stefano, G., Peteraf, M., & Verona, G. (2014). The organizational drivetrain: A road to integration of dynamic capabilities research. *Academy of Management Perspectives, 28*(4), 307–327.

Drnevich, P. L., & Kriauciunas, A. P. (2011). Clarifying the conditions and limits of the contributions of ordinary and dynamic capabilities to relative firm performance. *Strategic Management Journal, 32*(3), 254–279.

Duncan, R. B. (1972). Characteristics of organizational environments and perceived environmental uncertainty. *Administrative Science Quarterly, 17*, 313–327.

Dutt, N., & Joseph, J. (2019). Regulatory uncertainty, corporate structure, and strategic agendas: Evidence from the US renewable electricity industry. *Academy of Management Journal, 62*(3), 800–827.

Eisenhardt, K. M., & Martin, J. A. (2000). Dynamic capabilities: What are they? *Strategic Management Journal, 21*(10–11), 1105–1121.

Fainshmidt, S., Pezeshkan, A., Frazier, M. L., Nair, A., & Markowski, E. (2016). Dynamic capabilities and organizational performance: A meta-analytic evaluation and extension. *Journal of Management Studies, 52(8)*, 1348–1380.

Girod, S. J. G., & Whittington, R. (2017). Reconfiguration, restructuring and firm performance: Dynamic capabilities and environmental dynamism. *Strategic Management Journal, 38*(5), 1121–1133.

Gompers, P. A., & Lerner, J. (2004). *The venture capital cycle*. Cambridge, MA: MIT Press.

Grant, R. M., & Bakhru, A. (2016). Situating dynamic capabilities. In D. J. Teece & S. Leih (Eds.), *The Oxford handbook of dynamic capabilities*. Oxford, UK: Oxford University Press.

Heaton, S., Teece, D., & Agronin, E. (in press). Dynamic capabilities and governance: An empirical investigation of financial performance of the higher education sector. *Strategic Management Journal*. https://doi.org/10.1002/smj.3444

Helfat, C. E., Finkelstein, S., Mitchell, W., Peteraf, M., Singh, H., Teece, D., & Winter, S. G. (2009). *Dynamic capabilities: Understanding strategic change in organizations*, Hoboken, NJ: John Wiley & Sons.

Helfat, C. E., & Peteraf, M. A. (2015). Managerial cognitive capabilities and the microfoundations of dynamic capabilities. *Strategic Management Journal, 36*(6), 831–850.

Helfat, C. E, & Winter, S. G. (2011). Untangling dynamic and operational capabilities: Strategy for the (n)ever- changing world. *Strategic Management Journal, 32*, 1243–1250.

Hitt, M. A., Bierman, L., Shimizu, K., & Kochhar, R. (2001). Direct and moderating effects of human capital on strategy and performance in professional service firms: A resource-based perspective. *Academy of Management journal, 44*(1), 13–28.

Hoffmann, V. H., Trautmann, T., & Hamprecht, J. (2009). Regulatory uncertainty: A reason to postpone investments? Not necessarily. *Journal of Management Studies*, 46(7), 1227–1253.

Huber, J. P., Miller, C. C., & Glick, W. H. (1990). Developing more encompassing theories about organizations: The centralization-effectiveness relationship as an example. *Organization Science*, 1(1), 11–40.

Karim, S. (2006). Modularity in organizational structure: The reconfiguration of internally developed and acquired business units. *Strategic Management Journal*, 27(9), 799–823.

Kennedy, P. (2008). *A guide to econometrics*. Malden, MA: Blackwell.

Lavie, D. (2006). Capability reconfiguration: An analysis of incumbent responses to technological change. *Academy of Management Review*, 31(1), 153–174.

López-Gamero, M. D., Molina-Azorín, J. F., & Claver-Cortés, E. (2011). Environmental uncertainty and environmental management perception: A multiple case study. *Journal of Business Research*, 64(4), 427–435.

Knight, F. H. (1921). *Risk, uncertainty and profit*. New York, NY: Augustus Kelley.

MacMillan, I. C., Kulow, D. M., & Khoylian, R. (1989). Venture capitalists' involvement in their investments: Extent and performance. *Journal of Business Venturing*, 4(1), 27–47.

Makarevich, A. (2018). Performance feedback as a cooperation "switch": A behavioral perspective on the success of venture capital syndicates among competitors. *Strategic Management Journal*, 39(12), 3247–3272.

Matusik, S. F., & Fitza, M. A. (2012). Diversification in the venture capital industry: Leveraging knowledge under uncertainty. *Strategic Management Journal*, 33(4), 407–426.

Milliken, F. J. (1987). Three types of perceived uncertainty about the environment: State, effect, and response uncertainty. *Academy of Management Review*, 12(1), 133–143.

Norton, E., & Tenenbaum, B. H. (1993). Specialization versus diversification as a venture capital investment strategy. *Journal of Business Venturing*, 8(5), 431–442.

Pennings, J. M. (1975). The relevance of the structural-contingency model for organizational effectiveness. *Administrative Science Quarterly*, 393–410.

Peteraf, M., Di Stefano, G., & Verona, G. (2013). The elephant in the room of dynamic capabilities: Bringing two diverging conversations together. *Strategic Management Journal*, 34(12), 1389–1410.

Pollock, T. G., Lee, P. M., Jin, K., & Lashley, K. (2015). (Un)tangled: Exploring the asymmetric coevolution of new venture capital firms' reputation and status. *Administrative Science Quarterly*, 60(3), 482–517.

Ringov, D. (2017). Dynamic capabilities and firm performance. *Long Range Planning*, 50(5), 653–664.

Schilke, O. (2014). On the contingent value of dynamic capabilities for competitive advantage: The nonlinear moderating effect of environmental dynamism. *Strategic Management Journal*, 35(2), 179–203.

Schoemaker, P. J., Heaton, S., & Teece, D. (2018). Innovation, dynamic capabilities, and leadership. *California Management Review*, 61(1), 15–42.

Sutcliffe, K. M., & Zaheer, A. (1998). Uncertainty in the transaction environment: An empirical test. *Strategic Management Journal, 19*(1), 1–23.

Teece, D. J. (2007). Explicating dynamic capabilities: The nature and microfoundations of (sustainable) enterprise performance. *Strategic Management Journal, 28*(13), 1319–1350.

Teece, D. J. (2012). Dynamic capabilities: Routines versus entrepreneurial action. *Journal of Management Studies, 49*(8), 1395–1401.

Teece, D. J. (2014). The foundations of enterprise performance: Dynamic and ordinary capabilities in an (economic) theory of firms. *Academy of Management Perspectives, 28*(4), 328–352.

Teece, D. J., & Leih, S. (2016). Uncertainty, innovation, and dynamic capabilities: An introduction. *California Management Review, 58*(4), 5–12.

Teece, D. J., Peteraf, M., & Leih, S. (2016). Dynamic capabilities and organizational agility: Risk, uncertainty, and strategy in the innovation economy. *California Management Review, 58*(4), 13–35.

Teece, D. J., Pisano, G., & Shuen, A. (1997). Dynamic capabilities and strategic management. *Strategic Management Journal, 18*(7), 509–533.

Tung, R. L. (1979). Dimensions of organizational environments: An exploratory study of their impact on organization structure. *Academy of Management Journal, 22*(4), 672–693.

Wholey, D. R., & Brittain, J. (1989). Characterizing environmental variation. *Academy of Management Journal, 32*(4), 867–882.

Wilden, R., Devinney, T. M., & Dowling, G. R. (2016). The architecture of dynamic capability research identifying the building blocks of a configurational approach. *Academy of Management Annals, 10*(1), 997–1076.

Wilden, R., & Gudergan, S. P. (2015). The impact of dynamic capabilities on operational marketing and technological capabilities: Investigating the role of environmental turbulence. *Journal of the Academy of Marketing Science, 43*(2), 181–199.

Wilden, R., Gudergan, S. P., Nielsen, B. B., & Lings, I. (2013). Dynamic capabilities and performance: Strategy, structure and environment. *Long Range Planning, 46*(1-2), 72–96.

Williamson, O. E. (1985). *The economic institutions of capitalism.* New York, NY: Free Press.

Winter, S. (2003). Understanding dynamic capabilities. *Strategic Management Journal, 24*(10) 991–995.

Yang, B., Burns, N. D., & Backhouse, C. J. (2004). Management of uncertainty through postponement. *International Journal of Production Research, 42*(6), 1049–1064.

Zollo, M., & Winter S. (2002). Deliberate learning and the evolution of dynamic capabilities. *Organization Science, 13*(3), 339–351.

Zott, C. (2003). Dynamic capabilities and the emergence of intraindustry differential firm performance: Insights from a simulation study. *Strategic Management Journal, 24*(2), 97–125.

CHAPTER 7

MANAGING UNCERTAINTY IN ALLIANCES AND NETWORKS
From Governance to Practice

Jörg Sydow, Gordon Müller-Seitz, and Keith G. Provan

ABSTRACT

Alliances and networks formed by two or more organizations are an increasingly common means to cope with environmental uncertainty frequently resulting from incomplete knowledge. At the same time, alliances and networks must address uncertainty caused by the form itself, which unlike risk, is not calculable. Our review and analysis of the literature on the topic first distinguishes between the concepts of risk and uncertainty, and then identifies three gaps in the literature that offer directions for future research. First, dyadic alliances, rather than broader networks, have been the predominant focus of researchers, limiting our understanding of the scope of uncertainty. Second, previous research concentrates on vaguely defined interorganizational relations and not more in-depth collaborations, which are far more meaningful and have a greater impact on addressing uncertainty. Third, a governance perspective has typically been applied to deal with the risks and uncertainties ensuing from alliances and networks, limiting an understanding of the impact of uncertainty on practice. To address these concerns, we call for an emphasis on genuine uncertainties rather than risks, on consideration of alliances and networks of three or more organizations rather than only dyads, and moving beyond a governance perspective, considering also how managers actually "practice uncertainties" in face of their inability to control, reduce or even avoid the lack of knowledge.

Managerial Practice Issues in Strategy and Organization, pp. 195–233
Copyright © 2023 by Information Age Publishing
www.infoagepub.com
195

INTRODUCTION

Due to the absence of complete knowledge about both the internal and external environment, organizations are continually confronted with the need to recognize and deal with uncertainty. This observation is certainly not new and has been the focus of considerable research and theorizing over many decades. For instance, March and Simon (1958) initially pointed to the necessity of controlling sources of uncertainty internal to the organization (for a review, see Jauch & Kraft, 1986). Among others, Burns and Stalker (1961), Thompson (1967), and Duncan (1972) explored external uncertainty and the ways in which organizations might best be managed and structured to enable them to respond to and survive in an environment with sometimes high levels of uncertainty. The need to deal with uncertainty has gained prominence recently through some highly visible examples of unexpected events including 9/11, hurricane Katrina, the Deepwater Horizon oil spill, and the recent global financial crisis.

Since the early days of organization research, building and maintaining alliances and networks, or interorganizational relations more generally, has been considered an important means of organizational structuring as a way of coping with environmental uncertainty in the face of incomplete knowledge. Despite the benefits, it was soon recognized that this strategy introduces the dilemma of managing uncertainties by entering into dependencies that create new uncertainties (e.g., Aiken & Hage, 1968; Pfeffer & Salancik, 1978; Provan, 1982). More recently, interorganizational relations and networks, in the private as well as in the public sphere (and as public-private partnerships across these spheres) have been thought of as being a highly flexible, adaptive and fluid form of organizing that seems to be particularly well-equipped to deal with uncertainty (e.g., Huxham & Vangen, 2005; Moynihan, 2008; Powell, 1990; Rangan, Samii & van Wassenhove, 2006; cf. for recent reviews Borgatti & Foster, 2003; Provan, Fish, & Sydow, 2007; Zaheer, Gözübüyük, & Milanov, 2010). Hence, it comes as no surprise that uncertainty has been a major focus of research on alliances and networks, not only of an external/exogenous but also of an internal/endogenous nature (e.g., Beckman, Haunschild, & Phillips, 2004; Das & Teng, 1996, 2001a, 2001b). This research has even pointed to the power of alliances and networks as a mechanism for trading external for internal—and hence, allegedly more manageable—uncertainty. What is surprising, however, is that the present state of research is generally unclear with regard to the kind of uncertainties or risks taken into account (see Milliken, 1987, for an exception).

Our perspective in this chapter is consistent with that of Knight (1921), who viewed uncertainty as those situations when actors (in our case: organizational actors) face options whose likelihood of occurrence cannot be expressed by probabilities. This state results from a lack of knowledge about organizations and their environment and represents a sharp contrast to situations where actors are confronted with risk, in which known alternatives and probabilities can at least be estimated and oftentimes allegedly rational actors are deemed to have all the necessary knowledge available. As we will highlight, there is confusion about these different perspectives and their implications. Therefore, we examine and discuss a number of questions that have yet to be thoroughly addressed. First, how might uncertainty and risk be distinguished and assessed in research on alliances and networks, and at what level of analysis? Second, what approaches have been considered to deal with uncertainty in complex networks and how does this differ from dyadic alliances? And, third, what are the theoretical and practical implications of the current state of research in these respects?

The lack of a thorough understanding of organizational uncertainty with regard to alliances and networks is problematic for both theory and practice and motivates us to address this desideratum. Our focus here is not only to document the present state of research, but also to point out research gaps and avenues for future alliance studies. In particular, we draw attention to the relevance of a practice perspective (Floyd, Cornelissen, Wright, & Delios, 2011; Jarzabkowski, 2003, 2008) on uncertainty within alliances and networks—a perspective that nicely supplements present concerns about alliance and network governance.

The chapter is organized as follows: first, we define our object of study and clarify what we mean by uncertainty, how this concept can be distinguished from risk, and how it relates to ambiguity. In this context we also discuss the ambiguous role of knowledge as a source of certainty as well as uncertainty. Then we explain how we approach the review against the background of definitional ambiguities, presenting the results of the review regarding the questions posed above. These results lead to an extensive discussion of what we actually know about how alliances and networks are affected by exogenous and endogenous uncertainties and how these are dealt with or, to be more precise, how their managers deal with them. In addition, we discuss what else we still need to know about the concept. Based on this stocktaking, we come up with recommendations for future studies and, in particular, suggest a change of perspective from the dominant focus on relationship governance to a study of uncertainty practices. By this we mean how network managers actually practice the management of uncertainty in the face of their inability to control, reduce, or avoid uncertainty, even given the presumed advantages of organizations' involvement in alliances or networks.

UNCERTAINTY, RISK, AND
AMBIGUITY IN ALLIANCES AND NETWORKS

For the purposes of this chapter, we focus on alliances as a linkage between two or more organizations that are formally independent legal entities, regardless of whether the linkage itself is based on a contract or not (Cropper, Ebers, Huxham, & Ring, 2008). As opposed to most conceptualizations of alliances, which focus on dyadic relationships, an interorganizational network (or network, for short) is definitively made up of three or more organizations and their relationships (Provan et al., 2007). Related forms and terms in the literature are federations and associations (Aldrich & Staber, 1988), interlocking directorates (e.g., Beckman et al., 2004; Mizruchi, 1996) as well as regional clusters that represent a more aggregated phenomenon; studies that relate to these forms are incorporated in this review.

More often than not, the notions of uncertainty and risks, sometimes even of ambiguity, are used interchangeably in this literature. Take, for instance, Huxham and Vangen's (2000) analysis of the ambiguity of network membership, of status within the network, and representation in the network. Their focus on ambiguity could be easily substituted for one on uncertainty. As our review will show, this terminological indecisiveness and inconsistency is indeed quite common in research on alliances and networks. Nevertheless, we consider it a serious shortcoming of the literature not to distinguish between these concepts. With respect to risk and uncertainty, Knight (1921) long ago pleaded for a sharp distinction, and other, even more prominent economists like Keynes (1936) and Davidson (1988) have made the same argument (cf. Runde, 1990, 1998). This distinction is important also for research on alliances and networks, since genuine uncertainty, at least in its extreme form, requires different forms of governance (and practices) than when dealing with calculable risks.

Following Knight (1921), we focus on uncertainty, which includes the unexpected, as a state where organizational actors do not have complete knowledge, which is a key factor for causing uncertainty. As the "unknown unknown" this is obviously not measurable by its very nature. As a consequence, uncertainty is not only unpredictable but also unfathomable and impossible to insure against (cf. Froud, 2003, p. 572); "it is what is left behind when all the risks have been identified" (Cleden, 2009, p. 5). As such, uncertainty is clearly related to the agent's knowledge or lack thereof. However, it would be naïve to assume that an increase in knowledge necessarily helps to reduce uncertainties. That is often not the case. In contrast, additional knowledge often creates further uncertainties (Beck & Holzer,

2007), stimulating awareness of events and actions whose probabilities cannot be estimated either. In order to distinguish uncertainty from risk, some authors tend to speak of fundamental, genuine, ultimate, or simply "true" uncertainty.

Risk, then, is the probability estimate that something will go wrong times the size of the potential loss incurred (cf. Das & Teng, 1996; Nooteboom, Berger, & Noorderhaven, 1997). Hence, risk is calculable and, as a kind of "organized uncertainty" (Power, 2007), takes an intermediary position on a continuum marked by certainty on the other extreme. "Residual risk" clearly reflects the uncertainty that is "left over" even after meticulously carried out risk calculations. It should be noted that the notion of risk is widely and wildly used, not only in organization and network research, but also more generally in social theory (see Lupton, 1999, for a concise overview).

Ambiguity is often considered to be a cause of uncertainty and, via probability estimates, of risk. Sometimes, however, as noted by Huxham and Vangen (2000), ambiguity is considered either synonymous with, or a by-product of uncertainty. Quite like uncertainty, ambiguity relates to a lack of knowledge. With ambiguity, however, it is a lack of clarity regarding the interpretation of a particular event or situation, the possible effects of this on—in our case—alliances and networks, and possible feedbacks of these effects on further events/actions. Like uncertainty, ambiguity is a relational construct. That is, ambiguity cannot be defined without relating it to the agents, their mental models or idiosyncratic experiences, and accessible rules and available resources (cf. March & Olson, 1976; Schrader, Riggs, & Smith, 1993).

What is apparent from our cursory review of the literature on uncertainty and organizations, as well as from our systematic review of research on uncertainty in alliances and networks, is that there is insufficient clarity not only about the concepts but also about the level of analysis at which uncertainty is being assessed. In many studies, uncertainty, risk, and ambiguity are not only measured, but also conceptualized as perceptions of individuals; in particular, managers. Thus, it is unclear if research and theorizing is focusing on the uncertainty experienced by individual managers or by their organizations, however consensual the uncertainty perception may be (Huff, 1978). Given the importance of uncertainty for organizations, alliances, and networks and how these forms recognize, monitor, and manage risk and uncertainty, this individual manager focus is not satisfactory and mirrors similar problems in other fields of organization studies, such as organizational trust (cf. Kroeger, 2012). However, as we will show, focusing on alliances and networks reveals that the relevance and peculiarities of these organizational forms for responding to risk, uncertainty and ambiguity need to be examined in their own right.

REVIEW APPROACH

Our analysis rests on a number of different inclusion and exclusion criteria that were defined ex ante in order to narrow the scope of the review. Table 7.1 offers an overview of the different criteria.

Table 7.1

Hits Review Procedure

Type of criterion	Criteria	Reason for choosing the criteria	Exemplary evidence
Inclusion criteria	Search terms with truncation characters: uncertain*, risk* and ambigu* in connection with network*, allianc*, federat*, joint venture*, associate*, interorg*, cluster*, interlocking director*, partnership* and coalition*	Boolean logic with regard to uncertainty and interorganizational network related terms narrows down the number of articles to those that make use of the relevant key terms	Lee, Yeung, & Cheng (2009)
	Theoretical / conceptual papers	Previous conceptions and reviews serve to sensitize to research voids and constitute a valuable resource for suggestions of this review	Das & Teng (2001b)
	Empirical studies	Evidence from diverse empirical settings serves to capture a finer grained and diverse perspective on how networks are perceived to deal with uncertainty	Beckman, Haunschild, & Phillips (2004)
	Title and abstract	Serves to narrow down the focus of the studies to the relevant subject	Eisingerich, Bell, & Tracey (2010)
Exclusion criteria	Electronic database (EBSCOhost)	Enables transparency and replicability	/
	Double-blind reviewed articles in English-language journals	Insight into the international academic discourse	/
	Natural Sciences	Excludes articles that do not address managerial issues, e.g., related to the functioning of neural networks within the brain	Gudykunst, Sodetani, & Sonoda (1987)
	Interpersonal networks	These studies do not address interorganizational networks as defined for this review	Ford & Mouzas (2010)

The screening of the literature subsequently unfolded in three *search strategies* that were pursued by and large in parallel (cf. Figure 7.1). First, we started with the overall systematic database-guided procedure by which we approached the knowledge domain. In our systematic review we concentrated primarily on double-blind peer-reviewed articles in English-speaking journals from the data base EBSCOhost (http://web.ebscohost.com/ehost/). In order to remain open to the multifaceted phenomenon we were addressing, we did not distinguish between the quality of the respective outlets. However, the final subset of contributions reviewed is, apart from very few exceptions, from leading scholarly journals targeting managerial issues, for instance, *Strategic Management Journal*, *Academy of Management Journal* and *Administrative Science Quarterly*. Such an approach allows for transparency and replicability. The date of publication was not restricted. However, as we were interested above all in what is known about uncertainty regarding alliances and networks, we employed two further parallel search strategies. As a second strategy, we reverted to non-journal related publications like monographs or chapters in edited volumes and screened them in a less systematic manner than our approach for the journal articles. Third, we pursued a "snowball sampling" technique when checking the references of those articles, monographs, or chapters that were narrowed down as being relevant within the course of the systematic literature review. Though these three strategies (systematic search, random search, and snowball sampling) are by no means error-free, we believe that they offer adequate insight into the academic discourse on the topic, covering the most important aspects of that discourse.

In our first search strategy we relied on *keywords* that were culled from the above-given definitions of uncertainty/risk and alliances/networks. The application of these terms subsequently resulted in the inclusion or exclusion of publications in our literature review. As a result, we did not cover findings in this review that did not fit our definitions, such as those geared towards interpersonal networks (e.g., Ford & Mouzas, 2010). We did, however, consider these alternate perspectives to refine our comprehension of how uncertainty is practiced in alliances and networks.

In our search process, we used the following keywords as *inclusion criteria* with truncation characters: uncertain*, risk* and ambigu* in connection with allianc*, network*, federat*, joint venture*, associate*, interorg*, cluster*, interlocking director*, partnership*, coalition*, and collabor*. Using these keywords for an initial screening in the database-oriented search yielded 316,586 hits, which was too many to be considered for any kind of systematic analysis (cf. Table 7.2). Keywords are to some extent error-prone, as they are usually provided by the author(s) who might have had different perceptions than we did when considering uncertainty in connection with

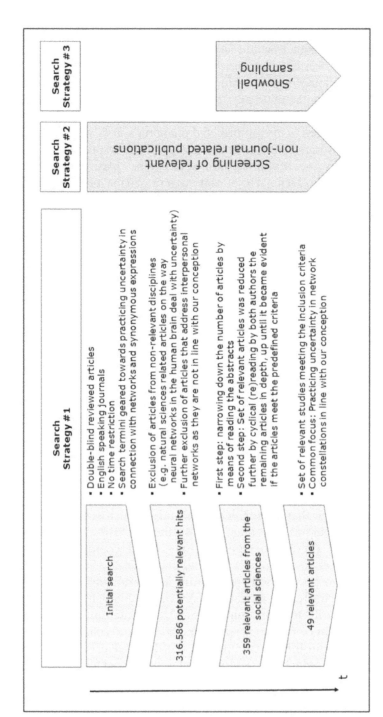

Figure 7.1. Review procedure.

networks. We tried to account for this challenge by making use of the two alternative search strategies as described above.

Table 7.2

Hits of the Systematic Literature Review (Initial Search and First Stage Hits)

Search termini #1	Search termini #2	Initial hits (limitation to abstract)	final hits to be reviewed (first stage, limitatinon to subject terms)
Uncertain* and...			
	network*	5521	49
	allianc*	2220	21
	federat*	612	8
	joint venture	274	10
	associat*	38311	26
	interorg*	875	21
	cluster*	9721	2
	interlocking director*	70	3
	partner*	3291	16
	coalition*	1358	3
Intermediate sum		*62253*	*159*
Risk* and ...			
	network*	11437	5
	allianc*	1374	18
	federat*	748	17
	joint venture	331	8
	associat*	202866	60
	interorg*	69	9
	cluster*	5531	26
	interlocking director*	0	0
	partner*	19161	12
	coalition*	659	6
Intermediate sum		*242176*	*161*
Ambigu* and ...			
	network*	1161	18
	allianc*	173	2
	federat*	55	0
	joint venture	19	0
	associat*	5620	10
	interorg*	27	6
	cluster*	421	0
	interlocking director*	1	0
	partner*	644	3
	coalition*	81	0
Intermediate sum		*8202*	*39*
Sum		*312631*	*359*

After checking the titles and, when appropriate, the abstracts, we narrowed the scope of our analysis down to 359 relevant articles. All these articles were then reviewed to determine whether they did, in fact, meet the criteria we established to achieve the aims of our research.

This restriction of the number of articles finally considered stemmed from the overall scope of the chapter. Specifically, we excluded a number of studies without an obvious focus on uncertainty, risk, or ambiguity in connection with alliances or networks. Given the more satisfactory result by keyword search, we proceeded to reduce our pool of results by means of the following *exclusion criteria*: first and foremost, we excluded articles from non-related fields of inquiry such as articles from the natural sciences on neural networks and the way the human brain reacts in connection with uncertainty (e.g., Gudykunst, Sodetani, & Sonoda, 1987). Moreover, we also excluded a number of studies in the social sciences that did not fit the criteria we set out above. For instance, intrapersonal networks (e.g., Ford & Mouzas, 2010) or interpersonal behavior (e.g., Gamson, 1961) or conceptual ambiguities (e.g., Knoben & Oerlemans, 2006) are not covered in this review. In order to increase the consistency and thoroughness of our findings, we surveyed previous reviews (e.g., Provan et al., 2007), special issues (e.g., Parkhe, Wasserman, & Ralston, 2006), monographs (e.g., Kilduff & Tsai, 2003), and edited volumes (e.g., Cropper et al., 2008) with similar foci in order to obtain the most comprehensive overview possible.

We also did not consider studies whose scope did not address uncertainty *and* alliances or networks and their close relatives. For instance, Drummond's (1995) title and abstract suggested that her study fits the scope of this review. However, on closer scrutiny this was not the case as uncertainty was not discussed in depth. In a similar vein, a number of studies mention uncertainty in terms of relational risks in networks, but did not discuss the role (and nature) of uncertainty per se (e.g., Powell, Koput, & Smith-Doerr, 1996). We also excluded articles that discussed the role of trust but made only fleeting reference to uncertainty (e.g., Sako & Helper, 1998; Zaheer & Venkatraman, 1995). Finally, and importantly, we did not include papers in the area of supply chain management because of its more applied, design-oriented nature. This decision is critical because otherwise we would have at least doubled our hits, especially because the field of global supply chain risk management has become quite popular since 9/11 and opened up to include not only calculable risks, but also generic uncertainties (see, for example, Brindley, 2004; Ritchie & Brindley, 2007; and in particular Paulsson, 2004, for a review).

We also eliminated studies from the field of technology and innovation management that are set in research and development intensive industries characterized by a high degree of uncertainty, which represents the raison d'etre for forming alliances and networks in the first place. However, uncertainty in these studies merely serves as information concerning the industry background. In particular, studies from the field of technology and innovation management rarely offer any further exploration or explanation of the governance approach to uncertainty (Robertson & Langlois, 1995; for an exception cf. Eisingerich, Bell, & Tracey, 2010).

Based on this procedure, we identified *49 journal articles* that matched our predefined search criteria and that constitute the *core of our review* (see Table 7.3). Because relatively few articles focused on uncertainty and networks, during the course of the review process we relaxed one initial selection criterion, in line with the definition offered above. Specifically, we considered articles on whole networks (Provan et al., 2007) that also focused on the core interest of this review, namely, uncertainty in alliances and networks, even though whole networks do not necessarily represent the empirical or conceptual phenomenon at stake. One example of such a study was by Beckman et al. (2004). These authors targeted primarily the organization and field levels of analysis, but they explicitly discussed how to manage uncertainty by broadening or deepening network relations.

The 49 articles were read in depth and classified with regard to 12 different criteria. Throughout the analysis, it turned out that not all criteria were actually central to our argument, which is why only a subset is presented for our final analysis. For instance, considering the different research settings proved to add no additional insights for our overarching observations, which is why we did not integrate it into the final table. Table 7.3 lists the 49 articles in alphabetical order.

RESULTS OF THE REVIEW

The review elucidates that previous research has provided reasonably detailed and convincing answers to many of our basic questions including the kinds of uncertainties considered (mainly as a result of a lack of knowledge), their measurement, the management approach taken or recommended, and the implications of the present state of research for the theory and practice of uncertainty in alliances and networks. Nevertheless, as we will show in our discussion following the review, the research on uncertainty has left some important questions unanswered.

Taking Stock of the Literature: Prima Facie Observations

As shown in Table 7.3, the number of articles (the number in brackets indicates the number of articles reviewed that address the respective criterion; multiple categorizations were permitted) addressing uncertainty (25) and risk/ambiguity (25) is equal, at least in terms of labeling these phenomena. In cases where the publications treated the key construct (uncertainty and/or risk or ambiguity) vaguely and no distinctive attribution was possible, we put the respective terms (Uncertainty, Risk, and Ambiguity) in brackets. In terms of the level of analysis, alliances

Table 7.3
Hits: List of the Literature Reviewed

Author/journal	Short title	Risk, ambiguity, uncertainty*	Level***	Status****	Uncertainty Types	Uncertainty Governance*****	Uncertainty practices	Network Relational/Social network analysis	Network Governance	Theoretical framework	Methodology Quantitative	Methodology Qualitative
Arts & Brush (2000), Journal of Economic Behavior & Organization	Asset specifity, uncertainty and relational norm	Risk	Alliance	Independent	Environmental uncertainty	Managing coordination cost	-	-	Buyer-supplier relationships	Transaction cost economics and relational exchange theories	+	-
Bayus-Beinensou, John & Venezra (2010), Journal of Economic Behavior & Organization	Uncertainty, networks and real options	(Risk)	Ego-network	Independent	Market uncertainty; technological uncertainty	Link formation or destruction	-	-	Strategic networks	Real options theory		Modeling
Baum, Rowley, Shipilov & Chuang (2005), Administrative Science Quarterly	Dancing with strangers	Risk	Alliance	Independent	Relational risk, partner selection uncertainty	Embedded or nonelectile	-	-	Syndicate	Learning theory; especially performance feedback models	+	-
Beckman, Heunschild & Phillips (2004), Organization Science	Friends or strangers?	Uncertainty	Field and organization	Independent	Market-level uncertainty, firm specific uncertainty	-	Broadening or deepening of network relations	-	Interlocks, alliance networks	Learning theory (exploitation and exploration)	+	-
Benssou & Anderson (1999), Organization Science	Buyer-supplier relations in industrial Markets	Uncertainty	Alliance	Independent	Technological uncertainty	Investing in supplier	-	-	Buyer-supplier relationships	Transaction cost economics	+	-
Burgers, Hill & Kim (1993), Strategic Management Journal	A theory of global strategic alliances	Uncertainty	Field	Independent	Demand and competitive uncertainty	Building a horizontal alliance	-	-	Alliance	Alliance	+	-

(Table 7.3 continued on next page)

Table 7.3 (Continued)

Hits: List of the Literature Reviewed

Author/ Journal	Short title	Risk, ambiguity, uncertainty*	Level**	Status***	Uncertainty			Relational/ Social network analysis	Network Governance	Theoretical framework	Methodology	
					Types	Governance****	Uncertainty practices				Quantitative	Qualitative
Camuffo, Furlan & Rettore (2007), Strategic Management Journal	Risk sharing in supplier relations	Risk Uncertainty	Alliance	Dependent and independent	Risk sharing regarding suppliers, supplier environmental uncertainty, supplier risk aversion and moral hazard	Risk allocation strategies concerning suppliers	-	-	Buyer-supplier relationships	Agency theory	+	
Carson, Madhok & Wu (2006), Academy of Management Journal	Uncertainty, opportunism, and governance	Uncertainty	Alliance	Independent	Uncertainty to be consisting of volatility and ambiguity	Designing (relational) contracts	-	-	Alliance	Transaction cost economics	+	-
Cui, Spielman & Kumar (1999), Journal of International Business Studies	Technological uncertainty; buyer preferences and supplier assurances	Uncertainty	Alliance	Independent	Technological uncertainty	Alliance structuring	-	-	Buyer-supplier relationships	Transaction cost economics and game theory	+	-
Das & Teng (1996), Journal of Management Studies	Risk types and inter-firm alliance structures	Risk	Alliance	Independent	Performance and relational risks	Equity and non-equity alliances	-	-	Equity and non-equity alliances	Alliance management, alternative to transaction cost economics		Conceptual
Das & Teng (2001a), Journal of Business and Psychology	Relational risk and its personal correlates in strategic alliances	Risk	Individual	Independent	Relational risk	Alliance structuring	-	-	Alliance	Trust approach, behavioral aspects	+	-
Das & Teng (2001b), Organization Studies	Trust control and risk in strategic alliances. An integrated framework	Risk	Alliance	Dependent and independent	Relational risk, performance risk	Alliance structuring	Coping via trust building and control mechanisms	Goodwill and competence trust, output, behavioral and social control	Strategic alliances, joint ventures, minority equity alliances and non-equity alliances	Alliance management		Conceptual
Delerue (2004), European Management Journal	Relational Risk Perception in European Biotechnology Alliances	Risk	Alliance	Independent	Relational risk	Alliance structuring	-	-	Alliance	Alliance management	+	-
de Man & Roijakkers (2009), Long Range Planning	Alliance governance	Risk	Alliance	Independent	Relational risk, performance risk	Alliance structuring	Coping via trust building and control mechanisms	-	Alliance	Alliance management	-	+

(Table 7.3 continued on next page)

Table 7.3 (Continued)
Hits: List of the Literature Reviewed

Author/ journal	Short title	Risk, own inquiry, uncertainty*	Level**	Status***	Uncertainty: Types	Uncertainty: Governance****	Uncertainty: Uncertainty practices	Network: Relational/ Social network analysis	Network: Governance	Theoretical framework	Methodology: Quantitative	Methodology: Qualitative
Dickson & Weaver (1997), Academy of Management Journal	Environmental determinants and individual-level moderators of alliance use	(Uncertainty)	Alliance	Independent	General (effect uncertainty), technological, 'issue', international and regarding future growth and profits	Alliance use	-	-	Alliance	Unclear, emphasizing individual differences	+	-
Bærgerich, Bell & Tracey (2010), Research Policy	How can clusters sustain performance?	Uncertainty	Cluster	Moderating	Market turbulence, competitive intensity, and technological turbulence	Network strength and openness	-	Clusters as networks	-	Network embeddedness theory	+	(+)
Gardet & Ambrister (2012), Organization Studies	Bridging uncertainty in management consulting	Uncertainty	Field	Independent	Institutional uncertainty and transactional uncertainty	-	Coping, but focus on sources of uncertainty	Regional networks, public and networked reputation, experience-based trust	-	Network embeddedness theory	-	-
Grabowski & Roberts (1999), Organization Science	Risk mitigation in virtual organizations	(Risk)	Network	Independent	Risk propensity of virtual organizations	Programs and practices of High Reliability Organizations, including prioritization of safety and reliability, redundancy in personnel and	-	-	Virtual organizations	Theory of High Reliability Organizations		Conceptual
Holma, Verhaus & Tourism (2002), International Journal of Production Research	Understanding mixed uncertainty in supplier networks	Risk	Alliance	Dependent	Transactional uncertainty	Strategies on how to reduce uncertainty within alliances	-	-	Buyer-supplier relationships	Transaction cost economics		+
Hirsch (1994), Administrative Science Quarterly	How much is that company worth?	(Risk)	Alliance	Independent	Valuation uncertainty	Interlocks	-	-	Interlocks and alliances with Professional Service Firms	Diverse streams	-	+
Haunschild & Miner (1997), Administrative Science Quarterly	Modes of interorganizational imitation	(Risk)	Alliance	Moderating	Transaction uncertainty, partner uncertainty	Use of advisor on acquisition	Imitation, in particular frequency-based imitation	-	Use vs. Non-use	Neo-institutionalism, resource dependence theory, network theory	-	+

(Table 7.3 continued on next page)

208

Table 7.3 (Continued)

Hits: List of the Literature Reviewed

| Author / journal | Short title | Risk, ambiguity, uncertainty* | Level** | Status*** | Uncertainty | | | Network | | Theoretical framework | Methodology | |
					Type	Governance****	Uncertainty practice	Relational/ Social network analysis	Governance		Quantitative	Qualitative
Heide & John (1990), Journal of Marketing Research	Alliances in industrial purchasing	Risk	Alliance	Independent	Volume unpredictability, technological unpredictability and performance ambiguity	Loose or tight coupling of relations	·	·	Buyer-supplier relationships	Transaction cost economics	·	
Hoetker (2005), Strategic Management Journal	How much you know versus how well I know you	(Risk)	Alliance	Independent	Technological uncertainty	Network or hierarchy		·	Buyer-supplier relationships	Transaction cost economics, relational and capability approaches combined	·	
Huxham & Vangen (2000), Human Relations	Ambiguity, complexity and dynamics in the membership of collaborations	Ambiguity	Network	Independent	Ambiguity in membership and status and ambiguity in representations	Designing collaborations, in particular regarding membership		·	Alliances and other types of organizational collaborations	Collaborative advantage		Action research
Joshi & Stump (1999), Journal of the Academy of Marketing Science	The contingent effect of specific asset investments on joint action in manufacturer supplier relationships	Uncertainty	Alliance	Independent	Decision-making uncertainty	Joint action arrangements (as a bilateral governance tool)	·	·	Buyer-supplier relationships	Transaction cost economics and relational exchange theories	·	
Kim, Yamada & Kim (2008), Decision Sciences	Search for alternatives and collaboration with incumbents	Uncertainty	Alliance	Moderating	Technological and volume uncertainty	Searching behaviors with regard to incumbent suppliers	·	·	Buyer-supplier relationships	Exit-voice-loyalty approach	·	
Koka, Madhavan & Prescott (2006), Academy of Management Review	The evolution of interfirm networks	(Uncertainty)	Ego network, whole network	Independent	Environmental uncertainty, apply Milliken's (1987) typology	Network change in terms of the creation and dissolution (network churning and network expansion)	·	·	Alliances and networks	Theory of network change		Conceptual
Lang & Lockhart (1990), Academy of Management Journal	Increased environmental uncertainty and change in board linkage patterns	Risk	Alliance, dyadic and triadic	Independent	Environmental, in particular competitive uncertainty	Interlocks	·	·	Interlocks	Resource dependence	·	

209

(Table 7.3 continued on next page)

Table 7.3 (Continued)

Hits: List of the Literature Reviewed

Author / Journal	Short title	Risk, ambiguity, uncertainty*	Level**	Status***	Uncertainty — Types	Uncertainty — Governance****	Uncertainty — practices	Network — Relational/ Social network analysis	Network — Governance	Theoretical framework	Methodology — Quantitative	Methodology — Qualitative
Lee, Yeung & Cheng (2009). International Journal of Production Economics	Supplier alliances and environmental uncertainty	Uncertainty	Alliance	Independent	Technological change and market uncertainty as two dimensions of environmental uncertainty	Joint financial and relation-specific investments	-	-	Alliance	Transaction cost economics and strategic management with conflicting propositions	-	-
Li, Boulding & Staelin (2010). Journal of the Academy of Marketing Science	General alliance experience, uncertainty, and marketing governance mode choice	(Risk)	Alliance	Independent	Market uncertainty and alliance-specific uncertainty (cultural distance, geographic scope, alliance partner experience)	Equity or non-equity alliances	-	-	Alliance	Transaction cost economics, knowledge based view, real options approach	-	-
Li, Chen, Shir & Mai (2010). Long Range Planning	Inter-network co-evolution	Uncertainty	Dyadic and network	Independent	Environmental uncertainty (cf. Koka et al 2006)	Network change in terms of its creation and dissolution (network churning and network expansion)	-	-	Alliances and networks	Theory of network change, complemented by mechanisms of inter-network co-evolution	-	-
Luo (2005). Academy of Management Journal	How important are shared perceptions of procedural justice in cooperative alliances?	Uncertainty	Alliance	Moderating	Structural (objective) environmental uncertainty	None, only alliance profitability	-	-	Alliance	Justice theory	-	-
Mizruchi (2000). International Journal of Organizational Analysis	Uncertainty in selecting alliance partners	(Uncertainty)	Alliance	Independent	Selection uncertainty, comprising uncertainty about technological aspects, behavioral aspects and commercial success	-	Reducing by relational, internal and contextual mechanisms	-	Alliance	Network-embeddedness theory	-	-
Noguine (2008). Public Administration Review	Learning under Uncertainty	Uncertainty	Network	Dependent	Substantive, strategic and institutional uncertainty	-	Develop learning strategies in particular standard operating procedures to reduce uncertainty	-	Alliance	Learning approaches	-	-

(Table 7.3 continued on next page)

210

Table 7.3 (Continued)

Hits: List of the Literature Reviewed

| Author / journal | Short title | Risk, ambiguity, uncertainty* | Level** | Status*** | Uncertainty | | | Relational / Network | | Theoretical framework | Methodology | |
					Types	Governance****	Uncertainty practice	Social network analysis	Governance		Quantitative	Qualitative
Nooteboom, Berger & Noorderhaven (1997), Academy of Management Journal	Effects of trust and governance on relational risk	Risk	Alliance	Dependent	Two dimensions of relational risk: size and probability of loss	Relational governance	-	-	Buyer-seller relationship	Transaction cost economics	-	-
Podolny (1994), Administrative Science Quarterly	Market uncertainty and the social character of economic exchange	Uncertainty	Field	Independent	Market uncertainty	Alliance investment related exchanges	-	Status and past experiences	-	Market sociology	-	-
Podolny (2001), American Journal of Sociology	Networks as the pipes and prisms of the market	Uncertainty	Field and alliance	Independent	Ego-altercentric market uncertainties	-	-	Markets as networks	-	Market sociology	-	-
Poppo, Zhou & Zenger (2008), Journal of Management Studies	Examining the conditional limits of relational governance	Risk	Alliance	Moderating	Performance ambiguity	Relational governance	-	-	Alliance	Transaction cost economics and agency theory	-	-
Provan (1982), Academy of Management Journal	Interorganizational linkages and influence over decision making	(Risk)	Alliance	Independent, but only implicitly	Generic uncertainty	Alliance with hub organization or others	-	-	Relations between agencies	Resource dependence approach	-	-
Ranger, Samii & van Wassenhove (2005), Academy of Management Review	Competitive partnerships	(Risk)	Alliance	Moderating	Not specified	Public Private Partnerships	-	-	Public Private Partnerships	Transaction cost economics and externalities theory	-	Conceptual
Santoro & McGill (2005), Strategic Management Journal	The effect of uncertainty and asset co-specialization on governance in biotechnology alliances	Risk	Alliance	Independent	Behavioral uncertainties (partner and task uncertainties) and technological uncertainty	Alliance governance: licensing, non-equity, minority equity, equity joint venture	-	-	Alliance	Transaction cost economics vs real option approach	-	-
Stark (1996), American Journal of Sociology	Recombinant property in East European capitalism	Uncertainty	Field and network	Independent	Uncertainty stemming from economic transformations	Ownership networks	Diversifying assets, redefining and recombining resources	-	Interorganizational ownership ties	Policy and sociological oriented perspective on interorganizational networks	-	-

(Table 7.3 continued on next page)

211

Table 7.3 (Continued)

Hits: List of the Literature Reviewed

Author/ journal	Shortdesc	Risk, ambiguity, uncertainty*	Level**	Source***	Uncertainty Types	Governance****	Uncertainty practices	Relational/ Social network analysis	Network Governance	Theoretical framework	Methodology Quantitative	Qualitative
Stark & Vedres (2006), American Journal of Sociology	Socialness of network spaces	Uncertainty	Field and network	Independent	Uncertainty stemming from economic transformations	Ownership networks	Usage of network resources/ sequencing of network formation	-	Interorganizational ownership ties	Structural network analytical approach	-	
Steensma & Corley (2000), Academy of Management Journal	On the performance of technology-sourcing partnerships	(Risk)	Alliance	Independent	Technological uncertainty, predominately generated by two factors, commercial uncertainty and dynamism of technology	Type of alliance (licensing agreement, joint development and acquisitions)	-	-	Alliance	Knowledge based view	-	
Steensma, Marino, Weaver & Dickson (2000), Academy of Management Journal	The influence of national culture on the formation of technology alliances by entrepreneurial firms	(Uncertainty)	Alliance	Independent	National and technological uncertainty (being similar to relational and performance risk respectively), moderating role of uncertainty avoidance as a property of national culture	Alliance use vs. Equity ties	-	-	Alliance	Transaction cost economics vs. resource dependence approach	-	
Sutcliffe & Zaheer (1998), Strategic Management Journal	Uncertainty in the transaction environment	Uncertainty	Alliance	Independent	Primary (i.e. stemming from external sources), competitive and supplier uncertainty	Decision making with regard to vertical integration	-	-	Alliance	Transaction cost economics, contingency approach and resource dependence (however, all of them implicitly given the focus on environmental uncertainty)	-	
Thomas & Trevino (1993), Journal of Management Studies	Information processing in strategic alliance building	Risk	Alliance	Moderating	Risk and equivocality/ambiguity		Knowledge search, design of knowledge-processing	-	Federations, joint ventures and joint programs	Knowledge-processing perspective	-	
Vercheva (2004), Managerial and Decision Economics	Behavioral uncertainty and investment in cooperative relationships	Risk	Alliance	Independent	Uncertainty about benefits and preferences	Cooperative relationship	-	-	Alliance	Decision theory		Formal modeling

(Table 7.3 continued on next page)

Table 7.3 (Continued)

Hits: List of the Literature Reviewed

Author / Journal	Short title	Risk, ambiguity, uncertainty[*]	Level[**]	Status[***]	Uncertainty				Relational / Network		Theoretical framework	Methodology	
					Types	Governance[****]	Uncertainty practices	Social network analysis	Governance			Quantitative	Qualitative
Walker & Weber (1984), Administrative Science Quarterly	A transaction cost approach to make-or-buy decisions	Risk	Alliance	Independent	Volume and technological uncertainty	Make-or-buy decisions in the face of uncertainty	-	-	Buyer-supplier relationships	Transaction cost economics	-	-

[*] Words in parentheses indicate that the respective contribution has no clear focus upon risk, ambiguity or uncertainty

[**] Relevant levels are organization, alliance, ego-network, whole network, cluster, field (incl. market, industry etc.)

[***] Status: independent, moderating or dependent variable

[****] Governance and discussion about early partnerships, joint ventures etc. all seen as attempts to deal with uncertainty

213

among two organizations dominate the discourse, with 35 entries. The field (6), network (9) or cluster (1), and individual (3) levels of analysis were addressed comparatively infrequently. What is more, uncertainty or risk were overwhelmingly considered as an independent (39) variable, and much less frequently as a dependent (5) or moderating variable (7). By and large, both uncertainty and risk stem from external sources, be it related to the market (e.g., Podolny, 1994), technologies (e.g., Eisingerich et al., 2010), or the respective partners themselves (e.g., Haunschild & Miner, 1997). Overall, however, the labels used by the respective authors were quite inconsistent and confusing, making it difficult to determine which specific sources or types of either uncertainty or risk and ambiguity they addressed.

Moreover, governance issues clearly dominate the discourse (39); in only a few cases was the discussion geared towards how uncertainty was actually addressed, or what we call "practicing uncertainty" (11). Those studies dealing with practicing uncertainty concentrate on the alliance or network partners, primarily in terms of trust-building mechanisms (e.g., Das & Teng, 2001b) or how to broaden or deepen network relationships (e.g., Beckman et al., 2004). In these studies, trust is typically viewed as a social lubricant serving to overcome the problems faced by incomplete knowledge. This observation echoes the finding that the majority of publications used theoretical approaches that favor considering risk and uncertainty in alliances or the form of dyadic relations as the key conceptual foundation, like transaction cost economics (18). Finally, the majority of the studies of this review utilized quantitative methods. From the set of 49 papers, qualitative methods were employed only nine times, while five articles we reviewed were conceptual pieces and two contributed to the literature by modeling.

Disentangling the Status of Uncertainty

What is the true object of the studies under scrutiny: uncertainty, risk, or some other close relative? At one extreme, studies could focus clearly on Knightian uncertainty and differentiate it sharply from calculable risk. At the other extreme, they could simply and vaguely deal with uncertainty, risk, or ambiguity or some mixture of these. Our review of alliance/network research shows that both occurred, although the latter approach seems to dominate. For instance, Beckman and colleagues (2004) did not differentiate but addressed uncertainty as "the difficulty firms have in predicting the future, when it comes from incomplete knowledge" (Beckman et al.,

2004, p. 260). Although they did not explicitly refer to Knight (1921), their view is consistent with our conception of uncertainty. Representative of studies that explicitly differentiate between both constructs are those by Stark and colleagues (1996; Stark & Vedres, 2006) who focused explicitly on the uncertainty due to the turbulence stemming from the economic transformation in post-socialistic Hungary. In contrast, Nooteboom and colleagues (1997) made use of the risk conception as set out above, analyzing trust- and risk-related issues from a transaction cost perspective concerning customer relations of suppliers in the electronics industry.

Regarding the formal status of uncertainty (or one of its relatives) as "variable," the choice is between independent, dependent, or moderating. As already indicated, most studies conceptualize uncertainty as an *independent* variable (see Table 7.3). An example of this is the study by Beckman and colleagues (2004) who analyzed how an interorganizational network and its members deepen or broaden their relationships depending on both market and firm specific uncertainty. Another example is Podolny's (1994) inquiry related to interorganizational investments, which varied in the face of uncertainty. Only five studies considered uncertainty as a *dependent* variable. For instance, Das and Teng (2001a, 2001b) not only looked at the influence of risk perception on trust and control, but also at the influence of the latter on the former. Distinguishing, therefore, between goodwill and competence trust on the one hand and between behavior, output, and social control on the other led them to a dozen detailed propositions about these relationships. Nooteboom et al. (1997) also studied trust as a dependent variable, investigating the effects of trust and governance in alliances on relational risk. So too did Moynihan (2008), who found that organizations could manage uncertainty by means of developing learning strategies; in particular, standard operating procedures that serve to reduce uncertainty.

At least six other studies considered uncertainty as a *moderator* variable. For instance, Haunschild and Miner (1997) analyzed the process of choosing an investment bank representative for advising investment decisions based on neo-institutional and learning conceptions. Their results highlight the role of uncertainty, which they argued could facilitate imitation. Another study representative of this strand is that of Eisingerich and colleagues (2010), who investigated eight regional clusters in different industries and countries. They found that the performance of these clusters was contingent on the strength and openness of network relationships within these clusters. More specifically, they discovered that as environmental uncertainty grew, the positive effects of network strength on cluster performance tended to decrease while the positive effects of network openness tended to increase.

Types of Uncertainties and Their Measurement

As stated in the introduction, from the beginning organizational research has been concerned with two types of uncertainty; external (e.g., Duncan, 1972) and internal (e.g., March & Simon, 1958). Regarding external or environmental uncertainty, the typology of Milliken (1987) has gained some prominence in the literature (e.g., Dickson & Weaver, 1997; Koka, Madhavan, & Prescott, 2006). Milliken (1987) distinguished three types of (perceived) environmental uncertainty: state, effect, and response. *State uncertainty* is defined as a situation when managers are not confident that they understand what the major events or trends in the organizational environment are, and unable to estimate the likelihood that particular events or changes will occur (cf. also Halinen, Salmi, & Havila, 1999). *Effect uncertainty* reflects what has been discussed elsewhere under the notion of causal ambiguity and refers to the inability of managers to predict the impact of a future state of the environment on the organization. Finally, *response uncertainty* describes their inability to predict the likely consequence of a chosen response to assessing state and effect uncertainties. These three types of perceived environmental uncertainty can be effectively measured and meaningfully distinguished (Ashill & Jobber, 2010).

Beyond Milliken's typology, several other types of uncertainties (or risks) have been considered by research on alliances or networks:

- *External to the network*: Market uncertainty (Lee, Yeung, & Cheng, 2009; Podolny, 1994, 2001) or, more specifically, demand uncertainty (Burgers, Hill & Kim, 1993); technological uncertainty as characteristic of an industry (Hoetker, 2005; Lee et al., 2009; Santoro & McGill, 2005; Steensma & Corley, 2000; Steensma, Marino, Weaver, & Dickson, 2000) and uncertainty avoidance as a property of national cultures (Steensma et al., 2000); competitive uncertainty as another dimension of environmental uncertainty (Burgers et al., 1993; Lang & Lockhart, 1990).

- *Internal to the network*: Task uncertainty or technological unpredictability as translations of technological uncertainty on the alliance or network level (Heide & John, 1990; Santoro & McGill, 2005; Walker & Weber, 1984); volume uncertainty as a respective translation of demand uncertainty, possibly complemented by performance ambiguity (Heide & John, 1990; Walker & Weber, 1984), the latter being similar to partner uncertainty (Haunschild & Miner, 1997; Santoro & McGill, 2005), behavioral risk (Vetschera, 2004), relational risk (Das & Teng, 1996, 2001a, 2001b), strategic and in particular institutional uncertainty (Koppenjan & Klijn, 2004; Moynihan, 2008), or supply uncertainty, this latter notion being popular in the literature on supply chain (risk) management.

In the studies surveyed, uncertainty, external as well as internal to networks, has been either simply *assumed* (e.g., Burgers et al., 1993; Stark, 1996; Stark & Vedres, 2006; and most studies of innovation and technology management) or *inferred* from the variation of some other variables (e.g., the volatility of an industry in terms of financial performance in Lang and Lochhart's 1990 study of board interlocks in the airline industry, or sales and profits in the industry in which an alliance participates, as in Luo's 2005 study of cross-cultural alliances in China). Most often, however, perceived uncertainty has been *measured* directly by asking managers about the market or other dimensions of environmental uncertainty or about partner-specific or other dimensions of network uncertainty. Hoetker (2005), for instance, represents this important line of inquiry when he studied the electronics industry, inquiring about notebook computer manufacturers' sourcing decisions for flat-panel displays. He conceptualized perceived uncertainty as "industry perceptions of the advance beyond existing technology that each innovation required" (Hoetker, 2005, p. 85).

Networks as Relations or Governance: Level of Analysis

The notion of network may either signify a relational perspective that tries to explain interorganizational reality by analyzing the structure of networks of relationships among organizations (i.e., who is connected to whom and in what ways), or a governance perspective focusing on how the relationship is coordinated and managed to achieve some goal (Grabher & Powell, 2004). As our review shows, only a few studies that have examined uncertainty conceptualized networks from a relational perspective and/or adopted structural network analysis (cf. e.g., Podolny, 1994; or Stark & Vedres, 2006) as a research methodology. Most followed the governance approach, highlighting the particular nature of the relationship itself (e.g., contractual, equity-based, or trust-based, etc.) rather than the overall structural pattern of the network (e.g., in terms of density or centralization). Most of these uncertainty studies focused not on multilateral networks, but on alliances and related constellations, either on a dyadic or ego-centric level of analysis. In particular, there have been relatively few studies that not only examine the governance and overall structure of whole networks (cf. Human & Provan, 2000; Provan & Kenis, 2008) but that also considered the effectiveness of the respective forms in dealing with uncertainty.

While alliances and networks can be studied at the levels of dyads, triads, more complex whole networks or organizational fields, research seldom extends beyond the dyadic level of analysis as our review shows. For instance, in their study of employing investment banks as consultants in the case of planned acquisitions, Haunschild and Miner (1997) focused on building up and maintaining a dyadic relationship; in this case, between the acquirer and the investment bank. Despite this predominant dyadic focus, at least seven of the papers we reviewed studied uncertainty at the network level of analysis. One example is the research by Bajeux-Besnainou, Joshi, and Vonortas (2010), who investigated the relationship of uncertainty and networks from a real option perspective and explained, among other things, why networks often display a hub-and-spokes architecture with small firms often sinking resources into relatively higher risk return investment projects. Huxham and Vangen (2000) also examined uncertainty at the network level of analysis focusing on what they call ambiguity in membership, status, and representation. Moynihan (2008) investigated uncertainty in his analysis of a crisis response network consisting of eight key actors, all public agencies. As pointed out above, this is one of the few studies that considered uncertainty as a dependent variable. Still another study of whole networks was a conceptual paper by Koka et al. (2006), who addressed the issue of network change (in terms of network expansion, network churning, network strengthening and network shrinking) in the face of different levels of environmental uncertainty and resource munificence. Lin, Chen, Sher, and Mei (2010) applied this same concept of network change in their longitudinal case study of two networks in the Central Taiwanese Science Park. They discovered the additional mechanism of "internetwork co-evolution" that, as an antecedent as much as a process outcome, linked changes in one network to those in another, providing an additional level of uncertainty coping capacity.

The studies of the transformation of interorganizational ownership networks in post-socialist Hungary by Stark and colleagues (e.g., Stark, 1996; Stark & Vedres, 2006) also addressed the structures of whole networks. They did not measure environmental uncertainty, however, but took it for granted based on the uncertain conditions organizations had to deal with during those transformation process. A few other studies addressed the cluster (e.g., Eisingerich et al., 2010) or field (e.g., Beckman et al., 2004) level and showed that even at aggregated levels of analysis, collaborations merit attention as they fostered coping with uncertainty. These studies also demonstrated that, depending upon whether firm-specific or market-level uncertainty prevails, firms tend to form new relationships with new partners for exploration and form additional relationships with existing partners for exploitation purposes (Harryson, Dudkowski, & Stern, 2008; Koza & Lewin, 1998; March, 1991; Vanhaverbeke, Gilsing, Beerkens, & Duysters, 2009).

Dealing With Uncertainty: Beyond a Governance Approach?

Almost all the studies reviewed focused on contractual or governance issues when it comes to dealing with uncertainty in alliances and networks. Typically, licensing, non-equity, and equity relations (the latter often including joint ventures) were distinguished on a market-hierarchy continuum (e.g., König, 2009; Santoro & McGill, 2005). Other research also focused on governance issues and looked at the influence of uncertainty on interorganizational ownership networks (e.g., Stark, 1996; Stark & Vedres, 2006) or board interlocks (e.g., Beckman et al., 2004; Lang & Lockhart, 1990).

Some of the studies reviewed, however, went beyond a pure contractual or governance approach. Stark and colleagues (Stark, 1996; Stark & Vedres, 2006), for instance, analyzed ownership structures among Hungarian companies over time subsequent to economic transformation stemming from the fall of the iron curtain. They elucidated how recombining resources fostered network formation. Das and Teng (2001b), based on their analysis of the relationships between trust, control, and risk, proposed a number of trust-building techniques and control mechanisms for reducing relational and performance risks in the face of a lack of knowledge in different types of alliances, which go well beyond the traditional governance approach (see also de Man & Roijakkers, 2009). Mitsuhashi (2002) explicitly addressed uncertainty in selecting alliance partners, discussing the possibilities of reducing this kind of uncertainty through relational, internal, and contextual mechanisms (cf. also Meuleman, Lockett, Manigart, & Wright, 2010). Relational mechanisms address the practice of firms embedding economic transactions in pre-existing or ongoing alliances and networks of personal relationships. While this mechanism, as well as the mechanism of relying on the reputation of the potential partner (regarding R&D competence and alliance history), is still quite close to the governance approach, using boundary spanning more consciously and building internal capability in the form of accumulating collaborative knowledge at the individual and organizational levels are significantly closer to a practice perspective (see below). Finally, Grabowski and Roberts (1999), while interested in the risk propensity in virtual organizations, that is, *temporary* networks of organizations, and basing their insights on research on high reliability organizations, addressed several uncertainty practices related to organizational structuring and design. These included the prioritization of safety goals, the intensification of communication at interfaces, the development of a decentralized yet shared and trusted culture of reliability, and the building up of redundancies (see also Staber & Sydow, 2002).

Behind the Curtain: Theory and Methodology

Because most of the research reviewed focused on alliance dyads, it comes as no surprise that transaction cost and resource dependence theory have been the dominant theoretical perspectives underlying discussion of uncertainty and risk in this domain. Some studies have even combined these two perspectives (e.g., Steensma et al., 2000) or included a third, like real option theory (e.g., König, 2009; Santoro & McGill, 2005). While studies of uncertainty in alliances and networks started out by using a single theory, the use of several theories seems to have become more common (see also Hoetker, 2005, for another example). Despite this trend towards a multi-theoretical approach regarding uncertainty in alliance/network research, a relational perspective that captures the complexity of networks has seldom been adopted. This is unfortunate because key aspects of the relational structure of a multi-organizational network, such as its centralization, density, or fragmentation, as well as an organization's specific position within the network (i.e., its centrality), are likely to have significant importance as endogenous sources of uncertainty for organizational participants. These and other relational network characteristics are likely to have considerable implications for practicing uncertainty, both relative to others in the network and to those external to the network.

In terms of methodology, quantitative studies dominate, with relatively little qualitative and ethnographic research on uncertainty in alliances or networks. Since alliances and networks are likely to be even more complex than large single organizations, qualitative approaches may be especially useful in developing a deeper understanding of the role of uncertainty in these settings. For instance, Thomas and Klebe Trevino (1993) offered an early but highly informative account of how deeper insights into complex organizational phenomena can be obtained by combining traditional data collection (e.g., interviews, archival data) with participating in strategy meetings and presentations. Such an approach has also been called for more recently by researchers interested in process (Langley, 1999) and practice phenomena (Feldman & Orlikowski, 2011; Jarzabkowski, 2003, 2008; Sydow & Windeler, 2003).

DISCUSSION: OPPORTUNITIES FOR RESEARCH

Reflecting on the findings, we suggest that three gaps in previous research on uncertainty in alliances and networks merit attention. These offer ample opportunities for research. First, most of the studies included in our review explicitly or at least implicitly target exclusively alliances consisting of interorganizational dyads (labeled as "Alliance(s)" in Table

7.3). While this approach has resulted in some significant advances in the study of uncertainty, a dyadic focus limits an understanding of how such multi-organizational arrangements as networks of three or more partner organizations (Grabher & Powell, 2004), or whole networks (Provan et al., 2007) confront and respond to uncertainty. We argue that this broader network perspective is often critical, as networks differ significantly from dyadic relations in a number of important ways. In arrangements of three or more partners, relationships assume a different social quality and are far more complex. For instance, structural holes may occur where there is the possibility of a tertius gaudens (Simmel, 1950), when an actor who benefits from maintaining a broker role can be positioned between two unconnected organizations, thereby having access to two different unrelated sources of knowledge (Burt, 1992; Müller-Seitz & Sydow, 2012). This is a clear example of how an organizational actor can practice uncertainty in a way that is not considered in traditional research on alliances. In addition, the complexities of managing in a multi-organizational context where collaboration is valued and goals are shared may well produce its own uncertainty, even if it helps to overcome knowledge barriers. Such uncertainty can certainly occur in dyadic alliances. However, since only two organizations are involved, the practice issues of addressing uncertainty are likely to be far less complex than in networks involving multiple organizations. Hence, targeting the network level of analysis, which occurred in only nine of the studies we reviewed, seems especially important for understanding how organizations actually practice uncertainty in alliances and networks.

One example of such a network-focused approach is the study, referred to earlier, by Moynihan (2008). This author elucidated how partners engaged with each other in a crisis response network dealing with animal disease outbreaks. Moynihan's network went beyond a dyadic perspective, not only because more than two participating organizations were considered (eight), but also because of the multilateral nature of their relationships, as members tried to help each other by developing joint standard operating procedures, creating a reflexively agreed-upon interorganizational division of labor while pursuing joint objectives (Sydow & Windeler, 2003). This was done to develop a network memory that fostered the joint storage and retrieval of knowledge collectively gathered and utilized in the case of the outbreak and subsequent containment of Newcastle disease, a highly contagious and generally fatal disease among poultry. Moreover, this specific case is important for our discussion as it represents horizontal cooperation. The discourse on knowledge and alliances is usually dominated by vertical relationships (e.g., Kim, Yamada, & Kim, 2008), like supply-chain networks or, in more general terms, by buyer-seller constellations where there is a quasi-hierarchical relationship among the engaged organizations. In these situations, the dominant buyer or supplier organization is typically able to force its partners to comply with its will, thus minimizing uncertainty in a way that is unavailable to organizations in horizontal networks. Currently, our knowledge of how horizontal and more heterarchical networks (Hedlund, 1986) operate in the face of uncertainty is limited. Nevertheless, due to the existence and relevance of such complex networks in praxis (Huxham & Vangen, 2000; Provan et al., 2007), analyzing uncertainty in these horizontal interorganizational constellations might prove especially beneficial (Boari & Lipparini, 1999; Müller-Seitz, 2012).

Second, most empirical research on alliances and networks relies on quantitative and theory-testing procedures focusing on whether or not a relationship exists and what is the extent of knowledge awareness. This work typically relies on large empirical data bases and samples, examining strategic alliances, and then making assumptions about how the existence of these alliances reduces uncertainty. Thus, the depth, extent, or frequency of interorganizational connections, or "interorganizational collaborations" (Huxham & Vangen, 2005; Ring & Van de Ven, 1994), and the subsequent actions and activities engaged in by partners to address uncertainty, are seldom analyzed. For instance, Hoetker (2005) made use of abstract categories (e.g., duration in years) and data capturing knowledge-related issues (like patent files) to depict the nature of the relationship between organizations. Given the predominance of this methodological approach, typically based on use of secondary sources, empirical studies have seldom offered a fine-grained picture of how more intensive interorganizational collaborations unfold over time, including how and when managers practice uncertainty and why.

One of the few exceptions to this common approach is the study by Mitsuhashi (2002), who conducted an in-depth case study to generate knowledge about how alliance partners seek to reduce selection uncertainty. Grounded in the data from his analysis, he pointed to the role of different mechanisms in coping with this specific form of partner-related uncertainty, elaborating on the practices these organizations employ—namely, relational (e.g., making use of pre-existing ties), internal (e.g., boundary spanning) and contextual mechanisms (e.g., the reputation of the potential partners). We suggest that comprehending the way different actors actually deal with uncertainty in interorganizational collaborations, as studied by Mitsuhashi, would be beneficial, as it would serve to offer a more grounded picture of what managers are actually doing once a relationship has been formed.

Third, and ensuing from the first two observations, approaches that adopt a governance perspective on how alliances and networks deal with uncertainty have dominated the literature. Most of the studies in our review have addressed governance related questions, with the presumption that solving governance issues will help alliances and networks to deal with uncertainty and/or risk. In the majority of these studies, designing the most adequate contractual format is deemed to alleviate if not prevent problems regarding uncertainty due to the lack of sufficient knowledge, as the study by Carson and colleagues (2006) demonstrated. In a similar vein, Santoro and McGill (2005) addressed licensing and equity issues that served to tackle the risk imbued in alliances and networks. It is not surprising that most of the studies that have adopted a governance perspective on uncertainty have been informed by transaction cost economics. Hence, the research object, method, and theoretical lens appear to make it almost inevitable that scholars who base their work on the transaction cost approach will be heavily concerned with governance issues, with the management of knowledge under conditions of uncertainty being discussed and analyzed predominantly as a contractual or trust-related issue (e.g., Das & Teng, 2001c).

We submit that complementing these studies—but not substituting them—with a practice perspective (Giddens, 1984; Jarzabkowski, 2003, 2008; Schatzki, Knorr Cetina, & von Savigny, 2001) would redirect the research agenda. Studying practices means paying attention to recurrent activities that are guided by structures, including government structures, and reproducing or transforming these structures (Feldman & Orlikowski, 2011; Giddens, 1984; Sydow & Windeler, 2003; Whittington, 2011). When studying uncertainty practices in alliances and networks, the focus shifts from the investigation of formal or informal governance mechanisms and/or cause-and-effect chains to the recurrent and dynamic activities of actually monitoring, coping, or even inducing uncertainty. In addition, prevention practices like the intentional preservation of organizational slack or emphasizing loosely over tightly coupled network relations (Staber & Sydow, 2002) can be more readily recognized and understood. These types of practice approaches are important because they are mechanisms that enable organizations in alliances or networks to buffer against unexpected challenges.

Summing up, adopting the complementary ideas set out above and incorporating them into research agendas on alliances and network uncertainty would mean moving from a narrow focus on dyads to a broader network perspective, from a governance perspective to one based on practice related issues, and from quantitative deductive studies to research that would require more process-sensitive, often qualitative methods. We believe these are steps that are worth pursuing as a way of broadening and extending how uncertainty is considered in relations between and among organizations.

CONCLUSION: FROM GOVERNANCE TO PRACTICE

The objective of this chapter was to review the literature dealing with the way uncertainty, primarily due to insufficient knowledge of the environment, affects and is affected by alliances and networks, identify research gaps, and discuss the ensuing implications for future research. At this point, we speculate in more detail about what a switch from the dominant governance perspective to a practice perspective on uncertainty in alliances and networks may entail.

Above all, a "practice-turn" (Schatzki et al., 2001) would allow researchers to study in detail how organizational actors embedded in complex and collaborative networks of relationships actually deal with uncertainty. This could be uncertainty that, due to a lack of relevant knowledge, exists at the outset, when a single relationship or a network of relationships is created, or develops during the course of the process, either in the network's external environment or within the network itself. The kinds of uncertainty addressed could cover a whole continuum marked at one extreme by genuine uncertainty ("unknown unknowns") in the Knightian (1921) sense, and at the other extreme, by risk that is much better understood and more or less calculable ("unknown knowns"). Actual risk calculations could provide a rationale for the means to organize and an approach to practice uncertainty reduction and management.

Complemented by the study of other "uncertainty practices" (see above) that could also do justice to the temporality intrinsic in dealing with uncertainty (Das & Teng, 2001c, p. 520), the analytic depth of the sort of practice focus we are recommending could and should go well beyond distinguishing, broadening, and deepening network relations (Beckmann et al., 2004) or noting the availability of redundant ties and slack resources (Staber & Sydow, 2002). Instead, it should unpack the processes by which such practices are used, reused, and eventually adapted or transformed. Theoretical approaches like structuration theory (Giddens, 1984) or more recent advances in neo-institutional theory under the rubric of institutional work (Lawrence & Suddaby, 2006), combined with qualitative research methods (Langley, 1999; Nicolini, 2011), would provide the necessary sensitizing devices and tools to analyze uncertainty practices in the way we envision— namely, as recurrent, socially, and recursively embedded activities. In this regard we have identified the studies of Beckman and colleagues (2004), Mitsuhashi (2002), and Moynihan (2008) as leading the way. While Beckman and colleagues took the notion of uncertainty very seriously and carefully differentiated between different levels of analysis, Mitsuhashi, in his in-depth case study, generated insights into how alliance partners, with the help of relational, internal, and contextual practices, seek to reduce the lack of knowledge with regard to selection uncertainty. Moynihan studied how the interorganizational collaboration in a public disease network faced with immense uncertainty unfolded over time and led to a shared knowledge base across the organizations involved.

While none of these studies adopted a practice-theoretical lens that captures simultaneously recurrent and embedded activities dealing with uncertainty over the course of time, all three studies are significantly closer to this envisioned future of uncertainty research in alliances and networks than most of the studies reviewed. Most prior work has focused on formal governance structures only and employed theories like transaction cost economics that favor quantitative-static research designs where knowledge is reduced to a measurable variable regardless of the research context (e.g., Hoetker, 2005). In addition, previous studies have primarily been based on the implicit or explicit assumption that increasing knowledge, either about or through the alliance partner, serves to reduce uncertainties and risks. In contrast, we suggest that while involvement in an alliance or network may be beneficial it may also induce uncertainty as, for instance, more alternatives become visible. This represents a perspective that has seldom been addressed (Beck & Holzer, 2007) and is a critical component of the practice of uncertainty.

Such a practice focus would not substitute for, but would complement the study of alliance and network governance by considering both economic and organizational approaches. A broader consideration of both risk and uncertainty (Hutter & Power, 2005; Renn, 2008), including development of an appropriate monitoring capacity, would need to draw on and extend research and thinking on both formal and informal governance mechanisms. Even more importantly and fundamentally, practicing uncertainty as we have envisioned the concept, relies on intelligent forms of network governance in which formal and informal structures would "guide" uncertainty practices and, in turn, would be reproduced or transformed by these very practices (Giddens, 1984; Jarzabkowski, 2008; Sydow & Windeler, 2003; Whittington, 2011).

Consistent with our plea for applying such a perspective for a deeper, more dynamic, recursive, and in the end, meticulous understanding of uncertainty practices, the full complexity of networks and network relationships must also be assessed and evaluated. In this regard, the work of Stark (1996; Stark & Vedres, 2006) is path-breaking. More than most other researchers, Stark's work has captured the complexity of interorganizational networks under conditions of extreme uncertainty and has at least touched on the question of how the network's organizational actors dealt with ambiguous and highly uncertain knowledge in practice. Capturing the complexity of reality is critically important since many uncertainties result exactly from the very interdependencies that characterize alliances and networks (Pfeffer & Salancik, 1978; Provan, 1982). However, in order to fully understand how organizational actors actually practice uncertainty, research methodologies would be needed that are not only able to condense complex relational realities, as with network analysis, but to study in detail their effects on network practices and processes (and vice versa; Langley, 1999; Nicolini, 2011). Such methodologies are needed to study this complex phenomenon, even if such investigations have to be restricted to particular episodes of the development of a particular relationship or network of relationships.

In sum, based on the results of our review we would like to encourage alliance and network scholars to study uncertainty practices more deeply, focusing on how managers actually and recurrently make sense of and cope with uncertainty in interorganizational collaborations. We acknowledge that this represents a challenge as engaging in practice research empirically is resource and time demanding. However, we believe it is essential if researchers are to become more reconnected to the objects they study (Feldman & Orlikowski, 2011; Nicolini, 2011). Such practice-oriented studies seem urgently needed in times like the present, in which the environments of organizations in all sectors have become increasingly uncertain and threats to survival due to a lack of knowledge are manifest.

ACKNOWLEDGMENT

This chapter, save some minor changes, was earlier published as Sydow, Jörg, Müller-Seitz, Gordon, and Provan, Keith G. (2013). Managing uncertainty in alliances and networks: From governance to practice. In T. K. Das (Ed.), *Managing knowledge in strategic alliances* (pp. 1–43). Charlotte, NC: Information Age Publishing. The authors are grateful for helpful comments by T. K. Das and Günther Ortmann on an earlier draft of this chapter.

REFERENCES

NOTE: Sources marked with a star ("") are included in the literature review (cf. also Table 7.3).*

Aiken, M., & Hage, J. (1968). Organizational interdependence and intraorganizational structure. *American Sociological Review, 33*, 912–930.
Aldrich, H., & Staber, U. (1988). Organizing business interests: Patterns of trade association foundings, transformations, and deaths. In C. Glenn (Ed.), *Ecological models of organizations* (pp. 111–126). New York, NY: Ballinger.

* Artz, K. W., & Brush, T. H. (2000). Asset specificity, uncertainty and relational norms: An examination of coordination costs in collaborative strategic alliances. *Journal of Economic Behavior & Organization*, *41*, 337–362.

Ashill, N. J., & Jobber, D. (2010). Measuring state, effect and response uncertainty: Theoretical construct development and empirical validation. *Journal of Management*, *36*, 1278–1308.

* Bajeux-Besnainou, I., Joshi, S., & Vonortas, N. (2010). Uncertainty, networks and real option. *Journal of Economic Behavior & Organization*, *75*, 523–541.

* Baum, J. A. C., Rowley, T. J., Shipilov, A. V., & Chuang, Y. (2005). Dancing with strangers: Aspiration performance and the search for underwriting syndicate partners. *Administrative Science Quarterly*, *50*, 536–575.

Beck, U., & Holzer, B. (2007). Organizations in world risk society. In C. M. Pearson, C. Roux-Dufort, & J. A. Clair (Eds.), *Organizational crisis Management* (pp. 3–24). Los Angeles, CA: SAGE.

* Beckman, C. M., Haunschild, P. R., & Phillips, D. J. (2004). Friends or strangers? Firm-specific uncertainty, market uncertainty, and network partner selection. *Organization Science*, *15*, 259–275.

* Bensaou, M., & Anderson, E. (1999). Buyer-supplier relations in industrial markets: When do buyers risk making idiosyncratic investments? *Organization Science*, *10*, 460-481.

Boari, C., & Lipparini, A. (1999). Networks within industrial districts: Organizing knowledge creation and transfer by means of moderate hierarchies. *Journal of Management and Governance*, *3*, 339–360.

Borgatti, S. C., & Foster, P. C. (2003). The network paradigm in organization research: A review and typology. *Journal of Management*, *29*, 991–1013.

Brindley, C. (2004). *Supply Chain Risk*. Aldershot, UK: Ashgate.

* Burgers, W. P., Hill, C. W., & Kim, W. C. (1993). A theory of global strategic alliances: The case of the global auto industry. *Strategic Management Journal*, *14*, 419-432.

Burns, T., & Stalker, G. M. (1961). *The Management of Innovation*. London, UK: Tavistock.

Burt, R. S. (1992). *Structural holes. The social structure of competition*. Cambridge, MA: Harvard University Press.

* Camuffo, A., Furlan, A., & Rettore, E. (2007). Risk sharing in supplier relations: An agency model for the Italian air-conditioning industry. *Strategic Management Journal*, *28*, 1257–1266.

* Carson, S. J., Madhok, A., & Wu, T. (2006). Uncertainty, opportunism, and governance: The effects of volatility and ambiguity on formal and relational contracting. *Academy of Management Journal*, *49*, 1058–1077.

* Celly, K. S., Spekman, R. E., & Kamauff, J. W. (1999). Technological uncertainty, buyer preferences and supplier assurances: An examination of Pacific Rim purchasing arrangements. *Journal of International Business Studies*, *30*, 297–316.

Cleden, D. (2009). *Managing project uncertainty*. Farnham, UK: Gower.

Cropper, S., Ebers, M., Huxham, C., & Ring, P. S. (Eds.). (2008). *The Oxford handbook of interorganizational relations*. Oxford, UK: Oxford University Press.

* Das, T. K., & Teng, B. (1996). Risk types and inter-firm alliance structures. *Journal of Management Studies*, *33*, 827–843.
* Das, T., & Teng, B. (2001a). Relational risk and its personal correlates in strategic alliances. *Journal of Business and Psychology*, *15*, 449–465.
* Das, T. K., & Teng, B. (2001b). Trust, control, and risk in strategic alliances: An integrated framework. *Organization Studies*, *22*, 251–283.
Das, T. K., & Teng, B. (2001c). Strategic risk behavior and its temporalities: Between risk propensity and decision context. *Journal of Management Studies*, *38*, 515–534.
Davidson, P. (1988). A technical definition of uncertainty and the long-run non-neutrality of money. *Cambridge Journal of Economics*, *12*, 329–337.
* Delerue, H. (2004). Relational risks perception in European biotechnology alliances: The effect of contextual factors. *European Management Journal*, *22*, 546–556.
* de Man, A.-P., & Roijakkers, N. (2009). Alliance governance: Balancing control and trust in dealing with risk. *Long Range Planning*, *42*, 75–95.
* Dickson, P. H., & Weaver, K. M. (1997). Environmental determinants and individual-level moderators of alliance use. *Academy of Management Journal*, *40*, 404–425.
Drummond, H. (1995). De-escalation in decision making: A case of a disastrous partnership. *Journal of Management Studies*, *32*, 265–281.
Duncan, R. B. (1972). Characteristics of organizational environments and perceived environmental uncertainty. *Administrative Science Quarterly*, *17*, 313–327.
* Eisingerich, A. B., Bell, S. J., & Tracey, P. (2010). How can clusters sustain performance? The role of network strength, network openness, and environmental uncertainty. *Research Policy*, *39*, 239–253.
Feldman, M. S., & Orlikowski, W. J. (2011). Theorizing practice and practicing theory. *Organization Science*, *22*, 1240–1253.
Floyd, S. W., Cornelissen, J. P., Wright, M., & Delios, A. (2011). Processes and practices of strategizing and organizing: Review, development, and the role of bridging and umbrella constructs. *Journal of Management Studies*, *48*, 933–952.
Ford, D., & Mouzas, S. (2010). Networking under uncertainty: Concepts and research agenda. *Industrial Marketing Management*, *39*, 956–62.
Froud, J. (2003). The private finance initiative: Risk, uncertainty and the state. *Accounting, Organizations and Society*, *28*, 567–589.
Gamson, W. A. (1961). An experimental test of a theory of coalition formation. *American Sociological Review*, *26*, 565–573.
Giddens, A. (1984). *The constitution of society*. Cambridge, UK: Polity Press.
* Glückler, J., & Armbrüster, T. (2003). Bridging uncertainty in management consulting: The mechanisms of trust an networked reputation. *Organization Studies*, *24*, 269–297.
Grabher, G., & Powell, W. W. (2004). *Networks*. Cheltenham: Elgar.
* Grabowski, M., & Roberts, K. H. (1999). Risk mitigation in virtual organizations. *Organization Science*, *10*, 704–721.

Gudykunst, W. B., Sodetani, L. L., & Sonoda, K. T. (1987). Uncertainty reduction in Japanese-American/Caucasian relationships in Hawaii. *Western Journal of Speech Communication, 51,* 256–278.

Halinen, A., Salmi, A., & Havila, V. (1999). From dyadic change to changing business networks: An analytical framework. *Journal of Management Studies, 36,* 779–794.

* Hallikas, J., Virolainen, V. M., & Tuominen, M. (2002). Understanding risk and uncertainty in supplier networks—A transaction cost approach. *International Journal of Production Research, 40,* 3519–3531.

Harryson, S. J., Dudkowski, R., & Stern, A. (2008). Transformation networks in innovation alliances – The development of Volvo C70. *Journal of Management Studies, 45,* 745–773.

* Haunschild, P. R. (1994). How much is that company worth? Interorganizational relationships, uncertainty, and acquisition premiums. *Administrative Science Quarterly, 39,* 391–411.

* Haunschild, P. R., & Miner, A. S. (1997). Modes of interorganizational imitation: The effect of outcome Salience and uncertainty. *Administrative Science Quarterly, 42,* 472–500.

Hedlund, G. (1986). The hypermodern MNC—A heterarchy? *Human Resource Management, 2,* 9–36.

* Heide, J. B., & John, G. (1990). Alliances in industrial purchasing: The determinants of joint action in buyer-supplier relationships. *Journal of Marketing Research, 27,* 24–36.

* Hoetker, G. (2005). How much you know versus how well I know you: Selecting a supplier for a technically innovative component. *Strategic Management Journal, 26,* 75–96.

Huff, A. (1978). Consensual uncertainty. *Academy of Management Review, 3,* 651–655.

Human, S., & Provan, K.G. (2000). Legitimacy building in the evolution of small-firm multilateral networks: A comparative study of success and demise. *Administrative Science Quarterly, 45,* 327–365.

Hutter, B., & Power, M. (2005). Organizational encounters with risks: An introduction. In B. Hutter, & M. Power (Eds.), *Organizational encounters with risks* (pp. 1–32). Cambridge, UK: Cambridge University Press.

* Huxham, C., & Vangen, S. (2000). Ambiguity, complexity and dynamics in the membership of collaboration. *Human Relations, 53,* 771–806.

Huxham, C., & Vangen, S. (2005). *Managing to collaborate.* London, UK: Routledge.

Jarzabkowski, P. (2003). Strategic practices: An activity theory perspective on continuity and change. *Journal of Management Studies, 40,* 23–55.

Jarzabkowski, P. (2008). Shaping strategy as a structuration process. *Academy of Management Journal, 51,* 621–650.

Jauch, L. R., & Kraft, K. L. (1986). Strategic management of uncertainty. *Academy of Management Review, 11,* 777–790.

* Joshi, A. W., & Stump, R. L. (1999). The contingent effect of specific asset investments on joint action in manufacturer-supplier relationships: An empirical test of the moderating role of reciprocal asset investments, uncertainty, and trust. *Journal of the Academy of Marketing Science, 27,* 291–305.

Keynes, J. M. (1936). *The general theory of employment, interest, and money*. New York, NY: Harcourt & Brace.

Kilduff, M., & Tsai, W. (2003). *Social networks and organizations*. London, UK: SAGE.

*Kim, S. K., Yamada, T., & Kim, H. (2008). Search for alternatives and collaboration with incumbents: Two-sided sourcing behavior in business markets. *Decision Sciences*, *39*, 85–114.

Knight, F. (1921). *Risk, uncertainty and profit*. Boston, MA: Houghton Mifflin.

Knoben, J., & Oerlemans, L. A. B. (2006). Proximity and inter-organizational collaboration: A literature review. *International Journal of Management Reviews*, *8*, 71–89.

König, F. (2009). *The uncertainty-governance choice puzzle revisited*. Wiesbaden, Germany: Gabler.

* Koka, B. R., Madhavan, R., & Prescott, J. E. (2006). The evolution of interfirm networks: Environment effects of patterns of network change. *Academy of Management Review*, *31*, 721–737.

Koppenjan, J., & Klijn, E.-H. (2004). *Managing uncertainties in networks: A network approach to problem solving and decision making*. New York, NY: Routledge.

Koza, M. P., & Lewin, A. Y. (1998). The co-evolution of strategic alliances. *Organization Science*, *9*, 255–264.

Kroeger, F. (2012). Trusting organizations: The institutionalization of trust in interorganizational relationships. *Organization*, *19*, 743–763

* Lang, J. R., & Lockhart, D. E. (1990). Increased environmental uncertainty and changes in board linkage patterns. *Academy of Management*, *33*, 106–128.

Langley, A. (1999). Strategies for theorizing from process data. *Academy of Management Review*, *24*, 691–710.

Lawrence, T. B., & Suddaby, R. (2006). Institutions and institutional work. In S. R. Clegg, C. Hardy, T. B. Lawrence, & W. R. Nord (Eds.), *The SAGE handbook of organization studies* (2nd ed. pp. 215–254), London, UK: SAGE.

* Lee, P. K. C., Yeung, A. C. L., & Cheng, T. C. E. (2009). Supplier alliances and environmental uncertainty: An empirical study. *International Journal of Production Economics*, *120*, 190–204.

* Li, N., & Boulding, W., Staelin, R. (2010). General alliance experience, uncertainty, and marketing alliance governance mode choice. *Journal of the Academy of Marketing Science*, *38*, 141–158.

* Lin, H.-M., Chen, H., Sher, P. J., & Mei, H.-C. (2010). Inter-network co-evolution: Reversing the fortunes of declining industrial networks. *Long Range Planning*, *43*, 611–638.

* Luo, Y. (2005). How important are shared perceptions of procedural justice in cooperative alliances? *Academy Management Journal*, *48*, 695–709.

Lupton, D. (1999). *Risk*. London, UK: Routledge.

March, J. G. (1991). Exploration and exploitation in organizational learning. *Organization Science*, *2*, 71–87.

March, J. G., & Simon, H. A. (1958). *Organizations*. New York, NY: Wiley.

March, J. G., & Olson, J. P. (1976). *Ambiguity and choice in organizations*. Bergen, Norway: Universitetsforlaget.

Meuleman, M., Lockett, A., Manigart, S., & Wright, M. (2010). Partner selection decisions in interfirm collaborations: The paradox of relational embeddedness. *Journal of Management Studies*, *47*, 995–1019.

Milliken, F. J. (1987). Three types of uncertainty about the environment: State, effect and response uncertainty. *Academy of Management Review*, *12*, 133–143.

* Mitsuhashi, H. (2002). Uncertainty in selecting alliance partners: The three reduction mechanisms and alliance formation processes. *International Journal of Organizational Analysis*, *10*, 109–133.

Mizruchi, M. S. (1996). What do interlocks do? An analysis, critique, and assessment of research on interlocking directorates. *Annual Review of Sociology*, *22*, 271–298.

* Moynihan, D. P. (2008). Learning under uncertainty: Networks in crisis management. *Public Administration Review*, *68*, 350–365.

Müller-Seitz, G. (2012). Leadership in interorganizational networks: A literature review and suggestions for future research. *International Journal of Management Reviews*, *14*, 428–443.

Müller-Seitz, G., & Sydow, J. (2012). Maneuvering between networks to lead—A longitudinal case study in the semiconductor industry. *Long Range Planning*, *45*, 105–135.

Nicolini, D. (2011). Practice as the site of knowing: Insights from the field of telemedicine. *Organization Science*, *22*, 602–620.

* Nooteboom, B., Berger, H., & Noorderhaven, N. G. (1997). Effects of trust and governance on relational risk. *Academy of Management Journal*, *40*, 308–338.

Parkhe, A., Wasserman, S., & Ralston, D. A. (2006). New frontiers in network theory development. *Academy of Management Review*, *31*, 560–568.

Paulsson, U. (2004). Supply chain risks management. In C. Brindley (Ed.), *Supply chain risks* (pp. 79–98). Aldershot, UK: Ashgate.

Pfeffer, J., & Salancik, G. (1978). *The external control of organizations: A resource dependence perspective*. New York, NY: Harper & Row.

* Podolny, J. (1994). Market uncertainty and the social character of economic exchange. *Administrative Science Quarterly*, *39*, 458–483.

* Podolny, J. M. (2001). Networks as the pipes and prisms of the market. *American Journal of Sociology*, *107*, 33–60.

* Poppo, L., Zhou, K. Z., & Zenger, T. R. (2008). Examining the conditional limits of relational governance: Specialized assets, performance ambiguity, and long-standing ties. *Journal of Management Studies*, *45*, 1195–1216.

Powell, W. W. (1990). Neither market nor hierarchy: Network forms of organization. *Research in Organizational Behavior*, *12*, 295–336.

Powell, W. W., Koput, K. W., & Smith-Doerr, L. (1996). Interorganizational collaboration and the locus of innovation: Networks of learning in biotechnology. *Administrative Science Quarterly*, *41*, 116–145.

Power, M. (2007). *Organized uncertainty*. Oxford, UK: Oxford University Press.

* Provan, K. G. (1982). Interorganizational linkages and influence over decision making. *Academy of Management Journal*, *25*, 443–451.

Provan, K. G., & Kenis, P. (2008). Modes of network governance: Structure, management, and effectiveness. *Journal of Public Administration Research and Theory*, *18*, 229–252.

Provan, K.G., Fish, A., & Sydow, J. (2007). Interorganizational networks at the network level: A review of the empirical literature on whole networks. *Journal of Management, 33,* 479–516.

* Rangan, S., Samii, R., & van Wassenhove, L. N. (2006). Constructive partnerships: When alliances between private firms and public actors can enable creative strategies. *Academy of Management Review, 31,* 738–751.

Renn, O. (2008). *Risk governance.* London, UK: Earthscan.

Ring, P. S., & Van de Ven, A. H. (1994). Developmental processes of cooperative interorganizational relationships. *Academy of Management Review, 19,* 90–118.

Ritchie, B., & Brindley, C. (2007). Supply chain risk management and performance: A guiding framework for future development. *International Journal of Operations & Production Management, 27,* 303–322.

Robertson, P. L., & Langlois, R. N. (1995). Innovation, networks, and vertical integration. *Research Policy, 24,* 543–562.

Runde, J. (1990). Keynesian uncertainty and the weight of arguments. *Economics and Philosophy, 6,* 275–292.

Runde, J. (1998). Clarifying Frank Knight's discussion of the meaning of risk and uncertainty. *Cambridge Journal of Economics, 22,* 539–546.

Sako, M., & Helper, S. (1998). Determinants of trust in supplier relations: Evidence from the automotive industry in Japan and the United States. *Journal of Economic Behavior & Organization, 34,* 387–417.

* Santoro, M. D., & McGill, J. P. (2005). The effect of uncertainty and asset co-specialization on governance in biotechnology alliances. *Strategic Management Journal, 26,* 1261–1269.

Schatzki, T., Knorr Cetina, K., & von Savigny, E. (2001). *The practice turn in contemporary theory.* London, UK: Routledge.

Schrader, S., Riggs, W. M., & Smith, R. P. (1993). Choice over uncertainty and ambiguity in technical problem solving. *Journal of Engineering and Technology Management, 10,* 73–99.

Simmel, G. (1950). *The sociology of Georg Simmel.* Glencoe, IL: Free Press.

Staber, U., & Sydow, J. (2002). Organizational adaptive capacity: A structuration perspective. *Journal of Management Inquiry, 11,* 408–424.

* Stark, D. (1996). Recombinant property in East European capitalism. *American Journal of Sociology, 101,* 993–1027.

* Stark, D., & Vedres, B. (2006). Social times of network spaces: Network sequences and foreign investment in Hungary. *American Journal of Sociology, 111,* 1367–1411.

* Steensma, K. H., & Corley, K. G. (2000). On the performance of technology-sourcing partnerships: The interaction between partner interdependence and technology attributes. *Academy of Management Journal, 43,* 1045–1067.

* Steensma, K. H., Marino, L., Weaver, M. K., & Dickson, P. H. (2000). The influence of national culture on the formation of technology alliances by entrepreneurial firms. *Academy of Management Journal, 43,* 951–973.

* Sutcliffe, K. M. and Zaheer, A. (1998). Uncertainty in the transaction environment: An empirical test. *Strategic Management Journal, 19,* 1–23.

Sydow, J., & Windeler, A. (2003). Knowledge, trust, and control. Managing tensions and contradictions in a regional network of service firms. *International Studies of Management & Organization*, *33*, 69–99.

* Thomas, J. B., & Klebe Trevino, L. (1993). Information processing in strategic alliance building: A multiple approach. *Journal of Management Studies*, *30*, 779–814.

Thompson, J. D. (1967). *Organizations in Action*. New York, NY: McGraw-Hill.

Vanhaverbeke, W., Gilsing, V., Beerkens, B., & Duysters, G. (2009). The role of alliance network redundancy in the creation of core and non-core technologies. *Journal of Management Studies*, *46*, 215–244.

* Vetschera, R. (2004). Behavioral uncertainty and investments in cooperative relationships. *Managerial and Decision Economics*, *25*, 17–27.

* Walker, G. and Weber, D. (1984). A transaction cost approach to make-or-buy decisions. *Administrative Science Quarterly*, *29*, 373–391.

Whittington, R. (2011). Giddens, structuration theory and strategy as practice. In D. Golsorkhi, L. Rouleau, D. Seidl, & E. Vaara (Eds.), *Cambridge Handbook of Strategy as Practice* (pp. 109–126). Cambridge, UK: Cambridge University Press.

Zaheer, A., & Venkatraman, N. (1995). Relational governance as an interorganizational strategy: An empirical test of the role of trust in economic exchange. *Strategic Management Journal*, *16*, 373–392.

Zaheer, A., Gözübüyük, R., & Milanov, H. (2010). It's connections: The network perspective in interorganizational research. *Academy of Management Perspectives*, *24*, 62–77.

CHAPTER 8

THE CHALLENGE OF DEVELOPING NEW META-MANAGEMENT PRACTICES OF FIRMS IN META-ORGANIZATIONS

Rick M. A. Hollen,
Frans A. J. Van Den Bosch, and Henk W. Volberda

ABSTRACT

Competitive and institutional pressures challenge established firms to create new ways to improve resource productivity, innovation and sustainability. One of these ways is through inter-firm collaboration, which requires firms to manage resulting (inter)dependencies beyond firm-level boundaries so as to achieve system-level goals. Being conceptualized by Gulati, Puranam, and Tushman (2012) as meta-organizations, collectives of multiple legally autonomous firms are found within and across a wide range of industries and geographies. Existing literature has emphasized the importance of developing new management practices (i.e., management innovation) to better align organizational design with changing environmental conditions in pursuing a firm's strategic goals. In a similar vein, new management practices at the level of the meta-organization are needed to enable its constituent firms to achieve their system-level goal over time. However, it remains largely unanswered how these firms can contribute to the development of such meta-management practices. We address this research gap by developing propositions based on a literature review. The propositions emphasize the enabling role of changes in the four core activities of management—direction, motivation, coordination and decision-making—in the meta-organizational context. We provide

Managerial Practice Issues in Strategy and Organization, pp. 235–257
Copyright © 2023 by Information Age Publishing
www.infoagepub.com

illustrative examples from the Port of Rotterdam. We discuss implications for the literature on meta-organizations and management innovation as well as for practice and suggest directions for future research.

INTRODUCTION

Established firms are continually triggered by competitive and institutional pressures to improve their resource productivity, innovation and sustainability. As the ability to do so within their organizational boundaries might be limited, these firms often choose for collaboration up, down or outside the production chain (Gulati & Kletter, 2005). For instance, inter-firm collaboration can improve resource productivity and sustainability by converting firm's waste effluents such as residual chemical compounds into useful input streams for each other's production process (Doménech & Davies, 2011; Esty & Porter, 1998). Externalization of certain activities may enable established firms to be more responsive to shifting environmental demands and to tap into outside knowledge sources (Gulati, Puranam, & Tushman, 2012a). By integrating dispersed knowledge and capacity to innovate within an interorganizational setting, firms can also enable more complex innovation (Dougherty & Dunne, 2011; Newell, Goussevskaia, Swan, Bresnen, & Obembe, 2008). The international competitiveness of established firms is therefore largely influenced by their embeddedness in interorganizational networks (Dyer & Singh, 1998; Gulati, 2007; Ireland, Hitt, & Vaidyanath, 2002).

Scholars in the strategy field have extensively examined how to manage interorganizational relationships from a firm's perspective in a way that strengthens the firm's competitiveness and minimizes coordination and transaction costs (e.g., Dyer, 1997; Gulati & Singh, 1998). Some have emphasized the importance of not only improving the focal firm's competitive position but also that of other firms in its network (Dyer & Singh, 1998; Madhok & Tallman, 1998; Ring & Van De Ven, 1994). Although these strains of literature have produced valuable insights, they pertain particularly to dyadic relations instead of collectives of multiple interrelated firms and their interrelationships. It is this latter level of analysis that is addressed in the emerging literature on *meta-organizations* (Ahrne & Brunsson, 2005, 2008; Gulati et al., 2012a; König, Schulte, & Enders, 2012). Conceptualized as collectives of multiple legally autonomous entities—such as firms—that are "characterized by a system-level goal" (Gulati et al., 2012a, p. 573), meta-organizations represent a strategically interesting but underexplored unit of analysis. As exemplified in Exhibit 8.1, system-level goals challenge established firms to strategize beyond their firm-level boundaries in order to remain competitive in the long term.

EXHIBIT 8.1

Illustrative Example of a Meta-Organization Within the Port of Rotterdam: System-Level Goal and Associated Managerial Challenges

Being one of the world's largest port-industrial complexes, the Port of Rotterdam hosts a large number of refineries (including some of the largest refineries in Europe), chemical and power generating firms, cargo terminals, transport companies and other businesses. Altogether, the port area and its urban surroundings, including the city center of Rotterdam, is responsible for more than fifteen percent of carbon emissions in the Netherlands. In 2007, the port's employers' association Deltalinqs and the Port of Rotterdam Authority, in collaboration with the municipality of Rotterdam and regional environmental protection agency DCMR, initiated the Rotterdam Climate Initiative (RCI). The RCI developed into a Rotterdam-based network that includes firms, knowledge institutions and other organizations as well as citizens that collaborate to achieve the RCI's goals. Its main goal is to drastically reduce carbon emissions by fifty percent (34 Mton) in 2025 compared to 1990 levels. This represents a system-level goal, and Deltalinqs can be seen as a meta-organization whose constituent members—more than 700 registered logistical and industrial firms and associations—need to collectively contribute to this goal to ensure that the Port of Rotterdam becomes more sustainable. This is strategically important for the firms involved, as they are required to reduce their environmental footprint so as to maintain their license to operate and grow, to lease land from the Port of Rotterdam Authority, and to ensure that the port remains attractive for future employees and investors. In order to enable large reductions in carbon emissions, these firms need to strategize beyond their firm-level boundaries. They are challenged, for instance, to jointly develop and implement sustainable measures, to support each other's sustainability initiatives, and to enhance utilization of each other's by-products and waste.

Sources: Documents of Deltalinqs and the Port of Rotterdam Authority; Van Den Bosch, Hollen, Volberda, & Baaij (2011)

Existing firm-level literature has emphasized the importance of developing new management practices, that is, *management innovation*, to better align organizational design with changing environmental conditions in pursuing a firm's goals (Birkinshaw, Hamel, & Mol, 2008; Damanpour & Aravind, 2012). By showing that management innovation may also take place in the interorganizational context, Hollen, Van Den Bosch, and Volberda (2013) took the observation of Birkinshaw and Mol (2006, p. 82) that management innovation seems to emerge "on the fringes of the organization rather than in the core" a step further. Yet, management innovation at the level of the meta-organization has remained mostly unexplored. Hitherto, the literature on meta-organizations has been primarily focused on conceptualizing meta-organizations, clarifying the antecedents of the emergence of meta-organizations, meta-organization design choices regarding key structural elements such as its boundaries and hierarchical differentiation, and on the related inertia and strategic behavior of meta-organizations in reaction to environmental change; see Table 8.1.

Table 8.1

Literature on Meta-Organizations: Research Topics

Research topic	Illustrative studies
Conceptualization of meta-organizations	Ahrne & Brunsson (2005, 2008); Gulati, Puranam, & Tushman (2012a)
Antecedents of the emergence of meta-organizations	Gulati, Puranam, & Tushman (2012a)
Meta-organization design choices	Ahrne, Brunsson, & Hallström (2007); Gulati, Puranam, & Tushman (2012a); Vifell & Thedvall (2012)
Meta-organizational inertia/renewal behavior	Ahrne & Brunsson (2005, 2008); König, Schulte, & Enders (2012)
Development of meta-management practices	This chapter

It remains largely unanswered how the development of new management practices on a meta-organizational level—for which we coin the term *meta-management practices*—can increase the meta-organization's ability to achieve its system-level goal over time. Meta-management practices are related to the concept of meta-governance practices as used in a recent article on meta-organizations by Vifell and Thedvall (2012). Vifell and Thedvall conceptualize these practices as "governance through bureaucratization" (p. 51) with which "meta-organizations are able to exercise authority over their members by effectively forcing them to comply with certain established processes," which is a way of coordinating activities (Birkinshaw & Goddard, 2009). New (meta-)management practices, however, not only imply new management practices in terms of new ways of coordination, but also new ways of setting objectives, motivating efforts, and decision-making regarding resource allocation (Birkinshaw & Goddard, 2009; Birkinshaw, 2010; Hollen et al., 2013; Van Den Bosch, 2012).

In this chapter we aim to contribute to narrowing this research gap by developing propositions based on a literature review. In the literature review, we first elaborate on the concept of meta-organization and—drawing on the study by Gulati et al. (2012a) on meta-organization design—its conceptual attributes, and then elaborate on the literature on management innovation and its conceptualization. Next, we develop a series of propositions that suggest how firms can improve the system-level goal of their respective meta-organization by contributing to the development of four core management activities (cf. Birkinshaw & Goddard, 2009; Birkinshaw, 2010) on a meta-organizational level. We provide illustrative examples from the Port of Rotterdam. Finally, we discuss implications for the literature on meta-organizations and management innovation as well as for practice and suggest several directions for future research.

LITERATURE REVIEW

Meta-Organizations

Although not entirely new, the concept of a meta-organization has been used increasingly in the strategy and organizational theory literature in the last decade. As Reveley and Ville (2010, p. 839) pointed out, "the recency of the meta-organizations category ... means that the attendant conceptual apparatus is underdeveloped." Table 8.2 provides illustrative examples of definitions of meta-organizations in the literature in the last decade.

Table 8.2

Illustrative Examples of Definitions of Meta-Organizations in the Literature

Study	Definition of meta-organization	Examples
Ahrne & Brunsson (2005)	"organizations-of-organizations that have assumed the form of associations" (p. 431)	United Nations, FIFA, European Union
Shekhar (2006)	"the combination of multiple organizations working towards common business objectives" (p. 477)	Extended virtual organizations
Ahrne & Brunsson (2008)	"organizations [whose members] are other organizations" (p. 2); "the members of meta-organizations may be states, firms, or associations" (p. 3)	International Chamber of Commerce, World Trade Organization
Reveley & Ville (2010)	"organizations whose constituent members are other organizations" (p. 837)	Industry associations
König, Schulte, & Enders (2012)	"associations whose members are organizations, rather than individuals" (p. 1327)	Industry associations
Gulati, Puranam, & Tushman (2012)	"a meta-organization [is] defined as an organization whose agents are themselves legally autonomous and not linked through employment relationships" (p. 573); "meta-organizations comprise networks of firms or individuals not bound by authority based on employment relationships, but characterized by a system-level goal" (p. 573)	OEM-supplier networks, franchising networks, developer/open-source software communities, technical standards committees

Table 8.2 shows that whereas there has been general consensus among scholars that meta-organizations consist of members that are not interconnected by virtue of employment contracts, ideas concerning the type(s) of these members vary considerably. For instance, Ahrne and Brunsson (2008) define meta-organizations as organizations whose members may be states, firms or associations, and Gulati et al. (2012a, p. 573) as comprising "networks of firms or individuals not bound by authority based on employment relationships." König et al. (2012, p. 1327, italics added), however, define meta-organizations as "associations whose members are organizations, *rather than* individuals." In this chapter, we reconcile these views by focusing on meta-organizations whose constituent members are firms. Furthermore, whereas Ahrne and Brunsson (2008) state that the constituent members have considerable autonomy, Gulati et al. (2012a) suggest that these are completely legally autonomous. Next, our main focus is on the recent conceptual research and contributions by Gulati et al. (2012a).

Conceptual Attributes of Meta-Organizations

Gulati et al. (2012a) used the concept of a meta-organization to conceptually capture a wide variety of interorganizational network arrangements comprising multiple legally independent entities (such as firms) which (1) are interlinked by a system-level goal and (2) lack an overarching formal authority structure based on employment contracts. Table 8.3 provides a structured overview of these and other conceptual attributes of meta-organizations as described by Gulati et al. (2012a) on which we will elaborate next.

Table 8.3

Overview of Conceptual Attributes of Meta-Organizations

• *Goal:*	meta-organizations are bound by a system-level goal.
• *Structure:*	meta-organizations comprise multiple legally independent organizational entities (members).
• *Membership:*	meta-organizations' membership is largely determined by approval and policing procedures, the specification of membership criteria, membership duration and membership exclusivity.
• *Governance:*	meta-organizational activities are governed by formalized control – except for employment contracts – and governance mechanisms associated with informal authority and bargaining power; the level of hierarchy in place can be high (hierarchical differentiation) or low (self-regulation).

Source: Adapted from Gulati, Puranam, & Tushman (2012a).

A *system-level goal*—which corresponds to the goals of the meta-organization's architects (Gulati et al., 2012a)—requires firms involved to not just focus on managing their firm-level interactions with the external environment so as to enhance their own competitiveness, but also on contributing to the relations with one another in such a way that they can properly respond to environmental demands as if they were a single entity. In this vein, König et al. (2012, p. 1327) posited that meta-organizations "aim to install a higher level of order to the interaction of actors within a field and to the interaction between the field and the environment." Having a system-level goal does not mean that firms necessarily share this goal (Gulati et al., 2012a), but collectively achieving this goal will improve their joint competitive position. It can hence be stated that a focus on a system-level goal contributes to interorganizational competitive advantage (cf. Dyer & Singh, 1998).

The notion of reciprocity—which was initially elaborated by Gouldner (1960) and a few years later by Thompson (1967/2003) in connection to interdependence—is an important one here. For instance, König et al. (2012, p. 1335) pointed out that a meta-organization's constituent firms share knowledge with each other "only when they are sure to receive some sort of an equivalent benefit." Moreover, the existence of a system-level goal implies that firms in meta-organizations are reciprocally interdependent in achieving this goal. As Gulati et al. (2012a, p. 573, italics added) point out, "meta-organizations resemble biological superorganisms, a multitude of individual organisms that coexist, collaborate, and coevolve via a complex set of *symbiotic and reciprocal relationships* which together form a larger organism" (Tautz & Heilmann, 2008). Reciprocal interdependence implies interactive transactions in which each firm or unit is "posing contingency for the other" (Thompson, 1967/2003, p. 55). Reciprocal interdependence requires the highest form of interorganizational interaction and is considered the most difficult to coordinate for management (Newell et al., 2008; Thompson, 1967/2003).

Das and Teng (2002a) pointed out that the meaning of reciprocity between more than two organizations could become less clear. For example, does each of the organizations reciprocate with all the others or are other reciprocal relationships possible? Taking a social exchange perspective, Das and Teng (2002a, p. 449) employs the construct "generalized reciprocity," defined as "a group-based exchange relationship in which members expect quid pro quo exchanges within the group but not necessarily with any specific member. Reciprocity becomes a generalized norm that all members are supposed to follow" (Gouldner, 1960).

As mentioned above, another defining feature of meta-organizations besides a system-level goal is "the absence of formal authority arising from an employment relationship between constituent entities" (Gulati et al.,

2012a, p. 573). Gulati et al. (2012a) mention several ways in which firms in meta-organizations can substitute for the use of formal employment contracts in exercising control over other constituent firms. These include bargaining power—which "stems from the possession of unique resources ... or investments in knowledge advantages" (p. 574) and the ensuing asymmetric dependence—as well as informal mechanisms based on such things as expertise, reputation, and gatekeeping privileges. They also indicate, however, that "it will be valuable to learn about other sources of authority in meta-organizations" (p. 581). In general, established firms can use several behavior and output control mechanisms (Das & Teng, 1998; Ouchi, 1977) other than employment contracts to exercise control over each other's activities (Vifell & Thedvall, 2012) and, by doing so, reduce the risks associated with interdependence. Examples are pre-established plans, standard operating procedures, dispute resolution procedures and non-market pricing systems (Gulati & Singh, 1998). A high level of formalization can be particularly important for those firms that are faced with high levels of asset specificity, transaction frequency and uncertainty (Poppo & Zenger, 2002).

Related to the use of these governance mechanisms is the degree of stratification: the level of hierarchical authority in meta-organizations. As Gulati et al. (2012a, p 578) point out, "a high degree of stratification gives rise to, and enables the exercise of, status- or role-based authority structure," whereas a low degree of stratification is associated with "heterarchical [rather than hierarchical] coordination arrangements." A high degree of stratification can help reducing the complexity of coordination between a meta-organization's constituent firms and can serve as a mechanism to motivate these firms to contribute to the envisioned system-level goal (Gulati et al., 2012a). Highly stratified meta-organizations, however, are also at risk of increased bureaucracy that may reduce the meta-organization's responsiveness to achieve this goal. Furthermore, a high degree of stratification discourages the adoption of "peer-based approaches to coordination" and associated "broad participation in vital design/supervisory tasks" (Gulati et al., 2012a, p. 578), which may complicate the consensus-building necessary to achieve the system-level goal. Hence, as stated by Gulati et al. (2012a, p. 579), stratification choices "have significant impacts on both motivation and coordination within meta-organizations." Most meta-organizations have a low level of hierarchy (Ahrne & Brunsson, 2008; König et al., 2012).

Whereas the system-level goal (goal attribute) and interrelatedness of multiple legally independent organizational entities (structure attribute) are inherent to all meta-organizations, the level of stratification (governance attribute) represents a dimension of meta-organizational design which can, hence, differ from one meta-organization to another. A second dimension of meta-organizational design considered by Gulati et al.

(2012a) is the degree to which the boundaries of a meta-organization are open for new entities to become part of it, that is, boundary permeability. This dimension, which determines meta-organization membership (membership attribute), is predominantly determined by approval and policing procedures, the specification of membership criteria, membership duration and membership exclusivity (Gulati et al., 2012a). Approval and policing procedures vary in particular with the extent to which membership of the meta-organization is self-selective or subject to the approval by one or several—or all—existing members. Membership criteria are mainly related to the resources of potential member firms and the redundancy of these resources within the meta-organization. Finally, membership duration is influenced by exit barriers such as contracts that specify a minimum engagement period, while membership exclusivity is determined by the degree to which contributions of a meta-organization's constituent firms are made exclusively to this meta-organization. Hence, as stated by Gulati et al. (2012a, p. 577), boundary choices "fundamentally alter the behavioral dynamics within a meta-organization, as well as the range of feasible governance arrangement."

Management Innovation: Change in Core Management Activities

Collaboration can be a complex and difficult endeavor that needs to be managed properly to reap its potential benefits (Dyer, 2000; Gulati, Wohlgezogen, & Zhelyazkov, 2012b; Newell et al., 2008). In so doing, executives make choices regarding management activities associated with setting objectives, motivating efforts, coordinating activities and decision-making regarding resource allocation. Combined, these strategic managerial choices reflect firms' management model (Birkinshaw & Goddard, 2009; Hamel, 2007; Van Den Bosch, 2012). Previous firm-level literature has emphasized the importance of developing new management activities—that is, management innovation—in order to enhance a firm's sustainable competitive advantage (Birkinshaw, 2010; Damanpour & Aravind, 2012; Hamel, 2006, 2007; Mol & Birkinshaw, 2009; Volberda, Van Den Bosch, & Heij, 2013). Birkinshaw, Hamel and Mol (2008, p. 829) defined management innovation as "the generation and implementation of a management practice, process, structure, or technique that is new to the state of the art and is intended to further organizational goals." They pointed out, however, that management innovation can equally be perceived as new to the organization rather than new to the state of the art. Also, Birkinshaw et al. (2008, p. 828) use the term "management practices" to cover the entire range of management practices, processes, structure and techniques.

Hence, management innovation could be concisely described as the development (including generation and implementation) of new management practices.

Although the often-referenced definition of management innovation by Birkinshaw, Hamel, and Mol (2008) might be conceptually appealing, the distinctions among practices, processes, structures and techniques are, as they point out themselves, not conceptually nor empirically clean, and "there are important similarities *across* the different forms of management innovation" (p. 828). In examining how meta-organizations' constituent firms can contribute to the development of meta-management practices to enable system-level goals, we therefore choose an alternative way to conceptualize management innovation. This alternative conceptualization—which is based on studies by Birkinshaw and Goddard (2009) and Birkinshaw (2010)—discerns four conceptually separate, context-neutral sets of management activities (i.e., practices) which were already mentioned earlier: (1) setting objectives; (2) motivating efforts; (3) coordinating activities; and (4) decision-making regarding resource allocation. Management innovation implies an adaptation of the existing management model by changes in these four generic types of management activities and their interrelations (Hollen et al., 2013; Van Den Bosch, 2012); see also Table 8.4.

Table 8.4

Conceptualizations of Management Innovation

Definition of management innovation by Birkinshaw, Hamel & Mol (2008, p. 829): "the generation and implementation of a management practice, process, structure, or technique that is new to the state of the art and is intended to further organizational goals."

Alternative conceptualization (used in this chapter) of management innovation: adaptation of the existing management model by developing new management activities in terms of:

- setting objectives (associated with short-term or long-term direction);
- motivating efforts (associated with extrinsic or intrinsic motivation);
- coordinating activities (associated with formal or informal coordination);
- Decision making (associated with hierarchical or decentralized decision-making).

Previous literature has mainly examined what are the processes through which new management practices come about within an intra-organizational context (Birkinshaw et al., 2008; Damanpour & Aravind, 2012; Hamel, 2006; Mol & Birkinshaw, 2009). Taking an inter-organizational rather than an intra-organizational perspective, Hollen et al. (2013) and Meuer (2014) showed how the development of new management practices of a firm can also be enabled by and come about in an interorganizational context. In this chapter, we go one step further (see Table 8.5) by introducing a meta-organizational perspective of management innovation.

In so doing, we examine the role of contributing to the development of new management practices on a meta-organizational level, that is, meta-management practices. These practices can be seen as the product of the joint efforts of the meta-organization's constituent firms, implying a meta-organizational perspective.

Table 8.5

Perspectives on the Management Innovation Process

Perspectives	Illustrative studies
• Intra-organizational perspective	Birkinshaw, Hamel & Mol (2008); Damanpour & Aravind (2012); Hamel (2006); Mol & Birkinshaw (2009); Vaccaro, Jansen, Van Den Bosch & Volberda (2012)
• Inter-organizational perspective	Hollen, Van Den Bosch & Volberda (2013); Meuer (2014)
• Meta-organizational perspective	Gap in the literature, addressed in this chapter

PROPOSITION DEVELOPMENT

Studies on meta-organizations differ from the mainstream literature on alliances and other forms of interorganizational relationships in that they explicitly treat a cluster of legally autonomous entities as an organization and acknowledge that such a meta-organization, like any other organization, "embodies key structural elements that can be designed" (Gulati et al., 2012a, p. 582). The key structural elements are associated with the management model that is in place, and the underlying design choices imply choices regarding the core management activities of management, i.e. activities associated with setting objectives (i.e. providing direction), motivating employees, coordinating activities and decision-making (cf. Birkinshaw, 2010). In order for a meta-organization and constituent firms to achieve an existing system-level goal in a complex dynamic environment (or, for instance, to pursue new system-level goals), the meta-organization's management model may need to change over time. This is especially needed when the meta-organization is faced with non-paradigmatic environmental change (König et al., 2012). As elaborated next, we argue that this requires the development of meta-management practices, that is, new management practices on a meta-organizational level, with regard to respectively direction, motivation, coordination and decision-making.

System-level goals are often relatively long-term, broad goals. These goals might not have been formulated very specifically as future conditions in which they should be attained are largely unknown. Hence, it is needed to also introduce system-level *objectives* that support attainment of these goals. Because objectives that clarify and refine system-level goals are usually more specific and measurable than these goals themselves, they can be more easily used for comparison and monitoring purposes within the meta-organization. The visibility of these objectives can be increased through published action plans and standards (Vifell & Thedvall, 2012). In this way, alignment of these objectives within the meta-organization can be facilitated, which in turn enables a more collective, comparable and controllable effort to achieve the system-level goal. New objectives need to be set and evaluated to change behavior of the constituent firms towards the desired direction (Gruber & Niles, 1974).

By setting and aligning new objectives, a meta-organization may legitimize the engagement in long-term projects needed to enable its system-level goal. Its constituent firms might be interested only in investing in projects with a limited payback time, while the system-level goal might need investments in projects with a longer payback time. By setting the objective that there should be a certain amount of longer-payback investments in order to achieve the system-level goal, these investments can be partly legitimized among the constituent firms. Managers also need to set objectives that motivate the constituent firms to acquire new knowledge and experience from outside the meta-organization to prevent meta-organizational inertia (König et al., 2012). Additionally, new objectives serve to direct the terms of the meta-organizational agreement, which is needed to secure the cooperation of all constituent firms in making an effort to enable the system-level goal. These arguments lead to the following proposition:

> **Proposition 1:** *The ability of a meta-organization to achieve its system-level goal is likely to increase if the constituent firms contribute to develop meta-management practices that improve alignment of their objectives related to this goal.*

As pointed out by Gulati et al. (2012a, p. 581), an "important question about the internal organization of meta-organizations is how particular linkages can be incentivized." New motivation schemes and incentives are needed that stimulate inter-firm collaboration within the meta-organization and the overall pursuit of the system-level goal. The motivation of the constituent firms can be based on extrinsic and intrinsic values. The firms involved need to be motivated to optimally contribute to the system-level goal. This may require both behavioral and output control mechanisms (Das & Teng, 1998; Dekker, 2004; Ouchi, 1977). The firms also need to be motivated to cooperate by increasing their involvement in achieving the set objectives (e.g., Leufkens & Noorderhaven, 2011). Incentives should therefore be synchronized with the newly set objectives as discussed above. One way to attain enhanced intrinsic motivation of the firms is by giving special importance to the extent of firm-level contribution to the system-level goal. If firms' efforts and accomplishments are highly valued by all other firms in the meta-organization—which may include their industrial customers—they will be more motivated. The employees involved should also be motivated to learn how to properly collaborate with each other across organizational boundaries inasmuch as this is valuable for their firm's competitive advantage. The meta-organization's constituent firms should be stimulated to exchange operational knowledge. Gulati et al. (2012a, p. 581) state that "privileged access to information or involvement in important decisions may serve as an intrinsic motivator for high priority relations in the collective." The larger the network of constituent firms, the more the meta-organizational context becomes a potentially rich knowledge base area in terms of both market and technology knowledge. The better the constituent firms can be motivated to communicate with and learn from each other, the more knowledge can be collectively generated, which may increase the meta-organization's ability to achieve its system-level goal. These arguments suggest the following proposition:

Proposition 2: *The ability of a meta-organization to achieve its system-level goal is likely to increase if the constituent firms contribute to develop meta-management practices that enhance intrinsic and extrinsic motivation to support each other in achieving this goal.*

König et al. (2012, p. 1327) pointed out that meta-organizations "encourage the networking and knowledge sharing between members, and are engaged in the collaborative build-up of knowledge and trust." Indeed, this increases the ability of a meta-organization to achieve its system-level goal as the associated mutual adjustment facilitates collaborative efforts to do so. Open interfirm communication and knowledge sharing, which is largely based on trust (Das & Teng, 1998), is associated with a relational approach to managing interorganizational relations (Dyer & Singh, 1998; Ireland et al., 2002; Macneil, 1974; Ring & Van De Ven, 1994). This approach reflects the idea that firms need to collaborate as their competitiveness depends on "reaching positive-sum solutions to inter-firm coordination problems" (Uzzi, 1997, p. 51), which is related to a focus on interorganizational competitive advantage (Dyer & Singh, 1998). As mentioned before, such a focus represents a system-level goal.

Interfirm relationships within the meta-organization have to be effectively coordinated, particularly in the case of a high degree of interdependence in achieving the system-level goal. Firm-level activities need to be aligned with each other and with this goal. Malets (2010, p. 1741) emphasized that "in order to survive, meta-organizations have to creatively manage differences and similarities between members ... and continuously balance their own identities with the identities of their members." Coordination might be focused on exploiting experiences and/or resources of each other (Liebeskind, Oliver, Zucker, & Brewer, 1996) and on the joint production of new experiences by engaging in collective explorative undertakings (Holmqvist, 2004; Santamaria & Surroca, 2011). Interrelated activities within the meta-organization need to be coordinated in such a way that the meta-organizational context provides incentives for both exploratory and exploitative activities in pursuing the system-level goal. This may require one or more entrepreneurial and ambidextrous meta-organizational staff members who will bear responsibility for all interorganizational activities that are associated with enabling the system-level goal. Relevant knowledge and experience of constituent firms regarding the achievement of goals comparable to the system-level goal needs to be integrated in order to realize the meta-organizational innovation's potential. Exchanging complex and tacit know-how within the meta-organization may require managers or technicians of the firms to visit each other. When objectives related to the system's level goal have been achieved, proceedings need to be monitored to see whether further changes are warranted. Coordination is also related to the means by which managers of the constituent firms value, assimilate and utilize new knowledge (Cohen & Levinthal, 1990) as acquired in the meta-organizational context. Besides coordinating communication and knowledge flows within its boundaries, meta-organizations also coordinate interaction of their constituent firms with external actors which, as pointed out by König et al. (2012, p. 1336), "can provide crucial information on the future of a field and on appropriate adaptation strategies, and act as catalysts for overcoming inertia". The above arguments give rise to the following proposition:

Proposition 3: *The ability of a meta-organization to achieve its system-level goal is likely to increase if the constituent firms contribute to develop meta-management practices that improve coordination by mutual adjustment based on communication and knowledge sharing related to this goal.*

Exhibit 8.2 provides an empirical context in which proposition 3 can be investigated.

The development of meta-management practices as mentioned above needs to be accompanied by putting in place new meta-management activities associated with decision-making about allocating resources, including human resources regarding meta-organizational projects. Resource allocation and commitment within the meta-organization is

EXHIBIT 8.2

Illustrative Example of the Development of Meta-Management Practices

Situated in the Port of Rotterdam, Plant One is a test facility—unique in Western Europe—enabling sustainable process technology. The test facility is an independent limited-liability organization that has been initiated by a consortium of various Dutch organizations, including the Port of Rotterdam Authority, and governmental agencies. It can be considered as a meta-organization that is open to all firms aiming to develop technologies that contribute to the system-level goal of more sustainable process technologies. It facilitates the development phase of promising chemical process technologies by enabling these to be tested on production scale and further developed for industrial applications. The facility offers equipped office space, a machine park and various industrial utilities, and intermediates the storage and handling of chemicals. Under the test facility's umbrella environmental permit, it can ensure that the legally autonomous firms in the facility receive required permits for their pilots within weeks instead of months. The test facility's staff consists of a managing director, an operations manager and a health, safety and environment manager which provide support, including maintenance and technical support, licensing and safety advice, and boundary spanning efforts to attract clients for the firm's process technologies. Communication and knowledge exchange takes place between firms within the test-facility, which is facilitated by informal meetings and informal talks between employees from the firms during their daily activities. As the number of firms within Plant One increased, these practices have been largely developed over time and most likely contribute positively to the system-level goal.

Sources: Documents of Plant One; Van Den Bosch, Hollen, Volberda, & Baaij (2011).

largely dependent on the constituent firms which, as pointed out by König et al. (2012, p. 1325), "typically have access to more resources than the meta-organization itself." The managers of these constituent firms are required to find and allocate discretionary time for effectively managing this endeavor (Gruber & Niles, 1974). New or adapted decision-making activities are required that take the interaction with other organizations within the meta-organization into account, for example by highlighting interorganizational decision-making (Tuite, Chisholm, & Radnor, 2009). Decision-making procedures on meta-organizational level should be clearly defined so as to prevent protracted decision-making that causes inertia in response to non-paradigmatic environmental change (König et al., 2012). In order to promote interorganizational knowledge sharing (e.g., Soekijad & Andriessen, 2003) in collective explorative undertakings, decision-making in meta-organizations may need to be less hierarchically structured than would be the case within the constituent firms themselves. Gulati et al. (2012a, p. 574) point out that "decisions about whom is collocated with whom are as important as decisions about who is grouped with whom in the organization's divisional structure." Based on these insights, we suggest the following proposition:

Proposition 4: *The ability of a meta-organization to achieve its system-level goal is likely to increase if the constituent firms contribute to develop meta-management practices that enhance interorganizational decision-making regarding resource allocation related to this goal.*

DISCUSSION AND CONCLUDING REMARKS

When established firms become more interdependent in reaching a certain goal, it is particularly the set of interrelated interorganizational relationships—in the form of a meta-organization—that needs to be examined, which goes beyond the viewpoints of the individual firms involved. Meta-organizations are an "increasingly important form of organizing" (Konig et al., 2012, p. 1325) that are continuously challenged to achieve system-level goals for the benefit of their constituent firms (Gulati et al., 2012a). In this chapter we examined how established firms can increase their meta-organization's ability to achieve this system-level goal by contributing to the development of new meta-management practices, i.e. management innovation on a meta-organization level. Drawing on a literature review in which we distinguished four conceptually separate, generic types of meta-management practices—that is, setting objectives, motivating efforts, coordinating activities and decision-making—that make up a *meta-organization's management model*, we developed a set of propositions that suggest how contributing to adaptation of this management model can increase the ability to achieve the meta-organization's system-level goal.

We particularly emphasized the importance of developing meta-management practices that enhance (1) alignment of objectives of the meta-organization's constituent firms related to the system-level goal; (2) intrinsic and extrinsic motivation to support each other in achieving this goal; (3) coordination by mutual adjustment based on communication and knowledge sharing related to this goal; and (4) interorganizational decision-making regarding resource allocation related to this goal. The speed with which choices are made regarding adaptation of the meta-management model in these ways and the chosen or emerging sequence (i.e., first changing decision-making, followed by changing motivation) are likely to be different for each meta-organization. We suggest that these differences in meta-organization-specific development of changes in the meta-management model result in differences in ability to achieve system-level goals and, hence, in the constituent firms' interorganizational competitive advantage. The fact that the distinguished meta-management practices are context-neutral (Birkinshaw & Goddard, 2009; Birkinshaw, 2010; Van Den Bosch, 2012) makes them applicable to various types of meta-organizations.

Enhanced collaboration between a meta-organization's constituent firms so as to achieve a system-level goal—which contributes to interorganizational competitive advantage (cf. Dyer & Singh, 1998)—requires a *relational approach* to managing interorganizational relationships and the associated interdependencies (e.g., Dyer, 2000; Ireland et al., 2002; Macneil, 1974; Ring & Van De Ven, 1994). Indeed, a relational approach is associated with a certain level of interorganizational knowledge sharing, disclosure of proprietary information, mutual adjustment and joint problem solving. Most established firms, however, are used to a more transaction-oriented (rather than relation-oriented) approach to managing interdependence relationships in order to protect their competitive advantage (Hollen & Van Den Bosch, 2013). Being principally motivated by self-interest from a short-term perspective, activities consistent with a transaction-oriented approach are embedded in "atomistic" network ties that lack social embeddedness (Uzzi, 1997, p. 36). A transition from a mainly transaction-oriented approach to a mainly relation-oriented approach emphasizes in particular the importance of trust-building efforts (Das & Teng, 1998; Neumann & Bachmann, 2011; Ring & Van De Ven, 1994) and, related to this, the importance of the development of a joint performance indicator (Hollen & Van Den Bosch, 2013).

Contributions

This chapter contributes in two related ways to the literature (see also Table 8.6). First, we contribute to the emerging *literature on meta-organizations* by distinguishing four generic and context-neutral types of meta-management practices that collectively define a meta-organization's management model, and by subsequently examining how adapting this management model improves a meta-organization's ability to achieve the envisioned system-level goal. König et al. (2012) have shown how general characteristics of meta-organizations cause inertia to non-paradigmatic changes in the external environment—which require achieving *new* system-level goals—and how these inertial forces can be partially offset by changes in meta-managements' constitution and routines. In this chapter, we examined how to improve meta-organizations' ability to achieve *existing* system-level goals by leveraging interorganizational collaboration within the meta-organization through the development of new meta-management practices.

Second, by examining the development of new management practices in a meta-organizational context, this chapter contributes to the *management innovation literature*, which is still focused primarily focused on an intra-firm level of analysis (Birkinshaw et al., 2008; Damanpour & Aravind, 2012; Hamel, 2006; Mol & Birkinshaw, 2009; Vaccaro et al., 2012).

Table 8.5

Perspectives on the Management Innovation Process

- *Contribution to the literature on meta-organizations* (1) by distinguishing four generic and context-neutral types of meta-management practices that collectively define a meta-organization's management model, and (2) by developing propositions on how adapting this management model improves a meta-organization's ability to achieve the envisioned system-level goal.
- *Contribution to the management innovation literature* by theorizing beyond a firm-level locus of management innovation: we examine how established firms develop new management practices at meta-organizational level in order to achieve system-level goals that cannot be achieved via management innovation at a firm level only.

Specifically, we examined how established firms develop new activities associated with setting objectives, motivating efforts, coordinating activities and decision-making at the level of their meta-organization in order to achieve system-level goals that cannot be achieved via management innovation at a firm level only. Accordingly, we theorize beyond a firm-level locus of management innovation. The focus on the interorganizational context of meta-organizations enables a broader recognition of the role of interorganizational interaction and the associated change agents (cf. Birkinshaw et al., 2008) in shaping and influencing the management innovation process.

How are these contributions related to a behavioral approach to strategy? This question is not easy to address because the definition and discussions about the delineation of such an approach with related approaches do not yet result in broadly accepted views. A recent Special Issue (December 2011) of the *Strategic Management Journal* illustrates two different views. The introductory article claims: "Behavioral strategy merges cognitive and social psychology with strategic management theory and practice" (Powell, Lovallo, & Fox, 2011, p 1371). The concluding article in the same Special Issue bears the provocative title: "A behavioral approach to strategy—what's the alternative?" In that article, Levinthal (2011, p. 1517) argues that "the divide between economic and behavioral approaches … is a false divide as any but the most trivial problems require a behavioral act of representation prior to invoking a deductive, 'rational' approach. In this sense, all approaches are behavioral." As the constructs and theoretical perspectives used in this paper are clearly related to the behavior of human actors, we believe our findings contribute to a behavioral approach to strategy in two ways. First, by focusing on meta-organizations as an interesting research context for such an approach, and second, by investigating management innovation in this context as an important behavioral lever to accomplish system-level goals of meta-organizations.

Limitations and Directions for Future Research

Several limitations of this chapter merit discussion and suggest directions for future research. Indeed, Gulati et al. (2012a, p. 582) state that "many areas of inquiry about meta-organizations remain fertile ground for further investigation." First, by emphasizing the active role of managers of the meta-organization's constituent firms in improving the meta-organization's ability to achieve the system-level goal, our propositions reflect a rational perspective on management innovation (cf. Birkinshaw et al., 2008). Hence, we have focused on the actions and choices of key individuals, that is, managers. Future research could also examine the role of institutional conditions and attitudes of major influencer groups (institutional perspective), suppliers of new ideas and their legitimacy (fashion perspective) and organizational culture (cultural perspective).

Second, in investigating the development of new meta-management practices, we have taken account of reciprocal interdependence among interconnected firms in achieving a system-level goal. In future research, it would be interesting to apply in a meta-organizational context the social exchange perspective proposed by Das and Teng (2002a, 2002b). Applying this perspective will contribute to an improved understanding of the role of generalized exchange processes and associated social control mechanisms. Another related issue would be to investigate the similarities and differences between alliance constellations (Das & Teng, 2002a; Gomes-Casseres, 1996) on the one hand and meta-organizations on the other hand.

Third, we have not looked into the effect of the size of the meta-organization (i.e., the number of constituent firms) on the development of meta-management practices. A larger number of interconnected firms will lead to more contingencies, requiring more network activities to be orchestrated through mutual adjustment, and a larger network also limits the potential development of informal management practices (Doménech & Davies, 2011). This will increase the complexity, difficulties and costs of coordination (Thompson, 1967/2003). Future research could examine to what extent meta-organization size has an effect on the constituent firms' behavioral strategy (Powell et al., 2011) regarding the management of interorganizational relations within the meta-organization.

Fourth, future research is needed to empirically examine how the development of meta-management practices can increase the meta-organization's ability to achieve its system-level goals over time. In particular, longitudinal case studies are required to properly investigate and illustrate the process dimension associated with this development. The empirical research could include examining secondary data sources (such as internal documents and publicly available archival sources) from the meta-organization and its constituent firms as well as conducting a series of in-depth, semi-structured interviews with key players within the meta-organization. In so doing, it is especially important to get a clear picture of key events associated with the development of new meta-management practices over time and to find yardsticks for measuring progress in achieving the system-level goal.

Notwithstanding the discussed limitations, we would argue that the conceptualization and examination of management innovation on a meta-organizational level of analysis extend and advance the literature on both meta-organizations and management innovation, and that this chapter contributes to a better understanding of the role of contributing to new ways of setting objectives, motivating efforts, coordinating activities and decision-making in improving the ability of meta-organizations and their constituent firms to achieve strategically important system-level goals over time and, in turn, to foster interorganizational competitive advantage.

ACKNOWLEDGMENTS

This chapter, save some minor changes, was earlier published as Hollen, Rick M. A., Van Den Bosch, FranzA. J., and Volberda, Henk W. (2014). The challenge of developing new meta-management practices of firms in meta-organizations. In T. K. Das (Ed.), *Behavioral strategy: Emerging perspectives* (pp. 105-127). Charlotte, NC: Information Age Publishing. The authors gratefully acknowledge the financial support of the Port of Rotterdam Authority in funding the PhD research of the first author. They are also grateful for the interviews and discussions held with (senior) managers of the Port of Rotterdam Authority and various other organizations and companies in the Port of Rotterdam.

REFERENCES

Ahrne, G., & Brunsson, N. (2005). Organizations and meta-organizations. *Scandinavian Journal of Management, 21*, 429–449.

Ahrne, G., & Brunsson, N. (2008). *Meta-Organizations*. Cheltenham, UK: Edward Elgar.

Ahrne, G., Brunsson, N., & Hallström, K. T. (2007). Organizing organizations. *Organization, 14*, 619–624.

Birkinshaw, J. (2010). *Reinventing management: Smarter choices for getting work done*. Chichester, UK: John Wiley & Sons.

Birkinshaw, J., & Goddard, J. (2009). What is your management model? *Sloan Management Review, 50*(2), 81–90.

Birkinshaw, J., Hamel, G., & Mol, M. J. (2008). Management innovation. *Academy of Management Review, 33*, 825–845.

Birkinshaw, J., & Mol, M. J. (2006). How management innovation happens. *Sloan Management Review, 47*(4), 81–88.

Cohen, W., & Levinthal, D. 1990. Absorptive capacity: A new perspective on learning and innovation. *Administrative Science Quarterly, 35*, 128–152.

Damanpour, F., & Aravind, D. (2012). Managerial innovation: Conceptions, processes, and antecedents. *Management and Organization Review, 8*, 423–454.

Das, T. K., & Teng, B. (1998). Between trust and control: Developing confidence in partner cooperation in alliances. *Academy of Management Review, 23*, 491–512.

Das, T. K., & Teng, B. (2002a). Alliance constellations: A social exchange perspective. *Academy of Management Review, 27*, 445–456.

Das, T. K., & Teng, B. (2002b). A social exchange theory of strategic alliances. In F. J. Contractor, & P. Lorange (Eds.), *Cooperative strategies and alliances* (pp. 439–460). Oxford, UK: Elsevier Science.

Dekker, H. C. (2004). Control of inter-organizational relationships: Evidence on appropriation concerns and coordination requirements. *Accounting, Organizations and Society, 29*, 27–49.

Doménech, T., & Davies, M. (2011). The role of embeddedness in industrial symbiosis networks: Phases in the evolution of industrial symbiosis networks. *Business Strategy and the Environment, 20*, 281–296.

Dougherty, D., & Dunne, D. D. (2011). Organizing ecologies of complex innovation. *Organization Science, 22*, 1214–1223.

Dyer, J. H. (1997). Effective interfirm collaboration: How firms minimize transaction costs and maximize transaction value. *Strategic Management Journal, 18*, 535–556.

Dyer, J. H. (2000). *Collaborative advantage: Winning through extended enterprise supplier networks*. New York, NY: Oxford University Press.

Dyer, J. H., & Singh, H. (1998). The relational view: Cooperative strategy and sources of interorganizational competitive advantage. *Academy of Management Review, 23*, 660–679.

Esty, D. C., & Porter, M. E. (1998). Industrial ecology and competitiveness: Strategic implications for the firm. *Journal of Industrial Ecology, 2*(1), 35–43.

Gomes-Casseres, B. (1996). *The alliance revolution: The new shape of business rivalry*. Cambridge, MA: Harvard University Press.

Gouldner, A. W. (1960). The norm of reciprocity: A preliminary statement. *American Sociological Review, 25*, 161–178.

Gruber, W. H., & Niles, J. S. (1974). How to innovate in management. *Organizational Dynamics, 3*(2), 31–47.

Gulati, R. (2007). *Managing network resources: Alliances, affiliations, and other relational assets*. New York, NY: Oxford University Press.

Gulati, R., & Kletter, D. (2005). Shrinking core, expanding periphery: The relational architecture of high-performing organizations. *California Management Review, 47*(3), 77–104.

Gulati, R., & Singh, H. (1998). The architecture of cooperation: Managing coordination costs and appropriation concerns in strategic alliances. *Administrative Science Quarterly, 43*, 781–814.

Gulati, R., Puranam, P., & Tushman, M. (2012a). Meta-organization design: Rethinking design in interorganizational and community contexts. *Strategic Management Journal, 33*, 571–586.

Gulati, R., Wohlgezogen, F., & Zhelyazkov, P. (2012b). The two facets of collaboration: Cooperation and coordination in strategic alliances. *Academy of Management Annals, 6*, 531–583.

Hamel, G. (2006). The why, what, and how of management innovation. *Harvard Business Review, 84*(2), 72–84.

Hamel, G. (2007). *The future of management.* Boston, MA: Harvard Business School Press.

Hollen, R. M. A., & Van Den Bosch, F. A. J. (2013). *Managing interorganizational interdependencies in industrial ecosystems.* Paper presented at the Academy of Management Annual Meeting, Lake Buena Vista, FL.

Hollen, R. M. A., Van Den Bosch, F. A. J., & Volberda, H. W. (2013). The role of management innovation in enabling technological process innovation: An inter-organizational perspective. *European Management Review, 10*(1), 35–50.

Holmqvist, M. (2004). Experiential learning processes of exploitation and exploration within and between organizations: An empirical study of product development. *Organization Science, 15*, 70–81.

Ireland, R. D., Hitt, M. A., & Vaidyanath, D. (2002). Alliance management as a source of competitive advantage. *Journal of Management, 28*, 413–446.

König, A., Schulte, M., & Enders, A. (2012). Inertia in response to non-paradigmatic change: The case of meta-organizations. *Research Policy, 41*, 1325–1343.

Leufkens, A. S., & Noorderhaven, N. G. (2011). Learning to collaborate in multi-organizational projects. *International Journal of Project Management, 29*, 432–441.

Levinthal, D. A. (2011). A behavioral approach to strategy—What's the alternative? *Strategic Management Journal, 32*, 1517–1523.

Liebeskind, J. P., Oliver, A. L., Zucker, L., & Brewer, M. (1996). Social networks, learning, and flexibility: Sourcing scientific knowledge in new biotechnology firms. *Organization Studies, 7*, 428–441.

Macneil, I.R. (1974). The many futures of contracts. *Southern California Law Review, 47*, 691–816.

Madhok, A., & Tallman, S. B. (1998). Resources, transactions and rents: Managing value through interfirm collaborative relationships. *Organization Science, 9*, 326–339.

Malets, O. (2010). Book review of Göran Ahrne and Nils Brunsson: *Meta-Organizations* (2008), Cheltenham, UK: Edward Elgar. *Organization Studies, 31*, 1740–1744.

Meuer, J. (2014). Archetypes of inter-firm relations in the implementation of management innovation: A set-theoretic study in China's biopharmaceutical industry. *Organization Studies. Organization Studies, 35*, 121–145.

Mol, M. J., & Birkinshaw, J. (2009). The sources of management innovation: When firms introduce new management practices. *Journal of Business Research, 62*, 1269–1280.

Neumann, K., & Bachmann, R. (2011). The containment of opportunism in the post formation period of interorganizational relationships. In T. K. Das (Ed.), *Strategic alliances in a globalizing world* (pp. 159–184). Charlotte, NC: Information Age Publishing.

Newell, S., Goussevskaia, A., Swan, J., Bresnen, M., & Obembe, A. (2008). Interdependencies in complex project ecologies: The case of biomedical innovation. *Long Range Planning, 41*(1), 33–54.

Ouchi, W. G. (1977). The relationship between organizational structure and organizational control. *Administrative Science Quarterly, 22,* 95–113.

Poppo, L., & Zenger, T. (2002). Do formal contracts and relational governance function as substitutes or complements? *Strategic Management Journal, 23,* 707–725.

Powell, T. C., Lovallo, D., & Fox, C. R. (2011). Behavioral strategy. *Strategic Management Journal, 32,* 1369–1386.

Reveley, J., & Ville, S. (2010). Enhancing industry association theory: A comparative business history contribution. *Journal of Management Studies, 47,* 837–858.

Ring, P. S., & Van De Ven, A. H. (1994). Developmental processes of cooperative interorganizational relationships. *Academy of Management Review, 19,* 90–118.

Santamaria, L., & Surroca, J. (2011). Matching the goals and impacts of R&D collaboration. *European Management Review, 8*(2), 95–109.

Shekhar, S. (2006). Understanding the virtuality of virtual organizations. *Leadership & Organization Development Journal, 27,* 465–483.

Soekijad, M., & Andriessen, E. (2003). Conditions for knowledge sharing in competitive alliances. *European Management Journal, 21,* 578–587.

Tautz, J., & Heilmann, H. R. (2008). *The buzz about the bees: Biology of a superorganism.* Berlin, Germany: Springer.

Thompson, J. D. (2003). *Organizations in action: Social science bases of administrative theory.* New Brunswick, NJ: Transaction. (Original work published 1967)

Tuite, M. F., Chisholm, R. K., & Radnor, M. (2009). *Inter-organizational decision making.* Chicago, IL: Aldine.

Uzzi, B. (1997). Social structure and competition in interfirm networks: The paradox of embeddedness. *Administrative Science Quarterly, 42,* 35–67.

Vaccaro, I. G., Jansen, J. J. P., Van Den Bosch, F. A. J., & Volberda, H. W. (2012). Management innovation and leadership: The moderating role of organizational size. *Journal of Management Studies, 49,* 28–51.

Van Den Bosch, F. A. J. (2012). *On the necessity and scientific challenges of conducting research into strategic value creating management models.* Rotterdam, Netherlands: Erasmus University Rotterdam, Erasmus Research Institute of Management (ERIM).

Van Den Bosch, F. A. J., Hollen, R. M. A., Volberda, H. W., & Baaij, M. G. (2011). *The strategic value of the Port of Rotterdam for the international competitiveness of the Netherlands: A first exploration.* Rotterdam, Netherlands: INSCOPE.

Vifell, Å. C., & Thedvall, R. (2012). Organizing for social sustainability: Governance through bureaucratization in meta-organizations. *Sustainability: Science, Practice & Policy, 8*(1), 50–58.

Volberda, H. W., Van Den Bosch, F. A. J., & Heij, C. V. (2013). Management innovation: Management as fertile ground for innovation. *European Management Review, 10*(1), 1–15.

CHAPTER 9

PROXIMITY IN INNOVATION NETWORKS

Mariane Santos Françoso, Matheus Leite Campos, and Nicholas Spyridon Vonortas

ABSTRACT

This chapter discusses the role of various dimensions of proximity on the structure and performance of innovation networks. Innovation is seldomly developed in isolation. Firms decide to engage in inter-organizational collaboration agreements to mitigate risks and costs as well as to access tangible and intangible assets that are not readily available inside their boundaries. Thoroughly accounting for the set of factors that determine the formation of ties inside the network and that also shape innovation outcomes is of high relevance for any given organization seeking to pursue external collaboration. An extensive literature review underscores the applicability of proximity dimensions for a better understanding of partnerships for interorganizational collaboration. Key insights on the impact of geographical, cognitive, institutional, social and organizational proximity on innovation network participants are introduced. Additional implications for management theory derived from the proximity framework, empirical gaps on these processes as well as avenues for future research are also highlighted herein.

INTRODUCTION

This chapter discusses the role played by proximity in innovation networks with special emphasis on the case of inter-organizational collaborations. Innovation networks represent those relational structures across

Managerial Practice Issues in Strategy and Organization, pp. 259–276

Copyright © 2023 by Information Age Publishing

www.infoagepub.com

organizations that emerge to jointly generate and advance knowledge. Inter-organizational collaboration has become a standard practice within innovation processes. Increased levels of technological complexity, strong competitive environments, pervasive uncertainties, and fast-paced market dynamics have routinized the formation of these types of networks. Firms engage on these collaborative projects to not only share risks and costs, exploit synergies and access larger pools of available knowledge and capabilities. They also participate in such innovation networks to access higher financial resources and penetrate markets thus increasing the likelihood of innovative ideas to come to fruition (Arranz & Fdez. de Arroyabe, 2008; Crespo & Vicente, 2016; Hagedoorn, 2002).

Empirical evidence suggests that these types of networks can also be characterized by the presence (or lack thereof) of several proximity dimensions (Broekel & Boschma, 2012; Lazzeretti & Capone, 2016). Proximity accounts for the similarities between connected organizations with regard to various features related to their physical closeness (geographical proximity), knowledge assimilation capabilities (cognitive proximity), set of rules and culture (institutional proximity), organizational settings (organizational proximity), as well as their social relationship structures (social proximity).

Building on this background, this chapter argues that the theoretical concepts derived from the proximity framework can play a pivotal role to further understand the performance and structure that governs innovation networks of inter-organizational collaborations. To this end, we conducted an extensive literature overview focusing on the interplay between proximity and innovation networks as well as on the set of managerial implications that stem from participation on these projects. Thoroughly accounting for the impact of proximity across networks of firms represents a pertinent subject due to the fact that the prevalence of poor protocols for partner selection might lead to high failure rates within the network of interorganizational projects that are being pursued (Morandi, 2013).

The rest of the chapter is divided as follows. The next section discusses key empirical findings on the link between inter-organizational collaboration and innovation processes. The following two sections, respectively, further elaborates on the idea of different proximity dimensions and discusses their impact on partnerships for innovation, and assesses the potential interplay between proximities and management. The last section discusses avenues for future research.

INTERORGANIZATIONAL COLLABORATION AND THE INNOVATION PROCESS

The last decades have witnessed an intense growth of collaborative agreements between independent organizations. Such process is seen in all production stages (ranging from product development to distribution) as well as through the presence of many organizational structures, such as joint-ventures and formal cooperation agreements (Powell, Koput & Smith-Doerr., 1996). Special attention has been paid to the type of cooperation that involves research and development activities (R&D), which are increasingly common in high tech-industries where keeping pace with technological advances is not a trivial task (Cantner & Graf, 2006; Cantner & Rake, 2014).

Firms decide to participate in projects for R&D collaboration not only to develop and disseminate new products and technologies. They also engage in these types of external projects to share risks and costs, develop synergies, and even foster knowledge spillover. Vonortas and Okamura (2009) show that organizations are more likely to collaborate when the perceived possibilities of knowledge spillovers are higher which, in turn, also highlights the existence of technological and market specialization similarities across those firms. When organizations are close in these two aspects, and already have a trust relationship based on previous collaboration, transaction costs become lower while the ability to learn from the partner gets higher. In addition, firms which have already experienced partnering with others, are also more likely to establish new cooperation agreements.

Inter-organizational collaboration is not a homogeneous practice as it might entail partnerships with different types of actors including suppliers (vertical cooperation), rivals (horizontal cooperation) and universities (Ahn et al., 2017; De Leeuw, Lokshin, & Duysters, 2014; Ritala, Golnam, & Wegmann, 2014). Vertical collaboration occurs inside the firms' value chain. These partnerships usually target the devising of cost-reducing technologies, the preparation of engineering projects for design optimization and, in general, any given strategy for process innovation (Belderbos, Carree, Lokshin, & Fernández Sastre, 2015; De Leeuw et al., 2014). Horizontal cooperation is set between competitors and seeks to generate new-to-market innovations, through the sharing of resources, risks, and costs (Hagedoorn, 2002). The downside to this latter collaboration is the risk of unwanted knowledge spillovers. Cooperation with universities, in turn, implies a search for state-of-the-art knowledge and, thus, the specific intention to conduct radical innovations (Bercovitz & Feldman, 2007).

Firms that choose to collaborate with external partners face, nonetheless, a tradeoff between accessibility and appropriability. On the one hand, organizations establishing external partnerships can exploit knowledge and capabilities which are not readily available inside their boundaries. They may benefit from accessing complementary resources and knowledge as this enhances their competitiveness and innovative performance. On the other hand, inter-organizational collaborations may also imply the emergence of costs for the firms, such as the need to monitor potential partners, additional learning costs, the risk of undesirable spillovers and even the partners' opportunistic behavior (Crespo & Vicente, 2016). Despite this tradeoff and the continuous presence of potential drawbacks, inter-organizational collaborations have become a standard procedure as many firms operating in different sectors are progressively willing to take part on these trends.

Considering this relevance, the phenomenon of inter-organizational collaboration has been approached by different theoretical perspectives. They seek to more deeply understand the main reasons that motivate a given firm to engage in innovation partnerships as well as define the set of benefits that stem from their participation in these practices. According to Lee and Vonortas (2002), some of these theoretical perspectives include the transaction costs view, the resource-based approach, the dynamic capabilities framework as well as key insights from network theory. In the next lines, we will explore in detail each of those.

The transaction cost approach investigates the circumstances under which external cooperation stands as the most efficient form of organization across companies. Pioneered by Coase (1937) and Williamson (1975), this approach evolves around the idea that firms aim at minimizing production and transaction costs. These two types of costs, in turn, also determine the extent of the firm's boundaries. Production costs are firm-specific and vary according to factors such as absorptive capacity, economies of scale and scope, as well as on the availability of tangible and intangible assets. Transaction costs are transaction-specific and differ depending on the type of expenses that are involved in contractual relationships. If the costs to internalize an activity are found to be higher than the costs associated to contract enforcing, the firm will then decide to carry out such transaction inside the market. The other way around, if those costs are lower, the firm will then expand its boundaries by internalizing this new activity (Hemphill & Vonortas, 2003; Lee & Vonortas, 2002).

External collaboration is then seen as a feasible organizational strategy that lies in between the enforcing of market contracts and the decision to internalize activities. This idea is built on the fact that the issuing of market contracts encompassing all potential contingences represents a daunting task on a rapidly changing business environment. Along the same lines, the process of internalizing activities can be time-consuming and might not allow for the exploration of economies of scale and scope. Therefore, collaborating with other organizations represents a valid alternative to these two latter practices. It is worth mentioning, however, that external cooperation is not free of costs. Some resources are partnership specific as they may be adapted to meet particular standards, as well as some specific requirements demanded by partners. In addition, changes in the environment may harm the estimation of costs derived from participation in these partnerships and even make some knowledge and resources obsolete (Li & Qian, 2018).

Although the theory of transaction costs has been a popular way to explain inter-organizational cooperation, some scholars argue that this approach does not fully capture some of the strategic aspects that are also involved in this phenomenon. The emergence of learning processes and the accumulation of dynamic capabilities constitute some of the key elements of network cooperation that are not thoroughly accounted for by this approach (Arranz & Fdez. de Arroyabe, 2008; Teece, Pisano, & Shuen, 1997). In light of this situation, the following three theoretical perspectives aim to fill such gap.

The resource-based approach switches the focus of analysis from transaction and production costs to account for the social and strategic dynamic aspects that are involved on the process of inter-organizational collaboration. Based on Penrose (1959), this approach portrays firms as a collection of resources, encompassing both tangibles and intangibles. The more valuable, rare, non-substitutable, difficult to transfer and imitate these resources are, the better the position of the firm. External cooperation thus constitutes a strategy to obtain those critical and complementary resources that are not available inside the boundaries of the firm. Hence, firms' competitive advantages not only depend on the resources they own, but also on the resources that they are able to mobilize with external partners (Arranz & Fdez. de Arroyabe, 2008; Lavie, 2006; Lee & Vonortas, 2002).

By focusing on the process of capability accumulation, the dynamic capabilities framework also addresses existing gaps within the transaction costs approach. Dynamic capabilities can be defined as the ability of a given firm to integrate, build as well as reset competences in order to cope with challenges stemming from the business environment. This framework explicitly deals with the potential issues of path-dependency that might emerge during the processes of learning and knowledge accumulation (Nelson & Winter, 1982). In this context, since the development of new capabilities is understood as a non-trivial task, processes for external cooperation then become a rather useful tool that enables firms access knowledge-based capabilities without the need of internalizing them. Furthermore, under this approach, partnerships are regarded as a way of learning and exchanging knowledge that even allows for the creation of new skills and capabilities inside the firm (Teece, 1992; Teece et al., 1997).

The network approach also contributes to a better understanding of inter-organizational collaborations by underscoring the relevance of interdependences across firms. Networks are relational structures whereby different nodes (in this case firms) are connected through a direct link. Under this framework, the sharing of resources and knowledge that is derived from a collaboration between two nodes can also benefit indirectly

connected firms, through the existence of a link with an intermediary organization (Newman, Barabási, & Watts, 2011; Owen-Smith & Powell, 2004;
Powell et al., 1996). This focus on the web of cooperative linkages across
firms permits a detailed assessment on the potential impact that increasing collaboration might have on the already established links and nodes
operating inside the network.

Taking into consideration concepts that explain network formation
(such as efficiency, synergy, and power) can also advance the analysis of
inter-organizational cooperation. The concepts of efficiency and synergy
of networks refer to the ability of firms to explore economies of scale and
scope. They highlight the importance of specialization in activities that
are essential to the competitive advantage of the firm as well as the need
to explore the capabilities of entities that coexist with them. Pursuing
networks of collaborations may lower transaction costs and increase the
opportunities for joint value creation (Jarillo, 1988; Miles & Snow, 1984).
The power dimension, on the other hand, indicates that firms can also
shape the structure and performance of the network depending on their
relative position, as some can enjoy an "early fit" that allows them to secure
resources and control flows inside the web (Miles & Snow, 1984). Thus,
achieving a central position in the networks can be as well a great source
of competitive advantage for the firm (Owen-Smith & Powell, 2004; Powell,
Koput, White, & Owen-Smith, 2005).

Having introduced these theoretical perspectives, we will now turn to
discuss the relevance of the proximity framework as a complement of our
understanding of inter-organizational collaborations. As will be observed,
based upon concepts built under the network approach, the proximity
framework provides additional insights on this phenomenon through its
emphasis on the attributes of the parties that are involved in such collaboration. Further elaborating on these ideas, as well as exploring the
managerial implications that are part of these processes, will be the main
objective of the next sections.

THE PROXIMITY FRAMEWORK AND INNOVATION NETWORKS

This section provides key definitions that are derived from the proximity
framework and introduces some of the empirical work that has utilized this
approach to describe inter-organizational collaborations.

The seminal work conducted by Boschma (2005) represents one of the
pivotal starting points on the discussion of how innovation networks are
impacted by factors of proximity across organizations. The formation of
networks requires the deliberate engagement of parties as well as the existence of some degree of coordination among these economic agents to

effectively succeed on the exchange of knowledge. Boschma (2005) characterizes the idea of proximity between organizations through the presence (or the lack thereof) of five distinctive dimensions: geographical, cognitive, organizational as well as social and institutional proximity.[1]

Geographical proximity accounts for the physical closeness that exists between different organizations and can be observed through the economies of agglomeration that emerge during innovation processes. Given the fact that some specific types of knowledge are territorially bounded (and thus difficult to transfer), geographical proximity emphasizes the spatial dimension that is involved in the formation of networks (Audretsch & Feldman, 1996; Feldman & Kogler, 2010; Jaffe, Trajtenberg, & Henderson, 1993). Cognitive proximity, on the other hand, deals with factors of absorptive capacities (Taalbi, 2020). Two agents seeking to exchange knowledge might encounter difficulties in doing it if they find themselves in different cognitive levels. For learning to take place, the receiver must have a sufficient degree of specialized knowledge to fully understand the set of ideas that are conveyed (Boschma & Frenken, 2010). In other words, it must possess well developed absorptive capacities. Therefore, the amount of knowledge being transferred might be irrelevant if low absorptive capacities prevail. Organizational proximity studies the process by which economic agents are connected through formal ties. Such formal ties are believed to play a pivotal role as they define the "extent to which relations are shared in an organizational arrangement, either within or between organizations" (Boschma, 2005). Therefore, organizational proximity relates to sharing similar organizational settings.

Even though the social and institutional dimensions of proximities seem to be closely linked to one another, their respective trends are conditioned by different environment settings. Social proximity has to do with the existence of informal and trust-based ties between agents of a network (Boschma, 2005). Trust is the main aspect shaping this kind of proximity, which is then powered by elements such as friendship, kinship, or past experiences (Tsouri, 2019). Institutional proximity, on the other hand, is configured by the degree through which economic agents share the same institutional environment (Broekel & Boschma, 2012; Boschma, 2005). This includes cultural aspects (such as language), social norms, rules and regulations, market standards and so forth. As can be inferred, the social and institutional dimensions of proximity then evolve around different scope of analysis (and thus have different implications for network collaboration) given the fact the first types of ties tend to form at the micro-level (between closely bonded agents), while the latter are determined by the macro-level institutional environment within which economic agents find themselves in.

At this point, it is worth mentioning that the different forms of proximity here described are not necessarily amalgamated across them. Instead, they possess a complementary nature as the absence of one may be compensated by the other (Bednarz & Broekel, 2019; Broekel & Mueller, 2018; Corradini, 2019; Françoso & Vonortas, 2022; Garcia, Araujo, Mascarini, Santos, & Costa, 2018; Makkonen, Williams, Mitze, & Weidenfeld, 2018; Santos, Garcia, Araujo, Mascarini, & Costa, 2021). Thus, the plural nature of proximity stands as an additional element that enables a more accurate interpretation of the mechanisms by which knowledge is constructed and shared within networks of people and organizations.

Acknowledging this relevance, a large body of empirical research has relied on the proximity dimensions to describe the set of elements that can foster increasing levels of cooperation on the development of innovation-related activities. Some of these analyses include case studies for business networks (Balland, Belso-Martínez, & Morrison, 2016; Morescalchi, Pammolli, Penner, Petersen, & Riccaboni, 2015; Tsouri, 2019), informal networks (Capone & Lazzeretti, 2018) as well research networks (Broekel & Boschma, 2012; Broekel & Hartog, 2013; Marek, Titze, Fuhrmeister, & Blum, 2017).

Further insights on the assessment of inter-organizational collaborations can also be obtained by taking into consideration the different subcategories that are present within some of the proximity dimensions. For instance, Werker, Korzinov, and Cunningham (2019) differentiate between the presence of pure physical proximity and systemic proximity. Unlike pure physical proximity, systemic proximity accounts for the effects that arise because of being geographically close, such as being allocated to the same innovation systems and being influenced by the same informal institutions. Along the same lines, while physical proximity impacts the likelihood of partnership formation, systemic proximity seems to be associated with the generation of a higher number of collaborative results thus positively impacting output performance of the agreements being pursued (Werker et al., 2019). Cognitive proximities also entail a large number of subcategories that are related to the presence of similarities in terms of common technical language, way of thinking about the technology/product, know what, know how, among others (Huber, 2012). Those latter skills, however, do not necessarily possess a similar degree of relevance in the process of tie-formation and may even be influenced by other factors such as the need for technological, spatial, and sectoral specificities inside the network.

Notwithstanding the importance of proximities for tie-formation, it is also important to highlight that the presence of too much proximity might also imply various shortcomings that can even erode some of the potential benefits of being engaged in networks. Too much cognitive proximity is detrimental to the innovation activity of firms that are too much alike in terms of the type of knowledge being utilized and type of internal processes being performed. In those cases, variations in knowledge sources tend to become scarce, making it difficult for new ideas to spur (Broekel & Mueller, 2018; Nooteboom, 2011). The same could be said about too much institutional proximity. Players operating on the same playing field, guided by the same strict set of rules tend to look inwards, thus providing for inertia and lock-in (Bercovitz & Feldman, 2007). Too much organizational proximity, by its turn, equals rigid organizational bonds, which discourages agents to seek new connections beyond the formally established ones (e.g., subsidiaries of firms with vertical and bureaucratic governance structures) (Broekel & Boschma, 2012).

Similarly, too much social proximity also discourages the formation of new bonds outside the socially established ones. This hinders the formation of other relations which could be fundamental for competitiveness and the acquisition of new knowledge (Balland, Boschma, & Frenken, 2015). Finally, too much geographical proximity does not allow for geographical openness, as agents will tend to develop relations within the same geographical clustering of organizations and lead, yet again, to a situation of lock-in (Boschma & Frenken, 2010; Broekel & Boschma, 2012).

Pursuing an optimal level of proximity then becomes an important goal for the successful performance of the innovation network (Fitjar et al., 2016). Achieving this objective, nonetheless, represents a challenging task because the optimal proximity level associated to a given network also varies depending on the specific type of tie being considered. Empirical evidence suggests that proximity dimensions are more important for tie-formation, while particular distances (i.e., absence of proximities) are more relevant for tie-continuation (Broekel & Bednarz, 2018; Fantino, Mori, & Scalise, 2015; Juhász & Lengyel, 2018). Broekel and Bednarz (2018) argue that institutional proximity might yield different results for the processes of tie-formation and tie-continuation in the context of collaborative agreements. In the view of those authors, institutional proximity might increase the likelihood of tie-formation, but also harms the continuation of existing links.

Along the same lines, acquiring an optimal degree of proximity is also conditioned by the different partnership stages. Lazzeretti and Capone (2016) investigated the expansion of innovation networks in the region of Tuscany (Italy) and found that social and institutional proximities were especially relevant during the initial stages of network formation, while cognitive and geographical proximities were far more important in latter phases. Similarly, on their analysis of the biomedical industry in the region of Guangzhou (China), Zhang, Qian, and Zhao (2020) pointed out that geographical proximity was more relevant during early phases of collaborations, while the cognitive and organizational proximity were more useful in the rapid stages of development.

The mechanisms that configure a balance between the levels of proximity and distance inside networks of collaborations can be better understood by focusing on their impact on innovation outcomes. Ties based on proximities may be more likely to generate incremental technologies, while ties based on distances are more related to radical innovations and technological breakthrough. Even more so, innovation outcomes are not only closely related to the presence of cognitive dimensions (such as the availability of similar technical competences) but also seem to shape the extent to which other types of proximity can take place inside the network. For instance, Bercovitz and Feldman (2007) show that firms manage to overcome institutional distance when their strategy is focused on exploring new innovation capabilities, rather than on exploiting existing competences. In these specific cases, firms prefer to engage in collaboration agreements with universities which, by definition, are institutionally distant partners. Radical innovation seems to be more successfully driven by distances rather by proximities (Arant et al., 2019), while partnerships for applied research benefit more from geographical proximity than those focused on basic research (Hinzmann, Cantner, & Graf, 2019).

PROXIMITY AND NETWORK MANAGEMENT

The relationship between the choice of a given partner and the type of innovation strategy being followed represents a particular subject within the field of management that could potentially benefit from the theoretical underpinnings of the proximity framework. Such relation constitutes a crucial topic for management analyses given the fact that poor partner choices on innovation related projects might both lead to high failure rates and below performance expectations (Morandi, 2013).

The screening method developed by Marra, Carlei, and Baldassari (2020) on the impact from similar cognitive competences on the process of partner selection, constitutes one of the few quantitative studies that have thoroughly addressed this issue. In line with this work, firms that aim at specializing on a specific technological field would most likely collaborate with other entities that share similar technical knowledge. On the opposite side, firms that attempt to diversify their innovation-related activities would seek to cooperate with those other entities that possess more distant knowledge with respect to theirs.

To further elaborate on the process to select strategic partners for successful partnership collaboration, we can refer back to our discussion on key proximity concepts. As advanced before, one important element stressed by literature is the compensating effect that each proximity dimension has with respect to others, which basically means that not all proximities need to be present on a given link at once. In light of these compensation mechanisms, firms might then decide to more accurately manage their portfolio of potential partners by trying to find a balance between their distances and proximities. For instance, if potential partners are found to be geographically close but cognitively distant, firms might be more likely to engage on diversification strategies as exemplified by Marra et al. (2020). By the same token, when seeking for partnerships with organizational distant entities, firms could potentially target institutional proximate partners that share similar communication channels, as well as key cultural and general values.

The degree of proximity that is shared across strategic partners can also vary not only with respect to the innovation strategy being set but also according to the time prospects and desired technological outcome stemming from such collaboration. Partnerships characterized by medium proximity levels are generally associated with high innovation rates (Fitjar et al., 2016). Institutional distant partnerships might also be more adequate for those projects involving disruptive technologies in the long-term. As shown by various studies, institutionally distant collaborations are particularly useful for those firms that seek to explore new production capabilities and conduct research activities at the technological frontier (Bercovitz & Feldman, 2007; Mitze et al., 2015; Morandi, 2013). Ensuring the existence of communication channels across the different entities and individuals that participate on these projects represents a major challenge for this type of collaboration. Therefore, firms pursuing a disruptive innovation strategy based on collaborations with institutionally distant partners could also aim to include in these projects other types of entities from which they share close social proximity (Jiang, Bao, Xie, & Gao, 2016; Ybarra & Turk, 2009; Zhang, Baden-Fuller, & Mangematin, 2007). Including firms that have already collaborated with either partner as well as individuals that share a common past may alleviate problems to communicate.

A final note regards to the importance of taking into consideration the different procedures through which proximity dimensions can be empirically operationalized. For instance, even though there is a large consensus on the feasibility to measure the presence of geographical proximity across economic agents, some of the indicators that are being used on such computation can also vary when accounting for factors such as physical distance, travelling distance, belonging to a specific territorial area and so forth. The ideas underlying the other proximity dimensions are more subjective and might then even imply more varied measures. Therefore, it should be kept in mind that all of the managerial and organizational implications discussed on this chapter are also strictly conditioned by the way in which each proximity dimension has been quantified according to the existing body of research here presented.

CONCLUSION AND FUTURE RESEARCH AGENDA

This chapter examined the extent to which the proximity framework might contribute to advance our understanding of innovation networks. Based upon concepts drawn from the network approach, the proximity framework focuses primarily on the the determinants of cooperation as well as on partner attributes that are more suitable to partnership formation, continuation, and dissolution. Empirical analysis has not only underscored the relevance of proximities between partners for successful tie-formation, but also highlight the need to balance out the presence of each proximity dimension in order to avoid situations of lock-in while ensuring tie-continuation

Although the applicability of the proximity framework is gaining increasing popularity on the assessment of innovation networks, there are still a number of interesting elements shaping these processes that nonetheless remain relatively unexplored. Our discussion suggests that a tighter exploration of the interplay between the various dimensions of proximity and management theory could potentially lead to the emergence of promising avenues of research. For instance, empirical studies on the configuration of projects for inter-organizational collaborations could be improved upon if they were to include concepts related to the negotiation position of firms (power dynamics, the existence of vertical/horizontal structures, and so forth) and their absorptive capacity regarding backward and forward knowledge in the web of alliances. Both of these items depend on various dimensions of proximity. Along the same lines, we also observe that some of the issues involved in the relationship between distances and failure to cooperate have not been extensively addressed. Cooperation failure can be regarded as the set of factors that lead to a premature termination of the project. Conducting thorough analyses on this particular area of research will be of importance to management as the existence of failing contracts not only implies money and time losses but also the presence of poor protocols for partner selection and inadequate planning inside the organization.

Yet another gap to be accounted for stems from the fact that quantitative appraisals linked to the proximity framework have mostly focused on the dynamics in Europe, the United States and China, without much discussion on other regions of the global south. This situation raises important questions on the extent to which the proximity dimension can also explain partnership formation in different environment settings that shape innovation systems across developing and emerging economies. Elements characterizing the performance of innovation activities in those parts of the world economy (such as the presence of weak institutions, low absorptive capacities and, lack of engagement from local firms on R&D activities, etc.) can seriously condition the impact of proximity dimensions, as the perceived risks and costs involved in cooperation networks can be significantly higher than otherwise anticipated.

Cooperation between firms and universities represents one complementary example that underlies the need to consider the prevalence of different institutional settings across developed and developing economies. Existing research in developed economies suggests that collaboration agreements between these two entities is less subject to risks given the fact that this type of institutionally distant partnerships are generally motivated by the pursuit of state-of-the-art research and the need of radical innovations. When it comes to the case of developing countries, however, these types of institutional distant partnerships involving universities might not necessarily be motivated by the aforementioned set of factors but rather constitute the firm's response to the prevailing local capabilities (insufficiency of local partners and higher uncertainties generated by institutional weakness, see Arocena & Sutz (2010) and Rapini, Alberquerque, Chave, Silva, Souza, Righi, and da Cruz (2009). Providing quantitative support on these claims is of high relevance, as the occurrence of those different settings might have an impact on the way by which proximities, inter-organizational collaborations and management practices are connected.

The analysis of sectors besides the science-based ones represents other avenue of research that could substantially benefit from the theoretical reasoning underlined within the proximity framework. As argued by Vonortas and Okamura (2009), the process of partnership formation across industrial sectors is also conditioned by the existing technology as well as by the productive structure that configures their performance. Proximity dimensions can assist on the efforts to identify the role played by those factors and can advance our understanding on the mechanism by which distinct industries engage on collaborative agreements.

Addressing partnership configuration in the context of macro-institutional distance constitutes one additional empirical gap that can be fed with ideas derived by proximity dimensions. Being part of an inter-organizational collaboration network represents a challenging endeavor for organizations due to the interaction of various complex factors related to the presence of different cultural baggage, legal frameworks, languages and so forth. A thorough assessment of the different proximity dimensions might lead to the devising of strategies that seek to mitigate the challenges derived from such macro institutional considerations. In doing this, future research will then be able to provide novel evidence that could guide areas for international cooperation management.

NOTE

1. Other types of proximity are also present in the literature. This is the case of industry proximity which represents the trade intensity between companies (Carboni, 2013). Nonetheless, these are less frequently mentioned as they can often be encompassed, to some extent, in the context of the above-mentioned five proximity dimensions

ACKNOWLEDGMENTS

The authors acknowledge support by The São Paulo Research Foundation (FAPESP) in connection to the São Paulo Excellence Chair "Innovation Systems, Strategy and Policy" (InSySPo) at the University of Campinas (grant numbers 19/04300-5; 20/12676-2 and 20/12704-6). They also acknowledge the excellent editorial support of Dr Juan Carlos Castillo, a postdoctoral researcher with InSySPo. None of the affiliated organizations is responsible for the contents of this article. Remaining mistakes and misconceptions are solely the responsibility of the authors.

REFERENCES

Ahn, J. M., Kim, D. B., & Moon, S. (2017). Determinants of innovation collaboration selection: A comparative analysis of Korea and Germany. *Innovation: Management, Policy and Practice, 19*(2), 125–145.

Arant, W., Fornahl, D., Grashof, N., Hesse, K., & Söllner, C. (2019). University-industry collaborations—The key to radical innovations? *Review of Regional Research, 39*(2), 119–141.

Arocena, R., & Sutz, J. (2010). Weak knowledge demand in the South: Learning divides and innovation policies. *Science and Public Policy, 37*(8), 571–582.

Arranz, N., & Fdez. de Arroyabe, J. C. (2008). The choice of partners in R&D cooperation: An empirical analysis of Spanish firms. *Technovation, 28*(1–2), 88–100.

Audretsch, D. B., & Feldman, M. P. (1996). R&D Spillovers and the Geography of Innovation and Production. *American Economic Review, 86*(3), 630–640.

Balland, P. A., Belso-Martínez, J. A., & Morrison, A. (2016). The dynamics of technical and business knowledge networks in industrial clusters: Embeddedness, status, or proximity? *Economic Geography, 92*(1), 35–60.

Balland, P. A., Boschma, R., & Frenken, K. (2015). Proximity and innovation: From statics to dynamics. *Regional Studies, 49*(6), 907–920.

Bednarz, M., & Broekel, T. (2019). The relationship of policy induced R&D networks and inter-regional knowledge diffusion. *Journal of Evolutionary Economics, 29*(5), 1459–1481.

Belderbos, R., Carree, M., Lokshin, B., & Fernández Sastre, J. (2015). Inter-temporal patterns of R&D collaboration and innovative performance. *Journal of Technology Transfer, 40*(1), 123–137.

Bercovitz, J. E. L., & Feldman, M. P. (2007). Fishing upstream: Firm innovation strategy and university research alliances. *Research Policy, 36*(7), 930–948.

Boschma, R. (2005). Proximity and innovation: A critical assessment. *Regional Studies, 39*(1), 61–74.

Boschma, R., & Frenken, K. (2010). The spatial evolution of innovation networks: A proximity perspective. In R. Boschma & R. Martin (Eds.), *The handbook of evolutionary economic geography* (pp. 120–135). Cheltenham, UK: Edward Elgar Publishing Limited.

Broekel, T., & Bednarz, M. (2018). Disentangling link formation and dissolution in spatial networks: An application of a two-mode STERGM to a project-based R&D network in the German biotechnology industry. *Networks and Spatial Economics, 18*(3), 677–704.

Broekel, T., & Boschma, R. (2012). Knowledge networks in the Dutch aviation industry: The proximity paradox. *Journal of Economic Geography, 12*(2), 409–433.

Broekel, T., & Hartog, M. (2013). Explaining the structure of inter-organizational networks using exponential random graph models. *Industry and Innovation, 20*(3), 277–295.

Broekel, T., & Mueller, W. (2018). Critical links in knowledge networks – What about proximities and gatekeeper organisations? *Industry and Innovation, 25*(10), 919–939.

Cantner, U., & Graf, H. (2006). The network of innovators in Jena: An application of social network analysis. *Research Policy, 35*(4), 463–480.

Cantner, U., & Rake, B. (2014). International research networks in pharmaceuticals: Structure and dynamics. *Research Policy, 43*(2), 333–348.

Capone, F., & Lazzeretti, L. (2018). The different roles of proximity in multiple informal network relationships: Evidence from the cluster of high technology applied to cultural goods in tuscany. *Industry and Innovation, 25*(9), 897–917.

Coase, R. H. (1937). The nature of the firm. *Economica, 4*(16), 386–405.

Corradini, C. (2019). Location determinants of green technological entry: Evidence from European regions. *Small Business Economics, 52*(4), 845–858.

Crespo, J., & Vicente, J. (2016). Proximity and distance in knowledge relationships: From micro to structural considerations based on territorial knowledge dynamics (TKDs). *Regional Studies, 50*(2), 202–219.

De Leeuw, T., Lokshin, B., & Duysters, G. (2014). Returns to alliance portfolio diversity: The relative effects of partner diversity on firm's innovative performance and productivity. *Journal of Business Research, 67*(9), 1839–1849.

Fantino, D., Mori, A., & Scalise, D. (2015). Collaboration between firms and universities in Italy: The role of a firm's proximity to top-Rated departments. *Italian Economic Journal, 1*(2), 219–251.

Feldman, M. P., & Kogler, D. F. (2010). Stylized facts in the geography of innovation. In B. H. Hall & N. Rosenberg (Eds.), *Handbook of the economics of innovation* (Vol.1, pp. 381–480). Amsterdam, Netherlands: Elsevier.

Fitjar, R. D., Huber, F., & Rodríguez-Pose, A. (2016). Not too close, not too far: testing the Goldilocks principle of "optimal" distance in innovation networks. *Industry and Innovation, 23*(6), 465–487.

Françoso, M. S., & Vonortas, N. S. (2022). Gatekeepers in regional innovation networks: Evidence from an emerging economy. *Journal of Technology Transfer, 47*(1). https://doi.org/10.1007/s10961-022-09922-4

Garcia, R., Araujo, V., Mascarini, S., Gomes Dos Santos, E., & Costa, A. (2018). Is cognitive proximity a driver of geographical distance of university–industry collaboration? *Area Development and Policy, 3*(3), 349–367.

Hagedoorn, J. (2002). Inter-firm R&D partnerships: An overview of major trends and patterns since 1960. *Research Policy, 31*(4), 477–492.

Hemphill, T. A., & Vonortas, N. S. (2003). Strategic research partnerships: A managerial perspective. *Technology Analysis and Strategic Management, 15*(2), 255–271.

Hinzmann, S., Cantner, U., & Graf, H. (2019). The role of geographical proximity for project performance: Evidence from the German leading-edge cluster competition. *Journal of Technology Transfer, 44*(6), 1744–1783.

Huber, F. (2012). On the role and interrelationship of spatial, social and cognitive proximity: Personal knowledge relationships of R&D workers in the Cambridge Information Technology Cluster. *Regional Studies, 46*(9), 1169–1182.

Jaffe, A. B., Trajtenberg, M., & Henderson, R. (1993). Geographic localization of knowledge spillovers as evidenced by patent citations. *Quarterly Journal of Economics, 108*(3), 577–598.

Jarillo, J. C. (1988). On strategic networks. *Strategic Management Journal, 9*(1), 31–41.

Jiang, X., Bao, Y., Xie, Y., & Gao, S. (2016). Partner trustworthiness, knowledge flow in strategic alliances, and firm competitiveness: A contingency perspective. *Journal of Business Research, 69*(2), 804–814.

Juhász, S., & Lengyel, B. (2018). Creation and persistence of ties in cluster knowledge networks. *Journal of Economic Geography, 18*(6), 1203–1226.

Lavie, D. (2006). The competitive advantage of interconnected firms: An extension of the resource-based view. *Academy of Management Review 31*(3), 638–658.

Lazzeretti, L., & Capone, F. (2016). How proximity matters in innovation networks dynamics along the cluster evolution. A study of the high technology applied to cultural goods. *Journal of Business Research, 69*(12), 5855–5868.

Lee, C. S., & Vonortas, N. S. (2002). Toward an integrated model of strategy formulation for strategic technical alliances. *International Journal of Technology Transfer and Commercialisation, 1*(3), 292–312.

Li, L., & Qian, G. (2018). Strategic alliances in technology industries: a different rationale. *Journal of Business Strategy, 39*(2), 3–11.

Makkonen, T., Williams, A. M., Mitze, T., & Weidenfeld, A. (2018). Science and technology cooperation in cross-border regions: A proximity approach with evidence for Northern Europe. *European Planning Studies, 26*(10), 1961–1979.

Marek, P., Titze, M., Fuhrmeister, C., & Blum, U. (2017). R&D collaborations and the role of proximity. *Regional Studies, 51*(12), 1761–1773.

Marra, A., Carlei, V., & Baldassari, C. (2020). Exploring networks of proximity for partner selection, firms' collaboration and knowledge exchange. The case of clean-tech industry. *Business Strategy and the Environment, 29*(3), 1034–1044.

Miles, R. E., & Snow, C. C. (1984). Fit, failure and the Hall of Fame. *California Management Review, 26*(3), 10–28.

Mitze, T., Alecke, B., Reinkowski, J., & Untiedt, G. (2015). Linking collaborative R&D strategies with the research and innovation performance of SMEs in peripheral regions: Do spatial and organizational choices make a difference? *Annals of Regional Science, 55*(2–3), 555–596.

Morandi, V. (2013). The management of industry-university joint research projects: How do partners coordinate and control R&D activities? *Journal of Technology Transfer, 38*(2), 69–92.

Morescalchi, A., Pammolli, F., Penner, O., Petersen, A. M., & Riccaboni, M. (2015). The evolution of networks of innovators within and across borders: Evidence from patent data. *Research Policy, 44*(3), 651–668.

Nelson, R. R., & Winter, S. G. (1982). *An evolutionary theory of change.* Cambridge, MA: Belknap Press of Harvard University Press.

Newman, M., Barabási, A. L., & Watts, D. J. (2011). *The structure and dynamics of networks.* Princeton, NJ: Princeton University Press.

Nooteboom, B. (2011). *Learning and Innovation in organizations and economies.* New York, NY: Oxford University Press.

Owen-Smith, J., & Powell, W. W. (2004). Knowledge Networks as Channels and Conduits: The Effects of Spillovers in the Boston Biotechnology Community. *Organization Science, 15*(1), 5–21.

Penrose, E. T. (1959). *The Theory of the Growth of the Firm.* New York, NY: John Wiley & Sons.

Powell, W. W., Koput, K. W., & Smith-Doerr, L. (1996). Interorganizational collaboration and the locus of innovation: Networks of learning in biotechnology. *Administrative Science Quarterly, 41*(1), 116–145.

Powell, W. W., Koput, K. W., White, D. R., & Owen-Smith, J. (2005). Network dynamics and field evolution: The growth of interorganizational collaboration in the life sciences. *American Journal of Sociology, 110*(4), 1132–1205.

Rapini, M. S., Alberquerque, E., Chave, C. V., Silva, L. A., de Souza, S. G. A., Righi, H. M., & da Cruz, W. M. S. (2009). University-industry interactions in an immature system of innovation: Evidence from Minas Gerais, Brazil. *Science and Public Policy, 36*(5), 373–386.

Ritala, P., Golnam, A., & Wegmann, A. (2014). Coopetition-based business models: The case of Amazon.com. *Industrial Marketing Management, 43*(2), 236–249.

Santos, E. G., Garcia, R., Araujo, V., Mascarini, S., & Costa, A. (2021). Spatial and non-spatial proximity in university–industry collaboration: Mutual reinforcement and decreasing effects. *Regional Science Policy and Practice, 13*(4), 1249–1261.

Taalbi, J. (2020). Evolution and structure of technological systems-An innovation output network. *Research Policy, 49*(8), 104010.

Teece, D. J. (1992). Competition, cooperation, and innovation. Organizational arrangements for regimes of rapid technological progress. *Journal of Economic Behavior and Organization, 18*(1), 1–25.

Teece, D. J., Pisano, G., & Shuen, A. (1997). Dynamic capabilities and strategic management. *Strategic Management Journal, 18*(7), 509–533.

Tsouri, M. (2019). Knowledge transfer in time of crisis: Evidence from the Trentino region. *Industry and Innovation, 26*(7), 820–842.

Vonortas, N. S., & Okamura, K. (2009). Research partners. *International Journal of Technology Management, 46*(3–4), 280–306.

Werker, C., Korzinov, V., & Cunningham, S. (2019). Formation and output of collaborations: The role of proximity in German nanotechnology. *Journal of Evolutionary Economics, 29*(2), 697–719.

Williamson, O. E. (1975). *Markets and hierarchies: Analysis and antitrust implications: A study in the economics of internal organization*. New York, NY: Free Press.

Ybarra, C. E., & Turk, T. A. (2009). The evolution of trust in information technology alliances. *Journal of High Technology Management Research, 20*(1), 62–74.

Zhang, J., Baden-Fuller, C., & Mangematin, V. (2007). Technological knowledge base, R&D organization structure and alliance formation: Evidence from the biopharmaceutical industry. *Research Policy, 36*(4), 515–528.

Zhang, K., Qian, Q., & Zhao, Y. (2020). Evolution of guangzhou biomedical industry innovation network structure and its proximity mechanism. *Sustainability* (Switzerland), *12*(6), 2456–2476.

CHAPTER 10

COPING WITH COMPETING INSTITUTIONAL LOGICS IN PUBLIC-PRIVATE ALLIANCES

Angel Saz-Carranza and Francisco Longo

ABSTRACT

Cross-sector inter-organizational partnerships, alliances and networks have become extremely popular. Such phenomena bring together diverse actors with differing, and often competing, institutional logics. Understanding how these logics interact and often hinder the collaborative is important for the management of the alliance. The management of competing institutional logics is central to alliance success. Competing logics are of particular relevance in alliances bring together public- and private-sector actors, as actors from these different sectors draw on very dissimilar premises, assumptions and valid rules. This chapter describes how competing institutional logics are present in public-private joint ventures, and proposes some managerial practices that allow participants in public-private joint ventures to successfully manage competing logics. The chapter draws on a case study of a private economic development company, PTB, set up by various town halls, a savings bank and a small group of leading local entrepreneurs near Barcelona, Spain.

INTRODUCTION

Cross-sector inter-organizational partnerships, alliances and networks have become extremely important. In today's complex society, full of "wicked

Managerial Practice Issues in Strategy and Organization, pp. 277–293
277

problems" (Rittel & Webber, 1973), no player can reach its goals alone. In the field of economic development policy, no single public or private organization can, by itself, undertake an enterprise such as the case presented in this chapter. Inter-organizational and cross-sector cooperation is therefore a necessary condition for economic development.

Cross-sector cooperation is made difficult by partner diversity (Huxham & Beech, 2003) and by the differences between the public and private sectors (Rainey & Bozeman, 2000). Cross-sector alliances, therefore, are governed by competing societal institutional logics, and the success of these alliances depends on the proper management of the competing logics. Yet, while research exists on how national and corporate cultures affect strategic alliances (Das & Kumar, 2010; Robson, Katsikeas, & Bello, 2008), little is known about precisely how competing societal institutional logics (Thornton, 2004), and attempts to manage them, affect public-private collaboratives.

This chapter aims to fill this gap by illustrating how competing logics co-exist in public-private collaboratives and how alliance managers cope with them.

A PUBLIC-PRIVATE JOINT VENTURE TO ENHANCE TERRITORIAL DEVELOPMENT: THE CASE OF PTB

In 2002, a bank and a local government, together with other public and private actors, set up a public-private joint venture called PTB, which was dedicated to developing strategic projects to stimulate local activity, drawing up strategic projects to foster business and development, and boosting economic activity. PTB was based in Manresa, a city of 70,000 inhabitants and the largest Bages county town. Bages county has a total of 155,000 inhabitants and is located about 50 kilometers inland from Barcelona, Spain. With the exception of Manresa, all of the county's 35 towns have fewer than 10,000 inhabitants.

PTB is open to all through public share subscriptions, with a required minimum subscription of 30,000 euros. PTB is governed by a General Assembly of Shareholders, which meets annually, and a Board of Directors, which meets four times a year. The management staff comprises a general manager, who reports to the Board of Directors, and an assistant to the general manager (see Figure 10.1). Neither the general manager nor the assistant belongs to nor comes from any of the shareholders.

After being successfully created by businesses and city councils and raising €15 million, in 2003 PTB bought land to develop a technology park in the hopes of attracting high value-adding businesses to the region. Shortly thereafter, however, PTB was in crisis: the media labelled PTB a

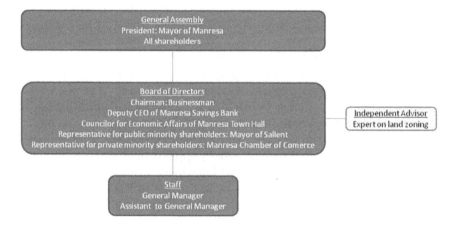

Figure 10.1. PTB's main actors.

mere speculative venture, disputes erupted between public and private shareholders, and environmentalist groups railed against the joint venture. PTB successfully navigated these events and, in 2008, broke ground on the Bages County Technology Park.

PTB is a high-performance case and an excellent example of how competing logics can be successfully managed. Five metrics can be used to measure the performance of international joint business ventures: survival, financial output, overall satisfaction, achievement of individual or joint goals, and learning (Ren, Gray, & Kim, 2009). We will apply these metrics to the case of PTB, as we are not aware of any specific performance measures for public-private joint ventures.

PTB has been successful in terms of survival, satisfaction, learning and joint goal achievement, and partially successful in terms of financial output. Survival, while clearly not the sole measure of a joint venture's success, is nonetheless an important indicator because unsuccessful partnerships tend to lose members. PTB has been active for eight years and has thus far attracted more than 40 members.

PTB's goal achievement appears to be high. Its objective is to invest in financially sound, environmentally friendly projects that spur the economy of Bages County and make the region attractive to businesses. At present, PTB is working on several economic development projects, including its star project, the Bages County Technology Park. There is no evidence that PTB has directly contributed to the region's economic development, but several international companies agreed to settle in the technology park.

PTB members have expressed a high level of satisfaction with the joint venture: "In one word: a success"; "It's a success story"; "I believe it is a success."

Similarly, PTB members say that they have learned from the joint venture. According to one public manager, "We, the public-sector people, have learned from the private parties." A private member said: "The process has made us better professionals by teaching us to cool down our impatience." The learning component is, nonetheless, a less critical factor in the success of a public-private joint venture like PTB. In international joint ventures, such as those to which Ren et al. (2009) applied their success measures, acquiring market- or product-related knowledge from the other partner may be an end in itself; this is not true in the case of PTB.

PTB has been partially successful in terms of financial output. Because the joint venture has yet to distribute profits to its shareholders, this measure of success is unsatisfactory. PTB has managed, however, to raise more than €15 million, with more than 75% coming from private shareholders. In this second sense, then, the financial measure is quite satisfactory.

UNITY AND DIVERSITY IN ALLIANCES

In collaborative contexts, managing means addressing the inherent paradoxes that emerge from the complex context itself (Agranoff & McGuire, 2001; Huxham & Vangen, 2000). The potential for collaborative advantage depends on each partner's ability to bring different resources to the alliance. However, these diverse resources are a function of institutional and organizational differences, which give rise to inherent tensions in the collaborative initiative (Das & Teng, 1998, 2000; Huxham & Beech, 2003; Ospina & Saz-Carranza, 2010). Difficulties arise precisely because collaboratives need to be simultaneously diverse and united. In the case of PTB, the alliance needed to generate unity among members (with regard to goals, strategy, and implementation) while at the same time building on the institutional and organizational differences that exist among the public and private members of the organization (Saz-Carranza, 2012).

COMPETING INSTITUTIONAL LOGICS

In public-private alliances, differences among partners tend to be large. Some of the difficulties arising from collaboration between the two sectors are due to differences between the various actors (Herranz, 2008; Klijn & Teisman, 2003). Intra-national strategic alliances have to deal with diverse corporate cultures and international alliances, in addition, have to confront different national cultures (Das & Kumar, 2010; Robson et al., 2008). Similarly, competing institutional logics are a key constraint to cross-sector collaboration process (Bryson, Crosby, & Stone, 2006).

Diverse cultures, logics, and norms are key for interpreting social reality. Diversity in such frames make joint sensemaking more difficult. "Alliance managers who have been socialized in different national cultures are likely to interpret and respond to their partners' behavior in conflicting ways" (Das & Kumar, 2010, p. 18). In cross-sector partnerships, competing sector logics—enacted by the different sector partners—may be expected to co-exist.

As "the basis of taken-for-granted rules guiding behaviour" (Reay & Hinings, 2009, p. 629), institutional logics apply to both the societal-sector level and the organizational field level (Thornton & Ocasio, 1999). At the societal level, there are six institutional logics—market, corporation, profession, family, religion, and state—each embodying a series of unique, taken-for-granted rules (Friedland & Alford, 1991; Thornton, 2004).

The PTB case study shows that the three logics most relevant to the public and private sectors are market, corporation and state. In the market institutional logic, self-interest is the basic norm, strategies are aimed at completing efficient transactions, and learning takes place through competition. In the state logic, citizenship is the basic norm, strategies are aimed at the notion of the common good, and learning occurs through popular opinion polls. Lastly, in the corporation logic, strategies are aimed at increasing the organization's size, the main norms are structured around employment relations, and learning occurs through competition. Table 10.1 shows the basic characteristics of the market, corporation, and state institutional logics.[1]

Competing institutional logics were present in PTB. Depending on which sector (public or private) they belonged to, managers held different taken-for-granted assumptions. This caused problems within the joint venture. The differing key assumptions were related to two main areas: the appropriate bases for strategy, and the functioning forms of control and organization.

Different Bases for Strategy: Efficiency Versus Legitimacy

Private and public actors tend to have different conceptions of time, and this can lead to problems. Inter-sector differences in terms of rhythms, speeds, temporal perspectives and timeframes hinder positive inter-partner interaction. The manager of PTB, recognizing that the main difficulties arose from tempo and pace, said:

Table 10.1

Basic Characteristics of the Market, Corporation, and State Societal Sector Institutional Logics

	Market	State	Corporations
Economic system	Investor capitalism	Welfare capitalism	Managerial capitalism
Sources of legitimacy	Share price	Democratic participation	Firm's market position
Sources of authority	Shareholder activism	Bureaucratic domination; political parties	Board of directors; management
Basis of norms	Self interest	Citizenship in nation	Employment in firm
Basis of strategy	Increase efficiency of transactions	Increase community good	Increase firm size and diversification
Learning mechanisms	Competition prices	Popular opinion leadership	Competition, training and routines
Informal control mechanisms	Industry analysts	Backroom politics	Organization culture
Formal control mechanisms	Enforcement of regulations	Enforcement of legislation	Board and management authority
Organization form	Marketplace	Legal bureaucracy	M-form organization
Logic of exchange	Immediate best bargain	Political power	Personal career advancement

Source: Thornton & Ocasio (1999)

> A private stakeholder with a private objective would trace a path in a straight line, until that objective is reached. And certain public shareholders might have a very clear objective but trace several zigzags so as not to bother others. They'll trace as many zigzags as they need to.

The mayor of a member city agreed: "In the private sector, they're used to putting everything in place and getting a return on it. But that isn't how it works in town-planning issues. Town planning is something that stews slowly, so it's not always easy."

A member businessman underscored the different conceptions of time: "I lay bricks. I come from a world where day-to-day work does not let you define long-term strategies."

Divisions among the private and public partners on time-related issues arose due to differences in the ultimate concept of value creation—here referred to as the *basis for strategy*—that persists in the public and the private sectors (Thornton, 2004). While efficient transactions are the basis for strategy under market logic, the common good is the basis used when strategizing under state logic. The implications regarding time and public participation in decision-making are conflicting: efficiency requires fast and straightforward decisions, whereas the common good requires involving diverse stakeholders—which takes longer—in order to generate legitimacy.

Formal Control Mechanisms and Organization Form: Total Versus Limited Internal Authority

Businesspeople tend to experience the political-technical divide within public administrations as incomprehensible and problematic. According to one businessman involved in PTB, "Political and technical priorities are often not aligned. In such cases, you have to deal with both the town hall's political and technical teams." The private sector has difficulties with the dual nature, typical of legal bureaucracies, found in the public sector: the political leadership, on the one hand, and the administration's technical core, on the other. A business representative described how private parties expected to encounter fewer obstacles to PTB's actions: "The most frustrating part of PTB was assuming that having the administration on board would help us." He had assumed, for example, that a mayor's support for a development project would mean a straight, quick re-zoning process. This, of course, was not so, since the re-zoning procedure is complex and requires the approval of several other officials in addition to the mayor. The business representative's thinking shows that the business partners perceived the mayor's power and role in the local administration as similar to that of a CEO at a private company. This led to frustration at the fact that the political head of an administration—and a local administration, at that – had less authority over his subordinates and autonomy in the use of resources than that enjoyed by business leaders.

Western-style public administration is necessarily dual and internally decoupled. One mayor argued,

> I have had problems with my technical people, but they don't raise issues just for the sake of it. They tell me, "Listen, there are rules, and I can't fit this project in." If we had had clear rules regarding technology parks, we would have finished a year earlier. Since we didn't have any rules, we had to make them up."

Another mayor added, "The fact that the town hall is a PTB member does not mean that it ceases to regulate PTB's development projects. This aspect generates confusion and needs to be well understood by PTB's private shareholders."

Competing logics are on display in PTB participants' assumptions about expectable control mechanisms and forms of organization. While formal control in a corporation is exercised by the board and management authority within a hierarchical business structure, control in the public sector is derived from the enforcement of legislation in the legal bureaucracy (Thornton, 2004). Although political leaders in local governments are far more involved in operational work than their counterparts in the central government, they still face important limitations to their hierarchical authority over civil servants and technical staff. These limitations are much greater than those faced by the leadership of private business enterprises.

Moreover, while control in the public sector focuses on processes and inputs, business organizations tend to exert control over results. Public administration has indeed shifted recently from a bureaucratic culture towards a more managerial one, but it is still far more procedural than the private sector.

In essence, these different logics create tensions and problems because private partners to public-private alliances, such as PTB, think of their public counterparts' organizational structure as being similar to their business structure. With such an assumption at work, the public organizations' lag in fulfilling their pledges is seen as a lack of commitment on the part of the political leadership. Table 10.2 shows the competing logics found at work in joint ventures such as PTB.

It should be no surprise that in this chapter we have only highlighted two areas (basis for strategy and organizational form and control) out of the 10 areas in which competing logics exist. Nor should it be surprising that business logic includes properties of both market and corporation societal-level institutional logics. The logics presented above are ideal types; therefore, pure representations of them do not exist empirically.

Table 10.2

Competing Logics Found at Work in the Joint Venture

	Private actors' institutional logic	Public actors' institutional logic
Basis of strategy	Increase efficiency of transactions (market ideal-type)	Increase community good (state ideal-type)
Formal control mechanisms and organization form	Board and management authority and M-form organization (corporation ideal-type)	Enforcement of legislation and legal bureaucracy (state ideal-type)

MANAGING COMPETING LOGICS IN COLLABORATIVES

There is a body of knowledge on the management of collaboratives and networks. There are four tasks that can help managers perform in the complex, uncertain context of collaborative networks (Saz-Carranza & Ospina, 2010). First, collaboration managers must attract new partners and support prospective members; this is referred to as *activating* (Agranoff & McGuire, 2001). Second, managers must secure the resources and support the network needs; they do this through a type of work called *mobilizing* (Agranoff & McGuire, 2001). Third, by *facilitating*, managers foster interaction among network member organizations; this includes tasks such as managing inequalities among participants and motivating network members to participate (Agranoff & McGuire, 2001; Kickert, Klijn, & Koppenjan, 1997). Lastly, *framing* refers to creating infrastructures for collaboration between member organizations; for example, managers try to influence the collaborative's rules, values, perceptions and processes (Agranoff & McGuire, 2001; Huxham & Vangen, 2000; Kickert et al., 1997).

The strategic alliance literature also contributes insights into the management of alliances, which may be applicable to cross-sector partnerships. Ring and Van de Ven (1994) describe an incremental teleological sense-making process among alliance partners, where trust-building increases as partners go through cycles conformed by three stages: negotiation, commitment, execution. Throughout these cycles, partners evaluate the alliance. Thus, procedural trust (Zucker, 1986) is built as partners jointly make sense of the alliance as they interact with each other. Similarly, Doz (1996) conceptualizes an alliance's process as iterative learning cycles among partners.

The literature on these activities makes no mention of how competing logics are managed. In fact, the body of knowledge on how competing logics are managed within a single organization is rather slim. Research on competing institutional logics has primarily focused on how prevailing logics are challenged and eventually modified by new logics in a given organizational field (Reay & Hinings, 2009).

The PTB participants were eventually able to cope with the competing logics and move forward. We can identify two practices that served to refocus the situation towards positive interaction among actors: (1) involving and communicating with stakeholders, and (2) creating mutual learning spaces.

Involving and Communicating With Stakeholders

One major way to cope with competing logics is by involving and communicating with stakeholders. PTB eventually became more permeable to its social context. The joint venture's management team went out and talked, explained and met with the various stakeholders and invited various non-profit and public actors to visit a variety of economic development projects around Spain.

Additionally, as the PTB stakeholder reshuffling diagram shows (Figure 10.2), the joint venture added several social and public figures to its structure: a panel of experts, including environmental and local economic opinion leaders; an independent advisor specialized in innovation; a representative of an innovation network; and the Association of Architects, which was included in the jury to select the winning technology park design.

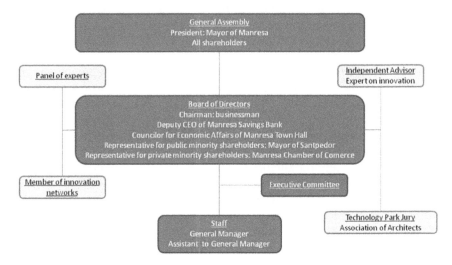

Figure 10.2.   PTB's main actors after reshuffle.

One businessman described how PTB opened up its analytic focus by incorporating the social context, by being receptive and open, and by communicating proactively with stakeholders:

> We understood that we needed to adopt a global consciousness. If someone has something to say, he can come and tell us, because the worst thing is to find out through the press. When this happened, we would tell ourselves, "We have to go see this person; we haven't explained our project well enough."

In short, public-private joint ventures can balance their economic and political objectives by involving their stakeholders.

Communication is essential to overcoming the tensions caused by sector differences. A for-profit member of PTB recognized the importance of having a communications strategy: "We had previously neglected communications. Only later did we start to manage communications seriously. The change was very positive."

A mayor involved in PTB highlighted the importance of providing information about the project: "At the end of the day, it's all about getting the largest possible number of people on board. We have worked hard to explain the project in this regard."

One of the founding businessmen explained the importance of communicating with external stakeholders: "We have been able to minimize the levels of internal divergence. If you don't do that, you can't hold such a thing together. I think we managed this by continually communicating with and convincing everyone." By better communicating with key external stakeholders, the joint venture reduced its internal tensions between public and private parties.

By taking into account its key stakeholders, a public-private alliance essentially combines legitimacy with efficiency, the public and private bases for strategy, respectively.

Creating Learning Spaces

Providing spaces for mutual learning makes it possible to bridge the differences between public and private partners. Learning, in turn, makes it possible for each actor to understand the others and alter their behavior accordingly. A mayor participating in PTB explained,

> The public and private sectors understand each other when they have a common space to debate and interact. Personally, as a politician, interacting with the private sector has made me grow, because I have seen how they suffer in their efforts to develop interesting projects for the region.

The manager of PTB agreed: "I believe that one key to success is to try to understand what the other party is seeing, perceives or is looking for, what is important to the other side and how we can reach both sides' goals." Another mayor described how learning occurs:

> The empathy element must be there from the very beginning. By empathy, I mean putting oneself in the other's place and understanding him. When I understand the other, I am able to see why he is pushing me one way or another. Empathy is achieved by having deep knowledge of the different elements involved in the project.

One businessman involved in PTB explained how he went from being frustrated to understanding the public sector:

In a small company, everything is more direct, everything is from today to tomorrow. Decision making is quicker. You search for information in order to be able to act. Here, obviously, if there is one thing we private business-people have learnt, it is the importance of reaching a consensus by starting from a broad range of possibilities.

This practice responds to the need to help the various participants understand the logic enacted by the partners from the other sector.

Our main assertion is that, in PTB, both business and public-sector institutional logics co-existed, rather than one logic imposing itself on the other. The co-existence of competing logics seems the only viable option in joint ventures where the partners belong to different societal sectors and are free to drop out if they feel their logic is diminished (Hirschman, 1970). Thus, public-private joint ventures are organizations in which different institutional logics must co-exist (Reay & Hinings, 2009).

Successful joint ventures manage to combine different institutional logics. The PTB partners, for example, did this by adopting two practices: (a) involving and communicating with stakeholders, and (b) providing mutual learning spaces. These two practices enabled the partners to cope with competing logics (a) by combining legitimacy (the public basis for strategy) with efficiency (the private basis for strategy) in the joint venture's bases for strategy, and (b) by helping the various participants understand the logic of the partners from the other sector, in particular with respect to organizational form and control. Table 10.3 illustrates these results.

Table 10.3
Practices for Coping With Competing Logics

	Private actors' institutional logic	Public actors' institutional logic	Practice for coping with competing key assumptions
Basis of strategy	Increase efficiency of transactions (market ideal type)	Increase community good (state ideal type)	Involving and communicating with stakeholders [mobilizing]
			Creating spaces for mutual understanding [facilitating]
Formal control mechanisms and organization form	Board and management authority and M-form organization (corporation ideal type)	Enforcement of legislation and legal bureaucracy (state ideal type)	Creating spaces for mutual understanding [facilitating]

The practice of communicating with and involving stakeholders builds legitimacy for the project and pays due tribute to the public nature of economic development. Collaborative and network managers build up legitimacy and support by mobilizing. Since the emergence of open-systems approaches to organizations (Katz & Kahn 1966), organizations have known that they need to attend to their contexts. Business strategizing must therefore take context into account (Bryson, 2004), just as public managers need to incorporate political management into their day-to-day work (Pearce, De Castro, & Guillen, 2008). Arguably, the more closely an organization interacts with the public sphere, the greater its need to attend to the social and political context. Not surprisingly, legitimacy-building is an important part of public managers' work (Moore, 1995).

Trust is an important condition in cooperation (Rousseau, Sitkin, Burt, & Camerer, 1999) and a determinant of the success of joint ventures (Ren & Gray, 2009). Communicating with and involving stakeholders—that is mobilizing external support—is key to building trust (Hardy, Phillips, & Lawrence, 1998), in part because this practice reduces non-decision-making space (Bacharach & Baratz, 1962), which helps stakeholders to better understand the joint venture's work.

Creating mutual learning spaces is in line with the current literature on inter-organizational management, which argues that interaction between diverse entities needs to be synthesized (Agranoff & McGuire, 2001), facilitated (Kickert et al., 1997), brokered (Lorenzoni & Baden-Fuller, 1995) and so on (Saz-Carranza & Ospina 2010). These activities serve to build bridges among the various actors and thus prevent clashes due to differing institutional logics. In addition, mutual learning spaces can instil trust—process-based trust, in particular—among partners (Zucker, 1986).

Mutual learning spaces also counteract the negative stereotypes that partners may hold of one another. Dissimilarities between team members tend to generate negative social categorization (Kearney, Gebert, & Voelpel, 2009; Williams & O'Reilly, 1998) and, in the absence of sufficient information, people tend to rely on stereotypes (Blatt, 2009). Mutual learning makes it possible to break down stereotypes and explore mutual gains (Ansell & Gash, 2008; Bentrup, 2001).

The practices found to be useful in coping with competing logics—(a) involving and communicating with stakeholders, and (b) providing mutual learning spaces—also resonate with the strategic alliance literature. The former is analogous to Das and Kumar's (2010) "sense-making of chaos," where information and planning are used to counter partner conflict. The practice of providing mutual learning spaces, however, is akin to Das and Kumar's "sensemaking in chaos" (2010), which counters disruptions in collaboration among alliance partners through symbolic and experimental interaction. Das and Kumar argue that sensemaking of chaos deals with complexity by reducing it, while sensemaking in chaos copes with complexity rather than trying to reduce it. The findings here presented suggest that successful public-private alliance managers attempt to both reduce and cope with complexity.

CONCLUSIONS

Different institutional logics co-exist in public-private joint ventures. The managers of these initiatives therefore face challenges in terms of partner collaboration. They can overcome these challenges by involving and communicating with stakeholders and by encouraging mutual learning. Both of these approaches essentially build trust, but more importantly they mobilise external legitimacy and facilitate interaction among the various members, respectively. Another way of looking at the practices is that they respectively reduce and cope with complexity.

If public-private cooperation initiatives were to take into consideration the different institutional logics followed by their public and private actors, both outsiders and subjects would gain a better understanding of the cooperation dynamics in these ventures. As Das and Kumar (2010) state, "Managers are often unaware of their own assumptions, much less the assumptions of their counterpart" (p. 31).

This chapter's recommendations to practitioners are as follows. First and foremost, managers should acknowledge sector-related differences—in particular, different institutional logics—when collaborating across sectors. Second, managers should aim to mobilize legitimacy by communicating with external stakeholders and facilitate partner interaction by providing mutual learning spaces.

NOTE

1. Sector differences derived from societal-sector institutional logics are in line with empirical findings by scholars who study the differences between the public and private sectors in terms of attitudes, personal values, motivation and organizational context (Crewson, 1997; Feeney, 2007; Houston, 2000; Lyons, Duxbury, & Higgins, 2006; Nutt, 2006; Poole & Gould-Williams, 2006; Rainey & Bozeman, 2000).

ACKNOWLEDGMENTS

This chapter, save some minor changes, was earlier published as Saz-Carranza, A., & Longo, F. (2014). Managing competing institutional logics in public-private alliances. In T. K. Das (Ed.), *Managing public-private strategic alliances* (pp. 171–188). Charlotte, NC: Information Age Publishing. The chapter is based on the authors' earlier article: Saz-Carranza, A., & Longo, F. (2012). Managing competing institutional logics in public-private joint ventures. *Public Management Review, 14*(3), 331–357. We have modified to adapt it for a general audience—as opposed to its former public-management orientation. They are extremely thankful to Adrià Albareda, who helped us in this adaptation process.

REFERENCES

Agranoff, R., & McGuire, M. (2001). Big questions in public network management. *Journal of Public Administration Research and Theory, 11*, 295–327.

Ansell, C. & Gash, A. (2008). Collaborative governance in theory and practice. *Journal of Public Administration Research and Theory, 18*, 543–571.

Blatt, R. (2009). Tough love: How communal schemas and contracting practices build relational capital in entrepreneurial teams. *Academy of Management Review, 34*, 533–551.

Bentrup, G. (2001). Evaluation of a collaborative model: A case study of analysis of watershed planning in the Intermountain West. *Environmental Management, 27*, 739–748.

Bryson, J. (2004). What to do when stakeholders matter. *Public Management Review, 6*, 21–53.

Bryson, J. M., Crosby, B. C., & Stone, M. M. (2006). The design and implementation of cross-sector collaborations: Propositions from the literature. *Public Administration Review, 66*, 44–55.

Crewson, P. E. (1997). Are the best and brightest fleeing public sector employment? Evidence from the national longitudinal survey of youth. *Public Productivity and Management Review, 20*, 363–371.

Das, T. K. & Kumar, R. (2010). Interpartner sensemaking in strategic alliances: Managing cultural differences and internal tensions. *Management Decision, 48*, 17–36.

Das, T. K. & Teng, B. (1998). Between trust and control: Developing confidence in partner cooperation in alliances. *Academy of Management Review, 23*, 491–512.

Das, T. K. & Teng, B. (2000). Instabilities of strategic alliances: An internal tensions perspective. *Organization Science, 11*, 77–101.

Doz, Y. (1996). The evolution of cooperation in strategic alliances: Initial conditions or learning processes? *Strategic Management Journal, 17*, 55–79.

Feeney, M. K. (2007). Sector perceptions among state-level public managers. *Journal of Public Administration Research and Theory, 18*, 465–494.

Friedland, R., & Alford, R. (1991). Bringing society back in: Symbols, practices, and institutional contradictions. In W. Powell & P. J. DiMaggio (Eds.), *The new institutionalism in organizational analysis*. Chicago, IL: University of Chicago Press.

Hardy, C., Phillips, N., & Lawrence, T. (1998). Distinguishing trust and power in interorganizational relations: Forms and facades of trust. In C. Lane & R. Bachmann (Eds), *Trust Within and Between Organizations* (pp. 64–87). Oxford, UK: Oxford University Press.

Herranz, J. (2008). The multisectoral trilemma of network management. *Journal of Public Administration Research & Theory, 18*, 1–31.

Hirschman, A. O. (1970). *Exit, voice, and loyalty: Responses to decline in firms, organizations, and states.* Cambridge, MA: Harvard University Press.

Houston, D. J. (2000). Public-service motivation: A multivariate test. *Journal of Public Administration Research and Theory, 1*, 713–727.

Huxham, C., & Beech, N. (2003). Contrary prescriptions: Recognizing good practice tensions in management. *Organization Studies, 24*, 69–93.

Huxham, C., & Vangen, S. (2000). Leadership in the shaping and implementation of collaboration agendas: How things happen in a (not quite) joined-up world. *Academy of Management Journal, 43*, 1159–1176.

Katz, D., & Kahn, R. L. (1966). *The social psychology of organizations.* New York, NY: Wiley.

Kearney, E., Gebert, D., & Voelpel, S. C. (2009). When and how diversity benefits teams: The importance of team members' need for cognition. *Academy of Management Journal, 52*, 581–598.

Kickert, W., Klijn, E.-H., & Koopenjan, J. (1997). Managing networks in the public sector: Findings and reflections. In W. Kickert, E.-H. Klijn, & J. Koopenjan (Eds.), *Managing complex networks* (pp. 165–191). London, UK: SAGE.

Klijn, E.-H., & Teisman, G. R. (2003). Institutional and strategic barriers to public-private partnership: An analysis of Dutch cases. *Public Money and Management, 23*, 137–146.

Lorenzoni, G., & Baden-Fuller, C. (1995). Creating a strategic center to manage a web of partners. *California Management Review, 37*(3), 146–163.

Lyons, S. T., Duxbury, L. E., & Higgins, C. A. (2006). A comparison of the values and commitment of private sector, public sector, and parapublic sector employees. *Public Administration Review, 66*, 605–618.

Moore, M. H. (1995). *Creating public value strategic management in government.* Cambridge, MA: Harvard University Press.

Nutt, P. (2006). Comparing public and private sector decision-making practices. *Journal of Public Administration Research and Theory, 16*, 289–318.

Ospina, S. M., & Saz-Carranza, A. (2010). Paradox and collaboration in network management. *Administration and Society, 42*, 404–440.

Pearce, J. L., De Castro, J. O., & Guillen, M. F. (2008). Influencing politics and political systems: Political systems and corporate strategies. *Academy of Management Review, 33*, 493–495.

Poole, M. M. R., & Gould-Williams, J. (2006). Public and private sector managers over 20 years: A test of the 'convergence thesis'. *Public Administration, 84*, 1051–1076.

Rainey, H., & Bozeman, B. (2000). Comparing public and private organizations: Empirical research and the power of the a priori. *Journal of Public Administration Research and Theory, 10*, 447–469.

Reay, T., & Hinings, C. R. (2009). Managing the rivalry of competing institutional logics. *Organization Studies, 30*, 629–652.

Ren, H., Gray, B., & Kim, K. (2009). Performance of international joint ventures: What factors really make a difference and how? *Journal of Management, 35*, 805–832.

Ring, P. S., & Van de Ven, A. H. (1994). Developmental processes of cooperative inter-organizational relationships. *Academy Management Review, 19*, 90–119.

Rittel, H. W., & Webber, M. (1973). Dilemmas in a general theory of planning. *Policy Sciences, 4*, 155–169.

Robson, M. J., Katsikeas, C. S., & Bello, D. C. (2008). Drivers and performance outcomes of trust in international strategic alliances: The role of organizational complexity. *Organization Science, 19*, 647–665.

Rousseau, D. M., Sitkin, S. B., Burt, R. S., & Camerer, C. (1998). Not so different after all: A cross-discipline view of trust. *Academy of Management Review, 23*, 393–404.

Saz-Carranza, A. (2012). *Uniting diverse organizations: Managing goal-oriented advocacy networks*. New York, NY: Routledge.

Thornton, P. (2004). *Markets from culture: Institutional logics and organizational decisions in higher education publishing*. Stanford, CA: Stanford Business Books.

Thornton, P., & Ocasio, W. (1999). Institutional logics and the historical contingency of power in organizations: Executive succession in the higher education publishing industry, 1958–1990. *American Journal of Sociology, 105*, 801–843.

Williams, K., & O'Reilly, C. (1998). Demography and diversity in organizations: A review of forty years of research. *Research in Organizational Behavior, 20*, 77–140.

Zucker, L. G. (1986). Production of trust: Institutional sources of economic structure. *Research in Organizational Behavior, 8*, 53–111.

CHAPTER 11

USING TECHNOLOGY TO TEACH BUSINESS COURSES IN GHANA

Managerial Practice Implications

Grace Abban-Ampiah,
Joseph Ofori-Dankwa, and Micah DelVecchio

ABSTRACT

The need for technology-oriented instruction in business schools is vital for both national development and corporate competitive advantage. The COVID-19 school closures have highlighted this importance. While several studies have described the diverse types of technologies business schools in African countries use for classroom instruction, relatively few have specifically focused on their practical managerial implications. Consequently, this chapter first sought to find out what type of technology is being used to teach business courses in universities in West Africa. We carried out a survey with professors, lecturers, and students in the business schools in two leading universities in Ghana. The survey found that while laptops are much used in teaching, other technologies, such as smart phones are relatively less used. The survey's respondents highlight the challenges associated with using technology in the business schools and make recommendations for improving its use. We highlight several managerial practice implications of the study. Specifically, we focus on how the current technology being used could have managerial practical implications on planning, organizing, leading and control in organizations.

Managerial Practice Issues in Strategy and Organization, pp. 295–316

INTRODUCTION

The use of technology educational institutions for classroom instruction is important for several reasons (Mitchell, Woleb, & Skinner, 2016). Effective use of technology in the classroom setting has been associated with substantial improvement in students' motivation, learning and engagement levels (Farag, Park, & Kaupins, 2015; Kruss, McGrath, Petersen, & Gastrow, 2015; Ng'ambi, Brown, Bozalek, Gachago & Wood, 2016). The diverse technologies available to effectively teach their students include the use of clickers (Farag et al., 2015; Rana & Dwivedi, 2018; Rana, Dwivedi, & Al-Khowaiter, 2016), digital technology (Cavanaugh, Giapponi, & Golden, 2016), and online services (Mitchell, Woleb, & Skinner, 2016).

Specifically, in the African context, several studies have described the specific technologies used for industry (Chege, Wang, & Suntu, 2020; Donbesuur, Ampong, & Owusu-Yirenkyil, & Chu, 2020; Tian, Otchere, Coffie, Mensah, & Baku, 2021), For example, some studies focused on Technology's impact on innovation and performance of SME in African countries like Ghana (Donbesuur et al., 2020; Tian et al., 2021). Other studies more specifically focused on technology use in the classroom instructional setting in Africa (e.g., Ng'ambi, et al, 2016; Kaliisa & Mitchelle, 2019; Kaliisa & Picard, 2017; Ocholla, 2008; Shambare, 2011). For example, Ng'ambi et al. (2016) focused on the impact of technology on students' learning and instruction in South Africa while Kaliisa and Picard (2017) provided an overview of mobile learning in Africa. Few studies have specifically and explicitly focused on highlighting the managerial practice implications of technology used in classroom setting in higher educational institutions in Africa.

Consequently, our first research question centers on the type of technology that is being used to teach business courses in West Africa. To answer this question, we carried out a survey with lecturers, and students in the business schools in two leading universities in Ghana. The survey identified the type of technology being used. This led us to our second research question that focused on identifying the managerial practice implications associated with the type of technology being used to teach in business schools in Ghana.

LITERATURE REVIEW

Incorporation of Technology to Teach Effectively

Technology is an important medium through which universities across the world engage students to ensure their success in learning (Farag et al., 2015; Kruss et al., 2015; Rana & Dwivedi, 2018). Specifically, in the

African context, diverse and wide range of technologies have been adopted in classroom instruction across the continent. Some African business and technical schools using statistical analysis software in teaching (Shambare, 2011). Other African universities use library information systems to provide access to technology-oriented teaching services (Ocholla, 2008). Bervell and Umar (2017) look at the adoption of learning management systems in sub-Saharan Africa. They find that the biggest challenges that teachers in African higher education face in adopting a learning management system for their classroom are the information and communications technology (ICT) infrastructure: LMS usage skills and training; LMS system quality, LMS use policy and management support. Adam (2003) and Bon (2010) also note the problems that African universities were having in establishing a workable ICT infrastructure throughout the first decade of the 2000s. Much of this had to do with the costs associated with these relatively new (at the time) technologies.

Not only can infrastructure be an additional challenge to technology-oriented teaching in African higher education, but the student body also presents unique challenges, as there is wide variation in exposure to technology among incoming university students in Africa (Byungura, Hansson, Muparasi, & Ruhinda, 2018). Kaliisa and Picard (2017) examine a possible solution to the above challenges by studying the use of mobile devices in higher education. The authors find that the technology can help provide distance learning and improve student engagement. Kaliisa and Picard (2017) observe institutional challenges and resistance to mobile learning that may also need to be addressed for this potential solution to come to fruition. Currently, due to the advancement in technology across the African continent, most institutions have emphasized incorporating different kinds of technologies in their classroom instructions. For example, Ng'ambi et al. (2016) focused on the impact of technology on students' learning and instruction in South Africa.

The need for and challenges to incorporating technology, especially methods of mobile learning, have been highlighted by the severe impacts that COVID-19 has had on the institutions of higher education. Kathula (2020) surveys Kenyan students and teachers affected by school closures and finds that access to internet and even electricity was a large impediment to learning during the pandemic. Iseolorunkanm et al. (2021) notes there are a variety of responses that instructors have taken in Nigeria to the COVID-19 closures. Specifically, instructors in private schools are more likely to adopt methods of distance learning than public school instructors, while younger instructors all around were more likely to adopt virtual learning.

Nonetheless, there are studies describing technologies used in teaching in Africa. For example, one study conducted in South Africa that have examined the effects of new technologies on learning or readiness of tertiary education institutions (Ng'ambi et al., 2016). Studies that have specifically focused on the managerial practical implications of classroom technological instruction has been limited. Ivala (2016) has also assessed staff development strategies used by tertiary institutions in South Africa. This study, therefore, attempts to fill this gap by specifically examining the classroom instructional technologies used in business schools of Ghana and to highlighting the managerial practice implications.

METHODOLOGY

In order to find out what types of technologies are being used in business schools in Ghana, an online survey platform (Survey Monkey) and self-completion questionnaires were administered in April 2019. This sample came from the lecturers and instructors of the two top business schools in Ghana: the Ghana Institute of Management and Public Administration (GIMPA) and the University of Ghana (UG). These two institutions were selected because, when compared to other business schools in Ghana, these two institutions are likely to have a wider level of available technological resources.

Faculty Sample

We sent surveys to approximately 170 lecturers from the two business schools. GIMPA has 70 lecturers while UG-Legon has roughly 100 lecturers. In order to reach lecturers teaching at these two universities' business schools, an online survey was delivered to all lecturers through email. The online survey was completed by 28 GIMPA teachers and two UG-Legon lecturers. With the low response rate from the online survey, lecturers were also provided with face-to-face questionnaires. Six of the ten face-to-face questionnaires provided to GIMPA lecturers were returned. Fifteen face-to-face questionnaires were distributed to UG Legon lecturers, and 11 questionnaires were returned. In total, 45 questionnaires (26% of total potential respondents) were received from the online and face-to-face surveys sent to lecturers at both business schools.

The number of online surveys and face-to-face questionnaires obtained from GIMPA lecturers is 32 (71.1%), whereas the number of questionnaires received from UG-Legon lecturers is 13 (28.9%). This made a total of 45 lecturers. 11 (24.4%) of the lecturers were female, while 34 (75.6%) were male. The majority of lecturers, 31 (68.91%) lecturers from the two institutions who took part in this study held PhD degrees, while master's degrees are held by 14 (31.1%) of the lecturers who responded.

Department of Lecturers

The lecturers from the two business schools who participated in this study came from diverse departments at the two schools. These include the Accounting and Finance, Business Management and Administration, Marketing, Organization and Management Information Systems, Organization and Human Resource Management, Public Administration, Public Service and Governance, and Social Science departments.

Most the lecturers who took part in this research did not disclose their departments, that is, about 18 (40%) out of 45 (100%) that took the survey. Twelve (26.7%) of the lecturers stated that they belonged to the Business Management, Business Administration, Management Science, and Marketing departments. Six (13.3%) of the lecturers were from the Organization and HRM, Organization and Management in Information Systems, and Social Science departments. Four (8.9%) are also part of the Public Administration and Public Service and Governance departments. Table 11.1 shows the different departments represented in this study.

Table 11.1

Department of Lecturers

Broad Disciplines	Frequency	Percent
Accounting and Finance	5	11.1
Business Management/ Business Administration/ Management Science/ Marketing	12	26.7%
Organization and HRM/ Organization and Management in Information Systems/Social Science	6	13.3%
Public Administration/Public Service and Governance	4	8.9%
Missing Value	18	40%

Length of Service of Lecturers

Table 11.2 presents the length of service of lecturers from the two business schools. About 13 (28.9%) lecturers did state their length of service. More of the staff have been working with their institution for 5 years (35.6%). In terms of length of service, more of the lecturers, about 15 (33.3%) from both GIMPA and UG-Legon, have been with the institution for less than five years. There are 12 (26.5%) lecturers who have worked for the last 6 to 10 years, and 4 lecturers who have worked for their institutions for 10 years or more.

Table 11.2
Length of Service of Lecturers

Department	Frequency	Percent
0–5 years	16	35.6%
6–10 years	12	26.6%
11 and above years	4	8.9%
Missing Value	13	28.9%

Questions in Survey for Lecturers

We asked the lecturers the following questions:

- *What are the different types of techniques that you currently use to teach in your classroom?*
- *What are the other types of technologies you use but not listed?*
- *What are the three most important factors that you consider when choosing the technologies you use in your classroom?*
- *What technologies would you like to use in your classroom in the future?*
- *What are the purposes of the technologies used in your classroom?*
- *What is the purpose of other technologies not listed as part of the technologies you often use?*
- *What are the challenges and barriers that you face when using technologies in teaching at your institutions?*
- *What are the key suggestion and recommendations for greater effectiveness of technology in your institution?*

Student Sample

Students participating were from the GIMPA Business School and the University of Ghana Business School.

Students from the GIMPA Business School targeted in this survey are 104 undergraduates from two classes. One class had 49 students and the other class had 65 students. Total number of responses received was 62 (81.6%). Out of the 104 students targeted for this study, two GIMPA students completed the online survey, while the remaining 60 completed the face-to-face interview, making a total of 62 respondents from the GIMPA Business school.

All students at the Business School at University of Ghana, Legon were targeted. Initially a link to the online survey was emailed to all business school students at the University of Ghana. There were no responses to the online survey by the University of Ghana undergraduate students, so questions were sent on the WhatsApp social platform. Twelve students responded to it.

Of the total number of student respondents, 81% were from the GIMPA business school. 45 (59.2%) of the students taking part in this study were male compared to 29 (38.2%) female. However, as a result of skipping the question given, two of the participants did not reveal their identity. The students who helped to conduct the survey were undergraduates.

Student's Academic Department

The students who participated in this research came from several departments, as stated in Table 11.3. Accounting, Business Management, Distant, Humanities, and Social Sciences formed the departments of the participants as shown in Table 11.3. Only 6 (5.2%) of the 76 participants, however, stated their departments. The other participants' representing 92.1% who amounted to 70 did not show their departments.

Table 11.3
Student's Academic Department

Department	Frequency	Percent
Accounting	2	2.6
Business Management	1	1.3
Distant	1	1.3
Humanities	1	1.3
Social Sciences	1	1.3
Missing Value	70	92.1

Questions in Survey for Students

These were the questions that were posed to the students:

- *What are the technologies that your lecturers currently use to teach in your classroom?*
- *How frequently do your lecturers use each of these technologies to teach?*

- *What other technologies do your lecturers use in the classroom that are not listed?*
- *Which of these technologies would you like your lecturers to use to teach in the future?*
- *What are the purposes of the following technologies used in your classroom?*
- *What are the purposes of the other technologies used in your classroom?*
- *What are the challenges and barriers that you face when the different technologies are used to teach in your classroom?*
- *What are the key suggestions and recommendations for more effective use of the technology in your institution?*

FINDINGS OF THE STUDY

Findings of Lecturer's Experiences of the Use of Technologies in the Classroom

Types of Technologies Used to Teach in the Classroom

Here are the findings of the different types of technologies used to teach in the classroom. From Table 11.4, lecturers used different types of technologies but the most (39 or 86.7%) used laptops, followed by smart phones (21 or 46.7%), online learning systems (18 or 40%) and social media (18 or 40%). They do not use clickers. For instance, about 36 (80%) of lecturers confirmed that they do not use clickers. About 36 (80%) lecturers also claim they do not use the telephone to teach in the classroom.

Table 11.4

Different Types of Technologies Used to Teach in the Classroom

Technology Type	Yes	Percent	No	Percent	Total
Smart phones	21	46.7	23	51.1	45
Online learning	18	40.0	25	55.5	45
Clickers	7	15.6	36	80.0	45
Social Media	18	40.0	25	55.6	45
Laptops	39	86.7	4	4.4	45
Traditional phone	7	15.6	36	80.0	45
Missing value	–	–	–	2 (4.4)	

Other Technologies Lecturers Use But Not Listed

Table 11.5 shows the other technologies that lecturers use apart from the ones that were not listed as part of the survey. About 35 (77.8%) did not answer this question. Three (6.6%) stated that they use projectors to teach in the classroom. The other technologies that the lecturers use but not listed are shown in the Table 11.5.

Table 11.5
Other Technologies Lecturers Use But Not Listed

Other Technologies	Frequency	Percent
Desktop	1	2.2
Facebook	1	2.2
Projectors	3	6.6
Traditional Media (e.g., television, radio, newspaper)	1	2.2
Open educational resource	1	2.2
Projector and Smart board	1	2.2
Projector and Case Video	1	2.2
Learning Management System	1	2.2
Missing value	35	77.8

Frequently Used Technologies

The technologies that lecturers regularly employ are listed in Table 11.6. In looking at which technologies are used "all the time," we can see that laptops, which account for 82.2% of the total, appear to be one of the most commonly used technologies by lecturers. Then there is the use of smart phones, which are used "all the time" by 13.3% of the respondents. Out of technologies which are used "not at all" by the lecturers, clickers are the most frequently mentioned (53.3%) followed by smart phones (42.2%) and then regular phones (40%).

Purpose of Technologies Used by Lecturers

Table 11.7 provides the purpose of technologies used by lecturers in the classroom. Only 6 lecturers (13.3%) admitted that they used smartphone

Table 11.6

Frequently Used Technologies

Technology Type	Not at all	Infrequently	Sometimes	Often	All the time	Missing Value	Total
Smart Phones	19 (42.2%)	7 (15.6%)	8 (17.8%)	8 (17.8%)	6 (13.3%)	1 (2.2%)	45 (100%)
Online Learning	13 (28.9%)	5 (11.1%)	9 (20%)	10 (20%)	3 (6.7%)	5 (11.1%)	45 (100%)
Clickers	24 (53.3%)	3 (6.7%)	4 (8.9%)	1 (2.2%)	4 (8.9%)	9 (20%)	45 (100%)
Social Media	12 (26.7%)	9 (20%)	10 (22.2%)	7 (15.6%)	3 (6.7%)	4 (8.9%)	45 (100%)
Laptops	1 (2.2%)	–	2 (4.4%)	3 (6.7%)	37 (82.2%)	2 (4.4%)	45 (100%)
Regular Phone	18 (40%)	3 (6.7%)	8 (17.8%)	3 (6.7%)	6 (13.3%)	4 (8.9%)	48 (100%)

for teaching. Thirty-nine (86.7%) did not respond to this question. Eight (17.8%) of those lecturers stated that they use online learning only for research and 4 (8.9%) said they use online learning system for only teaching. Also, about 5 (11.1%) use this technology for both research and teaching. Nonetheless 28 (62.2%) did not answer this question because they do not use online learning at all. As for clickers, 6 (13.3%) use it only for teaching, whereas, 2 (4.4%) claim they use it for both teaching and research. About 37 (82.2%) did not respond to this question. A total of 5 (11.1%) of the lecturers responded that they use social media only for teaching purposes. Thirty-eight (84.4%) did not respond to this question. They may not conversant with using social media to teach leadership and business management to their students. For laptops, a considerable number of lecturers responded to this question. For instance, 16 (35.6%) said they use their laptops for research and teaching, whereas, 23 (51.1%) said that they use their laptops for only teaching. While 5 (11.5%) did not state whether or not they used laptops for any of these purposes. Only 9 (20%) of the lecturers stated that they used telephone for only teaching. Nonetheless, 36 (80%) of lecturers did not respond this question. This might mean that they do not use this technology at all in carrying out either research or teaching.

Challenges and Barriers Faced With the Different Technologies Used in Teaching

Table 11.8 shows the results that internet connectivity issues are some of the major challenges facing lecturers in teaching at their institution.

Table 11.7

Purpose of Technologies Used by Lecturers to Teach in the Classroom

Technology Type	Purpose of Technologies			
	Combination	Research	Teaching	Missing Value
Smart Phone	–	–	6 (13.3%)	39 (86.7%)
Online Learning	5 (11.1%)	8 (17.8%)	4 (8.9%)	28 (62.2%)
Clickers	2 (4.4%)	–	6 (13.3%)	37 (82.2%)
Social Media	1 (2.2%)	1 (2.2%)	5 (11.1%)	38 (84.4%)
Laptop	16 (35.6%)	1 (2.2%)	23 (51.1%)	5 (11.1%)
Telephone	–	–	9 (20%)	36 (80%)

For instance, about 26 (57.8%) of the lecturers stated that there are issues with internet connectivity (e.g., slow internet, fluctuation in the network). Other issues included access to diverse technologies (2.2%), faulty devices (6.7%), and a limited number of technologies to help lecturers in teaching innovatively. However, 10 (22.2%) did not answer this question. This may mean that they do not have any challenges with the technologies that they utilized at their institutions.

Table 11.8

Challenges and Barriers Faced With the Different Technologies Used in Teaching

Challenges faced using technologies to teach in the classroom	Frequency	Percent
Access to Technology issues	3	6.7
Faulty device	3	6.7
General technical issues	2	4.4
Internet Connectivity issues	26	57.8
Unavailability of Technology	1	2.2
Missing Value	10	22.2

Example of quotes from some lecturers on the challenges and barriers faced with the different technologies used in teaching:

- "Sometimes no internet connectivity or the internet is rather slow. When memory stick (pen drive) is used on desktop set up in class, there is risk of virus infection. Other times no lights."
- "Accessibility: in that some of the students may not have access to some of the technologies."
- "Students abuse the use of technology in class."
- "Often outdated equipment, power challenges, sockets not working, lack of compatibility of set up with laptop."
- "Limited use of the technologies in class because of limited internet availability."
- "Low internet signal or lack of internet facility in the classroom."

Suggestions and Recommendations by Lecturers for Effective Use of Technology

Table 11.9 is a list of recommendations that lecturers provided to help improve teaching students with technologies in their institutions. Twenty lecturers (44.4%) suggested that management should provide better internet services such as fast internet to enable them to carry out their own research and to enable them to give their best to enable students to become more innovative in their quest for knowledge. Further, eight (17.8%) suggested that there should be more investment in technologies available to boost the acquisition of knowledge. Other suggestions included maintenance of equipment and building of infrastructure to better support the utilization of technologies in their institutions.

Table 11.9

Suggestions and Recommendations for Effective Use of Technology

Suggestions/ Recommendation	Frequency	Percent
Access to technology	2	4.4
Maintenance of equipment	3	3.7
Good internet connectivity	20	44.4
Training of lecturers on technology	2	4.4
More Investment in Technology	8	17.8
Other recommendations	3	6.7
Missing value	7	1.5

Examples of some of the quotes from lecturers on the suggestions and recommendations for effective use of technology in the classroom:

- "Institutions should purchase technologies to enhance course delivery."
- "Accessibility of technologies and their usage should be made part of school policy."
- "Update classroom equipment every 3–4 years, monitor and apply technologies in use by world class universities, and institution must proactively respond to the teaching needs of lecturers."
- "All classrooms should have the means to access the internet."
- "Institutions must invest more in teaching and learning technologies."
- "Lecturers should be educated on the technologies available for teaching."

Findings of Students' Experiences With the Use of Technologies in the Classroom

Different Types of Technologies Used to Teach in the Classroom

Here are the findings of students' experiences with the use of technologies in the classrooms. Respondents were asked to identify the different types of technologies adopted by their lecturers in the classroom. The respondents had the opportunity to list more than one type of technology used. Table 11.10 shows that participants use more laptops for teaching in their classroom at 66 (86.8%). Other technologies used are online learning and smart phones at 33 (53.9%) and 21 (27.6%) respectively. The technologies not often used in their classroom are social media, telephone, and clickers. The percentage ranges are 65 (85.5%), 65 (85.5%), and 64 (84.2%) respectively. Table 11.10 shows the different types of technologies used to teach in the classroom.

Other Technologies Students Used But Not Listed

In Table 11.11 respondents suggested some of the technologies that they use that are not on the list of technologies provided. Most of the respondents did not indicate other technologies that they use. This might mean they do not use other technologies apart from those listed. Only 8 (10.5%) stated that they use projectors and only 1 (1.3%) claimed to use blogs, pointers, and real items and materials.

Table 11.10

Different Types of Technologies Used to Teach in the Classroom

Type of technology	Yes	Percent	No	Percent	Total (n)	Percent
Smart phones	21	27.6	53	69.7	74	97.4
Online learning	33	53.9	41	43.4	74	97.4
Clickers	10	13.2	64	84.2	74	97.4
Social Media	9	11.8	65	85.5	74	97.4
Laptops	66	86.8	8	10.5	74	97.4
Telephone	9	11.8	65	85.5	74	97.4
Missing value					2	2.6

Table 11.11

Other Technologies Students Use But Not Listed

Other Technologies	Frequency	Percent
Blogs	1	1.3
Pointers	1	1.3
Projectors	8	10.5
Real items and materials	1	1.3
Missing value	65	85.5

Frequently Used Technologies

According to Table 11.12 the most frequently used technology is laptops at 53 (69.3%), followed by clickers, online learning, and social media which amounted to 3 (3.9%). This may mean that laptops are the technology that lecturers used in their delivery of courses to respondents. On the other hand, the technologies that are not used frequently in teaching are the clicker at 57 (75%), the telephone at 55 (72.4%), and social media 48 (63.2%).

Purpose of Technologies Students Experience in the Classroom

Table 11.13 indicates that about 25 (32.9%) respondents use smart phones only for research. About 8 (10.5%) students also reported that they use smartphones only teaching while 2 (2.6%) used them for both research

Table 11.12

Frequently Used Technologies

Type of technologies	Not at all	Infrequently	Sometimes	Often	All the time	Percent
Smart phones	54 (71.1%)	3 (3.9%)	14 (18.4%)	1 (1.3%)	–	3 (3.9%)
Online learning	24 (31.6%)	6 (7.9%)	32 (42.1%)	5 (6.6%)	3 (3.9%)	5 (6.6%)
Clickers	57 (75%)	1 (1.3%)	5 (6.6%)	1 (1.3%)	3 (3.9%)	9 (11.8%)
Social Media	48 (63.2%)	5 (6.6%)	9 (11.8%)	2 (2.6%)	3 (3.9%)	6 (7.9%)
Laptops	3 (3.9%)	4 (5.3%)	5 (6.6%)	6 (7.9%)	53 (69.7%)	5 (6.6%)
Telephone	55 (72.4%)	4 (5.3%)	5 (6.6%)	2 (2.6%)	2 (2.6%)	8 (10.5%)

and teaching. Nevertheless, 41 (53.9%) students, the majority, did not provide any response. This may mean that they are not conversant with the use of smartphones for either teaching or research. Many students, about 33 (43.4%), did not respond to what the purpose of online learning technologies are used for in their institution. They may not often use online learning technologies for their courses. Twenty-four (31.6%) claimed that online learning technologies are for research. While 10 (13.2%) admitted that they use online learning technology only for teaching, the other 9 (11.8%) said they use this technology for both research and teaching. Only 8 (10.5%) of students said that clickers were used for teaching. According to the response of students 18 (23.7%) claim that laptops are used for only teaching, whereas 5 (6.6%), stated that laptops are used for both research and teaching. However, 52 (68.4%) did not respond to this question. The majority of students 70 (92.1%) did not respond to this question of what a telephone is used for in the teaching of Leadership and Business Management. In Table 11.13 only 4 (5.3%) claimed that a telephone is used for teaching and 2 (2.6%) admitted that they used this technology is used for research.

Challenges and Barriers Students Faced With the Different Technologies Used in Teaching at Their Institution

Table 11.14 illustrates the challenges and barriers faced by students with the different technologies used in teaching at their institution.

Table 11.13

Purpose of Technologies Students Experience in the Classroom

Type of Technologies	Purpose of Technologies			
	Combination	Research	Teaching	Missing Value
Smart Phone	2 (2.6%)	25 (32.9%)	8 (10.5%)	41 (53.9%)
Online Learning	9 (11.8%)	24 (31.6%)	10 (13.2%)	33 (43.4%)
Clickers	–	1 (1.3%)	8 (10.5%)	67 (88.2%)
Social Media	2 (2.6%)	5 (6.6%)	4 (5.3%)	65 (85.5%)
Laptop	5 (6.6%)	1 (1.3%)	18 (23.7%)	52 (68.4%)
Telephone	–	2 (2.6%)	4 (5.3%)	70 (92.1%)

Approximately 18 (23.7%) did not respond to this question. About 17 (22.4%) said the issues they faced are internet connectivity issues. They normally experience fluctuations in the internet services at their institutions. Twelve (15.8%) students said they had no challenges with the technology and no training on the different technologies used in their institution. Eleven (14.5%) complained of faulty projectors during their lectures. Apart these challenges, lack of access to the internet and affordable technologies are some of the issues that students raised.

Table 11.14

Challenges and Barriers Students Faced With the Different Technologies Used in Teaching at their Institution

Challenges faced using technologies to teach in the classroom	Frequency	Percent
Access to internet	4	5.2
Affordable technology	2	2.6
Faulty Projectors	11	14.5
General technical issues	2	2.6
Internet Accessibility	4	5.2
No challenges with Technology	12	15.8
Technical Issues	2	2.6
No training for students on Technology	12	15.8
Internet Connectivity	17	22.4
Missing Value	18	23.7

Examples of the quotes from students on the challenges and barriers faced with the different technologies used in teaching at their institution:

- "Malfunction of gadgets."
- "Slow internet, students taking advantage and browsing the social media."
- "Network Issues."
- "Not all students are able to access the information because some technologies aren't available to them."
- "Affordability and technical challenges."

Suggestions and Recommendations by Students for Effective Use of Technology in the Classroom

Here are some suggestions and recommendations by students for effective use of technologies in the classroom shown in Table 11.15. Despite the challenges that students raised with the different technologies they use at their school, they provided recommendations to improve on the technologies they use their institutions. Some of the suggestions include provision of good internet connectivity by their institutions. This was suggested by 15 (19.7%) students who took part in this research while, 8 (10.5%) also recommended that there is the need for institutions to be able to get access to technology continuously on campus and these technologies need to go through maintenance. Eleven students (14.5%) also suggested that they be trained on how to use the different technologies. However, 15 (19.5%) did not respond to this question meaning they are alright with the services provided by their institutions.

Table 11.15
Suggestions and Recommendations for Effective Use of Technology

Suggestions/ Recommendation	Frequency	Percent
Access to technology	8	10.5
Availability of equipment	2	2.6
Good internet connectivity	15	19.7
Maintenance of equipment	8	10.5
Training students on technology	11	14.5
Other	17	22.4
Missing value	15	19.5

Examples of quotes from students on suggestions and recommendations for effective use of technologies in the classroom:

- "There should be stable network."
- "Use of properly function equipment."
- "The gadgets should be maintained periodically."
- "Technical faults should be looked at before usage of technologies."
- "I suggest that technologies should be used frequently during lecture to make learning easy."
- "There should be rule for all lecturers to use technologies when teaching."

MANAGERIAL PRACTICE IMPLICATIONS OF STUDY

There are several important managerial practice implications arising from the findings of this study. We highlight these managerial practice implications, with a specific focus on the often-referenced and key managerial functions of planning, organizing, leading, and controlling (Bateman & Snell, 2013). An important managerial practice implication arises from one of the important findings of this study. Our study indicates that both lecturers and students at the business schools surveyed substantially utilized laptops the most in the classroom instructions. In the current business environment and in corporations and organizations computers play critical roles in the key managerial functions (Bateman & Snell, 2013). Computers are increasingly used for planning projects and for the development of project-oriented charts and timelines. Similarly, computers play critical roles in managers organizing their human resources and for effectively carrying out the control function. Documentation, presentation, and report generation are examples of tasks that are part of a company's everyday operations. Laptops are also crucial since they are an excellent communication tool that most businesses utilize to store, manage, and maintain important data. Consequently, to the extent that laptops are consistently and frequently used by both lecturers and students in the class-rooms in business schools in Ghana, this will very beneficial and have positive managerial practice outside of the classroom.

A second important finding from this study indicates that both lecturers and students do not frequent user smart phones during class room instructions. This finding also has important managerial practice implications. From a business practice perspective, smart phone use offers potential positive managerial practice advantages as they enable the use of currently available social media platforms such as Facebook, Twitter, and so forth. The smart phones also have the strong advantage of being highly mobile and therefore increasing the flexibility and speed of getting managerial functions completed. Furthermore, smartphones currently have all the capabilities that will enable an organization to successfully undertake corporate promotion and branding, Furthermore, and increasingly, smart phones are used for important practical managerial actions such as carrying out inventory and money transfer (e.g., Momo). Consequently, the fact that both lecturers and students are not consistently use smart phones in the teaching and learning process suggests a potentially missed opportunity to further enhance the managerial practice capabilities and skillsets of the business students.

Another notable point is that the study's findings come from some of Ghana's top schools: UG Legon and GIMPA. In terms of financing, prestige, capital, and manpower, these institutions have a lot of resources. For example, the majority of the lecturers in these two business schools are highly qualified and are likely to adhere to best practices in terms of technology-assisted teaching. Ghana has more than 40 business schools. Consequently, if GIMPA and UG Legon are not using smartphones, it is safe to assume that these universities aren't either. As such, one of the managerial implications of this study is to recommend the usage of smartphones at business schools throughout Ghana.

Several technological problems were reported by both professors and students. Lecturers, for example, reported major challenges such as difficulty in getting online connectivity and very slow internet speeds when there is a connection. Students also highlighted network troubles and slow internet connection. In addition, students also had concerns over gadget malfunctions and internet affordability. Successfully address these technological issues will result in improved management practices when the business school students entered the workforce and obtain managerial positions.

Both lecturers and students provided several recommendations. For example, lecturers proposed that their institutions purchase technologies to aid in effective course delivery, as well as establish a school policy on technology access and use. In addition, all classrooms should have reliable access to faster internet service providers as part of their institutions' investments in teaching and learning technologies. Lecturers should be educated on the many educational technologies available. Students urged that there be a fast and reliable, that properly functioning technology be used, and that equipment/hardware be maintained on a regular basis.

This study has some notable limitations that we want to highlight. First, the survey of the use of technology in teaching was only carried out at business schools in Ghana, therefore its applicability to other African countries will be limited. Another limitation is that while Ghana has about 40 business schools, the survey focused on only two universities, namely GIMPA and UG-Legon which limits the generalizability of our findings to other universities. Third, the number of lecturers employed in this study is limited, with 45 lecturers accounting for roughly 25% of the faculty at the two business schools. Despite these limitations, there is a convergence of lecturers' and students' results, as both lecturers and students indicate that laptops, rather than other technology, are frequently employed in business school education. These types of common responses between students and lecturers tend to support the veracity of this study's results with respect to the types of the technologies employed in Ghanaian business schools.

In the end, this chapter points to opportunities to improve learning and managerial practices through better use of technology in the business schools of Ghana and likely other parts of Africa. Further, not all of the improvements need to come from better funding. For example, incorporating the use of smart phones into the teaching and learning process will be beneficial.

REFERENCES

Adam, L. (2003). Information and communication technologies in higher education in Africa: Initiatives and challenges. *Journal of Higher Education in Africa/Revue de l'enseignement supérieur en Afrique*, 195–221.

Bateman, T. S., & Snell. S. A. (2013) Management: Leading and Collaborating

Bervell, B., & Umar, I. N. (2017). A decade of LMS acceptance and adoption research in Sub-Sahara African higher education: A systematic review of models, methodologies, milestones and main challenges. *Eurasia Journal of Mathematics, Science and Technology Education*, *13*(11), 7269–7286.

Bon, A. (2010). Information and communication technologies in tertiary education in sub-Saharan Africa. In D. Teferra & H. Greijn (Eds.), *Higher education and globalization, challenges, threats and opportunities for Africa* (pp. 63–77). Maastricht, Netherlands: Maastricht University Centre for International Cooperation in Academic Development (MUNDO), and Boston, MA: Boston College International Network for Higher Education in Africa (INHEA), Center for International Higher Education (CIHE).

Byungura, J. C., Hansson, H., Muparasi, M., & Ruhinda, B. (2018). Familiarity with technology among firstyear students in Rwandan tertiary education. *Electronic Journal of e-Learning*, *16*(1), 30–45.

Cavanaugh, J. M., Giapponi, C. C., & Golden, T. D. (2016). Digital technology and student cognitive development: The neuroscience of the university classroom. *Journal of Management Education*, *40*(4), 374–397.

Chege, S. M., Wang, D., & Suntu, S. L. (2020). Impact of information technology innovation on firm performance in Kenya. *Information Technology for Development*, 26(2), 316–345.

Donbesuur, F., Ampong, G. O. A., Owusu-Yirenkyi, D., & Chu, I. (2020). Technological innovation, organizational innovation and international performance of SMEs: The moderating role of domestic institutional environment. *Technological Forecasting and Social Change*, *161*, 120252.

Farag, D. M., Park, S., & Kaupins, G. (2015). Faculty perceptions of the adoption and use of clickers in the legal studies in business classroom. *Journal of Education for Business*, 90(4), 208–216.

Iseolorunkanm, J., Adebola, F. B., Adebola, G., Rotimi, M., Nweke-Love, H., Adebisi, T. & Lawal, I. (2021). COVID-19 pandemic: Nigerian university lecturers' response to virtual orientation. *Cogent Arts & Humanities*, *8*(1), 1932041.

Ivala, E. N. (2016). Educational technology training: Staff development approaches. *International Journal of Educational Sciences*, *14*(3), 195–204.

Kaliisa, R., & Michelle, P. (2019). Mobile learning policy and practice in Africa: Towards inclusive and equitable access to higher education. *Australasian Journal of Educational Technology*, *35*(6), 1–14.

Kaliisa, R., & Picard, M. (2017). A systematic review on mobile learning in higher education: The African perspective. *TOJET: The Turkish Online Journal of Educational Technology*, *16*(1).

Kathula, D. N. (2020). Effect of COVID-19 pandemic on the education system in Kenya. *Journal of Education*, *3*(6), 31–52.

Kruss, G., McGrath, S., Petersen, I. H., & Gastrow, M. (2015). Higher education and economic development: The importance of building technological capabilities. *International Journal of Educational Development*, *43*, 22–31.

Mitchell, G. W., Wohleb, E. C., & Skinner, L. B. (2016). Perceptions of public educators regarding accessibility to technology and the importance of integrating technology across the curriculum. *Journal of Research in Business Education*, *57*(2), 14.

Ng'ambi, D., Brown, C., Bozalek, V., Gachago, D., & Wood, D. (2016). Technology enhanced teaching and learning in South African higher education: A rearview of a 20-year journey. *British Journal of Educational Technology*, *47*(5), 843–858.

Ocholla, D. N. (2003). An overview of information and communication technologies (ICT) in the LIS schools of Eastern and Southern Africa. *Education for information*, *21*(2–3), 181–194.

Rana, N. P., & Dwivedi, Y. K. (2018). An empirical examination of antecedents determining students' usage of clickers in a digital marketing module. *International Journal of Business Information Systems*, *27*(1), 86–104.

Rana, N. P., Dwivedi, Y. K., & Al-Khowaiter, W. A. (2016). A review of literature on the use of clickers in the business and management discipline. *International Journal of Management Education*, *14*(2), 74–91.

Shambare, R. (2011). Using projects in teaching introductory business statistics: The case of Tshwane University of Technology Business School. *African Journal of Business Management, 5*(11), 4176–4184.

Tian, H., Otchere, S. K., Coffie, C. P., Mensah, I. A., & Baku, R. K. (2021). Supply chain integration, interfirm value co-creation and firm performance nexus in Ghanaian SMEs: Mediating roles of stakeholder pressure and innovation capability. *Sustainability, 13*(4), 2351.

ABOUT THE CONTRIBUTORS

Grace Abban-Ampiah is a Lecturer and Doctoral student in Human Resource Management at the Ghana Institute of Management and Public Administration (GIMPA), Accra, Ghana. Her research interests include leadership, career development, succession planning, learning and development, as well as women entrepreneurship development. She holds a master's degree in Human Resource Management from the University of Sheffield, Sheffield, UK. She has published several chapters and made numerous presentations on women's roles and challenges faced in the workplace. Email: gabban-ampiah@gimpa.edu.gh

Susanne Braun is a Professor in Leadership and PhD Program Lead at Durham University Business School, Durham University, Durham, UK. She has research interests in leadership, identities at work, and positive organizational functioning at the interface of work and non-work domains. She currently co-leads a world-wide network of over 30 leadership researchers with Durham University as the hub of eight research projects funded by the US Army Research Institute for Behavioral and Social Sciences. She is Associate Editor at *Frontiers in Psychology* and Editorial Board Member of the *European Journal of Work and Organisational Psychology* and *Journal of Organizational Behavior*. Her research has been published in the *British Journal of Management*, *Organizational Behavior and Human Decision Processes*, *Journal of Business Ethics*, and *Leadership Quarterly*. Email: Susanne.braun@durham.ac.uk

Johan Bruneel is Professor of Entrepreneurship at IESEG School of Management, Lille, France, and KU Leuven, Leuven, Belgium. Since 2011, he has studied social enterprises as hybrid organizations and the tension between the "social" and the "economic" that they face. His current

Managerial Practice Issues in Strategy and Organization, pp. 317–326
Copyright © 2023 by Information Age Publishing
www.infoagepub.com

research interest lies at the intersection of strategy and governance focusing on board dynamics in hybrid organizations. Email: johan.bruneel@kuleuven.be

Matheus Leite Campos is a post-doctoral research fellow in the Innovation Systems, Strategies and Policy project (InSySPo) in the Department of Science and Technology Policy at the University of Campinas (UNICAMP), Campinas, São Paulo, Brazil. He holds a PhD in Business Administration from UNICAMP. His main research interest includes entrepreneurship and entrepreneurial ecosystems. Email: matleite@unicamp.br

Guoli Chen is a Professor of Strategy at INSEAD, Singapore. He received his PhD in strategic management from Pennsylvania State University, State College, PA. His research examines CEOs, top management teams, and boards of directors, and their influence on firms' strategic choices and organizational outcomes. He studies corporate governance and CEO–board dynamics in the contexts of organizational growth, renewal, and corporate development and sustainability. He has published academic articles in journals such as *Administrative Science Quarterly, Academy of Management Journal, Management Science, Organization Science,* and *Strategic Management Journal.* Email: guoli.chen@insead.edu

Dieudonnee Cobben is a PhD student in innovation ecosystems at the Management Department at the Open Universiteit, Heerlen, Netherlands. She has a double master's degree in Innovation Sciences and Innovation Management from the University of Technology, Eindhoven, Netherlands. Her research focuses on ecosystem governance, strategy, ecosystem health, and sustainability. Her articles have appeared in the *International Entrepreneurship and Management Journal, Journal of Business Research,* and *International Journal of Innovation..* Email: Dieudonnee.cobben@ou.nl

T. K. Das is Professor Emeritus of Strategic Management at the City University of New York, New York, NY, where he taught for over three decades and served concurrently as a member of the University's Doctoral Faculty. Prior to entering the academic life, Professor Das had extensive experience as a senior business executive. Professor Das received his PhD in Organization and Strategic Studies from the Anderson Graduate School of Management, University of California at Los Angeles, Los Angeles, CA (UCLA). He has a bachelor's degree in Physics (St. Xavier's College, University of Calcutta, Kolkata, India), a master's degree in Mathematics (Jadavpur University, Kolkata, India), a second master's degree in Management (Asian Institute of Management, Manila, Philippines), and a Professional Certification in Banking (C.A.I.I.B., Certified Associate of the Indian Institute of Banking and Finance [Life Member], Mumbai, India). His research interests are in strategic alliances, strategy making, organization studies, temporal studies, and executive development. Professor Das is the author or editor of 30 academic research books, mainly on strategy, organization, and management, and also 6 booklets on bank management for practicing executives. His research articles have appeared in over 45 journals, of which some of the later ones include *Academy of Management Executive, Academy of Management Review, Accounting, Organizations and Society, British Journal of Management, Cross Cultural Management: An International Journal, Entrepreneurship Theory and Practice, International Journal of Entrepreneurial Behaviour & Research, International Journal of Organizational Analysis, International Journal of Strategic Business Alliances, International Journal of Strategic Change Management, Journal of Business and Psychology, Journal of Business Ethics, Journal of General Management, Journal of International Management, Journal of Management, Journal of Management Development, Journal of Management Studies, Journal of Managerial Psychology, Long Range Planning, Management Decision, Management International Review, Organization Science, Organization Studies, Scandinavian Journal of Management, Strategic Management Journal,* and *Time & Society.* Also, by invitation, he has contributed book reviews in *Administrative Science Quarterly, Contemporary Psychology,* and *Journal of Management,* and authored the entry on "Strategic Alliances" in *Oxford Bibliographies in Management.* His work has been cited in nearly 1,600 journals published in a wide variety of disciplines. For a number of years now, he has been consistently ranked in the top 2 percent of scholars in his field of Business & Management in terms of research impact. Most recently, a Stanford University professor led a comprehensive study of the career-long research impact of more than 8 million researchers worldwide across 174 fields during the 60-year period 1960-2019, based on the article citations included in the well-known multidisciplinary citation database *SCOPUS,* and this study has ranked Professor Das among the top 1 percent of scholars (complete list published in the journal *PLOS Biology*). Professor Das is a former Senior Editor of *Organization Studies* and has previously served, or is serving, on the editorial boards of a number of other academic journals, and has been an *ad hoc* editorial reviewer for over 70 journals. He is the founding (and current) Series Editor of the three book series, *Research in Strategic Alliances, Research in Behavioral Strategy,* and *Research in Strategy Science* (all published by Information Age Publishing). Email: TK.Das@baruch.cuny.edu

Micah DelVecchio is Associate Professor of Economics at Saginaw Valley State University. He graduated in 2014 from Colorado State University, University Center, MI. He has worked as a policy consultant for energy and homelessness nonprofit organizations. His research is focused on macroeconomic and microeconomic determinates of economic development and income. His PhD thesis has been cited numerous times and his current papers establish a method which incorporates economic and political institutions into neoclassical growth models, providing a method to empirically estimate an economy's total factor productivity using measures of these institutions. Email: mpdelvec@svsu.edu

Frédéric Dufays is Assistant Professor at HEC Liège—University of Liege, Liege, Belgium, and at KU Leuven, Leuven, Belgium, where he is the co-promotor of the Cera-Boerenbond Chair on Cooperative Entrepreneurship. His current research interests include the implementation and impact of economic democracy and deliberative practices in cooperatives, the legitimation processes of alternative organizational models, and the collective internal dynamics at work in the emergence of hybrid organizations such as cooperatives and social enterprises. Email: frederic.dufays@ kuleuven.be

Mariane Santos Françoso is a post-doctoral research fellow in the Innovation Systems, Strategies and Policy project (InSySPo) in the Department of Science and Technology Policy at the University of Campinas (UNICAMP), Campinas, São Paulo, Brazil. She holds a PhD in Economics from UNICAMP. Her main research interests are global production networks, knowledge networks, and evolutionary economic geography. Email: marianef@ unicamp.br

Sohvi Heaton is a visiting assistant professor at Santa Clara University, Santa Clara, CA. She previously worked on poverty reduction for low-income countries and private-sector development at the World Bank in Washington, DC, and was recently a postdoctoral scholar at the University of California Berkeley's Haas School of Business, Berkeley, CA. She holds a PhD in management studies from the University of Oxford, UK. Her research on strategic management has covered dynamic capabilities, intellectual capital, corporate reputation, university entrepreneurship, and other topics. Her work has been published or is forthcoming in several management journals, including *Strategic Management Journal, California Management Review, Strategic Organization, Global Strategy Journal,* and *Academy of Management Perspectives.* Email: sheaton@scu.edu.

Rick M. A. Hollen is a Senior Researcher at the Faculty of Economics and Business, University of Amsterdam, Amsterdam, Netherlands. He obtained a PhD in Management from Rotterdam School of Management, Erasmus University, Netherlands, a master's degree in Strategic Management (cum laude) and a bachelor's degree in Business Administration at the same university. Before his doctoral studies, he worked as Project Manager

Business Development for a global technology and services company. He has published in *European Management Review, Maritime Economics and Logistics, and R & D Management*. Email: m.a.hollen@uva.nl

Peter Lok is an Associate Professor of Management at the University of Sydney's Business School, Sydney, Australia. His main research interests are in the areas of organizational change, cross-cultural management, Asian business, HRM and performance management. He has extensive consultancy and executive teaching experience, particularly in the Asian region. His publications are in the *Journal of Management Studies, Applied Psychology - An International Review, International Journal of HRM, International Journal of Cross-Cultural Management and Leadership*, and *Organizational Development Journal*. Email: pter.lok@sydney.edu.au

Francisco Longo has been an associate professor and former director of the Centre for Public Governance at Esade, Ramon Llull University, Barcelona, Spain. He was a member of the United Nations Committee of Experts on Public Administration (2011-2018). He has worked as an international consultant and joined committees of experts on public sector reform, university governance and organization of the public sector. He is a member of various editorial boards and author of several publications on governance, public management, and public-private partnerships. He makes regular appearances in a range of media outlets. Email: francisco.longo@esade.edu

Alex Makarevich is an associate professor of management at California State University East Bay, Hayward, CA. He was previously on the faculty at ESADE Business School in Barcelona, Spain. He earned his PhD from Stanford University, Stanford, CA. He studies how different aspects of embeddedness in the structure of markets shape firms' performance and outcomes in a variety of industries, such as the U.S. venture capital industry, the Japanese banking industry, and the global automotive industry. He has contributed to the following research areas: firm and alliance performance, new market entry, adoption of new organizational practices, and corporate venturing. His research has appeared in *Strategic Management Journal, Journal of Management Studies, Organization Studies*, and *Academy of Management Best Paper Proceedings*. Email: alex.makarevich@csueastbay.edu

Gordon Müller-Seitz is Chair of Strategy, Innovation and Cooperation at the Department of Business Administration and Economics, Technische Universität Kaiserslautern, Kaiserslautern, Germany. He is a management researcher focusing in his research upon interorganizational networks, open innovation and open strategy. Currently, he is focusing on business model innovations in light of the digital transformation and artificial intelligence in particular. His work has appeared in journals such as *Journal of Public Administration, Research and Theory, Research Policy, Organization Studies, Industry & Innovation*, and *R&D Management*. His research insights have been applied at large-scale organizations and small and medium sized enterprises. Email: gms@wiwi.uni-kl.de

Arash Najmaei is the head of the Centre for Applied Management Research and an adjunct lecturer at the Peter Faber Business School at Australian Catholic University, Sydney, Australia, as well as the International College of Management Sydney. He is currently working as a marketing consultant in Australia. He earned his PhD in strategy and entrepreneurship in 2014 from the Macquarie Graduate School of Management, Sydney, Australia. He also has an MBA and an undergraduate degree in civil engineering. E-mail: arash.najmaei@acu.edu.au

Joseph Ofori-Dankwa is the H. R. Wickes Endowed Chair of International Business Studies at Saginaw Valley State University, University Center, MI. He obtained a law degree from the University of Ghana, Legon, Ghana, a Master's Degree in Management and Technology from the University of Wales, along with a Master's Degree in Human Resource and Labor Relations, and a PhD in Management, both from Michigan State University, MI. He has published his work in the *Strategic Management Journal, Organization Science*, and *Academy of Management Review*. He has established the Makola Institute, a business and management enterprise in Ghana, and hopes to grow the institute to develop the future business leaders of Ghana. Email: oforidan@svsu.edu

Gabriella Padilla is currently studying for a PhD in Business Economics at KU Leuven, Leuven, Belgium. Earlier, she worked in corporate social responsibility as project manager and coordinator of strategic alliances, and conducted research on social enterprises, sustainability, and social impact. She holds a MSc in Environment and Sustainable Development from University College London (UCL), London, UK, where she graduated with honors, and a BA in International Relations, *magna cum laude*, at the University of Monterrey (UDEM), Monterrey, Mexico. Her doctoral research focuses on corporate governance, hybrid organizations, and board dynamics. Email: gabriella.padilla@kuleuven.be

Keith G. Provan was the McClelland Professor of Management at the Eller College of Management, University of Arizona, AZ. He held joint appointments in the Management and Organization Department and in the School of Public Administration and Policy. He was also a Senior Research Fellow at Tilburg University, Netherlands. Professor Provan's research focussed on interorganizational and network relationships. He published well over 70 journal articles and scholarly book chapters and was one of only 33 members of the Academy of Management's "Journals Hall of Fame." Until he passed away in 2014, he served on the editorial review board of the *Academy of Management Journal* and was coeditor for *Journal of Public Administration Theory and Research*.

Jo Rhodes is a senior lecturer in Macquarie Graduate School of Management (MGSM), Macquarie University, Sydney, Australia, and teaches in the MBA program. Her research interests include corporate strategy, e-commerce, competitiveness and performance, and Asian business strategy. She has published in journals such as *International Journal of Human Resource Management, Journal of Knowledge Management,* and *Asian Business & Management,* and *Journal of E-Commerce and Organizations, among others.* Email: jo.rhodes@mgsm.edu.au

Mark Robinson is a tutor in Science Diplomacy at the Centre for International Studies and Diplomacy at SOAS, London University, London, UK. He has a PhD in Government and International Affairs from Durham University, an MSc from Oxford University in Major Programme Management, and an MA in Global Diplomacy from London University. Previously, he worked in three inter-governmental organizations, namely, the ITER Nuclear Fusion Project in Cadarache, France, the European Southern Observatory in Munich, Germany, and the North Atlantic Treaty Organisation (NATO) Eurofighter 2000 and Tornado Management Agency (NETMA) in Munich, Germany. He has published in the *Global Policy* journal.mr39@soas.ac.uk

Nadine Roijakkers is a Professor of Open Innovation at the Management Department of the Open Universiteit, and the Director of the Expertise Center for Education, also at the Open Universiteit, Heerlen, Netherlands. She was a senior strategy consultant at KPMG consulting, Utrecht, Netherlands, for several years, advising companies on their collaborative strategies and practices. Her main research interests are focused on open innovation, sustainability, and healthcare organizations. Her research has been published in, among others, *Small Business Economics, Research Policy, Technological Forecasting & Social Change, Long Range Planning, California Management Review,* and *International Journal of Technology Management.* Email: Nadine.roijakkers@ou.nl

Angel Saz-Carranza is Associate Professor in the Department of Strategy and General Management, and Director of ESADEgeo Center for Global Economy and Geopolitics, Barcelona, Spain. He earned a PhD in

Management as a Visiting Scholar at Wagner School of Public Service, New York University, where he spent three years. Previously he earned a Master's degree in Aeronautical Engineering from Imperial College, University of London, London, UK. His research focuses on business-government relations, nonmarket strategy, intergovernmental organizations, and organizational networks. His research has been published, among others, in the *Journal of Public Administration and Theory*, *Public Administration Review*, *Global Policy*, and *Corporate Governance International Review*. Email: angel. saz@esade.edu

Wei Shi is an Associate Professor of Management and Cesarano Faculty Scholar at Miami Herbert Business School, University of Miami, Miami, FL. He obtained his PhD in business administration from Rice University, Houston, TX. His primary research interest focuses on the influence of corporate governance actors and upper echelons on strategic decisions. He coauthored the book entitled *Understanding and managing strategic governance* (2021/Wiley). His research has been published at outlets such as *Academy of Management Journal*, *Strategic Management Journal*, *Organization Science*, and *Journal of Management*, and covered by *Harvard Business Review* and *Wall Street Journal*. Email: wshi@bus.miami.edu

Jörg Sydow is a Professor for Inter-firm Cooperation at the School of Business & Econimcs, Freie Universität Berlin, Germany, and a Visiting Professor at Strathclyde Business School, Glasgow, UK. Moreover, he is the director of the Research Unit "Organized Creativity" sponsored by the German Research Foundation (DFG), a founding co-editor of two leading German journals, *Managementforschung* and *Industrielle Beziehungen—The German Journal of Industrial Relations*, and a member of the editorial review boards of *Organization Studies*, *Academy of Management Journal*, *Academy of Management Review*, *Journal of Management Studies*, and *Scandinavian Journal of Management*. He co-authored two recently published books: *Managing and Working in Project Society—Institutional Challenges of Temporary Organizations* (2015, Cambridge University Press) and *Managing Inter-organizational Relations—Debates and Cases* (2016, Palgrave-Macmillan). E-mail: joerg. sydow@fu-berlin.de

Frans A. J. Van Den Bosch has been a professor of management interfaces between organizations and environment at the Department of Strategic Management & Entrepreneurship, Rotterdam School of Management, Erasmus University, Netherlands. He holds a BA in Mechanical Engineering from the Polytechnic of Rotterdam (with distinction), received his Master's degree in Economics (cum laude) from the Erasmus University Rotterdam, and his PhD in Law from Leiden University, Netherlands.

Since 2012, he has a part-time appointment focusing mainly on research, PhD supervision, and MSc thesis supervision. He holds a BA in mechanical engineering with distinction from the Polytechnic of Rotterdam and a MSc in economics degree cum laude from Erasmus University Rotterdam. He has a PhD in law from Leiden University, Netherlands. His major research interests lie in the development of integrative strategy frameworks incorporating both the externally and internally-focused view of strategy, the application of these frameworks to general management issues such as management models, non-technological sources of innovations like management innovation; strategic renewal processes, organizational ambidexterity, and corporate governance. He has published in journals such as *Academy of Management Journal, Business and Society, Corporate Governance, European Management Journal, International Studies of Management and Organization, Journal of Management Studies, Long Range Planning, Management Science, Organization Science, Organization Studies, and Strategic Management Journal.* Email: fbosch@rsm.nl

Wim Vanhaverbeke is Professor of Digital Strategy and Innovation at the University of Antwerp, Antwerp, Belgium, and visiting professor at ESADE Business School, Barcelona, Spain. He is co-editor in chief of *Technovation*. His current research focuses on open innovation, innovation ecosystems, and digital strategies. He has published in many international journals, such as *Technovation, Research Policy,* and *Journal of Small Business Management,* and was co-editor of three books on open innovation. Email: Wim. vanhaverbeke@uantwerpen.be.

Henk W. Volberda is Professor of Strategic Management & Innovation at the Faculty of Business and Economics, Amsterdam Business School, University of Amsterdam, Amsterdam, Netherlands. Earlier, he was Professor of Strategic Management and Business Policy at the RSM Erasmus University. He obtained his doctorate in Business Administration (cum laude) from the University of Groningen, Groningen, Netherlands. He is the author of a number of books, including *Building the Flexible Firm: How to Remain Competitive* (Oxford University Press, 1998), *Rethinking Strategy* (SAGE, 2001), and *Reinventing Business Models: How Firms Cope with Disruption* (Oxford University Press, 2018). He has published in journals such as *Academy of Management Journal, Global Strategy Journal, Journal of International Business, Journal of Management, Journal of Management Studies, Management Science, Organization Science, Strategic Entrepreneurship Journal,* and *Strategic Management Journal.* Email: h.w.volberda@uva.nl

Nicholas Spyridon Vonortas is Professor of Economics and International Affairs at George Washington University, Washington, D.C. He is a faculty member of the Department of Economics, of the Institute for International Science and Technology Policy, and of the Trachtenberg School of Public Policy and Public Administration. He is currently the Director of the IISTP and the Director of PhD candidacy in Economics. His teaching and research interests are in industrial organization, the economics of technological change, and technology and innovation policy and strategy. He specializes in strategic partnerships/innovation networks, investment under uncertainty, technology transfer, knowledge-intensive entrepreneurship, and R&D program evaluation. Email: vonortas@gwu.edu

INDEX

A

Abban-Ampiah, G., 277–293
Abbott, K. W., 22
Absorptive capacity, 265, 271
Abuzaid, A. N., 79
Achtenhagen, L., 160, 162–163
Acs, Z. J., 171
Activities and actions, 149–153
Activity theory, 145, 150
Adam, L., 297
Adebisi, T., 297
Adebola, F. B., 297
Adebola, G., 297
Ades, C., 41
Adner, R., 161, 179
Africa, 295–297, 314
African universities, 295, 297, 314
Agency theory, 67–69, 72
Agency theory, board as monitor, 68–69
Agranoff, R., 280, 285, 289
Agronin, E., 183
Aguilera, R. V., 67
Aguinis, H., 10
Ahn, J. M., 261
Ahrne, G., 236, 238–240, 242

Aiken, M., 196
Akhtar, S., 110
Alberquerque, E., 271
Albors Garrigós, J., 41
Aldrich, H., 198
Alecke, B., 269
Alford, R. R., 163, 281
Al-Khowaiter, W. A., 296
Allen, V. L., 109
Allison, P. D., 119
Allison, P., 119
Allison, S. T., 37
Almandoz, J., 128
Altman, D., 106
Amason, A. C., 92–93, 114
Ambiguity, 77, 95, 113, 137, 198–199, 204–205, 214, 216
Ambiguity, uncertainty, and risk, 198–199
Ambrosini, V., 179
American Association for the Advancement of Science (AAAS), 2, 10, 26
Amit, R., 146, 150, 152, 156, 162–163, 165
Ampong, G. O. A., 296
Anderson, E., 206

Managerial Practice Issues in Strategy and Organization, pp. 327–351
Copyright © 2023 by Information Age Publishing
www.infoagepub.com
327

Lightning Source UK Ltd.
Milton Keynes UK
UKHW020800041122
411637UK00007B/449